Race Characters

Race Characters
Ethnic Literature and the Figure of the American Dream

Swati Rana

The University of North Carolina Press CHAPEL HILL

Open access edition funded by the National Endowment for the Humanities.

© 2020 The University of North Carolina Press

The text of this book is licensed under a Creative Commons AttributionNonCommercial-NoDerivatives 4.0 International License: https://creativecommons.org/licenses/by-nc-nd/4.0/

Set in Merope Basic by PageMajik
Manufactured in the United States of America

The University of North Carolina Press has been a member of the Green Press Initiative since 2003.

Library of Congress Cataloging-in-Publication Data
Names: Rana, Swati, author.
Title: Race characters : ethnic literature and the figure of the American dream / Swati Rana.
Other titles: Ethnic literature and the figure of the American dream
Description: Chapel Hill : University of North Carolina Press, 2020. | Includes bibliographical references and index.
Identifiers: LCCN 2020022354 | ISBN 9781469659466 (cloth : alk. paper) | ISBN 9781469659473 (paperback : alk. paper) | ISBN 9781469659480 (ebook)
Subjects: LCSH: American Dream in literature. | American literature—Minority authors. | Minorities in literature.
Classification: LCC PS169.A49 R36 2020 | DDC 810.9/920693—dc23
LC record available at https://lccn.loc.gov/2020022354

Cover illustration: Sa'dia Rehman, *Allegiance to the flag on picture day* (2018), canvas, charcoal fiberglass screen, velvet, carbon paper, oil pastel, chalkboard paint, white pencil and ink, 200 in. x 150 in., Byrdcliffe AIR, Woodstock, New York. Used by permission of the artist.

Portions of chapter 1 were previously published in a different form in "The Production of Nativity in Early Syrian Immigrant Literature," *American Literature* 83, no. 3 (September 2011): 547–70. They are used here with the permission of Duke University Press.

For Mummy, Papa, and Aarti

Contents

Acknowledgments xi

Introduction 1
Reading Race and Character

CHAPTER ONE
Superman of America vs. Ameen Rihani 42
The Hyperproduction of Character

CHAPTER TWO
José Garcia Villa's Book of Grotesques 66
Character and Compulsion

CHAPTER THREE
Many Parts of Pocho 92
The Discontinuous Characters of José Antonio Villarreal

CHAPTER FOUR
Building American Character 119
Dalip Singh Saund's Model of Minority

CHAPTER FIVE
Paule Marshall's Brown Girls 152
Structures of Character

Conclusion 183
The Old Constellation

Notes 197
Bibliography 221
Index 239

Illustrations

Portrait of Dalip Singh Saund 2

Illustration for *The Book of Khalid* 52

Photograph of José Garcia Villa at Gotham Book Mart 69

Painting by José Garcia Villa, *Boy with Bird* 89

Painting by José Garcia Villa, *Woman's Face* 90

Front cover of *Pocho* 93

Front cover of *Congressman from India* 120

Illustration from Dalip Singh Saund's campaign biography 130

Back cover of *Congressman from India* 135

Photograph of Brooklyn brownstones 175

Acknowledgments

I am humbled by how many people have helped this book along the way. To Paule Marshall, whom I know through her writing, I am very grateful for her staunch wisdom and dedication to community and to craft. *Brown Girl, Brownstones* has been with me for as long as I can remember as a student of literature, from Sanborn House to Wheeler Hall to South Hall. I came to this project through Selina Boyce and am honored to end it with her, as a character in all the ways I have learned to query and explore.

My deepest thanks go to my advisors at University of California, Berkeley, where this project first began. Colleen Lye, thank you for your inestimable rigor and dedication to critique, which continue to inspire me to be the best thinker I can be. Thank you Gautam Premnath, Marcial González, and Rebecca McClennan for your careful readings and for your generosity as you guided me through the many twists and turns of my analysis. For their pedagogy and scholarly praxis, I thank Elizabeth Abel, Anne Anlin Cheng, Kevis Goodman, Steven Lee, Jennifer Miller, and Samuel Otter. Nadia Ellis and Namwali Serpell continue to sustain me with the dynamism they bring to their writing and being in the world. Thank you Marisa Libbon for sharing in this adventure from the first day we arrived at Berkeley.

To my colleagues at University of California, Santa Barbara, I am very grateful for your warmth and support. Thank you Stephanie Leigh Batiste, Jeannine Marie DeLombard, Bishnupriya Ghosh, and Avery Gordon for your invaluable mentorship, your thoughtful readings, and your ability to draw out the best version of my argument. Julie Carlson, Enda Duffy, Shirley Geok-lin Lim, Christopher Newfield, Ben Olguín, Rita Raley, and Teresa Shewry helped guide and keep this work on track when I needed it most. Felice Blake curated matchless spaces for generative thought. I am grateful to Ninotchka Devorah Bennahum, Kum-Kum Bhavnani, and erin Khuê Ninh for their excellent guidance and company. For their humor and encouragement, I thank Heather Blurton, Nadège Clitandre, Brian Donnelly, Andrew Griffin, and Rachael Scarborough King. Thank you to Mona Damluji, Rebecca Powers, and Elana Faye Resnick for their expansive vision and sustaining perspective.

Tremendous thanks go to University of North Carolina Press, its editorial board, and its staff. I thank my editor, Lucas Church, for his dedication to the book and for masterfully seeing it through. Thank you to Andrew Winters for his expert help. Many thanks to Mark Simpson-Vos for appreciating the potential of this project. Thank you to Ihsan Taylor at Longleaf Services for his meticulous attention to all aspects of production and to Paula Durbin-Westby and Regina Higgins for their work indexing and proofreading the book. I am very grateful to my reviewers who read so carefully and helped me to sharpen my analysis at every stage. Susan Koshy, Vanita Reddy, Elda María Román, Stephen Hong Sohn, and Eleanor Ty lent me their counsel and their support at the eleventh hour, for which I am deeply grateful. Thank you especially to Sara Jo Cohen and Gordon Hutner for believing in this work and moving it forward.

I would like to thank the National Endowment for the Humanities (NEH) for their generous support of this project, although any views, findings, conclusions, or recommendations expressed in this book are my own and do not represent those of the NEH. I am also very grateful to the Academic Senate, the Division of Humanities and Fine Arts, the Interdisciplinary Humanities Center, and the Regents' Junior Faculty Fellowships Program at University of California, Santa Barbara, which supported my work. Grants from the Hellman Fellows Fund and the Townsend Center for the Humanities at University of California, Berkeley were also indispensable for my research. I would like to thank Felicia Wivchar and her associates at the Office of Art and Archives at the U.S. House of Representatives for their fascinating tour and for their help obtaining materials; Lance Villa for granting me permission to use paintings by José Garcia Villa; and the Filipinas Heritage Library as well as the U.S. National Archives and Records Administration for their quick work procuring photographs. I am very grateful to Sa'dia Rehman for permission to feature her powerful wall drawing *Allegiance to the flag on picture day* on the cover.

Several undergraduate and graduate students helped this project to fruition. I warmly thank Amanda Burns, Diana Hernandez, Julia Olson, and Alexandra Peterson for the energy and thoroughness they brought to the book as part of the Faculty Research Assistance Program (FRAP). Many thanks go to Nicole Dib for her research and to Jessica Zisa for going above and beyond to see this project to the end.

Jonathan Crewe, Ivy Schweitzer, and Melissa Zeiger nurtured my early thinking and supported me endlessly. I am very grateful to Serin Houston for her genius and spirit, and for helping to bring this work in balance with life. For teaching me to argue and to write in the first place, I thank Hamish Guthrie.

Biji and Darji, Dadi and Dada, you are with me as you have always been, reaching back to places I never knew and ahead to stories I hope to tell. To the Londergan, Makhni, Springer, and Rana clans, my hearty thanks for your verve and merriment, for your nourishing curries and chowders, and for your acceptance and love. Mom and Dad, thank you for your unstinting welcome and for your abiding and anchoring values. You have been there from the very beginning, Mummy and Papa, and steadied me with your immovable love and belief. Even though I became a different sort of Indian doctor, you never once questioned my choices. You have held my hand, opened my path, and led by the example of your care and attention. Aartu, your voice on the line has pulled me through. For our closeness I am utterly grateful. Life is all the richer with your love, your savvy, your belief, and your example.

Christopher, best friend, soulmate, partner in all things, the best of this book is yours. I thank you for your brilliance and your humor, your steadying hand and freeing spirit, your skill in seeing through to what is done and what remains, for the many readings and conversations that crystallized these ideas, and for your devotion to our family in all kinds of weather. Sharing this journey has been a marvel and a thrill. Anaya and Shasta, my dears, you bring magic into my life and make every moment shine. For taking me away from this book into the world of unicorns and excavators, across the creek and to the nesting birds, over the bluffs and out to the ocean, thank you.

Race Characters

Introduction
Reading Race and Character

A remarkable portrait greets visitors to the U.S. Capitol. The East Grand Staircase features a painting of Dalip Singh Saund, in which he stands in the balcony of the Cannon Rotunda behind a trompe l'oeil frame. Though the painting is not large, it is captivating. On the first floor landing where it hangs, there is space to pause for a closer reading. Saund appears casual at first, as though stopped in a customary round of his office building. But the portrait is not casual. Luminaries such as Mahatma Gandhi, Abraham Lincoln, and Woodrow Wilson adorn the border, along with another image of the young Saund. Laden with maps, flags, and monuments, the frame charts Saund's triumphal journey from the fields of Punjab to the U.S. House of Representatives, where he represented California from 1957 to 1963. The brown of Saund's skin stands out against the white of his collar and the whiteness of the many faces that surround his in the halls of the Capitol building. Saund's presence in the inner sanctum of American democracy astonishes. The painting elicits admiration for the success of this immigrant from India who, during a period of immigration restriction and nativist violence, achieved the pinnacle of social mobility and did so with an impressive political program, committed to his constituency as well as to civil rights and to global self-determination. Commissioned by the House of Representatives and unveiled in 2007, the painting commemorates Saund's historic election: he was, as the plaque below the portrait declares, the "First Asian American in Congress."

It is difficult not to admire Saund and be compelled by his singular achievement. During his lifetime, news of Saund's congressional victory spread far and wide. He served as an emissary for the United States during the Cold War, presenting his own success story to audiences around the world who were skeptical of the promise of American freedom and democracy. The 2007 portrait is but one commemoration amid a range of others, including posthumous awards and banquets, the renaming of a post office in Temecula, a California state resolution commemorating his birthday, an exhibit at the Smithsonian featuring materials from his election campaigns,

Portrait of Dalip Singh Saund by Jon R. Friedman (2007). Courtesy of the Collection of the U.S. House of Representatives.

and the installation of a bust at the American Center Library in New Delhi. Saund is hailed as a paragon in the American tradition: a "real American hero out of Horatio Alger," "an Asian American hero," "a source of inspiration," "the perfect person to organize around," and a "political pioneer" who "truly lived the American dream."[1] He is evoked across the political spectrum—by Bobby Jindal (patterned as another Punjabi "wonder-boy") for whom Saund "personifies the idea that every person can, through hard work and dedication, achieve amazing heights"; and by Barack Obama who, even as he cautions against the temptation "to buy into the myth of the 'model minority,'" has praised the "young man from India who, in 1920, came to study agriculture, stayed to become a farmer, and took on the cause of citizenship for all people of South Asian descent."[2]

The figure of Saund does troubling cultural work. Although he is put to several, often incommensurable uses, Saund overwhelmingly represents a protagonist of the American dream. His example evokes its commonplaces: including individualism and opportunistic success, the bootstrap narrative of upward mobility, and the heroic saga of immigrants' rights. As a figurehead, he is made to serve multiple ideological functions. He appeals to liberals and conservatives, to the first African American Democratic president as well as to the first Indian American Republican governor. No matter the caveats that accompany mentions of Saund, his allure persists as a type of model minority who obfuscates structural racism. There are public figures following him who represent the triumph of the American dream and of the immigrant and refugee generations that produced them, albeit in very different ways, and who have also constructed elaborate literary personas, including Nikki Haley, Kamala Harris, Darrell Issa, Eric Liu, Bharati Mukherjee, Colin Powell, Richard Rodriguez, Marco Rubio, and Amy Tan, not to mention Jindal and Obama.[3]

The painting captures the particular fantasy of racial assimilation that Saund represents. Symbols of the "East" become progressively Western as our gaze moves from top to bottom. Displayed in miniature, Saund's turbaned image is overshadowed by the much larger figure of Saund at the center. Backed by the trappings of neoclassical architecture, this large central figure is shorn of his hair and enveloped in the drapery of a Western suit. His suit and tie seem to fit like a second skin. Despite his visibly dark appearance, he assumes the mantle of Americanization with the sartorial ease of assuming new clothes. In a context that saw the successful transformation of European immigrants into white ethnics, Saund's racial difference is not effaced but incorporated. The quotation at the bottom affirms the exceptional status of American democracy. Painted on "multicolored stone," as the description of the painting attests, the quotation helps to recruit Saund to the cause of multiculturalism at the turn of the twenty-first century.[4]

Race Characters considers figures like Saund who circulate within U.S. literature and culture. Visibly racialized immigrants who have an attenuated relationship to minority identity, they embrace certain shibboleths of the American dream, whether individualism, assimilation, upward mobility, or imperialism. Conventional and stereotypical, imitable and replicable, these figures have archetypal appeal. Race is crucial to this appeal. Partly effaced or pointedly displayed, the racial identity of such figures subtends the ethos of liberal multiculturalism that they represent. Because they are underexamined and ineffectively critiqued, they pose an ongoing problem, in that their facile deployments perpetuate the hegemonic ideal of the American dream. To engage with such figures is to engage with the volatility of ethnic literature. To engage with such figures is to confront how they populate the public imaginary as interchangeable archetypes that subordinate the politics of race to ideologies ranging from conservatism to exceptionalism, from neoliberalism to colorblindness.

I propose a new way of reading these figures by enlisting the concept of character and its formal, discursive, and theoretical range. As literary theories of character show, character is a formal as well as a social construct. I adapt this double valence to the study of ethnic literature and race, fashioning a method of race character critique that links literary representations of character to the biographical contexts and diasporic histories that shape them. My chapters focus on immigrant writers—Paule Marshall, Ameen Rihani, Saund, José Garcia Villa, and José Antonio Villarreal—who represent vexed attachments to the American dream either in their work or within the historical record and are therefore ripe for appropriation. Situated in a relatively understudied period from 1900 to 1960, they have a troubling relationship to the archive of ethnic literature, which tends to be mined for dissent and resistance. Each chapter grapples with characters that are eccentric to this oppositional framework in a different way, because they champion imperialist intervention, sever art from biography, betray racial identity, assume the mantle of model minority, or embrace upward mobility. Taken together, my readings reveal an archetype of American character that, to the extent it has been considered, has been viewed in terms of isolated literary figures. Comparative analysis shows how pervasive this archetype is, and how constraining it is, and how ethnic writers confront this archetype in their work.

To return to Saund's portrait, we can study the many parts that character plays. To begin with, characters abound in their basic sense: as persons, portrayed. While Saund occupies pride of place, politicians, public leaders, and nondescript farmers also appear in the frame. The young Saund is here as well, referencing a prior version of himself. Then there are the alphabetic characters at the bottom, painted in such a way as to evoke the Greek root of character, meaning to engrave or furrow. Taken from Saund's autobiography, *Congressman from India* (1960), which was the impetus for the portrait, the words lettered here gesture to other multiples of Saund: protagonist, narrator, and author.[5] Character is not just descriptive of this image, but also constitutive of it. For one, Saund appears to be a character, in that his life is unusual, extraordinary even, when compared to the lives of many others who journeyed to the United States in the early part of the twentieth century. The painting also conjures all that we think of when we think of someone as having character: strength of will, stalwart dedication, moral fortitude, illustrious personality. In addition, character mediates not just what we see but how we perceive it. While the outward person of Saund takes prominence, we are invited to read in his face the lineaments of his inward personality, to attribute character from the appearance of it. In this way, characterization subtends racialization, for we infer who Saund is from the perceptible mark of his skin, aided by the symbolic array beside him. Another slippage happens between individual and nation, as we read in Saund the character of American democracy itself. "There is no room in the United States of America for second-class citizenship," the painting declares, showcasing not only Saund's character but also the purported character of the United States.

Read in this way, the highly wrought figure of Saund comes into view. Character is not just a way of denoting this figure but is central to its very formation, for character drives the ideology of the American dream even as it shapes how racialized subjects are read. Having achieved the pinnacle of success and of self making, Saund appears to be unassailable. Understood as a character, however, he is revealed as a racialized archetype of the American dream, evolving yet persistent, even as his archetypal figure is refracted into multiple parts. The autobiography is key to this breakdown, for it features the author as distinct from his literary and social incarnations. This jostling of parts dislodges the archetype that seems to encompass them all. By studying the interplay of these many versions of Saund's character, we can show that Saund is not identical to himself and, through him, develop a critique of the ideology that he appears to represent.

What my readings show is that the dynamics of characterization are also those of contestation. We can critically engage with the American dream precisely through characters that appear to exemplify its ideology. The chapters that follow demonstrate this—that writers who carry the representational burden of such characters do not merely reproduce it in their work. Rather, they reveal the protagonist of the American dream to be an impoverished and unsustainable archetype, enabling a fuller understanding of the American dream, of its protean forms and their vulnerability. Their writings expose the vagaries of identification that arise when minorities are disenfranchised by majority culture and help create a more complete picture of minority identity shaped by compulsion and necessity.

Characters that are discomfiting have much to teach, as *Race Characters* demonstrates, working with rather than through figures that do not fit neatly into a resistance-based model of ethnic literature. This mode of attention generates a fundamental shift in focus from personality to society. Race character critique understands character as a social construct of individuality and thinks with this construct, considering how it continues to be nationally appealing as it bespeaks assimilation and compromise. Through literary structures of characterization, there emerges a structural reading of how sociohistorical constraints act upon the outliers who appear to evade their reach.

Brown Uncle Tom

Ethnic literature is peopled by figures like Saund. His precursor, Abraham Mitrie Rihbany, who immigrated to the United States from Ottoman Syria in 1891, was also politically minded. During World War I, Rihbany called for the United States to intervene in the Middle East and thwart the advance of European colonialism, attending the Paris Peace Conference in 1919 as a representative of Syrian societies in the United States.[6] Rihbany's autobiography, *A Far Journey* (1914), entwines his conversion to Protestantism with his deepening Americanism. "I was born in Syria as a child, but I was born in America as a man," Rihbany writes, producing a type of American whose Syrian nativity is no impediment to his effortless naturalization.[7]

Rihbany was joined in the Syrian diaspora by Salom Rizk and Rihani, who voiced their devotion to their adoptive land.[8] Similarly, Manuel Buaken's *I Have Lived with the American People* (1948), while deeply aware of colonial oppression and its extension into the diaspora, fashions the Filipino as a type of ideal American, "one with America."[9] For Villa, the heart of empire holds out the promise of "a white cool birth in a new land" as the "Young Writer" (in a story thus titled) dreams of being unfettered by race, nation, or coloniality.[10] The United States is a horizon of hope for Younghill Kang and Dhan Gopal Mukerji as well, insofar as it represents an alternative to the colonial regimes that they leave behind. Despite the daily struggle with poverty and racism that they dramatize so vividly in their work, they invest in a cosmopolitan, syncretic American ideal. In *East Goes West* (1937), New York inspires in Kang's protagonist a vision of "life reaching out and up in a scope unrestricted, north and south to the Poles, east, west, to a meeting place of divided hemispheres . . . broad, cosmopolitan, fresh, a rich spiritual emanation from material wealth."[11] Mukerji, while considerably more ambivalent about his sojourn in the United States than Saund, nonetheless ends his autobiography, *Caste and Outcast* (1923), with a remarkable invocation of America. "All the world and all the nations are planting their best and worst seed in this spring-smitten island," he writes, imbuing this "seed continent" with the expectation of global synthesis.[12] While he claims to offer an insider's view of "Indian life from within," his relationship to India is anything but transparent, and so too is its rendering for American audiences.[13] Like Rihbany's depictions of the Holy Land, Mukerji's view of the "East" calls to mind the work of other writers (like Sui Sin Far, Sadakichi Hartmann, C. Y. Lee, Yone Noguchi, Onoto Watanna, and Jade Snow Wong) who trade in Orientalist stereotypes. Others like Claude McKay, Ved Mehta, and Villarreal are anywhere from capricious to taciturn about the politics of race. Reading beyond the specific intersection of immigration and race yields other accommodationist, apologist, and assimilationist figures who strain the bounds of an oppositional framework (Mary Antin, Abraham Cahan, María Ruiz de Burton, Jean Toomer, Booker T. Washington, Anzia Yezierska) or throw the terms of racial identification into crisis in their writings (James Weldon Johnson, Nella Larsen).

More recently, the controversy around Mukherjee's novel *Jasmine* (1989) encapsulates something of what is at stake. Likened to Horatio Alger, the novel's eponymous heroine goes from being a penniless widow, driven to a perilous migration, to becoming the desired object of multiple, wealthy white men and a substitute for their wives.[14] Jasmine traces the arc of Westward expansion from Punjab to Florida and eventually to California, adopting identity after identity and trading in one romance for another. "Watch me re-position the stars," she declares, for "the frontier is pushing indoors," and Jasmine must push ahead with it, "a tornado, rubble-maker."[15] The disruptive momentum of the protagonist extends to the novel and to the author herself, who is notorious for her claim to unhyphenated American identity. "I choose to describe myself on my own terms, as an American, rather than as an Asian-American," Mukherjee has written, partly addressing those academics who would see this "rejection of hyphenation" as "race treachery."[16] Her rejection has its uses. A U.S. Department of State publication, *Writers on America* (2002), which was meant to "illuminate in an interesting way certain American values—freedom, diversity, democracy—that may not be well understood in all parts of the world," relies on Mukherjee to serve this propaganda function by rehearsing her rejection of minority identity.[17] Rodriguez, too, has provoked controversy through similar demurrals. "I remain at best ambivalent about those Hispanic anthologies where I end up," he writes in *Brown*, a 2002 volume of essays that looks instead to "be shelved Brown."[18] Like Mukherjee, Rodriguez has been called to task for his bourgeois liberalism, embrace of assimilation, and capitulation to white hegemony.[19]

Chang-rae Lee's *Native Speaker* (1995) explores some of this terrain, featuring a character who circles back to the figure of Saund. John Kwang is another unexpected protagonist of the American dream who, with a measure of luck and charity, transforms himself from a stowaway and refugee of the Korean War into an enigmatic and wildly popular candidate for mayor of New York. John embodies the possibility that an Asian American might become a representative American; that, being "effortlessly Korean, effortlessly American," he might claim not only the name (of the generic John Doe) but also the allegiance of everyman.[20] His appeal, like that of Saund, hinges on the calculated display—part revelation, part effacement—of just the right degree of multicultural savor.

How are we to reckon with such figures? For those intrigued by the entanglements of personality and race, by the dilemma of political recalcitrance, or by outliers within literary and public culture, these figures are something of an enigma. They have potent appeal, for they promise to expiate the country's racial sins and augur a new era of global domination for the United States, however questionable this promise might appear at the end of the American century. To denounce them can be satisfying. But censure inadequately considers the position of immigrants who must negotiate whiteness and hegemony, no matter what reserves of cultural capital they are themselves able to draw upon. To recuperate them as heroes of a progressive history, where this is possible, hides their reluctance around occupying such roles. Their own ambivalence as historical figures drops out of view, as do the gaps and inconsistencies between the revolutionary and reactionary uses to which their figures are put. In Saund's case, we risk losing sight of the dynamic tension among the historical person, his autobiographical self-representation, and the many ways in which his character is resurrected and deployed. Whether we rally around or against such figures, we accept the inducements of character and remain trapped within circuits of admiration and condemnation.

Ethnic studies recognizes the limits of oppositional critique for making sense of these troubling figures. Guided by the imperatives of racial solidarity and resistance to oppression, and seeking to imagine through ethnic literature just future worlds, literary critics have confronted the challenge of apprehending figures that contravene such imperatives. María Carla

Sánchez grapples with "the Color of Literary History" in her suggestively titled essay on the work of early Mexican American writers whose identifications with whiteness call into question not only "the utility of resistance theory" but also "the notion of a genealogy of Mexican American literature as a whole"; these early writings "are not simply not resistant in the same ways as post-1960s writings," she claims, "they're not Chicano."[21] Similarly, Viet Thanh Nguyen points to "ideological rigidity" within Asian American studies that defines Asian America as "*only* a place of ethnic consensus and resistance to an inherently exploitative or destructive capitalism" (that divides the subversive "bad subject" from the assimilationist "model minority") and in so doing fails to account for "the *flexible strategies* often chosen by authors and characters to navigate their political and ethical situations."[22] And Stephanie Leigh Batiste refuses to presume "an inherent moral rectitude of black cultural expression that ignores how African Americans have been implicated in configurations of power in ways more complicated than (only) domination or (only) resistance."[23] These scholars underscore how domination and racial exclusion delimit the scope of literary critique and look to enlarge it. They propose less binary and more versatile models of subjectivity, and call for yet more models, attuned to how minorities confront and channel hegemonic power.

More and more, scholarship in ethnic studies and adjacent fields is grappling with work that does not fit an oppositional mold. Historically, many of the enduring models of subaltern identity—whether Frantz Fanon's reverberant topos of "black skin, white masks," Gloria Anzaldúa's reclaiming of La Malinche, Houston Baker Jr.'s excursus on modernist minstrelsy, or Homi Bhabha's concept of colonial mimicry—have at their core a subtle sense of dissent shaped by constraint.[24] Nuanced theories of minority identification have emerged at the intersection of literary criticism, affect studies, performance studies, psychoanalysis, and queer studies.[25] Other scholarship foregrounds the politics of negotiation by exploring how ethnic literature answers conflicting creative, ideological, and material demands, as well as by mapping the social fields and institutional frameworks that shape its interpretation.[26] Another vein of critique complicates the model minority myth—by unearthing counternarratives, reconfiguring assimilationist archives, or exploring the extensions and limits of its critique.[27]

My book builds on these studies by bringing into focus the troubling figures that are at the heart of many of these projects. I am drawn to archives of ambivalent identification on which the work of Batiste, Heather Love, José Esteban Muñoz, Sianne Ngai, Crystal Parikh, and others is centered—work that exhumes controversial texts, enlarges the scope of minority subjectivity, and imagines a politics attuned to accommodation and recalcitrance. As Love argues, we must understand "backwardness as an alternative form of politics—one that is consonant with the experience of marginalized subjects."[28] Whereas these studies work through figures of vexed identification with a view to develop fuller models of affect, ethics, performance, or queerness, I propose that we recenter them as literary characters.

To this project, literary formalism has something important to contribute. Broadly speaking, literary criticism has made much of character study, but comparatively little has been said about ethnic characters as objects and agents of theorization in their own right. New work on race and form provides a useful point of departure, for it is guided by the sense that literary studies has particular insights for understanding racial identity. In Asian American studies, Colleen Lye's theorization under the rubric of "racial form" of historical formalism rooted in cultural materialist critique has inaugurated a rich body of work that links the aesthetics of race to its social modes.[29] Although her work predates this formulation (and has a different lineage in poststructuralism), Kandice Chuh makes a related claim proposing that we think of the term "Asian American" as a "*metaphor* for resistance and racism," "connotative and evocative, and in that way, perhaps even poetry in itself."[30] Literariness grounds Chuh's "call for conceiving Asian American studies as a *subjectless discourse*," a "strategic *anti*-essentialism," which "points to the need to manufacture 'Asian American' situationally" to avoid "problematic assumptions of essential identities" that have shaped the field.[31] Stephen Hong Sohn arrives at a similar strategy as he curates an archive where the identity of Asian American writers is not coextensive with the fiction that they create. He, too, pursues "strategic antiessentialism" to press "the limits of cultural nationalist models" and undermine the draw of the "authenticity paradigm . . . assuming unification among the author, narrative perspective, and narrative content" in the literary market.[32] These scholars address themselves to a particular challenge. How can criticism of ethnic literature honor its oppositional formation in ethnic studies while ordering archives in terms other than those of identity-based resistance? Christopher Lee makes the case that an "idealized critical subject . . . operates throughout Asian American literary culture and cultural criticism as a means of providing coherence to oppositional knowledge projects and political practices"; this, too, is a literary figure, a "flexible trope, a position that gets occupied by a range of subjects including fictional characters, writers, artists, activists, students, critics, and intellectuals."[33] Gene Andrew Jarrett and Ralph Rodriguez take up these considerations in the fields of black and Latinx studies, respectively. Jarrett aligns the demand for ethnic authenticity with the "racial realism" of the "deans" of African American literature that the "anomalous quality of the texts written by truants" contravenes.[34] And Rodriguez proposes that a formalist taxonomy of genre do "the work of unbinding Latinx literature from the usual critical, racial, and sociological perspectives" ("there are more satisfying taxonomies and heuristics for grouping and analyzing literature than what scholars now recognize as the biological fiction but social reality of race").[35]

Race Characters builds on this momentum. Although these critics have yet to use character as a hermeneutic, they provide many openings onto character. "Subjectlessness" as a critical orientation appears to preclude reinvesting in character, except that Chuh asks not that we jettison subjectivity but examine its "discursive constructedness."[36] Similarly, the work of Lee, Sohn, and Jarrett begs the question of how to develop better models for reading across literary and authorial—and even critical—subject formations. Expanding theories of character, my study creates one such model, using formalist analysis to transform social analysis, and vice versa. I take a literary approach to an archive whose literariness has been questioned, an archive historically read in terms of essentialist identities that conflate writer and text. Ethnic literature does not, however, reflect social minorness but redefines it. The dual valence of character as both authorial and textual, formal and social, brings this transformative capacity to the fore and enables us to explore how writers confront in their writing the very characters they are meant to represent. This confrontation is particularly important for writers whose work exceeds an oppositional paradigm of ethnic studies and features complex negotiations, daring yet precarious naturalizations, and ambitions despite (and because of) visible difference to symbolize the American ideal.

Rodriguez's memorable reflection on his own problematic figure speaks to this point, as he adapts one set of stock characters to name another. Referencing the critiques of affirmative action and bilingual education that made him so well known and, for many scholars, even infamous, he describes himself thus in the prologue to his autobiography *Hunger of Memory* (1982): "I have become notorious among certain leaders of America's Ethnic Left. I am considered a dupe, an ass, the fool—Tom Brown, the brown Uncle Tom, interpreting the writing on the wall to a bunch of cigar-smoking pharaohs."[37] Rodriguez recruits the figure of the roguish yet reformed British schoolboy, the titular hero of Thomas Hughes's 1857 novel (whose last name, as it turns out, has broader symbolic uses). To this appellation, he conjoins Harriet Beecher Stowe's legendary figure of servility and piety, who first appeared in her famous 1852 novel. These stock characters come together to describe a twentieth-century type of "scholarship boy" whose schooling in the American dream leads him to disavow his working-class Mexican immigrant upbringing, his mother tongue, and his familial intimacy.[38]

Is Rodriguez trying to piece together the name for a character for whom no name exists? Certainly there are other names that he might use. "Tio Taco" is the "Mexican-American equivalent of an Uncle Tom," although possibly of recent derivation.[39] "Pocho" is another choice as a commonly used term for an assimilated Mexican American, and it is an epithet that attaches to Rodriguez at multiple points in the autobiography. But Rodriguez is drawn to the modifier "brown," which begins as a surname and is then transformed into a signifier of race. It denotes not only Rodriguez's own Mexican American identity (even as he disclaims that identity), but it also encompasses other ethnic groups that are neither black nor white and that have a contentious relationship to whiteness. Elsewhere in the autobiography, he finds other ways to symbolize this relationship: he is a "'coconut'—someone brown on the outside, white on the inside."[40] Rodriguez names a distinct figure of racialized sycophancy that foregrounds immigration rather than slavery and, being "brown," transforms the binary model of race relations in the United States.

Whatever we call such figures, they appear across ethnic literature. Diffused by immigration from Asia, Africa, and Latin America, they extend the imaginative genealogy of Uncle Tom into the twentieth century. I am not especially interested in framing a typology of this array, as this approach risks reproducing such figures as static—a type or set of types. Instead, I propose that we look to character theory, particularly those aspects that bridge aesthetic forms and social formations, to develop a hermeneutic for reading figures that exceed an oppositional configuration of ethnic studies. This method emerges out of the problem that these figures pose as readymade devices, or reproducible archetypes, into which visibly racialized minorities are slotted in order to advance the fiction of the American dream. Character theory can be equipped to engage critically with these figures through the work of writers who represent them in a double sense—as historical persons and literary personas. To read in this way is to grapple with minority identity under the sign of its own erasure. This interpretive practice maps out the discontinuities between Rodriguez the author, Rodriguez the narrator, and Rodriguez the protagonist. It brings into view characters who blur our interpretive categories and refuse to inhabit race in ways that can be named in advance. To read in this way is to apprehend both the scope of such characters and their specificity by restoring the continuities and disjunctures between literary and social worlds.

Burden of Signification

Adapting character theory to the study of ethnic literature involves more than diversifying the characters we read. Rather, we must rethink both the study of character and ethnic literature. How do ethnic characters transform our habits of character analysis? How does the concept of character deepen our reading of ethnic literature? Developing race character critique requires a double move, forging theoretical links between character and race on the one hand, and showing how literary critique of character navigates these links on the other. The burden of signification of character enables us to interpret the burden of representation of ethnic literature. Considerations of race, power, and difference broaden our readings of literary character. Exploring how authors translate their own social character into their literary work reorients character theory around questions of autobiography and authorship. While attuned to ethnic literature, these hermeneutics are relevant to a range of projects centered on literature and characterization.

Toni Morrison lays the foundation for this work in *Playing in the Dark* (1992), which urges readers and scholars to consider the "Africanist persona" within American literature.[41] This is not necessarily an anthropomorphic figure, but "a dark and abiding presence," a "shadow" that "hovers in implication, in sign, in line of demarcation," shaping the formation of "American character" and serving as "a metaphor for transacting the whole process of Americanization."[42] Character theory opens up one approach to this task by linking minor and minority characters. Through readings in the nineteenth-century novel, Alex Woloch develops a system of character distribution that includes two minor types, traced to industrialization and social stratification: the worker (a single-use character, flat and unremarkable) and the eccentric (a fragmentary character, unruly and unmanageable). Charlotte Brontë's *Jane Eyre* (1847) illustrates this typology, for Grace Poole plays the role of the worker and Bertha Mason that of the eccentric. Bertha is a minor character in more ways than one. Locked in an attic apartment by her husband, and marginal to much of the narrative, she also hails from the margins of the British Empire. She is a Creole woman, transplanted from colony to metropole, whose racial identity remains ambiguous. As a character, Bertha has many afterlives. As Woloch points out, she features centrally in Jean Rhys's novel *Wide Sargasso Sea* (1966) and has become a touchstone for feminist thought.[43] Elsewhere, Woloch extrapolates his analysis to twentieth-century fiction: "What kind of narrative centrality is possible for characters who are structurally subordinated within the social system," he asks, and "how should the modern novel negotiate the configured relationship between minority characters and minor characters"?[44]

There is a productive assonance between "minor" and "minority" here that critics such as Ulka Anjaria and Sohn have also pursued in order to understand the stock characters of Indian realism and ethnic literature, respectively. As Anjaria argues, building on Woloch's work, "minorness" can be understood as an aesthetic "strategy to account for the different degrees to which citizens are incorporated into the body politic.[45] These critics open up a term that denotes relative textual priority to modes of contextual priority, asking how socially and racially marginalized characters occupy narrative space. The example of *Wide Sargasso Sea* generates further considerations, as the lineaments of Rhys's life and identity are recognizable in those of her protagonist. How do writers negotiate their own minority character through their work, particularly in those instances where authorial character and literary character overlap? Here is a possibility for adapting character theory to analyze the relationship between literary and social minorness.

In taking this opening, I begin broadly. The meaning of character is multivalent, which makes it both theoretically rich and conceptually challenging, its range of connotations shown in my reading of Saund's portrait. The origin of the word "character" can be traced back to the Greek for mark or engraving (*kharakter*), the act of marking or engraving (*kharassein*), and the instrument of marking or engraving (*kharax*). As the *Oxford English Dictionary* (OED) defines the term, its meanings can be divided along literal and figurative lines. In the literal sense, character is a mark, brand, stamp, sign, emblem, symbol, token, feature, or trait. Characters are legible at many different sites, such as astrological symbols, letters of the alphabet, ideograms, musical or mathematical notation, computer data, or handwriting. In the figurative sense, character signifies distinguishing traits or properties that typify particular things, individuals, or species; distinctive or peculiar features of someone or something; the mental or moral qualities that set apart peoples, groups, or cultures; strong or striking personalities linked to appearance or representation, and sometimes to face or features; rank, position, status, or capacities relative to other people or things; reputation or broad estimation; as well as types of persons, particularly those who are odd, extraordinary, or eccentric. Locutions such as "having character" or "being quite a character" follow from some of these meanings, describing people who are extraordinary, either because they outperform social standards or (in a more neutral, often negative sense) because they transgress accepted norms. The concept has considerable discursive range. The literary meaning is only one of fifteen possible variants: "A person portrayed in a work of fiction, a drama, a film, a comic strip, etc.; (also) a part played by an actor on the stage, in a film, etc., a role."[46]

To these dictionary definitions, literary theory adds considerable insights. Scrutinizing OED'S taxonomies of character, J. Hillis Miller questions the neat partitioning of literal and figurative senses of the term. He points out those sites where the meaning of character is redoubled: *kharassein*, for instance, names an act of human transformation whereby the world is "marked with the mark which makes it a mark, a sign, a 'character'"; or that characters beget characters in an interpretive spiral such that to "interpret someone's character (handwriting) is to interpret his character (physiognomy) is to interpret his character (personality) is to interpret his character (some characteristic text he has written), in a perpetual round of figure for figure."[47] "To read character is to read character is to read character is to read character," Miller declares, inhabiting the *mise en abyme* or recursive mirror of characterological interpretation.[48] Similarly, John Frow observes that these definitions entail "a series of metonymic transfers from the more concrete to the more abstract, without ever quite losing the sense of the impressed physical mark."[49] "Metonymic displacement" ranks, according to Morrison, among the key techniques "that displace rather than signify the Africanist character" (along with various condensing modes like the fetish and the stereotype).[50]

In effect, the concept of character carries a burden of signification, which these critics underscore in different ways. Character is a reflexive sign, one that revolves around the making and reading of signs. The OED divides character into its literal and figurative aspects, as though character qua sign is separable from character qua signification. But this division is unsustainable. All characters, no matter how straightforward they may appear to be, have a surfeit of *character*—associated and associative meanings that cannot be delimited to the concrete sense of the term. There is an overdetermination of meaning at work here, an interpretive excess that, while bound to the literal mark, ranges both deep and wide (metaphorically and metonymically) along axes of association that link signifier and signified.

So we continue to return to this enigmatic term, despite the many deaths that character has suffered as a concept. For Hélène Cixous, writing in 1974, characters are marionettes, ideological constructs that appeal to readers because they perpetuate the myth of a selfsame, singular, and masterful "I." Characterization, in Cixous's words, "conducts the game of ideology," and we must understand this game for what it is: "reality as simulacrum," "mask as mask."[51] In her introduction to a 2011 volume of *New Literary History* devoted to new work on character, Rita Felski points out that, although a certain version of character—"an idea of a unified, unchanging, intrinsic, or impermeable personhood"—is no longer tenable, "character has become newly intriguing."[52] Its resurrection neither involves staid character studies nor restores old typologies of character (although these continue to be the standard stuff of the study guide), nor does it revoke the concept as such, as might be expected in the wake of poststructuralist critique. Instead, critics are redefining and using the concept of character to find new ways of reading in a range of historical fields from medieval to contemporary, as well as a range of conceptual fields, including cognitive literary studies, ethics, genre studies, and literary criticism itself.[53]

In this context, it is helpful to consider scholarship that can be loosely grouped under the category of "socioformal" approaches to character.[54] While Woloch uses this term to talk about the sociality of narrative form, I use it to describe a method of reading character (which Woloch also employs) that bridges literary and social worlds and thus enables their articulation.[55] How do characters mediate the fictive and the real? What are the contexts out of which characters emerge and what work do they do in these contexts? How does character function as the expression of a varied and variable set of social dynamics? How can we extrapolate from the basic literary understanding of character as a representation of personhood to understanding how persons are represented outside of literature? These are some of the questions that preoccupy socioformal critiques of character. These critiques offer some ways out of the theoretical contradictions that surround the concept of character—particularly the tension between character as *person* (agent of human subjectivity, verisimilar individuals we love to love or to hate, who jump off the pages of the text and lead whole lives beyond them) and character as *device* (structural element, set of textual effects, illusory, repressive agent of bourgeois hierarchy)—by articulating its literary and social modalities through a new vocabulary that links textual structures of characterization to extratextual worlds.[56]

With a few exceptions, the inventive force of this criticism has not yet been mustered to read ethnic literature; conversely, we have yet to extend our theories of character through ethnic literature. "Characterology," as Jarrett points out, "needs more diverse perspectives attentive to race."[57] Jennifer DeVere Brody's approach to punctuation is illuminating, for she rethinks "typography as a form of experimental (and perhaps even experiential) blackness," reading "characteristics of the ellipsis" in Ralph Ellison's work "as analogues to the character Invisible Man."[58] Formulating race character critique involves forging a similar set of conceptual links. Returning to the dictionary definition reveals that character is tied to appearance. As a "distinctive mark impressed, engraved, or otherwise made on a surface," a "brand, stamp," "an outward sign," a "distinctive indication, a visible token, evidence," "a feature, trait, characteristic," or "the distinguishing features of a species or other taxon," character implicates physiognomy. Its attachment to what Frow calls the "impressed physical mark" opens up character to theorizing of race. Built into the idea of character, Miller tells us, is "the presumption that external signs correspond to and reveal an otherwise hidden nature," that the "visible designs made by the features of a face—nose, mouth, eyes, lines of forehead, cheek, or chin—are taken as a hieroglyphic sign telling accurately what that person is like inwardly."[59] Thus, Tamburlaine reads in Theridamas the "characters graven in thy brows" in an attempt to enjoin him to his destiny.[60] These points have particular relevance for racialized subjects, for whom the relation between outward and inward character is both feeble and overdetermined. The OED tells us that this extrapolation of personality from appearance ("face or features as identifying a person; personal appearance as indicative of something") is rare or obsolete.[61] But in practice this is not the case. While these locutions of character might be uncommon, outward appearance continues to function as an index of inward character for visibly racialized subjects. This is what racism is in a fundamental sense—the extrapolation of all manner of essentialist assumptions from the apparent "mark," "brand," or "stamp" of race.

Although not focused on character, Fanon's phenomenology of race in *Black Skin, White Masks* (1952) helps link race to character. In his famous fifth chapter, "The Fact of Blackness," Fanon vividly describes the fragmentation of the black colonized subject under the white colonizer's gaze and subsequent attempts to reconstitute subjectivity and formulate a response.[62] This fragmentation is the outcome of a reading of character that entraps the black subject in a web of significations. "I am overdetermined from without.

I am the slave not of the 'idea' that others have of me but of my own appearance," Fanon writes, concerned to dramatize the relationship between "appearance" and "idea."[63] Carefully charting the movements of his body under the white gaze, Fanon shows how he is compelled to fashion his "corporal schema" (a "slow composition of my *self* as a body in the middle of a spatial and temporal world") out of a "historico-racial schema" ("a thousand details, anecdotes, stories") that violently substitutes for it a "racial epidermal schema."[64] The phenomenology of character overdetermines its ontology, as the racial history of colonialism is inscribed upon the surface of black skin, precluding unselfconscious embodiment.

This scene casts the recursive mirror of characterological interpretation in a new light. The black subject is rendered in entomological and scientistic terms: "I progress by crawling. And already I am being dissected under white eyes, the only real eyes. I am *fixed*. Having adjusted their microtomes, they objectively cut away slices of my reality."[65] He becomes a specimen on a slide under the microscopic lens of the colonial gaze. "I slip into corners," Fanon writes, where his "long antennae pick up the catch-phrases strewn over the surface of things" that might at any moment attach to him and leave him "locked into the infernal circle," liked "in spite of my color" or disliked "not because of" it.[66] An excess of interpretation, which Fanon tries and fails to evade, is provoked by his appearance. He is indescribable except in the language of racism, hypervisible as a type (a sample, an insect) even as he is rendered invisible by a surfeit of figuration, or "perpetual round of figure for figure," in Miller's terms.

Mustering a fundamental typology of character, we might say that Fanon describes the making of a flat character—stereotypical, imitable, and replicable.[67] The conceit of microscopic fixation captures this rendering, as the three-dimensional subject is flattened into the two dimensions of the slide and readied for examination. This metaphor questions the pretensions of scientific racism even as it evokes a particular impress of character—the stereotype, which derives its meaning from the casting of formes of type into metal plates for mass production. There are at least two things happening here. The gap between outward and inward character, between appearance and personality, is leveled. And this flattened character is reduplicated and widely circulated.

Stepping back from this scene, it is possible to see that characterization and racialization are linked practices of social reading. In essence, we read racial figures through characterological templates. This reading is also misreading, as Fanon shows. Race, as the outward impress of character, eclipses ontology. The black colonial subject is assailed by the overdetermination of his own character, vulnerable to an apprehension that is only skin deep. Racialization operates by way of interpretive excess, as a web of metaphorical and metonymic linkages (repeatedly invalidated by humanist and scientific critique) are reinvented and conjured out of the depths of a single reading of race and generalized to an entire people. This has a parallel in the interpretive movement of characterization, for racialization and characterization extrapolate from a concrete mark to a range of figurative meanings. While tethered to a particular encounter, these figurative meanings are broad and excessive. This propensity for generalization is built into the definition of character itself, which in one of its aspects designates the "sum of the moral and mental qualities which distinguish an individual or a people, viewed as a homogeneous whole."[68] Consider how racial profiling works: a profile, in the sense of physical outline or feature, is relied upon in order to produce a profile, in the sense of biographical record or description, which is then extrapolated to an array of racialized subjects in order to police them. "Character is a system for creating distinctions between things," Sara Ahmed notes.[69] Linked to race, character becomes a system for denoting and managing visible racial difference. It functions as an important technology of the construction of race, as a social device that makes race happen in certain ways. Yet, this system is not unassailable. According to Ahmed, "fictional characters ... might still reveal the truth *about* character, as a system for creating truth."[70] Mediating fiction and truth is a key task of adept literary criticism and one way that it contributes to the study of race. Literary criticism helps navigate what Michael Omi and Howard Winant describe as the tendency to understand race "as a mere *illusion*" when we "should think of race as an element of social structure," "a dimension of human representation rather than an illusion."[71] Well practiced in the study of illusion and its structural determinants, character analysis elucidates representational truths. Literary reading thus creates a fuller social reading of race.

Burden of Representation

Ethnic literature, then, consists of characters that are likely to be in dialog with their apprehension as characters. This apprehension signals a particular combination of discernment and arrest; as flat characters, marked out by their difference, they are meant to stand in for the whole of a given ethnic group. Ethnic writers are perhaps especially vulnerable to this trap of signification, insofar as they, too, must inhabit an overdetermined social field. Their being, their function, is often centered on their character. No matter where their work is located on a spectrum from fiction to autobiography, ethnic writers are often taken to be representing themselves. This assumption often entails another: that they represent the character of a given ethnic group as a whole and must not only tell their own story but that of the collective to which they presumably belong. In effect, their literary and social worlds are collapsed. This is one way of parsing what critics in postcolonial and ethnic studies commonly refer to as a burden of representation, the demand for broad social representativeness that attaches of necessity to minority cultural production within the dominant public sphere to which minorities have limited access. In this context, there emerges a corollary demand that ethnic literature achieve particular political imperatives, that it revise racist records, serve as a sociological corrective, or right past wrongs.

Writing on black British culture, Kobena Mercer argues that "the artistic discourse of hitherto marginalized subjects is circumscribed by the assumption that such artists speak as 'representatives' of the communities from which they come," which "creates a burden that is logically impossible for any one individual to bear."[72] "Representations thus become allegorical," argue Ella Shohat and Robert Stam in the context of postcolonial popular culture: "within hegemonic discourse every subaltern performer/role is seen as synecdochically summing up a vast but putatively homogenous community."[73] Anglophone literature obscures vernacular forms, Aijaz Ahmad notes: "The retribution visited upon the head of an Asian, an African, an Arab intellectual who is of any consequence and writes in English is that he or she is immediately elevated to the lonely splendour of a representative—of a race, a continent, a civilization, even the 'Third World.'"[74] This "'retribution' includes the scorn of the ethnic community as well," adds Rey Chow, theorizing "ethnic *ressentiment*": how the psychic damage of colonialism is displaced onto "those who ethnically most resemble oneself," evincing a "deep-rooted anxiety and defensiveness about what the ethnic culture amounts to and how it ought to be represented to the world at large."[75]

Some of the more memorable controversies within the U.S. ethnic canon have revolved around this burden and this *ressentiment*. In his scathing 1937 review of McKay's work, Alain Locke presents "representative character" as an ideal based on "the acceptance of some group loyalty and the intent, as well as the ability, to express mass sentiment."[76] While informed by the vagaries of their personal relationship, and Locke's own radical turn, the essay implicates what Claudia Tate calls the "manifest text of black literary discourse," shaped by "protest-oriented directives" and the call to "manifest the sociological factors of an oppressive 'black experience'" (which her own archive of black novels counters).[77] Commenting on the controversy around Maxine Hong Kingston's autobiography, *The Woman Warrior* (1976), Sau-ling Cynthia Wong makes a similar claim: "The individual loses his or her uniqueness and becomes a sociological category," she writes, as she probes the aporias that the demand for "representativeness" creates for ethnic autobiography.[78] "What if the single individual's life happens to confirm or even endorse white perceptions instead of challenging them?" asks Wong in her assessment of critiques of Kingston for lack of authenticity and reliance on stereotype: "*Bios* is of little worth unless it is 'representative'—averaged out to become sociologically informative as well as edifying."[79] These considerations continue to animate criticism of ethnic literature that probes the "*assumption* of representation" (Mark Chiang) and its "culturalist" limits (Cynthia Wu), and forays outside its "knowable boxes" (Rodriguez).[80]

The concept of character offers a way of exploring how social minorness translates into ethnic literature on multiple levels. At a conceptual level, because character traverses literary and social worlds, it helps us to articulate these worlds. Again, the literary meaning of character is only one of fifteen dictionary variants. As a concept, character helps to link literary representations and social persons: reading ethnic characters on the page, we read the social character of race and ethnicity. At a discursive level, character is a key feature of public culture, particularly as it takes up questions of national belonging and social reform. Not only is there an ongoing preoccupation with the elusive yet captivating construct of "American character," character has long been the stuff of the American dream, in a genealogy stretching from Benjamin Franklin through Alger to Washington.[81] As Cathy Schlund-Vials points out, "good character" is enshrined within the Naturalization Act of 1790, where it "masks a decidedly racist citizenship matrix."[82] Linked to trials adjudicating racial identity, the evolution of scientific racism, projects of racial uplift, and narratives of the self-made man, the discursive dimensions of character have particular relevance for ethnic literature and for the sorts of characters studied here.[83] The confluence of race and character has historically served to dislodge particular forms of racial stigma even as it generates others, opening up the possibility of social mobility unconstrained by race. In James Salazar's words, "while the discourse of character detached race from the surface features of the visible body through which it had been traditionally construed, it also lodged race more deeply in the body by identifying it with the subtle signs and manners of character."[84]

At a theoretical level, the burden of signification of character throws the burden of representation of ethnic literature into relief. As I discuss above, character magnifies the recursive relation of signifier and signified. The term denotes an interpretive excess, in that it represents not only the making and reading of signs but also the sign itself as well as the range of meanings that attach to that sign. Due in part to its tenacious, if loose, attachment to the physical mark, character has particular significance for racially marked figures who are, following Fanon, "overdetermined from without." Characterization thus discloses racialization. The burden of signification that attaches to the concept of character attaches in specific ways to racialized subjects. A given literary representation of ethnic character is part of a chain of metonymic and metaphorical associations that is proliferating and expansive. To return to the recursive mirror of characterization, character begets character. This chain encumbers ethnic writers as well. Drawn into the ambit of these volatile significations, they vanish in the infinite mirror of their own characterization.

This shared disclosure of character through race and race through character is on view in a scene from Rihbany's *A Far Journey*. Rihbany is set to depart from the Syrian enclave in New York when he appeals to a local pastor for a reference. "Dr. van Dyke met me very cordially, but felt some hesitancy about giving a recommendation to one who was an entire stranger to him. But I said to him, in my broken English, not to be afraid because 'I was very good man.'"[85] This transaction foregrounds the discursive importance of character to Rihbany's Americanization, for he must build his character before he can journey West. The exchange is allegorical in that it points to the reading of the autobiography itself: Rihbany is appraised not only by the clergyman but also by the reader. Because his audience hardly knows him, Rihbany must supply his own character reference in anticipation of receiving the one that he desires. At this point in the narrative, something odd happens. Upon hearing Rihbany's halting self-endorsement, which exposes his lack of facility with the English language, the clergyman presents to him a text that is likely to be incomprehensible to Rihbany. "Reaching to the bookcase behind him he took out a book of a very strange character and asked me whether I could read that," Rihbany writes; "I said 'No. This must be Babylon writing.' Shaking with laughter, he said, 'It is shorthand.'"[86] The book, which Rihbany cannot read and consequently misinterprets, occasions their camaraderie. Although they laugh at Rihbany's expense, their exchange ends happily, as the clergyman proceeds to add his name to a letter of support for Rihbany. But why is this book proffered and, in turn, featured within the span of the autobiography? The answer has to do with the burden of signification of character. At bottom, "character" references the printed script of the book. But the term, in its singular form, evokes the "very strange character" that the autobiography features—the character of Rihbany as he appears to the clergyman and to his readers who are unsettled by his palpable, if unspoken, racial difference. The interpretive excess of character signals the interpretive excess to which Rihbany is subject, and which he seeks to manage and contain. In the response of the clergyman, Rihbany models the response he desires from his readers: that the visible threat of racial difference might be diffused by convivial, if one-sided, laughter.

If the act of conjoining character to ethnic literature discloses these shared burdens, character theory offers ways to grapple with them. Miller's exegesis understands the chain of signification of character through readings in continental philosophy and nineteenth-century literature. "Character (in the sense of self) is never present. It is always over there, somewhere else pointed to by characters (signposts) that cannot be followed to reach an unmediated access to what they indicate," he writes, noting that "characterological signs do not stand for anything beyond themselves," and that "the manifest signs of character must both presuppose and constitute what they signify."[87] The relationship between sign and signifier that the concept of character throws into relief, and that Miller explores through the deconstructive insight that signs do not reveal but construct reality, has a specific instantiation in ethnic literature since ethnic literature is so often read as denoting a particular extrasemiotic order. Ethnic characters are taken for signs that stand for selves—authorial selves in particular. Or they are taken as parts that represent the whole of ("synecdochically summing up," as Shohat and Stam put it) a given minority group. How might we read *with* such characters rather than *through* them to some representative order? How might we rethink the potential of their indexical value to reshape the very reality they are taken to simply denote? Rihbany's own shorthand suggests as much—while his "strange character" might well be on display, its meaning is not readily decipherable, and we must learn to read *A Far Journey* (another "book of a very strange character") if we are to understand Rihbany's meaning.

Socioformal critiques of character help to answer these questions, particularly when retooled to consider authorial character. Found in these critiques are rich vocabularies and methods for articulating literary and social worlds, whether by creating casts of characters who allegorize social mobility (Elda María Román), confronting social fictions of personhood through literary fictions of character (Frow), articulating the "rhetoric of character" across literary and social worlds (Salazar), mapping social stratification onto the fictive distribution of characters (Woloch), reading literary characters as referents for "social persons" (Elizabeth Fowler), or showing how the "pragmatics of character" enables writers and readers to come to terms with social change (Deirdre Shauna Lynch).[88] What can drop out of view of these articulations is the way in which the author functions as a character, which character criticism with its basis in fiction can ignore. For authors who are caught up as characters within the literary historical record, who are perceived to be peculiar, morally and ethically suspect, and who appear to have an excess of personality—a reading through the lens of character has much to offer. At issue is how these authors inhabit the nexus of literary persona and social personhood, and how they grapple with this relationship in their writings in a range of fictive and autobiographical modes.

In his foundational treatment of character, E. M. Forster offers a relevant provocation. Describing the particular relationship of the novelist and the novel, he writes that the "novelist, unlike many of his colleagues, makes up a number of word-masses roughly describing himself (roughly: niceties shall come later), gives them names and sex, assigns them plausible gestures, and causes them to speak by use of inverted commas, and perhap to behave consistently. These word-masses are his characters."[89] There is a certain daring to this provisional claim that the "word-masses" that constitute literary characters "roughly" describe novelists themselves. An inert equivalence is out of the question, as Forster's promise of "niceties" indicates, as does the basic New Critical precept of the "intentional fallacy" (which impresses upon the student of literary criticism the relative autonomy of the literary text), and its iterations in poststructuralism (with the "death of the author" predicted by Roland Barthes or the "author function" formulated by Michel Foucault) and cultural materialism (where the author, for Raymond Williams, is "trans-individual" or "a complex of active relations").[90] Yet the tendency to equate author and character is of concern, given that ethnic writers are often assumed to be writing about themselves or, through themselves, about the ethnic group to which they are presumed to belong. When it comes to ethnic literature and this burden of representation, we need a methodological framework that can articulate these positions.

Studies of autobiography, and of ethnic autobiography in particular, are helpful in this respect. While the assumed identity of author and textual character (whether narrator or protagonist) is a defining feature of the horizon of expectations of autobiography, the tension that inheres in this relationship has been a source of rich hermeneutics attuned to the ways in which these positions are both coextensive with and discrete from one another.[91] This tension takes particular form within ethnic autobiography, as Wong points out, adapting W. E. B. Du Bois's theory of "double consciousness" for Kingston's work. "The discursive space occupied by *The Woman Warrior* is between the two poles of 'double consciousness,'" Wong writes, referencing the incommensurability of self-awareness and outward scrutiny for racialized subjects.[92] Race character critique offers a new perspective on this subjective and social landscape by mapping out a spectrum of gradations between author and character. At one end resides the character function of the author within the text. This language is resonant with that of Foucault, but it concentrates on one aspect of his argument. Among the four characteristics of the "author function" that Foucault identifies—its economy of ownership, its spatial and historical variability, its constructed (rather than spontaneous) nature, and its breakdown of the author as individual—I am concerned primarily with the fourth, that it "does not refer purely and simply to a real individual, since it can give rise simultaneously to several selves, to several subjects—positions that can be occupied by different classes of individuals."[93] Foucault uses the example of a "novel offered as a narrator's account," where "neither the first-person pronoun nor the present indicative refers exactly to the writer or to the moment in which he writes, but, rather, to an alter ego whose distance from the author varies, often changing in the course of the work"; the "author function is carried out and operates in the scission itself, in this division and this distance."[94] So too do literary characters serve as multiples of the "real individual" who creates them. As character functions of the author, they are not reflections or doubles. Alike, yet irreducibly different, they can represent the author in different guises.

At the other end of the spectrum resides the author as a character within the biographical and historical record. In this respect, Woloch's definition of *"character-space"* can be extended into the social field, for "that particular and charged encounter between an individual human personality and a determined space and position within the narrative as a whole," translates into extraliterary worlds.[95] This is in part because biography and history often take their bearings from the narrative form of literature and also because authors (particularly those perceived as having an excess of personality) feature in these social narratives as characters. Drawn into the orbit of their own fictive characters, they are not identical to themselves but are, to adapt Woloch, "implied" persons, "partially inflected" but "never directly reflected."[96] Fowler, too, has this sense, that the "social persons" who form the template for literary characters shape authors themselves: the "human Chaucer," in her words, "fitted his own natural body to many social persons and died."[97] By integrating theories that explain how authors operate in social worlds with theories that explain how characters operate in literary worlds, we can better understand ethnic literature. Ethnic writers are in creative dialog with forces of social characterization, which perforce include their own characterization within the social field and implicate their own status as characters.

To situate character on a spectrum is to refract a singular sense of personhood into plural, heterogeneous personas. This is character in difference, other to itself. Attuned to doubling and triangulation of character, to its crossing and divergence, race character critique thus maps out the relation of these many parts of character—including especially the character of the author, which it disarticulates from fictive character—even as it brings these parts into a conversant whole. This method reads variation across context and text, making space for literature to speak to the deployments of literary characters, to biography and history, as well as to how authors feature as characters within these spheres. These are the sites critics disentangle as they "venture in biography, history, and literature" in search of a "more complicated portrait," as with José Aranda Jr. writing on Ruiz de Burton; or explore the *"conjunction"* of "racist reality" and the "protagonist's (as well as Wright's) personality," seeking to "resist any analytical flattening of his character and career," as with Tate's and Jarrett's work on Richard Wright, respectively; or navigate the "danger of conflating the author specifically with historian, autoethnographer, or autobiographer—roles that do not grant the possibility of Asian American creativity and artistry," as with Sohn.[98] Reading in this way illuminates a range of works beyond those I study here, where literary and authorial character intersect and race overdetermines their intersection both within the text and without, as to how the text is produced, marketed, and circulated. Think of relatively recent forays into autofiction by Pamela Lu and Ocean Vuong, or classic works by

Anzaldúa, Du Bois, and Audre Lorde, that blur the boundaries of autobiography, ethnography, and historiography.[99]

This method of reading also has particular relevance for the characters I study here. As protagonists of the American dream, who exceed an oppositional framework of ethnic literature, these characters serve an archetypal function. I do not employ this word as archetypal criticism does, to describe how universal psychic forms or elemental material worlds manifest in a fairly inert and autonomous literary sphere.[100] But the literary heft of this word is suggestive, in that it denotes not just an outmoded interpretive tradition but also the inheritance of American literature writ large—a story of the American dream featuring a quintessential American character. This is the specific representational burden that the term carries here. "The original pattern or model" that the archetype denotes is a pattern of power, an ideological model that is not determinative but constitutive.[101] It is the norm through and against which ethnic literature does its work.

The phrase, "having character," takes on a particular valence for the characters I focus on who are admired (as Saund's display shows) precisely for the shibboleths of the American dream for which they stand. As ideals of individualism, singular personhood, and masterful self-sufficiency, such figures appear monolithic. They obscure the variegated conditions of their production and appear to encompass the writers who create them. But literary characters do not mirror their writers so much as hold up a mirror to their social function. *Race Characters* reveals this gap by foregrounding the formal richness of literature and articulating it to authorial biography. It disaggregates the archetype of the American dream, refracting this figure into its various parts, unearthing sites of ideological ambivalence, places where the exemplar breaks down and signals its own impossibility. The writers I study negotiate their own social character in their work. Through literary characterization, they develop, manage, and subvert dominant ideologies of nation, race, and belonging. What we find in the tension between literary and authorial character is a critical perspective on such figures and on their role within ethnic literature and a broader social imaginary. This way of reading is relevant to popular and national culture, where the spectacle of racial disavowal circulates, personality and politics appear entangled, and the dilemma of political recalcitrance surfaces. Race character critique helps navigate these highly visible yet confounding scenes where the American dream pervades and where its racialized protagonist continues to allure and compel.

Attending to the Past

The readings in this book are based in a nascent period of ethnic identification. Spanning the first half of the twentieth century, this is a time in which ethnic studies had not yet been shaped by civil rights activism, cultural nationalism, and third worldism of the 1960s and 1970s. Coupled with new immigration laws and demographic changes, these social movements brought new visibility and urgency to ethnic literature as part of a nationwide effort to democratize the production of cultural knowledge.[102] Prior to these pivotal decades at midcentury, claims to minority status were subject to different regimes of disenfranchisement and violence, including racially restrictive naturalization, Jim Crow segregation, and overtly racist and repressive immigration policies. For the relatively small numbers of immigrants from non-European countries in these early decades, the horizon of negotiation with whiteness was limited and minority identity fraught and inchoate. Writers and works from this period are part of a controversial prehistory that, to varying degrees, contravenes the imperatives of antiracism and resistance that governed the formation of ethnic studies. From the vantage of oppositional critique, such figures appear to be moving backward. Because they are ostensibly retrograde, recalcitrant, and compromised, they can be appropriated as archetypes that sustain the ideology of the American dream. How are we to attend to this past?

The decades from 1900 to 1960 from which my readings are drawn are part of a story of the American dream that features European immigrants. As studies of this period show, the shared experience of immigration and upward mobility formed the basis for a socially constructed model of "white ethnicity" with which immigrants from Southern and Eastern Europe were identified and which was a key feature of their Americanization.[103] "'Ethnic inclusion,' 'ethnic mobility,' and 'ethnic assimilation' on the European model set the standard upon which 'America,' as an ideal, is presumed to *work*," Matthew Frye Jacobson points out, in his long view of the "saga of European immigration."[104] The literature of European immigration during this period is shaped by the prospect of assimilation, as are many of its literary critical appraisals. Mary Antin's *The Promised Land* (1912) is a touchstone in this regard, with its unflagging patriotism and dogged pursuit of assimilation. William Boelhower bases his analysis of immigrant autobiography partly upon Antin's work, arguing that the genre is governed by the interpretive practice of "constitutional allegoresis," whereby the immigrant narrator becomes a claimant to American citizenship by repeating a set of constitutional maxims.[105] Other studies (by Werner Sollors and Thomas Ferraro, for instance) emphasize imaginative consent over social constraint and take ethnicity as their ultimate horizon, even insofar as they complicate the teleology of Americanization.[106]

The concept of the American dream was also popularized around this time and associated with a range of evolving aspirations. James Truslow Adams is often credited with introducing the phrase into everyday parlance with his popular history *The Epic of America* (1931). Adams's notion couples a (somewhat pragmatic) frontier individualism with Jeffersonian liberalism, and entails critiques of materialism motivated by the onset of the Great Depression.[107] But the American dream has its antecedents, which have been traced as far back as the Puritan migration and the American Revolution, and have been linked to figures such as Franklin and Lincoln who represent the achievement of economic and social mobility. In one aspect, the American dream involves the bootstrap narrative, with a vision of self making that rewards hard work and perseverance. Another aspect, not entirely compatible, involves the romance of rags to riches made popular by Alger, in which fame and fortune are to be had overnight, much like lottery winnings. As a central tenet of American exceptionalism and of the civil rights movement, the American dream takes even more diametrically opposed forms in the second half of the twentieth century.[108]

What the American dream has signified is protean and changeable and as varied as those who dream it. While not empty of content, it functions, rather, as a horizon of endless possibilities. The American dream is that whatever your dream is will come true. Because its themes are highly substitutable, what the American dream is matters less than the form it takes. In the Althusserian model of ideology, the American dream represents an imagined relationship to reality that more often than not elides its obverse: systemic inequality, entrenched class divides, ongoing racial discrimination, lack of social advancement, the decline of U.S. hegemony, and so on—nightmares that are never too far from the dream discourse. Lauren Berlant has called it a "machine" and a "cliché."[109] Following Donald Pease and Jacqueline Rose, the American dream is a "state fantasy" that governs wants and hopes concerning the nation.[110] Upon yet another register, it is a national mythos, involving a set of recurrent themes and plots. What interests me here is that, regardless of how it is defined, the American dream is so often imbricated with character. As Sarah Churchwell points out, the

"American Dream, according to Adams, was about the power of character, not purchasing power."[111] Characters drive the American dream, in that it represents outsized personalities to whose life stories we look to enrich our own. In Adams's estimation, these are the "frontiersman and the old-type farmer" who "remain America's legendary heroes," and even "the business type," as he grudgingly concedes, who personify the ideals and contradictions of liberal individualism.[112] Often these personalities are immigrants. As Jim Cullen and Jeffrey Louis Decker have shown, the "Dream of the Immigrant" and "Immigrant Aspirations" are central to the American dream and to the ethos of self making that is its key feature.[113] It should come as no surprise that Adams closes his book by asking that his reader "hearken to" a tribute to the American dream by none other than Antin.[114]

What is less clear is how non-European immigrants fit into this American dream trajectory. We now know that these immigrants were not assimilated in the same pattern as European immigrants, but there is some question as to whether they were entirely unassimilable. As historians and sociologists have shown, not only is the history of European immigration at bottom a racial history, the ethnicization of European immigrants (premised upon the Chicago school of sociology's "race relations cycle" of contact, conflict, accommodation, and assimilation) did not work for non-European immigrants who were racialized in a different way.[115] The restriction of immigration during the tenure of the national origins quota system from 1924 to 1965 generated a climate favorable to European assimilation that also produced Asian, Mexican, and other non-European immigrants as racial aliens, as Mae Ngai has shown.[116] Despite "an intense will to pound the square peg of race into the round hole of ethnicity," in Omi and Winant's words, the experiences of these very different immigrant groups have not paralleled one another.[117] As Vilna Bashi Treitler points out, "ethnic projects" designed to climb the racial hierarchy (while keeping it intact) are not equally available to all minority groups.[118] This disjuncture is apparent in literary criticism, as scholars based in ethnic studies have critiqued Eurocentric readings of immigrant literature for their emphasis on the incorporative promise and consensual agency of ethnic formations, and their corresponding lack of attention to race and to the vastly different constraints that non-European writers face.[119]

But there is considerable ambiguity and variation in how the diverse non-European immigrant groups have been historically positioned across the race and ethnicity divide. "Who it is that is bound to be racialized—all non-European populations, as it turns out, in Omi and Winant's concern to draw a line between the hard exclusions of race and the soft assimilability of ethnicity—seems to be geographically predetermined," as Lye notes, critiquing their emphasis on the "foundational status of racism to U.S. society at the expense of describing its historical variability."[120] Susan Koshy grapples with this variability in her study of key sites that illustrate the "permeability of the white-Asian boundary": we must contend with "the morphing of race into ethnicity," she argues, as "European American ethnicity has achieved dominance as the paradigm of Americanness" and "represents a very powerful solicitation to incoming immigrant groups"—"a mythology of the American Dream that allows for their ethnicization rather than their racialization and ties the comforting vision of a continuity with the past (through ethnicity) to a promising future (through class mobility)."[121] As Treitler argues, "mythmaking" and *characterization* are key to ethnicization, for ethnic projects rely on social characterizations "meant to convince that upward mobility may be achieved by hard work and moral righteousness (a.k.a. the 'bootstrap' or 'model minority' myths)."[122]

A broad view of naturalization and national belonging during this period underscores the liminal position of many non-European immigrants. The racial prerequisite cases present a striking example. From 1878 to 1952, of the fifty-two reported cases, "all but one ... turned on whether the applicant was White," as Ian Haney López points out, even though the right to naturalize—limited since 1790 to "any alien, being a free white person"—had been amended in 1870 to include "aliens of African nativity" and "persons of African descent."[123] To take a few examples pertaining to my readings, Syrian immigrants were found to be white in 1909, 1910, and 1915, but not in 1913 and 1914. When Bhagat Singh Thind brought his case before the Supreme Court in 1923, the Court allowed that he might well belong to the Caucasian race based on the racial pseudoscience of the period, but that he was nonetheless *not*, in the popular understanding of the term, white for the purposes of naturalization. Annexation and colonization gave rise to other indeterminate identities, as Mexicans granted citizenship by federal treaty were juridically but not socially white, and Filipinos (as "U.S. nationals") were neither citizen nor alien, although they had the right to freedom of movement within the United States.

Through coordinates such as these, it is possible to understand non-European immigrants during this period as part of a vexed genealogy of Americanization. Distinctly racialized, and unable to participate in the cultural assimilation that transformed Southern and Eastern European immigrants into white ethnics in the first half of the twentieth century, many of these immigrants had an asymptotic relationship to the American dream. Their relationship to whiteness was undecidable and contingent. Trapped between a biologized and unassimilable mode of difference, viewed as inferior and threatening, and a cultural and incorporable mode of difference that was attractive to and constitutive of U.S. exceptionalism, these immigrants were situated at the *pivot* of race and ethnicity. Their racial and ethnic identifications were not necessarily incommensurable (as the rigid model of the square peg and round hole suggests) and even oscillated in response to the demands of racial hegemony. As Linda Joyce Brown demonstrates, Sui Sin Far, among other women writers in the late Progressive Era, inhabited this juncture, "constructing ethnicity and questioning the racial essentialism of her time."[124]

The archive of ethnic literature is peopled by figures who must negotiate the undecidability of ethnicity and race. The question of how best to read these figures is still an open one. It is crucial that we incorporate writers and works in this early period into given genealogies of ethnic literature, particularly for fields such as Arab American and South Asian American studies that are still finding their literary coordinates. To only read such figures through these canalized formations, however, is to not fully read them. Identifying early twentieth-century writers as part of a given ethnoracial grouping can obscure sites where they put the very terms of such identities into question. Not only are many of the ethnoracial classifications that developed in the post–civil rights era anachronistic in this early period, many of these early writers rejected minority identity, even in its embryonic forms, and fashioned assimilative allegiances. When we apprehend such writers through genealogies that emphasize racial affiliations, it is not always apparent how they challenge these affiliations. Their classification in terms of racial identity obscures their recalcitrance around precisely those politics through which they are made legible. Nor is it easy to bring into view how these writers are recruited, irrespective of their distinct identities, to serve an archetypal function within hegemonic culture as representatives of the American dream.

As Audrey Wu Clark points out in her study of Asian American writers and artists before the civil rights era, "deconstructive readings of political resistance and melancholic abjection" do not necessarily elucidate this archive and "disregard the extent to which these authors laid claim to America"; given "the anachronism of the term Asian American," Clark works to "reconstruct the term rather than to deconstruct it."[125] Cynthia Tolentino brings African American and Asian American writers into conversation through their shared objectification by sociologies of race during this period. "As important as the 1960s and 1970s history of institutionalization is," Tolentino writes, "it does not account for the ways that intellectuals of color were interpellated by transnational and comparative race discourses of assimilation and racial reform. We need an analysis that allows us to consider the tenuousness, incompleteness, and contradictory nature of these identifications."[126]

Alongside these studies, *Race Characters* posits minority identity as a dynamic question, discovering its answer in the interrelation of literary persona and social personhood. The chapters that follow are not organized around racial groupings but around distinct facets of identification with the American dream, ranging from imperialism to individualism, racial betrayal to upward mobility. They do not represent an exhaustive survey of the early twentieth-century period. Rather, I focus on writers situated in ways that are similar to their literary characters. Marshall, Rihani, Saund, Villa, and Villarreal are all first-or second-generation immigrants who were part of a non-European genealogy of racialization. They each struggled in their own way with their minority status and their desire for the American dream, traveling the false trajectory of American belonging in idiosyncratic ways. Their desire is gendered, as this primarily male constellation reveals, driven by the masculinist imperative to build character even as it is undercut by male surrogacy, queer desire, and intersex fantasy. Retroactively ordered as Arab American, Asian American, black, or Chicano, the writers I consider have a troubled, even consternated, relationship to these identities. Eccentric to an oppositional paradigm in different ways, their work generates different openings for critique. Attuned to their eccentricity, *Race Characters* brings together figures who are relatively neglected alongside those who are notorious for their assimilative character. Taken together, they represent concessions and aberrations that have been marginal to the constitution of ethnic studies while at the same time populating the social field in ways that have yet to be fully grasped.

My objects of inquiry are fundamentally autobiographical in that they implicate authorial character. But they are also varied in that they combine genres such as fiction and autobiography to which criticism of character customarily attaches with genres to which it does not, including epistles, interviews, media coverage, memoirs, personal essays, paintings, photographs, and political speeches. I am drawn to particularly compelling concatenations of literary and authorial personae, where writers contend with their own production as characters within the literary historical record and in so doing open up a creative dialog between literature and society. While organized around single authors, these readings undermine the ideal of individualism and self-sufficiency that attaches to them. I read these figures as multiples of character—doubles, triangulations, and crossings through which authorial personality is diffused. Situated within particular histories of immigration and racialization, my readings excavate the troubling identifications of a given writer and his or her work from these histories. Thus, history is not incidental to the formation of these characters but crucial to understanding how they are shaped by social compulsion and structural necessity. The resulting pan-ethnic assemblage features pioneering works (the first Arab American novel in English and the autobiography of the first Asian American member of Congress) as well as unexpected juxtapositions (little-known missives to Uncle Sam alongside more canonical works of ethnic literature, including the 1959 novels *Pocho* and *Brown Girl, Brownstones*). It also represents a new mode of comparison geared toward urgent social questions rather than divisions of identity. While each chapter explores a distinct problem of character that a given writer represents, my readings collectively illuminate the overarching ideological framework within which these characters are deployed.

The first chapter opens with a surprising citation by a sitting U.S. president of an early twentieth-century Syrian immigrant writer. Appearing almost one hundred years after its initial publication, this short excerpt from Rihani's work appears to justify American exceptionalism to an audience that is well aware of the hypocrisy of U.S. empire. In this moment, Rihani is reduced to an archetype of American character. Discovered among the archives of ethnic literature, this character is made to solicit the audience's support of the ideology of empire. Who was Rihani and what would he have to say about being enlisted in this way?

Chapter 1 rethinks this scene of appropriation as a problem of characterization, seeking to counter Bush's motivated reference. This chapter begins at a key juncture in World War I, when the United States has decided to enter the war and Rihani speeds back from a hiatus in Europe to offer himself up to the war cause, describing his newfound patriotism in *Letters to Uncle Sam*, written from 1917 to 1919. This autobiographical piece gives a rare view into the author's motivations, as Rihani champions imperialist intervention and represents something of a mortification for the emergent canon of Arab American literature. This is a posture that Rihani's *The Book of Khalid* (1911) contravenes. Published a few years earlier, this wild and fantastical novel voices some of Rihani's disquieting attachments through its titular, picaresque hero who also identifies with U.S. empire. But Khalid's desire is destabilized by the hyperproduction of his character. Building on psychoanalytic theories, my analysis reveals Khalid to be a manic figure with a proliferating array of cathexes. At the root of his mania is the loss of the American dream. This is a psychosocial condition, an indictment of the impossible identifications that the American dream demands of its diasporic subjects, and of Syrian immigrants in particular—a demand that Rihani confronts through fictive characterization in his early work.

The manic embrace of Khalid gives way in chapter 2 to a different character: the minority writer who severs art from biography. Villa famously disavows the particulars of his life—or transcends them, as he would have it—in writings that are rarefied, abstract, and unmarked. Drawing on work that links this creative sublimation to the history of Filipino colonial subjection, I rethink Villa's writing in terms not of transcendence but of exposure by looking at the grotesqueness of the characters within his work. My focus is on a loosely autobiographical short story cycle in *Footnote to Youth* (1933), which is modeled on Sherwood Anderson's *Winesburg, Ohio* (1919), originally titled *The Book of the Grotesque*. Villa's characters are similarly exaggerated and distorted. Much like Fanon's specimen on microscopic view, they draw attention to their own twisted forms and expose the social characterization of minorities and of Filipinos in particular, who are caricatured in primitivist and Orientalist terms. I offer a new view upon Villa's consummate character and reveal his insistent negation of biography to be the result of social compulsion rather than eccentric choice.

This reading orients itself around a famous photograph of Villa among a panoply of modernism's greats, taken in 1948 at the Gotham Book Mart. He is conspicuously inconspicuous. Where he might be expected to stand out as the only non-white, colonial subject in this montage, he does not. Suited much like the other men in the photograph, he makes himself (or is made to be) quite small. The exposure of the flash reflects back at the viewer just above where Villa is positioned, drawing our gaze to him even as it blinds our field of vision. How can we meet Villa's glare, read with this figure who is legible only through categories that he utterly disavowed?

Villarreal, too, paints an evocative picture in *Pocho*, his semiautobiographical novel upon which chapter 3 is focused. In a stream of consciousness occasioned by his twelfth birthday, Richard, the protagonist, makes a show of his manliness while confessing his effete fears, even entertaining the possibility of intersex identity. Much of this nuance is lost in the characterization of Richard and, by extension, Villarreal as the quintessential pocho, notorious for betraying racial identity. Building on feminist and queer critiques that reappraise writers like Villarreal in the context of the Chicano movement, my reading maps out the discontinuities between the character of the author and that of his protagonist. I discover two dynamic and interrelated fields of characterization within the novel: the queer figure of El Malinche, who emblematizes assimilative desire and who (much like Khalid) wants to be part of everything; and the masculinist figure of El Macho, who has a revolutionary consciousness of colonial subjection. Corresponding roughly with Richard and his father, these two fields ultimately generate a critique not only of assimilation but also of machismo. *Pocho* does not behave as Villarreal or his detractors would have this text behave. The charge of treachery obscures *Pocho*'s subtle concessions to assimilation, which reveal but do not necessarily reproduce the dominant heteropatriarchal order from which minority masculinity takes its bearings.

Chapter 4 also explores male adolescence in Saund's *Congressman from India*, which is equal parts autobiography and political treatise. What does it take to transform a poor immigrant farmer into a successful member of Congress, sanctioned to speak nationally and internationally as a representative of the United States? I find the answer to this question in the autobiography's discourse of character building, which foregrounds masculinist discipline and conceals the racial body, reframing structural inequities as tests of individual character. The landmark contest that precedes Saund's election represents the ascendency of a distinct archetype, as the romance of rags to riches loses out to a different success story—one in which the visibly racialized immigrant champions the American dream, takes up the mantle of model minority, and augurs the successful transformation of race into ethnicity. Even as the autobiography builds up this particular American character, it shows us how to break it down. Saund brackets sites of racial oppression and occludes his own racial presence. But the autobiography reveals how precarious Saund's representative posture is by pivoting between race and ethnicity, thus destabilizing the model of minority that Saund seeks to build.

That Saund went on an international tour at the behest of the U.S. government during the Cold War is unsurprising, but it is astonishing that Marshall did so as well. Unlike Saund, she had a clear sense of her propaganda function and used her platform to inform audiences worldwide about violence and discrimination facing black people in the United States as the civil rights movement gained momentum. As this brief contrast suggests, my reading of Marshall in chapter 5 occupies a very different place in this study. Unlike the other authors I consider, Marshall is not drawn into the ambit of her troubling characters. Nonetheless, her loosely autobiographical novel, *Brown Girl, Brownstones*, has been cited to justify arguments about black pathology. What prompts such appropriations is the powerful character of Silla, who stands out in Marshall's work for her embrace of upward mobility. Although the bildungsroman features Silla's daughter Selina, Silla maintains her hold on the novel and on its criticism, which is organized via the conflict between mother and daughter. Moving away from this paradigm, I consider not only how the characters of mother and daughter are opposed as to their orientation toward the American dream but also how they are drawn together in their common experience of racism, which interprets character through race. This chiastic structure integrates Silla's character rather than disavowing it, imagining an oppositional politics that is responsive to shared social constraints.

This reading offers a new gloss on the chapters that precede it. The chiasmus of character that links mother and daughter is refracted through the architectural space of the Brooklyn brownstone. Housing immigrants from both old world and new, the brownstones emblematize the difficult succession of European and non-European immigration. Built into their design is not only the incongruity of ethnicity and race but also the disturbing possibility of their congruence—that Barbadian immigrants might well follow in the footsteps of Jewish immigrants upon whom their upward mobility is modeled. Ensconced in the umber reaches of the house, or illuminated by streaks of shadow and light from its windows, mother and daughter both take their lineaments from this symbolic structure. They occupy a brown space of ideological indeterminacy and muddled allegiance. Following in the absence of Saund's structural critique, *Brown Girl, Brownstones* provides a powerful rejoinder. It brings the spectacular archetype of self making into focus as a constrained character, shaped not just by individual will but also by determinative social forces.

The conclusion highlights the double movement of *Race Characters* as it reveals an archetype of the American dream on the one hand and refracts this archetype into variegated parts on the other hand. Ethnic literature's shared engagement with and inevitable difference from this archetype brings out both ubiquity and unevenness. Constellating distinct literary traditions in this way transforms comparative ethnic scholarship, destabilizing the field of comparison and the ethnoracial formations across which it extends. A new orientation develops toward the archives of ethnic literature, as does a better understanding of how race and ethnicity are being realigned in the present. Interweaving a reading of the final scene of Marshall's novel, I return to what characterization accomplishes: how the interplay of the many facets of character within literary and social worlds breaks down persistent archetypes, foregrounds social constraint, and attends to figures who exceed our interpretive models.

The Other of Character

The pervasiveness of the American dream ("an idea that seems to envelop us as unmistakably as the air we breathe," to quote Cullen) is such that ethnic literature already participates in its mythos.[127] Ethnic characters might be said to contain at their very core a fragment of the protagonist of the American dream. This archetype of American character calls out from the center to the margins, seeking to appropriate the social field and stabilize forms of social difference. As a norming mechanism, it generates a trajectory toward the American dream even as it produces the framework for comparison across ethnic literature. As a dream construct, however, this archetype is subject to being imagined and reimagined. In its creative aspect, ethnic literature reveals its varied features, destabilizes its telos, and opens up paths to critique.

The literary theory of character enables such critique. Returning to insights Ahmed, Miller, and Frow offer, character undermines character. "The fictional character might help us to reveal the fiction of character," Ahmed writes.[128] Miller points out that "even a resolute commitment to a single theory of character"—namely one that holds character to be expressing a "central presence of a fixed personality," or "a preexisting, nonlinguistic self"—"will not keep out its differential other, the notion that characters (in the sense of signs) generate character (in the sense of selfhood). The one is not the opposite of the other but its inseparable ghostly companion, like a double reflection in a double-paned window at night."[129] Frow, too, unearths this twofold aspect, proposing that character is "shadowed by a daemonic other," what he calls "the paredros: the familiar who accompanies a group, the non-human but figured absence from which all narrative figuration emerges."[130] Instead of stable egos and interpersonal relationships, we find elements and devices in this space of absence, "transpersonal forces that make up individual human beings: the web of connections through which they belong to a generational structure, for example, which joins them to a past and a future, or to the 'horizontal' patternings of the age cohort, of gender, of social class, of race and ethnicity."[131]

These evocative passages, and their resonance with one another, help to frame the analysis that follows. These critics suggest that character has the capacity to make as well as undo. Character builds itself up as a fictive center, a coherent self, in which we invest personhood and personality. But character also breaks itself down into the other of itself, an impersonal zone of structural elements that are beyond its reckoning as a figure centered on the ego. It is through this double work that the concept of character serves readings of troubling figures in ethnic literature.

To return to Saund's portrait, the other of Saund's character disrupts the predominant figuration of Saund. Looking out in miniature from the margins, the image of the turbaned Saund represents multiples of Saund's character over and against itself. It signals the rhetorical work of the autobiography, which must build the character of the young Saund and American character besides. The turban conjures the very difference that the central portrait has apparently effaced. Inasmuch as the other characters on the frame are meant to chart Saund's progressive assimilation, their awkward juxtaposition also points up the difficulty of bridging "East" and "West." So too the characters engraved on the bottom register the history of colonialism, racism, nativism, and exclusion of which Saund was well aware, and that the portrait disavows, opening up the possibility that there is in fact room for second-class citizenship in the United States. These plurals of character that the principal image attempts to aggregate are cast into relief by the marbled paneling. While the trompe l'oeil frame is meant to set off the vividness of Saund's example, it ends up collapsing his archetypal character.

Essentially, characterization reveals as it refracts. On the one hand, it makes manifest an archetype of American character that is otherwise difficult to define. Within an archive of ethnic literature that serves as the basis for oppositional politics and pedagogies, it can be a challenge to perceive figures who disregard this imperative. They appear to be outliers, for they spurn minority identity or group solidarity and cultivate this disavowal as a feature of their eccentricity. When recruited to the cause of resistance, they often become unrecognizable, perhaps even to themselves. Locating these figures across a range of ethnoracial formations shows the pervasiveness of this position of undecidability. Comparative analysis tells a different story of immigration where non-European immigrants inhabit the juncture of race and ethnicity. It also brings into view a shared burden of appropriation, as these immigrants are recruited as protagonists of the American dream on the basis of a racial identity at once visible yet incorporable. In this incarnation, they often find notoriety and gain social currency. Indiscriminate, reductive, and dispiriting, this archetype is the norm against which minority identity is measured and with which it must contend.

On the other hand, ethnic literature does not merely index this archetype but refracts it. Taking a multifaceted view upon the protagonist of the American dream exposes the distortions to which this figure is subjected and offers strategies to contend with how it is deployed. Sites of appropriation are reframed through the dynamics of characterization, bringing this archetypal construct into view as a character. Analysis that is both close and situated develops a fuller picture of this ostensibly flat figure, anchoring its troubling identifications in social history and authorial biography. Out of the productive tension between authorial and literary characters emerge different ways of engaging critically with the American dream—whether by exposing its constraints upon minority identity, voicing critiques of hegemony through the embrace of its forms, or discovering politics based in communities rather than singularities. Because these figures are made equivalent and interchangeable, reading them as characters foregrounds their specificity and incommensurability and shows how they exceed such facile deployments.

Race Characters creates a fuller picture of the ideological complexity of ethnic literature. It begins with a social problem of characterization and, through it, discovers new applications and uses of character theory. I aim not just to diversify the characters we study but also to develop race character critique, reimagining the study of character and of ethnic literature both—adding to character theory considerations of immigration, race, and difference, and unearthing the vagaries of minority identity across the archive of ethnic literature through the rubric of character. The work of reading reveals the uses of literature and literary analysis. By attending to its characterization across formal and social spheres, we can apprehend an archetype of the American dream and contest its uncritical deployments. Through character theory's practiced linkage of these spheres, we can read with this archetype, not around or against it, and discover beyond the draw or repulse of personality the structural forces that shape it.

In this light, characters such as Saund take on a different aspect. They not only evoke familiar platitudes of hard work, determination, and individual success. Instead, their production is reoriented in a field of characterization whose formal and social elements are in productive tension with one another. Far from representing instances of poor judgment or misguided allegiance, they draw their lineaments from creative impulses, biographical exigencies, and historical necessity. They are revealed to be in negotiation with an archetype to which minorities are recruited, an archetype that is interracial in scope and contingent upon the erasure of the very specificity of race. Reading such characters demonstrates the particular agency of the literary, opening up a critique of the American dream and a broader perspective upon minority identity.

CHAPTER ONE

Superman of America vs. Ameen Rihani
The Hyperproduction of Character

In a speech delivered in Abu Dhabi in 2008, President George W. Bush addressed the people of the Middle East, vowing that the United States would support economic and democratic freedom in the region. The entente proposed by Bush was not received warmly by an audience familiar with the violence and hypocrisies of U.S. neocolonial intervention.[1] Bush closed by setting a familiar scene in New York Harbor, where the vision of the Statue of Liberty greets newcomers to the United States: "One of these immigrants was a poet-writer named Ameen Rihani. Gazing at her lamp held high, he wondered whether her sister might be erected in the lands of his Arab forefathers. Here is how he put it: 'When will you turn your face toward the East, oh Liberty?' My friends, a future of liberty stands before you. It is your right. It is your dream. And it is your destiny."[2] Bush's remarkable evocation of Rihani underscores the difficult legacy of Rihani's life and work. Having left Ottoman Syria for the United States in the early twentieth century, Rihani is called upon to voice the appeal that would bring "the lands of his Arab forefathers" within the reach of the United States. The symbology of immigration works to justify U.S. intervention in the Middle East. Helped by Rihani's literary mediations, the Statue of Liberty threatens to leave her customary post at the gateway to the nation of immigrants and encompass the entire Arab world. The Arab immigrant becomes, in effect, the herald of U.S. imperial aims.

Bush invokes a particular archetype of American character: the immigrant who champions imperialist intervention. "For most of the world," Bush contends, "there's no greater symbol of America than the Statue of Liberty." But the fact that he closes with a quotation by Rihani suggests that Rihani might be a formidable symbol of America in his own right: the immigrant who, in appraising the beacon of liberty, appears to conceive the global hegemony of the United States. Rihani's utility in this moment is as this caricature. In his proximity to the Statue of Liberty, he is imbued with something of its symbolic value, his pen transformed into another version of her torch. He returns by way of Bush's speech to the Middle East to make a case for the American cause. Through the character of Rihani, Bush vouches for the national character of the United States. Much can be said by way of Rihani that might be difficult to say otherwise.

This chapter reframes Rihani's appropriation by Bush as a problem of characterization. It focuses on the character of the imperialist immigrant that Rihani represents and with whom he can be identified, especially in his early work. A slim epistolary volume written from 1917 to 1919, *Letters to Uncle Sam* offers a rare glimpse into Rihani's embrace of the American dream, which is in part a dream of imperial intervention. Prompted by the entry of the United States into World War I, Rihani styles himself as a prodigal son who renews his devotion to the United States and to the Allied cause, imagining the United States as a benevolent force for Arab self-determination. To generate a critical view upon this figure, I turn to Rihani's novel *The Book of Khalid* (1911), whose titular protagonist seeks to found an Arab empire on the American model. Much like Rihani, this "Superman of America" appears to champion the cause of imperialism.[3] The novel devotes itself to making the character of Khalid, proliferating natal tropes and origin stories as it tries to construct a teleology that would work for this character. But through these exertions, Khalid is also unmade. The unceasing and obsessive hyperproduction of Khalid has the effect of undercutting this character and exposing the madness of his imperialist vision. Key to this subversion is the character function of Rihani himself, who frames Khalid's aspirations in the guise of a wry, bemused Editor. The archetype of the American "Superman" is ultimately stalled in Rihani's work. Try as he might, the imperialist immigrant cannot move forward along the course of his own ambition. Through his characterization of this figure, Rihani indicts the American dream and the impossible identifications that it demands of ethnic subjects.

Adopted Child, Native Son

There is much that is missing in Bush's calculated depiction of Rihani's life and work. Rihani was a complex figure with dubious claim to being an "immigrant." After his initial arrival in the United States in 1888, he returned on multiple occasions to Freike, his birthplace in present-day Lebanon, coming back to the United States periodically as part of a broader itinerary that took him to Europe, North America, and the Middle East. At the time of his death in 1940, he was a pioneer in Arab diasporic literature, in both Arabic and English, as well as poetry and prose; an astute observer of and commentator upon the spiritual and cultural life of Arabia and America; and a principled, committed, and astute social critic whose politics were adaptive and evolving. Bush's depiction of Rihani gazing in ardent admiration at the Statue of Liberty is misleading, for Rihani's career was devoted to critiquing Western imperialism and championing Arab self-determination.

Yet, it is not hard to see why the figure of Rihani proves serviceable in defense of U.S. empire. While critical of aspects of American society, Rihani's early work was written during a period of transition from Ottoman rule to the French mandate, when the prospect of Syrian independence seemed quite near and Rihani was enamored of the possibility that the United States would right the balance of power within the Middle East.[4] The essay from which Bush's quotation is likely drawn, "From Brooklyn Bridge," was published as part of a 1910 collection of essays, *Ar-Rihaniyat*. It contains an extended meditation on the benevolent expanse of Western progress shining like a "moon around the earth," or borne in "sacred water" in boats from New York harbor to distant seas and coasts.[5] Voicing the more sanguine hopes surrounding immigration at the turn of the century in another collection of essays published around this time, Rihani imagines a "Melting Pot" vision of America, "impregnated with alien influences," fusing "Orient" and "Occident" and embodying "a universal consciousness, multifarious, multicolored, prismatic."[6] Rehearsing Orientalist divides, Rihani's rhetoric lends itself to being appropriated in the context of the war on terror. In a metonymy that links immigration and imperialism, and advances the ideology of American exceptionalism, "America" becomes a figure (and substitute) for the world.

This expansionist metonymy finds expression in the eponymous hero of Rihani's *The Book of Khalid*. Khalid conjoins universalist and imperialist desire. His migration from the old world to the new and back again pivots around a climactic scene in which he has a vision of the American dream, yoked to the dream of empire. Affirming his "faith in the future world-ruling destiny of America," he prophesies the rise of "the Superman of America" who represents an amalgamation of Asia, Europe, and America, and augurs material and spiritual progress (BK, 95). This Columbian figure "shall ray forth in every direction the divine light," Khalid proclaims, attempting to realize this imperial mission in the remainder of the novel (BK, 95). Emboldened by this prophecy, Khalid returns to Syria where his "Dream of Empire" is elaborated in a chapter of that title: "He could not think: he could only dream. The soul of the East—The mind of the West—the builder of a great Empire. The triumph of the Idea, the realisation of a great dream: the rise of a great race who has fallen on evil days; the renaissance of Arabia; the reclaiming of her land; the resuscitation of her glory;—and why not? especially if backed with American millions" (BK, 220).

In many ways, *The Book of Khalid* represents a character that Rihani himself tried to inhabit. There are assonances between Rihani's eclectic spiritual and cosmopolitan intellectual formation and that of Khalid.[7] Rihani immigrated and wrote in the context of a complicated history of mediations between Syria and the United States. He was part of a migration of approximately six hundred thousand immigrants who arrived in the Americas between 1860 and 1914 from the Ottoman province of Greater Syria, encompassing modern-day Israel, Jordan, Lebanon, Palestine, and Syria.[8] Educated by American missionaries, many Syrians were schooled to desire the United States as they fled the economic depravations of the deteriorating Ottoman Empire, divided by European interference, and sought to realize the promise of the American dream.[9] Rihani wrote *The Book of Khalid* when he returned to Syria for a second time after his initial immigration to the United States, in the course of peregrinations much like those Khalid undertakes. The entente between America and Arabia that Khalid seeks was in some ways pursued by Rihani as well. This was particularly true of the period following the publication of *The Book of Khalid*, when Rihani found U.S. intervention in the Middle East to be an appealing prospect given the designs of European colonial powers over the region.[10] Hopes for Arab self-determination flared with the collapse of the Ottoman Empire, but the popular Arab regime installed after the war was overthrown, and French mandatory rule was instituted over Syria.

Letters to Uncle Sam offers an indispensable window into Rihani's understanding of his own calling. While Rihani has been something of "an unpatriotic citizen, wanting in all the civic virtues," the prodigal resolves henceforth to "redeem" himself, show "gratitude," and repay his "debt" to his adoptive county.[11] He attempts to join the war cause, dashing off two letters: one to President Woodrow Wilson, offering his services to the government, and a second to Theodore Roosevelt, offering to join his volunteer army. When these avenues prove fruitless, he travels instead to Mexico to organize its Syrian immigrant community into a league resolved to serve the "sacred cause of the Allied powers" and "to seek through France and her Allies the liberation of Syria from Turkish rule" (LUS, 45).

Letters to Uncle Sam charts a troubling transformation, as Rihani tells Uncle Sam exactly what he imagines the latter wants to hear. Rihani's aim is quite nuanced, for he hopes to link Syrian and American interests in the arena of the war and ultimately to enjoin the United States to the Syrian anticolonial struggle. The resonance of *Letters to Uncle Sam* with *The Book of Khalid* is unmistakable, however, in that Rihani claims the prerogative of the reformed nephew and fashions his autobiographical character as a version of the American "Superman." He insists that he is irreversibly transformed: "I have torn up my birth certificate, Uncle," he writes; having "never really felt up to the present time that I am one of your children, a recognized member of your esteemed household," but rather "an adopted child, an outsider, an alien American at best," he now declares that "the complex consciousness and psychology of your adopted son" are "changed completely" (*LUS*, 11–12). His rhetoric is patriotic, even jingoistic. His swift return from Spain to the United States retraces the familiar topography of immigration with renewed vigor and commitment, as he tries to rejoin the teleology of the American dream. Rihani is so eager to demonstrate his assimilability that he takes on the prerogative of assimilating the Syrian immigrant community in Mexico to the American cause. In one particularly discomfiting scene, an encounter with a white officer ("a fine specimen of your native children, Uncle") prompts him to imagine a new genealogy for himself that would render him unmistakably American and white (*LUS*, 14). It is not hard to imagine this version of Rihani gazing up at the Statue of Liberty in awe, if only to affirm his fitness for the imperial mission.

Reckoning with the difficulty Rihani poses is not easy. Because criticism on Rihani must often make him known, it is governed by the need to commemorate his life and work. In this context, Rihani is lauded as a mediator who aspires to universalism, and who bridges, synthesizes, and reconciles "East" and "West," as even a quick glance at the contents of a 2004 volume of essays on Rihani shows.[12] Khalid is also read as exemplifying an amalgamative ideal. The introduction to the 2000 edition affirms that Khalid is "a citizen not of the Occident nor of the Orient" but "a poet singing to the universe and to the Superman."[13] This appraisal was reiterated around the centenary of the publication of the novel, which is seen (in the words of the organizers of Project Khalid, formed to commemorate this occasion) as an "extraordinary opportunity" for Rihani's legacy, "to raise his cultural profile and communicate his message of dialogue and unity between East and West."[14] Bush's quotation of Rihani often surfaces as part of this commemorative project, appearing among other "tributes" to Rihani on the website of the Ameen Rihani Organization and as one among many reasons why Rihani should be honored by Congress as part of a congressional resolution proposed in 2012.[15]

This vein of critique can obscure not only much that is oppositional about Rihani's legacy but also much that is vexing about it. Speaking against the grain of the 2004 collection, Halim Barakat emphasizes Rihani's revolutionary politics, which are occluded by the commemorative framework of the collection, and criticizes "celebrants of Rihani's work" who "do him a disservice by seeking to wedge him into a contemporary framework of pragmatic reconciliation" when his "career was one of dissent rather than accommodation to the prevailing realities of East or West."[16] Moreover, the terms in which Rihani's recovery is couched obscure the fact that he is not a seamlessly oppositional figure. His unabashed Orientalism, as well as his imperialist and occasionally racist Americanism, does not lend itself to easy incorporation within the emergent field of Arab American studies, which is charting the cultural and historical coordinates of its own resistance to U.S. empire.[17] Insofar as Bush's appropriation of Rihani is repeated and circulated in order to justify Rihani's recognition, the important work of engaging with Rihani risks becoming limited to Rihani's archetypal function: to promulgate a banal universalism updated for our multicultural order that is of a piece with the new Orientalism.[18] Driven by the imperative to honor Rihani, it becomes difficult for literary criticism to apprehend the gaps and distortions of his amalgamative vision, to read the expansionist metonymy of his transcendental aspirations, and to understand how he represents the prerogatives of an imperialist U.S. order.

Recent criticism on Rihani offers a richer assessment of the logics of Rihani's work. The 2016 critical edition of *The Book of Khalid* explores some of the historical and intellectual motivations behind Rihani's amalgamative vision.[19] In addition, Paul Jahshan situates his 2011 edited collection along a "pre-Saidian" and "post-Saidian" spectrum, demarcating a shift in Rihani criticism toward poststructuralist and postcolonial theory to make sense of his legacy.[20] Reprinted in both of these collections, Waïl Hassan's reappraisal of Rihani via the Saidian paradigm of Orientalism points out that much of the criticism about Rihani remains trapped within Orientalist binaries of "East" and "West," even as it looks to Rihani to transcend them. Hassan foregrounds the politics of translation in Rihani's work and offers an illuminating account of the latter's "reconstructed Orientalism" that reevaluates these binaries while remaining invested in their fundamental distinction.[21] He concludes with a damning assessment of Rihani's legacy: "Rihani's sublimation of Orientalism led Arab-American literature to a dead end," and his work, while "pioneering," is "hopelessly unsustainable" for generations of writers following him who continue to be "haunted... by a sense of burdensome, embarrassing" and "dislocated past."[22]

I intervene in this context by way of the richness of Rihani's characterizations. What might it mean to reassess Rihani's legacy by foregrounding his literary self-production? Is it possible to find in his writing sustenance for future projects in ethnic studies? Bush's appropriation of Rihani assumes that the character of Rihani within the historical record is coextensive with the characters Rihani represents, whether fictive or autobiographical. My analysis reveals that this is not the case. In the reading that follows, I come back to the autobiographical and historical figure of Rihani by way of the fictional character of Khalid. *The Book of Khalid* takes pains to make and unmake Khalid, exposing through his impracticable identifications the impossible demands of the American dream. While Rihani in some guises represents an archetypal investment in the American dream, his writings suggest otherwise and open up avenues for critique.

Making and Unmaking Khalid

The Book of Khalid announces itself as a book about the making of character. The opening passages set the reader upon this task. We are introduced to an Editor who has stumbled upon a mercurial and mystical manuscript in Cairo, "The Book of Khalid," written in Arabic. He sets out to look for its author and finds himself, upon the advice of a clairvoyant, at a local hashish den where the name of Khalid evokes much speculation and laughter. Everyone it seems has "something to say on the subject" (*BK*, 25). Someone points him to Shakib, Khalid's poet-companion, whom he tracks down shortly. It seems Khalid has disappeared. But Shakib offers the Editor his adoring *Histoire Intime*, originally in French, which supplies the biographical detail lacking in Khalid's account. It falls to the Editor to translate and reconstruct the story of his protagonist from these multiple sources and to produce *The Book of Khalid* in novel form. This task is drawn out through an elaborate conceit. Khalid's manuscript is "the warp of our material," the Editor states, the "Loom" being his own contribution, supplemented by Shakib's *Histoire*, and the material a "mixture" of "the raw silk of Syria" and "the cotton and wool of America" (*BK*, 17).

As this conceit suggests, the literary traditions that Rihani draws upon are manifold. A pioneering example of Arab American literature, *The Book of Khalid* interweaves a dizzying array of religious, literary, and philosophical traditions including American transcendentalism, classical Arabic poetry, French Enlightenment, German philosophy, Romanticism, Sufism, and Wahhabism.[23] Even Rihani was unsure as to how to categorize this vast project. "Just what is the nature of the work? I can scarcely say," he remarked in 1911, describing *The Book of Khalid* as "a sort of romance in philosophy."[24] The prelude ("Al-Fatihah") opens with a gesture to the Qur'an and to Miguel de Cervantes's *Don Quixote* (1605), whose metafictional conceits the framing of the Editor calls to mind. With its antecedents in the Arabic genre of maqāma, the picaresque serves as an important template for *The Book of Khalid*, which also combines elements of the bildungsroman and the immigration novel. As a type of picaro, Khalid is a rebel and a rogue. He tries to follow the surest path of upward mobility for Syrian immigrants by peddling goods from the Holy Land.[25] But he breaks dramatically with this teleology, setting fire to his peddling box in an act of protest, and relies mostly on Shakib's finances and his own Orientalist cultural capital.[26] While his journey has a discernible arc, it proceeds in fits and starts. The episodic plot is richly allusive and layered with Khalid's own commentary and that of the other characters, chiefly the Editor and Shakib. The popular appeal of this picaresque hero would become apparent a few years later with the astounding success of Kahlil Gibran's *The Prophet* (1923), whose protagonist Khalid in some ways prefigures.

As the wild speculations that initially greet the Editor suggest, Khalid is quite a character. *The Book of Khalid* follows his many adventures from his birth in Baalbek to his eventual disappearance in the Libyan desert. We learn of his youth; his immigration to New York (through Beirut and Marseilles) where he settles with Shakib in a basement apartment in the Syrian quarter; his stint peddling goods purported to be from the Holy Land; his period of voracious self-education (with a reading list as varied as the Old Testament and Thomas Paine, generally consigned at the end to a fire by which Khalid warms himself); his diligent attendance of lectures in atheism; his brief clerkship in a law office from which he is shortly fired; his stint peddling his exotic charms to the mediums and writers of bohemian New York; his short-lived and ignominious turn as a political canvasser of the Syrian District for Tammany Hall, which ends with Khalid being jailed on trumped-up charges of misappropriating public funds; his episode selling fruit from a pushcart in the Bronx in order to amass enough money for his return passage; his return journey to Syria where he is denounced by the Jesuit establishment as an anarchist, and eventually excommunicated, his planned marriage to his childhood love, Najma, thwarted; his second stint in prison, this time in Damascus, for defying the religious establishment; his period of solitude and recovery in the Lebanon mountains, whereupon, being presumed dead, he returns to the fray of Syrian revolutionary politics with a new companion, Mrs. Gotfry, an American adherent of the Baha'i faith; his infamous speech at the Mosque of Omaiyah (Umayyad Mosque) in Damascus, at which he incites a riot and is forced once again to flee, this time escaping to Egypt; and his final encampment in the Libyan desert where he eventually disappears. A description that Rihani reserves for Khalid's contemplation of his own fame, as he eyes a stack of newspapers that reference him, applies also to the novel for they are both "simmering, as it were, with Khalid's name, and Khalidism, and Khalid scandals" (*BK*, 219).

A key feature of Khalid's characterization is that he is constantly being birthed and rebirthed. Natal tropes proliferate around him. Battery Park is an important site of expectancy, where Khalid and Shakib ogle promenading women. This gendered scene of spectacle and consumption turns out to have an unexpected reverse, as Khalid is launched into a nostalgic reverie. In the form of a free verse poem, "Dream of Cyclamens" is a pastoral interlude that returns him to an Edenic Baalbek and his youthful intimacy with its feminized landscape, only to be interrupted by a "goblin" who leaves him bereft among the women of Battery Park, longing for his "own land" (*BK*, 54, 53). Freed from a set of prose constraints, Khalid seems stirred by his imaginary homecoming. This poetic detour within the prose generates a new feeling in Khalid: "He feels the embryo stir within him," the Editor writes, "and in the squeamishness of enceinteship, he asks but for a few of the fruits of knowledge" (*BK*, 54). Khalid feels out of place not only within the new world landscape but also within his gender identity, which the narrative proceeds to bend. Rihani uses a rarefied vocabulary to figuratively impregnate Khalid with the possibility of his own rebirth: he is in a state of "spiritual enceinteship," carrying a "palingenetic burden" or "soul-fetus," constantly suffering from "puerperal pains of mind" (*BK*, 50, 56, 63, 65). He portrays Khalid as a feminized surrogate who is at once expecting and expected, as though pregnant with a new version of his character.

Along with these natal tropes, *The Book of Khalid* reveals a penchant for telling and retelling origin stories about Khalid. The Editor finds that the manuscript version of "The Book of Khalid" reveals very little of Khalid's ancestry. Bemoaning this lack of information ("'Tis very well to endeavour to unfold a few of the mysteries of one's palingenesis, but why conceal from us his origin? For is it not important, is it not the fashion at least, that one writing his own history should first expatiate on the humble origin of his ancestors and the distant obscure source of his genius?"), the Editor tries as well as possible to fill in the gaps (*BK*, 24). Much to his dismay, Shakib is largely speculative on this point. Getting his "boys" on *Histoire Intime*, the Editor is able to confirm the "truth" of Khalid's existence, that "though he conceals from us his origin after the manner of the Prophets, that he was born and bred and fed, and even thwacked, like all his fellows there" (*BK*, 28). Khalid is similarly preoccupied with his self-conception, although on a grander, more inventive, scale. His vision of the "Superman of America" shows Khalid's proclivity for imagining new futures for his own character, midwifed by the vicissitudes of his own immigration. Obsessed with the task of rebirthing his own character, he fashions, in a reversal of Orientalist dichotomy, a matrilineal claim to a feminized version of America: "this dumb-hearted mother, this America, in whose iron loins I have been spiritually conceived"—what the Editor elsewhere refers to as his "iron-loined spiritual Mother" (*BK*, 105, 117).

A pivotal scene in this construction of origins, Khalid's vision of the "Superman of America" remakes him in the image of the imperialist immigrant. When Khalid is jailed after being involved with Tammany politics, the Editor quotes in translation from Khalid's manuscript a long diatribe against American materialism and the corruption of democracy, which ends in a remarkable "prophecy." Affirming his confidence in America's "world-ruling destiny," Khalid heralds the rise "in this New World" of "the higher Superman": of both old world and new, steeped in the spirit of Asia, Europe, and America, this figure shall from "his transcendental height" issue a "divine light, which shall mellow and purify the spirit of Nations and strengthen and sweeten the spirit of men" (*BK*, 95).[27] This is a timely vision, coming as it does with the announcement of the end of the American frontier by Frederick Jackson Turner at the World's Columbian Exposition in Chicago in 1893. It resonates with aspects of cultural pluralism that conjoined American transnationalism with exceptionalist imperialism. Randolph Bourne's famous 1916 description of America as a "trans-nationality of all the nations" comes to mind, for Bourne celebrates the American as "a colonial of the world," claiming that "the returning immigrant is often a missionary to an inferior civilization."[28] In this expansionist metonymy, the combinative, Columbian figure of the "Superman of America" stands in for a new global order. Illustrations by Gibran scattered throughout the text also cultivate this impression, portraying human figures reaching toward mythical and cosmic landscapes, as though they encapsulate in their gestures the fate of the entire universe.

Illustration by Kahlil Gibran accompanying the original edition of *The Book of Khalid* (1911).

Khalid seeks out the destiny that he has envisioned as he leaves the United States and returns to Syria. It seems it is his own future that Khalid has prophesied as he references his rebirth "in the very loins of New York" (BK, 105). He is the "returning immigrant" in Bourne's conception, schooled in American exceptionalism and poised to fulfill a new civilizing agenda. When Khalid rejoins the world of politics in Damascus after a considerable retreat in the Lebanon mountains, it is with a new imperial mission, which is revealed in a series of feverish visions and overexcited conversations with Mrs. Gotfry. Hailed by the newspapers as the prospective "builder of a great Asiatic Empire," he puts his proposal thus: "With my words and your love and influence, with our powers united, we can build an Arab Empire, we can resuscitate the Arab Empire of the past. Abd'ul-Wahhab, you know, is the Luther of Arabia; and Wahhabism is not dead" (BK, 219, 221). Styling himself as the new Saladin, he seeks to build an Arab empire with American support, represented here by Mrs. Gotfry. "The Turk must go—at least out of Arabia," he avers (BK, 221). This protest against the Ottoman Empire is ironically framed as a new imperialism, and relies in an even greater historical paradox upon a puritanical form of Islam in order to shape this new future.

Aptly, Khalid routes his return to Syria through a fanciful genealogy that authorizes his imperial mission. He glorifies the Phoenicians of ancient Syria, their advanced civilization as well as their innovations in art, culture, and science. This tribute evokes a contemporary discourse of Phoenicianism that linked the *mahjar*, or diasporic, Syrian communities to their fabled Phoenician past, casting the Syrian immigrant trader in the image of the seafaring Phoenician merchant. "The history of Syrian migration to the United States began to be written as a classic 'rags to riches' story," Sarah Gualtieri points out, "and Phoenicianism became a kind of 'Mayflowerism'—a mythology of noble and ancient immigrant origins and exaggerations of the successes and contributions to the host societies."[29] Khalid seeks a warrant not only for his immigration but also for his imperial mission. He reserves particular praise for Phoenician voyages of trade and colonization, and for their purported discovery of the Americas (a popular theory at this time). "Ah, if we but knew the name of their Columbus!" he intones (*BK*, 113). No matter, for their "activity of the industry and will" lives on in Americans, "for they are my Phœnician ancestors incarnate," Khalid claims; a "mysterious recurrence which makes for a continuous, everlasting modernity" ensures that "the spirit which moved those brave sea-daring navigators of yore" persists in "the steam engine, the electric motor, the plough, and in the clinic and the studio as in the Stock Exchange" (*BK*, 113–14). Khalid's "palingenetic burden" is unpacked in this recapitulation of ancestral forms. Tracking this "mysterious recurrence" with Khalid through ancient Phoenicia to pre-Columbian America and through the Syrian immigrant to the modern American, we arrive in the end at Khalid himself: "Superman of America," heir apparent to Columbus, poised to realize a new imperial dream.

At the same time, *The Book of Khalid* unmakes Khalid. The novel raises the prospect of Khalid fraudulence from the very beginning, when the Editor inquires into Khalid's whereabouts only to be jeered and mocked at by the locals. As the Editor worries over the provenance of the manuscript, he is flooded by doubts as to whether Khalid is "a literary hoax" or "a myth" (*BK*, 24). Of course, this is exactly what he is, as Rihani and the reader (who are in on the joke) well know. There is a double movement in *The Book of Khalid* between the making of Khalid and his unmaking. Much of the novel is devoted to the imperative to seek, find, and construe Khalid as a character.

The Editor appears immersed in this work, as he meditates over Khalid's birth and rebirth, reconstructs his genealogy and his origins, and fleshes out exactly what Khalidism is at the level of philosophy. Yet, this work is constantly undone at the levels of both story and discourse. In this, the episodic and multilayered structure of the picaresque serves Rihani well. Nothing quite comes of the exertions that follow, which are ironized and undermined at every turn. Khalidism accretes to the point of absurdity, as Khalid's grandiose aspirations amount to very little.

Whether in the cellar, the prison, the return voyage, the Lebanon mountains, or the moment of Khalid's triumphant return to Syrian politics, each climactic production and reproduction of Khalid's character proves fruitless. The ambition of the "Superman of America" to found a great Arab empire turns out to be a spectacular failure. In a speech at the Umayyad Mosque, Khalid denounces political revolution and calls for Wahhabi reform. This is an unpopular view during what is likely the period of the Young Turk Revolution of 1908, in which a coalition of various reform groups brought about the restoration of the constitution and sought to advance in place of the absolutist rule of Abdülhamid II a more liberal and modernizing program of Turkish nationalism, which was often in tension with Arab nationalism and with Islam.[30] Driven from the stage by his enraged audience, and eventually forced to flee Damascus, Khalid disappears by the end of the novel. Although he is briefly reunited with Najma and her son (and with the interrupted marriage plot), both die under tragic circumstances, Najib from a case of cerebral meningitis and Najma from tuberculosis likely contracted from Khalid. *The Book of Khalid* appears to conclude that the world is not ripe for Khalidism, condemning its progenitor to an exilic fate. The Editor speculates that Khalid "might have entered a higher spiritual circle or a lower; of a truth, he is not now on the outskirts of the desert: deeper to this side or to that he must have passed" (*BK*, 252). Khalid might well be above or below, to one side or another, but he is nowhere to be found. Despite his excess of origins, Khalid does not belong. Even within the fantasy of the text, Khalidism, with all its grand ambitions, remains a fantasy once removed.

The tripartite structure of Khalid's characterization is a profound force in his unmaking, for it challenges and renders unstable the fiction of Khalid's character. The novel draws attention to this construction from the very beginning in the conceit of weaving as it conjoins Khalid's manuscript with Shakib's *Histoire* and the Editor's gloss. These many strands of commentary undercut the possibility of Khalid being a singular and cohesive character, particularly insofar as the Editor's ironic perspective challenges Khalid's self-involved writing and Shakib's fawning descriptions.

This divided structure of characterization is apparent in the iconic scene of Khalid's entry into New York Harbor, when it is only by piecing together the perspectives of the various characters that we learn of Khalid's melancholic orientation toward his immigration. Shakib endeavors to describe the spectacle of the "gate of Paradise," this "marvel of enchantment," and "this superterrestrial goddess, torch in hand," urging Khalid to "wake up" and "behold these wonders. Salaam, this enchanted City! There is the Brooklyn Bridge, and here is the Statue of Liberty which people speak of, and which are as famous as the Cedars of Lebanon" (BK, 42, 43). But Khalid is downcast in sight of this much awaited port, his gaze trained into the water, looking "as impassive as the bronze goddess herself" (BK, 43). The preceding pages reveal that, even as his American dream is unfolding, Khalid is besotted with a very different dream. He is in the grip of a vision of his triumphant march into the "City on the Hills of the Cedar Groves," where he is to be crowned King (BK, 40). Even as his ship sails into his longed-for destination, he thinks of "the paper-boats" he "used to sail down the stream in Baalbek" (BK, 41). "Poor Khalid!" the Editor intones, "For though we are approaching the last station of the Via Dolorosa, though we are nearing the enchanted domes of the wonder-working, wealth-worshipping City, he is inexplicably sad" (BK, 41).

Jostling perspectives of multiple characters orient the reader toward Khalid's inward character in this moment. The posture he strikes is very different from the posture that Bush evokes in his encomium to Rihani, for Khalid does not look up to the Statue of Liberty but looks down at the water, "impassive" like the statue itself. The Editor and Shakib endeavor to make out his character. Khalid's nostalgic vision, it turns out, is the "first event recorded by our Scribe, in which Khalid is seen struggling with the mysterious and unknown," for there are signs that Khalid is "showing a latent phase, hitherto dormant, in his character" (BK, 41). This language resonates with that of Shakib, who also tracks this transformation: "from the time he related to me his dream, a change in his character was become manifest" and a "new phase was being gradually unfolded" as the "hard-headed, hard-hearted boy, stubborn, impetuous, intractable" now "looked pensive and profound" (BK, 41). To this, the Editor adds: "Not in our make-up, to be sure,—not in the pose which is preceded by the tantaras of a trumpet,—do the essential traits in our character first reveal themselves. But truly in the little things the real self is exteriorised" (BK, 42). As they try to grasp Khalid's evolution, the Editor and Shakib draw the reader away from the external spectacle of New York Harbor. *The Book of Khalid* focuses our attention on what other characters see in him, rather than what Khalid sees around him. It concerns itself not with where Khalid has arrived as an immigrant but where he has arrived as a character.

Khalid's vision of the "Superman" is similarly refracted, as the other characters counterpose a "subtranscendental" corrective to Khalid's transcendental aspirations and effectively diagnose him as mad. I take this term from the title of the chapter immediately following this vision, in which Shakib visits Khalid and observes his mercurial states of mind. At times, Khalid berates Shakib and snaps at him to "withhold" his "favours"; at other times, he calmly resolves to start a business with Shakib's capital (*BK*, 97). Faced with these "spasms and strange hallucinations," as Shakib understands them, he promptly takes Khalid to a doctor upon his release to find a cure (*BK*, 97). The Editor supplies his characteristically ironic commentary upon Khalid's "tears and rhapsodies," his "soliloquising, tearing a passion to rags," which he likens to William Shakespeare's prototype of madness, "Hamlet himself" (*BK*, 98, 96). Other characters comment upon Khalid's madness at multiple points: the Syrian woman who manages their cellar believes that Khalid should be taken to a monastery to be dispossessed of the devil within him; the Jesuit priest in Baalbek would have him committed to an asylum and thereafter consigned to hell; the monk at a monastery where Khalid recovers from a bout of illness finds that the "clock in him was not wound right"; and Mrs. Gotfry dismisses his ambitions as "chimeras" (*BK*, 153, 248).

This commentary upon Khalid's character invites us to read him through mania and its distinctive alternation with melancholia. Sigmund Freud's descriptions of mania are plainly appropriate to Khalid, as he undergoes all the states associated with mania ("joy, triumph, exultation," "high spirits," "discharge of joyful emotion," "increased readiness to all kinds of action") and "runs after new object-cathexes like a starving man after bread."[31] The syncretic, universalist, transcendental, and expansionist figure of the "Superman of America," Khalid's ego ideal in one sense, clearly expresses Khalid's manic hunger. The obverse of mania is at work in the novel as well. Descriptions of Khalid's depressive swoons resonate with Freud's description of the melancholic state: "profoundly painful dejection, abrogation of interest in the outside world, loss of the capacity to love, inhibition of all activity, and a lowering of the self-regarding feelings to a degree that finds utterance in self-reproaches and self-revilings, and culminates in a delusional expectation of punishment."³² This alternating structure shapes Khalid's ambivalent reception of Shakib during his incarceration, as he asks his friend to join in his self-reproach.

But what is it exactly that occasions Khalid's madness? Freud makes a well-known distinction in "Mourning and Melancholia" (1917) between these two psychic states: mourning is a conscious, healthy relation to loss in which the subject is able, after a period of bereavement, to find substitutes for the lost object; on the other hand, melancholia is a largely unconscious, pathological state of despair and inhibition in which the object-cathexis is withdrawn into the ego in narcissistic self-identification. What distinguishes mourning from its pathological forms is this unconscious, introjected loss. A regression is involved when the loss of the libidinal attachment to the love object, itself structured by ambivalence, cannot easily be endured. Rather than being transferred to a new object, the libido is withdrawn into the ego, which becomes identified with the abandoned object in a narcissistic relation. The ego treats itself as an object (the lost object), bringing the ambivalence of the original libidinal attachment to bear upon itself. "The shadow of the object has fallen upon the ego," Freud reiterates in *Group Psychology and the Analysis of the Ego* (1921), describing the ego divided from itself by an "ego ideal" that denigrates the ego.³³

Freud has comparatively little to say about mania. Although he is fascinated by the alternation between melancholia and mania, his thoughts on the subject are speculative and provisional. Drawing upon the psychoanalytic consensus that mania and melancholia share the same "content" or "complex," he notes that in "melancholia the ego has succumbed to it, whereas in mania it has mastered the complex or thrust it aside."³⁴ In trying to make out the structure of this mastery, Freud conjectures that "the ego must have surmounted the loss of the object (or the mourning over the loss, or perhaps the object itself), whereupon the whole amount of anti-cathexis which the painful suffering of melancholia drew from the ego and 'bound' has become available."³⁵ Returning to this subject in *Group Psychology*, he clarifies that mania involves a coincidence of ego and ego ideal, which produces the feelings of triumph and exultation characteristic of a manic state (the gap between which conversely produces the misery and self-deprecation of melancholia). In his words, "it cannot be doubted that in cases of mania the ego and the ego ideal have fused together, so that the person, in a mood of triumph and self-satisfaction, disturbed by no self-criticism, can enjoy the abolition of his inhibitions, his feelings of consideration for others, and his self-reproaches."³⁶

The Freudian structure of mania helps reveal that Khalid has lost precisely what he seems to affirm in his vision—namely, his belief in the American dream. Coming back to the jailhouse scene, this proposition seems counterintuitive: "'But my faith in man,' he swears, 'is as strong as my faith in God. And as strong too, perhaps, is my faith in the future world-ruling destiny of America'" (BK, 95). His faith in America is apparently "strong." But he hesitates in using the word "perhaps," and he repeats the word "faith," providing a clue to the traumatic loss. This repetition compulsion suggests that the encomium that follows does not affirm Khalid's achievement of the American ideal but, rather, his loss of it. His resplendent vision of the American dream is in fact a "shadow" cast upon Khalid's ego by the loss of that dream. The hyperbolic form of the "Superman of America" represents the short-lived coincidence of ego and ego ideal, with all its attendant delusions of mastery and triumph. Working backward from this coincidence points the way to the lost object and to Khalid's ambivalent relation to that object. Khalid's degrading experience with Tammany Hall, his impersonation of the Orientalist parody of himself, the travails of peddling and keeping himself dry in a flooding basement cellar, the terror of nearly failing the Ellis Island medical inspection, and the "via Dolorosa" of his cramped and exploitative journey are the subtext of his hollow triumph. These torments are masked by the "Superman of America" and encoded in the ferocity of Khalid's alternation between manic and melancholic states. The libidinal energy freed by Khalid's manic identification undergirds the syncretic expansiveness of the "Superman." Khalid's transcendental aspirations are an attempt to surmount his essential loss of the American dream, and his imperialist ambition is an attempt at reinvesting in that dream.

The Book of Khalid diagnoses not only Khalid's individual pathology but a psychosocial condition. It provides a "sociodiagnostic," per Frantz Fanon, that links Khalid's madness to his emotional investment in the American dream.[37] By unmaking Khalid, Rihani exposes the difficulty of fashioning an American dream that conjoins "East" and "West," particularly American and Arab empire. Such a dream consists in cathexes that are impossible to sustain—they do not hold in the person of one character. Khalid's vision obscures, even as it tries to overcome, the fundamentally deidealizing relation of the Syrian immigrant to this dream. This vision delays the apprehension of loss and extends the fiction of mastery. But Khalid's libidinal freedom is a parody of freedom, which reaches an apotheosis at the very moment when Khalid is jailed. As the prophetic structure of deferral built into this vision indicates, the fusion of ego and ego ideal that Khalid appears to achieve is impossible to sustain.

Stepping back from the novel reveals a hyperproduction of character that further undermines the fiction of Khalid. Rihani takes pains to draw attention to the production of Khalid's character through an energetic, double movement within *The Book of Khalid*. In one sense, Khalid is birthed and rebirthed, compelled by transcendental and syncretic imperatives to fashion multiple origin stories for himself. But this movement to make and remake Khalid is also accompanied by a "subtranscendental" drive that unmakes his character. Natal tropes find no fruition. Interruptive narration derails, by way of a series of ironic outbursts, the possibility of any tangible outcome of Khalid's exertions. Even as the "Superman of America" is countenanced within the space of his self-characterization, he is undercut in ways that expose, partly by exaggerating, the scaffolding of his character.

This hyperproduction of character renders Khalidism impossible. Following John Frow, Khalid is dogged by a "zone" of characterization that mobilizes the other of his character: "the realm of textuality itself, a structure of resemblances, correspondences, repetitions, and variations striving for but never achieving narrative coherence."[38] Narration by multiple characters, vociferous character commentary, and Khalid's own self-important musings all center on Khalid's character, whether on his role as a literary persona or on the ethics of his philosophical ruminations. They serve to explode the fiction of a coherent, selfsame, archetypal immigrant, particularly in those iconic moments such as the arrival into New York Harbor or the rise of the American "Superman" that rely on this character. They foreclose the teleology of Americanization that seeks to achieve an imperialist synthesis of America and Arabia. As readers, we cannot inhabit the fiction of Khalid. Instead, we are forced along with the textual apparatus of his characterization to question and reappraise his character.

Stalled Protagonists

The Editor offers one way to arrive at Rihani through *The Book of Khalid*. At one point in the novel, he comments at length upon Khalid's character, urging us to read against the grain of Khalid's proclamations. "Khalid, though always invoking the distant luminary of transcendentalism for light, can not arrogate to himself this high title," he writes: "Hallucinated, moonstruck Khalid, your harmonising and affinitative efforts do not always succeed"

(*BK*, 181). The Editor points to a fundamental gap between Khalid and his vision: "we can not conceive of how the affinity of the mind and soul with the senses, and the harmony between these and nature, are possible, if not exteriorised in that very superman whom Khalid so much dreads, and on whom he often casts a lingering glance of admiration" (*BK*, 181–82). The two figures are not coincidental. The "Superman" represents an exteriorization of Khalid's ambition to which the latter has only precarious and ambivalent access.

A small detail in this passage opens up the recursive mirror of characterization and brings us to the function of Rihani as a character within the text. Note the slip of the following word: "Hallucinated." Khalid is not hallucinat*ing*, as we might expect as part of the Editor's diagnosis, but he is hallucinat*ed* by the Editor himself. Even as Khalid's vision is "exteriorised" as the "Superman," so too is the Editor's vision "exteriorised" as Khalid. Rihani is not far behind this precipitous alignment. The figure of the Editor poring over Khalid poring over his "Superman" cannot help but evoke the figure of Rihani confronting his own relationship to the American dream through this assemblage of characters.

Viewing the autobiographical figure of Rihani through *The Book of Khalid* opens up a critical perspective upon the former. Consider the scene of Rihani's undisguised admiration for the white officer in *Letters to Uncle Sam*, in which the lineaments of Rihani's troubling identifications are apparent. On its return voyage, Rihani's ship is intercepted by a U.S. destroyer, which encircles the vessel and sends a naval officer on board to inspect it:

> The officer, a fine specimen of your native children, Uncle—a ruddy-cheeked, blue-eyed, raw-boned, chin-in-the-air lad of not more than twenty five,—made me regret for a moment that my father had not emigrated sooner than he did and adventured as I did with one of your native daughters. I might have been born under the flag then and with a countenance that no German spy or French official could mistake.
>
> But the hand of Fate, which shapes the destinies of individuals as well as of nations—No, no: this savors of a homily. I will cut out the-hand-of-fate-motive then. Brother or no brother, my heart thrilled with joy, swelled with pride, when he boarded our ship, your young officer Boy, with a pistol in his belt, silent, erect, sculptural, firm of step and gesture, a credit to the authority he represents. In silence he was received by the passengers and officers of the boat, in silence he proceeded to discharge his duty, in silence he exchanged with the captain a farewell salute. It was one of those intense, dramatic moments

when the human emotions well and overflow, drowning the faculty of human speech. We did not cheer your brave Boys, Uncle, although many of us their brothers were on board. But we remain on deck watching from the stern your flotilla steam away, half-concealed in the clouds of its own making, until it disappeared completely beyond the horizon, carrying with it the flutterings and silent vales of our hearts, pent-up, palpitating with a mixed sentiment of sadness and joy. (LUS, 14–15)

In this scene, *Letters to Uncle Sam* offers a window into Rihani's disquieting attempt to fit the recognizable prototype of American character. Enraptured by the young officer who boards the ship, Rihani pays him an unreserved tribute, perhaps looking to further endear himself to Uncle Sam. The officer's militaristic display of patriotic and nationalist duty rouses in Rihani religious and erotic fervor. As Rihani searches out ways to approximate the appearance of the officer, it seems he is attracted to the look of racial hegemony. If the circumstances of his own birth were different, Rihani conjectures, he would look more like this officer—more American that is, and implicitly more white.

On the face of it, the officer is a singular "specimen" of an American. But Rihani is also captivated by the vertiginous alchemy of character, which likely accounts for some of his intense feeling in this moment. The naval officer carries with him a proliferating set of significations. He is the metaphor and metonym for America. For one, his "countenance" is unmistakably American. So too are his carriage, his gestures, and his regalia. Sanctioned to block the returning vessel, even possibly to destroy it, or on the other hand to allow for its onward journey and that of Rihani, the officer wields the military might of the United States. That Rihani views the officer as a "credit to the authority he represents" indicates the seamless interweaving of individual and national character, as the person and personality of one officer affirms the entire war mission. Because this racial and cultural capital is denied to Rihani, he is all the more awed by it. He desires for himself this warrant to represent his adoptive nation. By approximating the appearance of the officer, he imagines that he too can advance the cause of war abroad.

Although race is an unspoken aspect of this encounter, it mantles Rihani's desire. The appeal of the officer's "countenance" is what provokes Rihani to imagine a different line of descent. The "ruddy-cheeked, blue-eyed" officer is plainly racialized as white. Faced with this ideal of American character, Rihani constructs a new origin story for himself. Here, as in the novel, the liminal space of the ocean enables such conjectures, as this scene recalls

Khalid's return voyage and his recourse to Phoenicianism, as well as *The Book of Khalid*'s repeated attempts to fashion new origins for its protagonist. Rihani wishes that the circumstances of his own conception were different: if he had been born the child of his immigrant father and a "native" daughter, he supposes that he would be recognizable to other nations as being properly American. Is the officer brother to him or "no brother"? Rihani understands that whiteness cements national brotherhood. Not only is American character encoded in the outward impress of racial character, but this character (in the sense of physical mark) is undeniably white. Looking ahead to his self-appointed mission to promote the Allied cause among Syrians in Mexico, Rihani creates a genealogy that would authorize this mission and present him as a definitive American character. As with Khalid's vision of the "Superman of America," the imperial project requires that the immigrant protagonist claim a hybrid lineage but one that is effectively white. This explains the absence of Africa from the transcontinental synthesis that Khalid conceives, as well as the appeal of Phoenicianism, which is in part an appeal to whiteness, as Phoenicians were thought to be the "first Caucasians to land in America."[39] Phoenicianism serves Rihani's diplomatic efforts among the Syrians of Mexico as well, for he presents them as a mobile, mercantile class whose wealth "goes to the American manufacturer and the American merchant" or "is safely deposited in U.S.A. banks" (*LUS*, 34).

The history of Syrian racialization and naturalization subtends Rihani's reverie, for the racial identity of Syrians was indeterminate. "Others didn't know whether to call us white, brown, or yellow," one Syrian immigrant recalled; an article describing the inhabitants of the Syrian enclave in New York in 1895 registered this confusion, noting that a "good many of them are easily distinguishable by a rather dark complexion, and might by some be taken for Italians or Frenchmen from the South of France, but not a few are of quite light complexion, with light-colored hair."[40] Disparaged in a variety of ways by the general populace (as "dago," "sheeny," "Turk," or "niggers"), these immigrants met with an inconsistent fate in the offices of immigration as well: they were classified alongside other Ottoman subjects under the category "Turkey in Asia" before 1899; distinctly as "Syrian" and "Palestinian" after 1899; as "Asiatics" by the U.S. Census Bureau in 1910; and as "Foreign-born white" in 1920.[41] Syrians were not included in the "Asiatic barred zone" formalized in the Immigration Act of 1917 and were thereby associated with a new formation, that of the Near or Middle East, as opposed to the Far East, the prime target of exclusion.[42] The classification of Syrians as "Asiatics" brought about what Alixa Naff refers to as a "'yellow race' crisis" in Syrian naturalization, threatening to include Syrians within the purview of Asian exclusion. Their status within the national polity would be adjudicated in a series of cases from 1909 to 1915, which addressed whether or not Syrians could naturalize, contingent upon their ability to prove themselves to be white. In this context, judges routinely "read" the petitioners' appearance, trying to fit them to extant racial formations. In his 1909 decision, despite the fact that he ultimately ruled that skin color was irrelevant to claims for naturalization, Judge Newman took pains to describe the appellant, Costa Najour: "He is not particularly dark, and has none of the characteristics or appearance of the Mongolian race, but, so far as I can see and judge, has the appearance and characteristics of the Caucasian race."[43] Syrians employed various racial, cultural, and legal logics to make their claim to whiteness, and partly prevailed. One judge noted "the consensus of opinion . . . that they were so closely related to their neighbors on the European side of the Mediterranean that they should be classed as white."[44] This was not "the triumph of assimilation," as Gualtieri cautions, underscoring "the dialecticity of immigrant adaptation"; despite the success of their juridical claims, Syrians continued to bear the brunt of nativist and racist violence.[45]

This history helps elucidate Rihani's desirous vision of the prototype of American character. His detailed study of the officer's face is a version of the courtroom scene of naturalization as he attempts to "see and judge" the marks of whiteness upon which the claim to being American depends. As Rihani perceives, "countenance" is everything. Not only was the ability to naturalize tied to whiteness, gaps in racial science were supplemented and even overruled by "common sense" readings of race, shaped by individual proclivities and the social imperative to maintain the balance of white power.[46] Rihani's evocation of the "hand of Fate" gestures to the Heraclitan maxim ("character is fate"), as though he perceives that his outward character, essentially the apparent impress of race, would circumscribe the fate of his diplomatic mission. To speak the word white in the autobiography, historical conventions aside, would be for Rihani to allow that he is not already white. Rihani's new story of origins partakes of his elision. It claims whiteness without appearing to do so. Reimagined as the son of a "native" mother, Rihani would not only be partly white but also American by birth, and would therefore be able to circumvent racial restrictions on naturalization altogether.

Reading this autobiographical figure through *The Book of Khalid* serves to guide our understanding of the problem Rihani poses. At bottom, the likeness of Khalid and Rihani is illuminating. Rihani, too, is a stalled protagonist

Superman of America vs. Ameen Rihani 63

of the American dream. The futility of the origin stories in the novel, Khalid's unrealized prophecy of the "Superman," and the novel's indictment of the American dream inform the interpretation of this autobiographical scene. Try as he might to cathect around a similar version of the American dream script (even one that he transforms for his own uses), Rihani is thwarted in his attempts to play the prodigal son. His bold, self-avowed metamorphosis from adopted child to native son in the opening pages is continually challenged by the fact that he does not fit the hegemonic template of American character, particularly in the racist and jingoist climate of the war. Uncle Sam, much like Khalid's "iron-loined spiritual mother," withholds his favor.

Alongside the multivoiced characterization of the novel, with its self-conscious hyperproduction of character, the single-minded longing of the autobiographical "I" appears suspect. In the guise of the droll and ironical Editor, Rihani is able to open up a gap between himself and his literary characters that is harder to access in his motivated address to Uncle Sam. Mapping the character function of the author allows for the fact that Rihani might be divided against his own autobiographical character. This strategy of race character critique locates what James Phelan calls the "implied authorial I" who lives somewhere between the historical author and the narrator, "the one who determines which voices the narrator adopts on which occasions—and the one who also provides some guidance about how we should respond to those voices."[47] The grammar of *Letters to Uncle Sam* offers a clue. While written in past tense, the passage above has it that Rihani must "remain on deck" along with the other passengers as the naval ship disappears from view in a cloud (another figure for inaccessible whiteness). This slip into the present tense in the 2001 edition widens the already immense distance between Rihani and the white officer.[48] It underscores their asymptotic relationship: to achieve the definitive appearance of Americanness and of whiteness is not possible for the Syrian immigrant at this historical conjuncture. Somewhere between the historical author, who has obviously moved beyond this scene, and the narrator who will shortly do so as well, is someone who has stayed behind. This is the character function of Rihani, the "differential other" (following J. Hillis Miller) of Rihani's singular autobiographical "I," who refracts Rihani into more than one place and more than one figure.[49] Try as he might to refigure his origin, Rihani cannot venture forward as his desire demands. The dynamics of characterization reveal this other of Rihani's character, locked in the present tense of this encounter, unable to progress along the teleology of the American dream that he imagines.

Within the biographical record, Rihani would go on to outdistance his archetypal function. After he left the United States, he wrote and advocated internationally on behalf of myriad concerns, ranging from Ottoman reform to Arabism, Syrian independence to pan-Arab unity, and secular nationalism to the Palestinian Arab cause.[50] While he saw the necessity of U.S. intervention and Anglo-Arab cooperation more broadly, this was a strategic concession in service of his overarching commitment to Arab self-determination. As he said in 1930 to an audience in Chautauqua, New York, "the politicians of Europe and America can not right the wrongs of the world. They have done enough already to make this international task an official impossibility."[51] Rihani moved away from "his earlier *mahjar* universalism" in the final decade of his life and became "more the polemicist than the conciliator, more the agitator than the mediator," as Geoffrey Nash writes.[52]

But we need not turn to Rihani's biography to develop a fuller view of his legacy. As this chapter shows, Rihani's early writings guide us to an apprehension of his character. Reading across Rihani's fictive and autobiographical characters reveals not one and the same figure in an endless repetition but a refraction of the archetype upon whose invariability and selfsameness Bush's appropriation depends. *The Book of Khalid* opens a view onto the grand narrative of the American dream, yoked to the dream of empire. It features a formidable and awe-inspiring protagonist. But the novel scaffolds Khalid with a hyperproduction of character that checks its own excess. It gives form to Khalid only to explode his character. Loss is at the heart of Khalid's vision of the "Superman" in ways that become apparent due to the character function that Rihani performs in the guise of Editor. Khalid's manic hunger is driven by his grief-stricken relationship to the American dream. This is an immigrant's dream of empire, much like the one that Rihani has: a dream that conjoins American imperialism to the unexpected aim of Arab self-determination. But these are both stalled protagonists, as their comparison reveals. Despite their propensity for fashioning new genealogies and origins, they cannot imagine their way to their desired ends. Race character critique thus leads us to understand where the archetype of the imperialist immigrant holds and fall apart—a feature that constitutes but does not define Rihani's literary career.

CHAPTER TWO

José Garcia Villa's Book of Grotesques
Character and Compulsion

The short story "Young Writer in a New Country" announces its basis in José Garcia Villa's biography. The unnamed narrator, much like Villa, appears to travel from the Philippines to the United States after being estranged from his father. Twice he lies in bed, trying to make out the meaning of the words, "America, America."[1] Finally, he appears to find what he seeks:

> Do you see America getting clearer in my mind? Do you see myself getting articulate, getting voice? Little by little calm comes to my mind. Little by little comes my white birth—a white cool birth in a new land.
>
> It was then that my stories were born—of the homeland and the new land. Some of you may have read them—they were cool, afire with coolth.
>
> I, father of tales. Fathering tales I became rooted to the new land. I became lover to the desert. Three tales had healed me. (*FTY*, 302–3)

Villa's sparse, enigmatic prose is in full evidence here, replete with poetic assonances, made-up words, and indulgent metaphors. He deals in abstract settings and unmarked characters prone to abstruse epiphanies. It appears the narrator has turned a corner. Even as the idea of "America" is clarified, the displaced exile is "healed" and grows "articulate." He finds not only his "voice" but also a new paternity. His "white birth" is key to this transformation. This phrase evokes the whiteness of the page upon which the narrator's creative empowerment is inscribed. Something must be effaced for something else to emerge. Race is implicit here, for it is by affirming whiteness that the minority subject finds the dissolution and absolution that he seeks.

While far less explicit, this scene calls to mind Ameen Rihani's desirous encounter with the white officer in his missive to Uncle Sam and its construction of a new genealogy for the immigrant writer. Villa's sparse and rarefied characters stand in contrast to Rihani's "Superman of America," with his voracious appetite for identification on an imperial scale.[2] While Rihani has no compunction about alluding to his life story or confronting the dilemmas of his adoptive American identity in his work, Villa's art is estranged from his biography.

"Biography I have none and shall have none," Villa famously wrote in ,,A Composition,, (1953).³ As its title suggests, the essay recomposes the figure of the author. Villa begins by stating his name and place of birth ("My name is José, my name is Villa. / I was born on the island of Manila, in the city of Luzon") but then takes on a new name and new coordinates: "My true name is Doveglion. . . . My country is the country of Doveglion."⁴ His identity is made unfamiliar, rendered as the "I of Identity, the Eye of Eternity," "the *ore*-I, the fundamentalizer I," the "I that cannot discontinue itself," "the truefarer amazer I," the "voyager, ransomer and parablist I," the "I that accosts and marauds eternity—the covenantal I," "the true and classic I, the I of Upward Gravity."⁵ Neologisms, gaps in punctuation, overturned quotation marks, and reversal of gravity upend received notions of identification. Villa's disavowal is infamous. "He would have hated the tag 'Asian American,'" his contemporary Luis Francia writes, noting that "Villa deliberately avoided any references to his ethnicity, or to his own experience as a person of color in the United States."⁶ "Villa, in short," as Christopher Lee notes, "is difficult to recognize and classify as an 'Asian American' writer."⁷

This chapter studies a resonant character in Villa: the minority writer who severs art from biography. Called upon to carry the burden of representation of coloniality, ethnicity, nationality, or race, he demurs. He refuses to represent not only himself but also others of the minority group with which he is identified. He dreams the American dream of being an unmarked artist, of creating art that is transcendent. While this dream of sublimation is part of Villa's sense of his work, and guides critiques of Villa as well, my analysis centers on what Villa exposes through his characters. I focus on a set of interlinked stories in *Footnote to Youth* (1933), the collection from which "Young Writer in a New Country" is drawn, and their modeling on Sherwood Anderson's *Winesburg, Ohio* (1919). Villa's grotesque characters draw attention to their own twisted forms. In so doing, they show how the social characterization of minorities works, in that their plenitude is reduced to an emblematic function. Returning to Villa's biography, and to the specific history of Filipino subjection, race character critique reveals how Villa's art is utterly identified with his otherness, despite his own insistence to the contrary. As one definition of the grotesque has it, Villa's characters are "ludicrous from incongruity." They disclose the incongruousness of Villa's own position within his artistic and social milieu and reveal his insistent negation of biography to be governed by social compulsion rather than eccentric choice.

Villa's Glare

No one glosses his work quite like Villa himself. The prefatory remarks to his annual selections of Philippine short stories and poems provide a view into Villa's dream of transcendence and sublimation. "Great art," he writes in 1931, in a preamble to a selection of short stories, "is the spiritual sublimation of the unassimilable reality: it has to do with spiritual experience, with internal crucifixions, with visions transcendent."[8] Bad writing, conversely, has "the characteristics of life, but not its essence"; "it is epidermal," "surface concern," oblivious to "the anguishing blood beneath the skin," according to Villa's preface to the 1934 selections.[9] Contemptuous of critics who fault his work for being unrealistic, Villa responds that his characters are "untrue, for they are all *noble, heroic* characters"; "*I do NOT write about the Filipino*," he declares, "*I write about MAN*.... The citizen holds no interest for me, whether American, Filipino, or Slav; I am interested in the *human being that God created*. I disbelieve in a Filipino literature as a special type of literature: *a national literature is valid only insofar as it is world literature*."[10] In this version of literary humanism, Villa prefers his characters to be unmarked and universal. He eschews particularity and seeks broad relevance for his work beyond national boundaries.

For a time, Villa's ambitions seemed to be realized, as he was both the dean of Philippine letters and the darling of the American modernist establishment. Although he lived in New York from 1932 onward, Villa dictated the course of Anglophone literature in the Philippines from his diasporic vantage. His eagerly awaited and highly contentious annual selections of Philippine short stories and poems, published between 1927 and 1940, were calculated to steer a new generation of writers in the Philippines. *Footnote to Youth* was published a year before the Tydings-McDuffie Act of 1934, and two years before the establishment of the Philippine commonwealth. While nowhere near as successful as his later work, it was the first collection of short stories by a Filipino writer to be published in the United States, and it introduced an innovation in the numbered prose segments that structure a subset of its stories. Villa undertook one generic experiment after another in subsequent collections, moving from short stories to poetry and ultimately to aphorisms (which he called Xocerisms, in derivation of his first name). His inveterate avant-gardism found admirers in the modernist moment.

Gotham Book Mart reception photographed by Lisa Larsen (1948). José Garcia Villa is standing in the back row, just right of center. Copyright © Getty Images.

His work won many accolades—among them a Pulitzer Prize nomination, a Guggenheim Fellowship, and a Shelley Memorial award—and was widely praised and anthologized, garnering favorable comparisons to E. E. Cummings, Emily Dickinson, Gerard Manley Hopkins, and Muriel Rukeyser, to name a few.[11] Villa's successes as a diasporic writer were assiduously tracked in the Philippines.[12] He received official recognition as cultural attaché to the Philippine mission to the United Nations from 1952 to 1963, served as Presidential Adviser on Cultural Affairs beginning in 1968, and was appointed National Artist of the Philippines in 1973, a year after Ferdinand Marcos declared martial law.[13]

In the famous 1948 Gotham Book Mart photograph, it appears Villa's artistic vision is realized. Standing in the back row, below and to the right of the glare on the glass-paneled bookcase, he seems at ease with this panoply of midcentury literary greats, gathered to celebrate Edith and Osbert Sitwell (seated in the middle). Rendered in black and white, and dressed in the prevailing fashion, Villa seems to not stand out. His pose recalls the commemorative painting of Dalip Singh Saund in that his racial and colonial difference is largely effaced. The photograph exemplifies the artist's dream of assimilation. He is not the minority artist but simply the artist, one who has found an entrée into the colonial metropole and been incorporated into modernism's transcultural imagination of itself.

But Villa's journey from periphery to metropole was anything but straightforward, as a broader look at his biography shows. His father, Simeon Villa, was personal physician and aide to Emilio Aguinaldo, leader of the anticolonial resistance to Spain and the United States, and first president of the short-lived Philippine Republic. Staunchly opposed to the occupation, and inflexible in his determination that his son study medicine, Simeon refused to support his son's desire to be an artist and writer, creating a rift that might have fostered Villa's antirevolutionary tendencies. E. San Juan Jr. describes Villa as a "lonely deviant," who grew up alienated from the vernacular in an era of colonial repression and protonationalist compromise, and who came to the United States as something of an outlier, being neither a migrant worker nor *pensionado*, or a government-sponsored student.[14] As Jonathan Chua has shown, Villa's star rose and fell in the Philippines along with the vicissitudes of nationalist struggle: colonial tutelage in Western, individualist models of writing coincided in the early decades of the twentieth century with Villa's popularity as writer and critic, but he was increasingly charged with "irrelevance, neocolonialism, and elitism" in the post-independence period when Philippine literature became a key site of anticolonial struggle.[15] In one of the great ironies of his career, he was both "proto-postcolonial champion" and a figurehead for "the neocolonial state and its oligarchic retainers/clients for the U.S. imperial power," as Chua and San Juan Jr. note, respectively.[16] Villa's relentless experimentation proved difficult to stomach, even for the modernist establishment. His lavish use of the caesura after almost every word in the infamous "comma poems" took Villa's devotion to innovation to the point of absurdity.[17] Tracking the changing tenor of Villa's reception, Timothy Yu points out that he underwent a dramatic transformation "in a generation from modernist cutting-edge to conservative old-guard."[18] The clash between Villa's insistently unmarked formalism and the emergent ethnic American literary tradition was inevitable in some respects, as his persistent disavowal of Filipino identity rendered Villa both notorious and irrelevant to scholars of ethnic literature.[19] The sense of Villa as an "incorrigible aesthete," as Martin Joseph Ponce notes, remains widespread and has "impeded approaches that exceed the colonialism/nationalism, aestheticism/proletarianism binaries."[20]

Critics have grappled in different ways with Villa's rarefied aesthetics. Since 1996, when San Juan Jr. proclaimed Villa to be "probably the most neglected twentieth-century writer on the planet," a reassessment of his work has been underway.[21] San Juan Jr. takes Villa's elevated view of artistic production as a point of departure rather than an end in itself and articulates the aesthetic and sociopolitical dimensions of his life and work. "To say Villa is concerned only with art or poetry is to say nothing much," he writes in a more recent article that situates Villa's writing in a historical-materialist frame of "large contexts . . . 'conditions of possibility,' lived collective situations" that inform his work, the most fundamental being the exploitative colonial relationship of the United States and the Philippines.[22] In *Footnote to Youth*, San Juan Jr. finds "reconciliation via aestheticism," as the "crisis of exile" is "dissolved by metaphorical sublimation": "Art then functions as the resolution of the conflict between solitary ego and community, unconscious drives and the fixated body, symbolic exchange and the imaginary fetish; between subjugated people and despotic conqueror."[23] Critics have built on this momentum to explore the disruptive potential of Villa's aestheticism and his disavowal of identity, arguing that Villa's work subverts colonialism and Orientalism (Chua, Yu); opens up the possibility of decolonial critique by staging nonnormative masculinities and queer affective bonds (Denise Cruz, Ponce); and reconfigures Asian American studies as a process of mediation with figures who exceed its bounds (Lee).[24]

Villa is a consummate character, but one that somehow keeps disappearing from view. He clearly thrived on his cult of personality. His eccentricity is apparent in *The Anchored Angel* (1999) collection, which juxtaposes selections from Villa's work alongside reminiscences from writers who entered his orbit, whether during his visits to the Philippines, or when he lived in New York and presided over poetry salons at his Greenwich Village apartment. Villa's contemporaries offer vivid descriptions of Villa's excess of character: "the grand poet, the flamboyant avant-gardist, the reclusive exile/ex-pat, the intimidating teacher, the bold flirt, the frail spectre," as Jessica Hagedorn describes him in her foreword, taking stock of a figure she sighted along Greenwich Street, feeding pigeons, or encountered at White Horse Tavern, drinking his signature martinis.[25] In Alfred Yuson's words, reconstructing a scene from the Café Los Indios Bravos in Malate, "Villa, silver-maned literary lion, puffs daintily, trendily at a thin, black, plastic cigarette holder, making sure his pinkie protrudes in aristocratic stiffness through all that smoke, above the palpable, mock-cavalier efforts at subtle snobbery."[26] His tremendous personality is readily perceptible in such accounts. As Cruz notes, the "mythos of Villa as bad boy, rebel, and iconoclast—now the stuff of Philippine literary legend—stemmed in part from a carefully crafted persona that reveled in controversy."[27]

It is surprisingly difficult to bring this larger than life figure into focus. There is a recurrent sense of a "vanishing Villa," which has become something of a trope in the literary criticism. Hagedorn's description gestures toward this paradox, describing a "grand," "bold," "flamboyant," and "intimidating" figure who is also a "frail spectre" who can only approximate his cultivated self-image. San Juan Jr.'s appraisal in the late 1990s of Villa as "probably the most neglected twentieth-century writer on the planet," or "the now 'disappeared' inventor of modern Filipino expression in English" makes sense, but the fact that he repeats this claim almost verbatim in a 2010 article ("Now virtually unknown, he is probably one of the most neglected twentieth-century writers in the English-speaking world") indicates that there is a deeper impulse at work in Villa criticism.[28] Other critics reiterate this idea as well, "'recovering' José Garcia Villa from obscurity" (Eileen Tabios), rediscovering the "unknown" (Yu) or the "enigmatic" Villa (Cruz), or seeking the reasons for "Villa's vanishing" (Ponce).[29] Villa's evanescence relates to the persistent disavowal of the colonial history of the United States and Philippines, but there is also something particular to Villa's work and life that makes it difficult to keep him in view.[30] Frequent reference to the Gotham bookshop image in Villa criticism and compilations suggests a repetition compulsion of the original trauma of Villa's disappearance, as though Villa's apparent inclusion among the who's who of modernist luminaries renders all the more poignant his relative exclusion from the literary historical record.[31]

The fact that Villa is both spectacular and disappearing indicates an ongoing problem of character linked to Villa's disavowal of his biography. The Gotham bookshop image captures the unforgettable yet vanishing Villa. While Villa ostensibly blends into his surroundings, he also draws our attention. He appears aside the brightest point of exposure, below the blaze of the flash reflected in the bookcase behind him. The image testifies to Villa's bizarre incongruence as the colonial migrant who comes to occupy the heart of the American literary canon, to shine briefly there, and then to vanish as though he never existed. He is illuminated by the light but also overshadowed by it. Partly eclipsed and partly overexposed, his face glares at the viewer, as though challenging us to develop the conditions for Villa's legibility. It provokes us to bring into view the minority artist without making him legible through the categories that he disavows.

I take up this provocation in the readings that follow by focusing on the dynamics of characterization across Villa's life and work. My readings shift away from Villa's dream of sublimation and its critiques and focus on what he makes visible through characters that are also grotesques. Villa contorts his characters, effaces their particularity, and renders them in highly visual terms, as part of a nonhuman landscape. These characters do not sublimate the "unassimilable reality" but expose it, revealing how Filipinos and other minorities are characterized socially as mere emblems and fitted to limited symbolic functions. Through Villa's work, we can take in the bright shadow of his glare. We can see the author himself as one version of the grotesque, compelled by the history of Filipino subjection to distort his relationship to his own biography.

Characterizing the Grotesque

The stories that I focus on within *Footnote to Youth* are part of a linked series that resonates with Villa's biography: "Wings and Blue Flame: A Trilogy" (consisting of "Untitled Story," "White Interlude," and "Walk at Midnight: A Farewell"), "Song I Did Not Hear," and "Young Writer in a New Country." Embedded within the larger volume, these stories deal with immigration and exile and share a matrix of themes, settings, plot, and characters. They feature an unnamed narrator who has left Manila at the behest of his father, who seeks to obstruct his love affair with Vi. He travels through California and Arizona to New Mexico to study at an unnamed university in Albuquerque. The stories reflect on the narrator's relationship with his parents and Vi, and follow the narrator as he develops new relationships with an array of characters, mostly students like him in the stratified society of the Depression-era Southwest, who participate in the narrative to varying degrees. Almost all of these characters inhabit subaltern positions within society, as women, poor whites, or immigrants. The central drama of the stories involves the narrator coming to terms with his father's injunction and subsequent exile, even as he wrestles with his unreciprocated attraction to Jack.

Like the narrator, Villa, too, came to the United States near the start of the Great Depression in 1930 after a break with his family and his father in particular. He attended the University of New Mexico (upon which the unnamed university is likely based) for two years and received a bachelor's degree, subsequently moving to New York to pursue graduate work at Columbia University. The autobiographical element is apparent in "Young Writer in a New Country," which is set apart from the other stories and functions as something of a gloss on them. The characters, themes, and settings of the preceding stories continue here, but not in their numbered serial form. Written as an uninterrupted narrative, "Young Writer in a New Country" appears to fit these earlier prose segments into the continuous life story of the writer, synthesizing them retrospectively from the vantage point of New York, where it seems he has finally arrived. The scene with which this chapter opens is drawn from this story and plainly features the character function of the author. The narrator's creative rebirth evokes Villa and his writing of the *Footnote to Youth*, even gesturing to the "Wings and Blue Flame" trilogy ("Three tales had healed me").

Given his dream of artistic transcendence, it is not surprising that Villa chose to render the lineaments of his autobiography in highly abstract terms. Little seems to happen to the people in these stories. The segmented fragments read like prose poems, sparse and aloof. Their sequencing is often arbitrary, and the storyline must be largely inferred. What unites these fragments is a shared cast of characters and a highly stylized, idiosyncratic symbology in which these characters are enmeshed. While they are not exactly unmarked, even their most literal descriptions seem freighted with metaphorical meaning. Villa takes pains to avoid anything that smacks of realism. "Young Writer in a New Country," which is most overt in its gesture to Villa's biography, is set apart from the other stories, as though Villa would rather not admit to the autobiographical figure that presides over this assemblage.

A theory of character informs these rarefied aesthetics, as Villa's critical writings reveal. In prefaces to short story compilations he published around the same time as *Footnote to Youth*, Villa argues that character, rather than plot, is the dramatic vehicle that propels the short story forward. "Plot is merely a literary device," he writes, and its "collapse . . . leads to a greater, more sincere personalisation"; the "superior artist sees people—character—first, and the situation—plot, if at all—afterward."[32] For Villa, dramatic action is the provenance of character development, and it is to this that the short story must devote itself. "Only insofar as it aids spiritual progress, only insofar as it unfolds character, is external action valuable," writes Villa, exalting the "inner man" and "the "adventure of his personality."[33] Not only is Villa uninterested in what happens to these characters, appearance and action are relevant only insofar as they unfold the inner drama.

Villa found something in Anderson that helped him develop this theory of character. He professed his admiration in a letter to Anderson dated

February 1930: "I want to be like you because you are the greatest of them all."[34] Villa was drawn to the idea of the grotesque in particular. Upon his suspension from the University of the Philippines on the charge of writing obscene poetry, he cited Anderson's poetry in his letter of defense and proclaimed "grotesqueness" to be key to artistic sublimation: "Artists find beauty even in physical ugliness, in grotesqueness, in what is dark—it is the beauty behind, the beauty transcendental. This the ordinary mind, the untutored, cannot see."[35] Responding to critiques of his work in 1932, Villa appears to reference some of Anderson's imagery. To charges that his characters are "freaks," Villa responds by evoking a higher order: his characters are "queer" he claims, they "are *aware* of life," and "the trembling of their hands, their unsureness of feet, their inarticulateness, their helplessness—I know—is a cry, a grasping for higher things."[36] He evokes Anderson's story, "Hands," in which a teacher whose hands move uncontrollably is falsely accused of fondling his students and seeks refuge under a new name ("Wing Biddlebaum," named for his fluttering hands), a hounded and broken man. Features that appear to be monstrous are signs of an exalted truth, according to Villa, a truth that the artist is uniquely capable of recognizing. Villa's description calls to mind John Ruskin's descriptions of the grotesque in art and architecture, which vaunt the "noble" form of the grotesque (not to be confused with its "ignoble" cousin) that "arises out of the use or fancy of tangible signs to set forth an otherwise less expressible truth; including nearly the whole range of symbolical and allegorical art and poetry."[37]

Anderson theorizes his concept of character in the preamble to *Winesburg, Ohio*, for Biddlebaum is one of a number of "grotesques" in his stories. Titled "The Book of the Grotesque" (the title Anderson originally proposed for the entire collection), the preamble features a narrator who tells a story about an old writer and a carpenter who has come to raise his bed. The project is something of a failure, but the bed occasions a reverie in which the writer sees a parade of grotesques that are both "horrible" and "beautiful."[38] He depicts these characters in a book, to which the title of this section refers. Glimpsing this volume, the narrator is struck by a parable in it about what makes people grotesque: "when the world was young there were a great many thoughts" composed into "truths" that were "snatched up" by people; when one of them "took one of the truths to himself, called it his truth, and tried to live his life by it, he became a grotesque and the truth he embraced became a falsehood."[39] Two other moments within the story bring this concept into view. First is the suggestion that the old man has narrowly averted becoming a grotesque due to his obsession with his book. Second is the figure of the carpenter ("the nearest thing to what is understandable and lovable of all the grotesques in the writer's book") who is grieving over the loss of his brother and is described thus: "He, like the old writer, had a white mustache, and when he cried he puckered up his lips and the mustache bobbed up and down. The weeping old man with the cigar in his mouth was ludicrous."[40] What is grotesque about these characters is their obsession with once freeform truths that become inert and encompassing. The revelation that Villa and Ruskin intuit is of a second order—the *truth* of truth, its perversion by desire. The result is both laughable and pitiable, linked to the emblematic and excessive feature of the "white mustache" that the carpenter and the writer both share. Other stories also present characters who are bound to a hyperbolic or repetitive "truth." Their fixation is often emblematized by physical features (Biddlebaum's "nervous" fingers, Doctor Reefy's knuckles that look like "twisted little apples," or Joe Welling's "fits") that are admired and caricatured by turns.[41]

There are many correspondences between the characters that people Villa's and Anderson's stories. Compare, for instance, the description of Biddlebaum's hands ("restless activity, like unto the beating of the wings of an imprisoned bird") to the narrator's growing awareness of himself in *Footnote to Youth*: "I could hear in myself the slow beating of wings against blue flame" (*FTY*, 117–18).[42] Here, Anderson's imagery plainly mantles that of Villa. *Footnote to Youth* and *Winesburg, Ohio* both feature lonely and searching figures who retreat periodically from the confines of life in the heartland or the frontier and have fervent, spiritual epiphanies about the edge of town, while rambling through empty fairgrounds and open mesas. Some characters are calculated to elicit a combination of empathy and disgust, like the "crippled woman selling pencils on a sidewalk" or the "nigger in the Pullman" who "was automatic like a machine," deformed in the lens of Villa's own racist imagination (*FTY*, 74). Others are physically exaggerated, much like Anderson's grotesques, and linked to emblematic movements and motifs. Jack, for instance, says "'Gosh' beautifully" and "Epa," phrases which the narrator rehearses in admiration (*FTY*, 102). Joe Lieberman has a "long narrow face" and "thin rigid lips," and is obsessed with horses (*FTY*, 246). The narrator's father's mouth is "thin" (much like that of Joe) and his teeth "tobacco-stained," whereas his mother's mouth is "fuller," her lips "blooming with ripeness" (*FTY*, 107, 108). Particular emblems are associated with particular characters: David with "soft" eyes; Georgia with "golden hair"; God with a "white flower" and with the title conceit of "wings against blue flame"; Aurora with "hands" that are "soft like flowers and thin like roots" and "dark" hair; his father with a "tree"; David with a "seed"; Johnny with "dark eyes" and "olive skin"; and the narrator with "long fingers," a "purple flower," "a great white wing," and "handkerchiefs" (*FTY*, 76, 78, 83, 117, 86, 89, 94, 95, 103, 114, 80, 95, 97).

Villa also conjures a painterly sense of the grotesque in *Footnote to Youth* through the interweaving of human and nonhuman forms. In visual art, the grotesque style combines human, animal, and natural forms to fantastical and, sometimes, comical effect: "an artistical pottage," as Ruskin has it, "composed of nymphs, cupids, and satyrs, with shreddings of heads and paws of meek wild beasts, and nondescript vegetables."[43] It is often unnatural or bizarre, and verges on the absurd. Villa painted, so it is likely that he had this visual technique in mind. He often analogized his writing to painting, describing his "comma poems" as similar to Georges Seurat's pointillism, likening his "duo-technique" to Cubism, and peppering his poems with references to prominent artists and art movements.[44] "The fine grotesque," writes Ruskin, bridging verbal and visual elements, "is the expression, in a moment, by a series of symbols thrown together in bold and fearless connection, of truths which it would have taken a long time to express in any verbal way, and of which the connection is left for the beholder to work out for himself; the gaps, left or overleaped by the haste of the imagination, forming the grotesque character."[45] In Villa's sparse prose, images serve a similar function. Action unfolds in a symbolic universe, suggestive yet obscured.

The narrator's anger at his father is symbolized in *Footnote to Youth* by a purple flower ("In fancy my anger became a gorgeous purple flower"), which he transmutes into "God's white flower" by way of his attachment to Aurora ("As the purple petals kissed the soft dark of her hair, my flower turned silver, then white—became God's white flower. Then I was no longer angry with my father") (*FTY*, 80, 84, 89). Similarly, his estrangement from and imagined reconciliation with his father is described through a tree motif: "In America I nourished the tree of my father till his love had branches and although I had never played before under the gentleness of his shade now I played in fancy under the coolness of his branches," the narrator claims, as the space of "fancy" serves to open up a sought-for intimacy with his father (his ancestral "branches") and to imagine the possibility that his "father's leaves are trembling with contrition" even, and precisely when, it is not possible for him to imagine his father as contrite (*FTY*, 94, 109). The narrator also makes sense of the central drama of the stories—his frustrated desire for Jack—through a succession of architectural and geographical features, claiming that Jack's "life was walled thickly," that the "house of his life was strong but it was empty of people," that "he did not understand" when "people knocked at the gate of his life," and that his "life was an arena: all soil and no sky: only the unresponsiveness of earth without sky" (*FTY*, 256).

Not only are flowers, trees, seeds, wings, earth, and so on linked to various anthropomorphic characters, the stories broadly intermingle organic and inorganic forms. The narrator likens the winds on the mesa to "helpless young puppies" or to "flowers blown from the fingers of God" (*FTY*, 75, 125). Of David, the narrator says at one point, combining animal and plant motifs, that "the shelter of my white wing had made of him a flower" (*FTY*, 95). As the opening scene from "Young Writer in a New Country" suggests, the narrator derives a particular aesthetic and sensuous pleasure from the effects of such juxtapositions: walking on a moonlit beach, he wishes he "were naked" to better "see how the silver of its rays would melt against my form" (*FTY*, 299).

Much of this imagery comes together in the final, climactic scene of the trilogy, in which the narrator grapples with his rejection by Jack and seems to transform his anger and grief into forgiveness. When Jack leaves the narrator to go for a walk with Dick instead, the narrator is plunged into deep grief, frenzied with tears, as he recalls another occasion when Jack rejected him. He describes his state thus: "The beating of wings within me rose to a tumult and died into a silence of death" (*FTY*, 127). He seeks out Johnny, and they go out on the mesa together, whereupon the narrator hears "a faint beating of wings" that becomes "louder and louder till it was music of silver and of flames of blue"; he grows frantic with the desire to see the bearer of these wings, which seem to represent beatific absolution ("'I want to see the bird! I am hungry for him!' . . . —I am hungry for You, O God!'") (*FTY*, 129, 130). As the beating of the wings reaches a crescendo, the drama at the heart of the trilogy is transmuted: "I was no longer unhappy and the thought of Jack and the walk I had made alone did not hurt any more. And I knew that when I lay on the ground, with the sky wet with stars above me, I was taking Jack out of me and giving him to the earth and to the sky, and the white flowers in my hands were my gifts of forgiveness" (*FTY*, 130). This scene appears to fit with Villa's exalted and transcendental aesthetics, as the narrator unburdens himself of the pain of his breach with Jack.

Read as a grotesque tableau, however, this scene both captivates and perturbs. The narrator's epiphany interweaves human, plant, animal, and physical forms. Wings beat in the narrator. In the fragments immediately preceding this moment, he lays down on the ground as though he has become part of it, "weak with earth and sky"; he then sets out to pick flowers and is weighed down by them as the "fragrance and starshine" make his hands "heavy" and "let drip gorgeously to earth" what he cannot hold; the sky on "the breast of the earth" grows "jealous"; flowers, "unstill with dew" and "love," take on his emotions until he is "flowing into flowers, filling them with love, draining myself of love"; God's "white wings" make "kind winds" that are to him like "fingers through my hair" (*FTY*, 128, 129, 130). Eventually, Jack flows out of him with "white flowers" into the surrounding landscape. These linked forms are unnerving. What defines them as grotesque is that they are "[l]udicrous from incongruity," "fantastically absurd," "odd or unnatural in shape, appearance, or character," "fantastic in the shaping and combination of forms."[46] Partly, it is the overlap of poetic and narrative forms that unsettles, as the story of the narrator's metamorphosis is punctuated by terse, epigrammatic verse. In addition, the passage conjoins an idealized apostrophe ("O God") to a sobriquet for that most conventional of names (John). In a world where nonhuman objects are imbued with anthropomorphism, agency seems displaced. Enmeshed in an expansive symbolic geography, the narrator seems fixated by it. What appears to be a "natural" resolution to the stories is also highly ornamental and contrived.

What Is Exposed

Villa's book of grotesques demands a different reading than the one Villa proposes. For Villa, the grotesqueness of his characters is coextensive with his rarefied aesthetics. As he claims in his letter defending against the charge of obscenity, theirs is a "beauty transcendental," their bizarreness a "grasping for higher things." Critics have found Villa's emphatic declarations to be suspect. Ponce, for instance, links Villa's "insistence on grotesque darkness" to the queer erotics of his work, mediated by coloniality and race; and Cruz points out that Villa's characters symbolize in their deviation from the norm a set of "irreconcilabilities—the uneasy, the troubling, and the disruptive within representational practices," figured in a series of "raced, classed, gendered, and sexed differentials."[47] The tension between Villa's stated ambition and the formal contrariness of his work inheres partly in the dynamics of characterization. Villa's grotesque characters open a view onto the social characterization of Filipinos and minorities, exposing the very reality that he would eclipse.

To clarify how this works, take together the concept of character and of the grotesque. "The grotesque," Leonard Cassuto argues, "is born of the violation of basic categories" for "it is both one thing and another, and thus neither one."[48] Justin Edwards and Rune Graulund also understand the concept as indeterminate and transgressive, blurring self and other, normalcy and deviance, civilization and savagery.[49] As it pertains to character, the grotesque collapses a distinction fundamental to the concept. Recall the double sense of character as both emblem and personality. The bifurcation of the meaning of character rests on this distinction, which is not always quite so neat: character has "literal senses" as emblem, token, feature, or trait; it also has "figurative senses" that encompass the features of someone's personality, or their mental and moral constitution.[50] What makes Villa's (and Anderson's) characters grotesque is that the plenitude of their personality is reduced to an emblematic function, to an inert, calcified "truth" linked to a perceptible external feature. The grotesque tableau works in a similar way—on a broad scale, as human characters are conjoined to plant, animal, and geographical features. Whether exaggerated along a single dimension or enmeshed in a symbolic plane, Villa's characters become flat: "types," "caricatures," "constructed around a single idea or quality," or "two-dimensional people," as E. M. Forster has it.[51] What Villa describes as the "adventure of personality" is actually an adventure in emblems, rendered in the detailed and fantastical patterning of the stories in *Footnote to Youth*.

This elaborate symbology is immanent rather than transcendent. Where Villa would have us link these emblems to their apparent referents in the inner drama of the narrator's development (purple flowers for anger, white wings for love, white flowers for forgiveness, and so on), they perform a different function. They do not denote the telos of sublimation but rather expose how the social characterization of minorities works. Like the narrator, minorities are not transported by the emblems to which they are linked but transfixed by them. Stripped of personality, of inner plenitude, they are reduced to what is outwardly perceived. The grotesqueness of Villa's characters is the grotesqueness of the characterization of minorities writ large: a disruption on the horizon of social expectations, two parts abruptly yoked, perspectives distorted by foreshortening or lengthening, an unthought of misshaping, the manifestation of unimaginable forms.

For racialized bodies, the grotesque has particular relevance. As Cassuto argues, the grotesque as a site of "racial objectification"—"the attempt to turn a person into a thing on the basis of race"—shapes the imagination of colonialism and slavery in the United States even as it reveals the impossibility of such a transformation.[52] Aliyyah Abdur-Rahman foregrounds this productive tension in millennial African diasporic cultural production.

While her object and moment of analysis is different, her insights into the aesthetics of racial grotesqueness and its social function resonate here. Black grotesquerie, she argues, "undermines the prevailing social order by confounding its representational logics"; it "discomfits the world, disarranging and reforming the official order of things" and does so through "disturbed form more than it does disturbing content."[53] Similarly, the grotesqueness of Villa's stories is shaped by their form more so than their content. Excrescence, corporality, carnality, mutilation, and degradation do not feature as such in the sublimated and ethereal landscape of these short stories. Nonetheless, Villa creates recombinant forms that register social hierarchies and expose reductive modes of representation.

Several extended examples reveal how grotesque character performs this work of exposure in *Footnote to Youth*. The narrator decides to hitchhike to Santa Fe upon Joe's advice because he does not have money for the bus. Joe tells him, "somebody might pick you up," which prompts a reverie as he waits by the roadside: "It made me think of handkerchiefs: I am a handkerchief on the road and somebody will pick me up. . . . Who would my picker be? . . . If a man picks up a lost handkerchief it belongs to him. But I would not belong to my picker" (FTY, 97). As it turns out, no one picks him up. In another example, Joe not only looks like a horse (with his "long narrow face" and "thin rigid lips") but is obsessed with horses. "In college there is too much idolatry of playground horses. . . . Everybody wants to be a horse because beautiful girls are priestesses of horses. Who does not want to have girls? I myself want girls—but I will not be venerated as a horse! Who truly wants to be a horse!"; later, it seems he is a horse, "a different kind of horse. Girls do not get wild over me. I get no ovations, no applause. It is that I sell my horsepower instead of merely displaying it" (FTY, 246, 248).

Where we might expect an interpretive path from characters to the particular identity that they represent, what we get instead is a juxtaposition that is grotesque. The narrator, a poor Filipino immigrant, finds himself standing by the side of the road in Albuquerque watching cars drive by instead of picking him up—a likely scenario in the Southwest during the Depression. Joe, who is Jewish, is working his way through college and struggling to find his place among his more affluent peers. But these characters do not perform the indexical function of pointing to a representative order. Instead, their epigrammatic, compressed rendering conjoins them, in turn, to handkerchiefs and to horses. It is not hard to read into these emblems. The narrator is like a handkerchief, lost by the wayside of the American thoroughfare, waiting for his homoerotic fantasy to be realized, or, by

José Garcia Villa's Book of Grotesques 81

extension to the author, flagging (waving his handkerchief) his ideal reader and asking that this reader pick him up. The horse represents hegemonic masculinity to which Joe has limited access, for he is a workhorse and not a show horse, condemned to labor even as he chafes against the hierarchy of status he wants to ascend.

Like the readings they provoke, these juxtapositions are both fascinating and discomfiting. There is no clear warrant to read from the emblem of character to its personality, from the appearances of the narrator and Joe to their individual and contextual identities. Their grotesque characters sideline us. In combination with their human forms, the handkerchief and the horse redirect our attention, much like Anderson's bobbing mustache. To read from these symbols back to the representative order—to race, ethnicity, biography—feels like a stretch. Our interpretive contortions are, in a word, grotesque. I am reminded of the scene of colonial migration in *Black Skin, White Masks* (1952) in which Frantz Fanon describes how the colonial subject is entrapped by racist schemas. In one sense, the subject is rendered grotesque, "dissected" like a specimen on a slide, "crawling" and probing with "antennae" in language that entwines human and entomological forms.[54] And the imposition itself is also grotesque, the desire to encapsulate character within character—to apprehend subaltern subjectivity from the outward appearance of it.

Several of Villa's stories feature a brown dog, displacing the colonial history of the Philippines while circuitously evoking this history as well. While going to school one morning, the narrator realizes he is not alone: "a brown dog followed me. I became afraid of him because he had panthery eyes. I wanted to run but I did not want to show I was afraid. I would not be afraid of a dog" (FTY, 106). The dog reminds the narrator of a puppy a friend gives him; the puppy is not allowed inside the house by the narrator's father, and it dies outside in the cold a few days later. The narrator then appears to have a vision of his father's contrition and is no longer afraid of the dog. He and Johnny adopt the dog for a while, which the narrator names "Wicki," after Jack. One day, he abandons Wicki to go watch a movie with Jack, and Wicki never comes back again. The dog has a corollary in Villa's biography, for the young Villa also had "a little brown dog," as Nick Joaquin reports, who was at the center of a furious fight between Villa and his father; when the dog disappeared after complaints by Simeón's tenants, Villa accused his father of having disposed of it.[55]

The emblematic figure of the "brown dog" cannot help but conjure the Orientalist, paternalist, and primitivist contours of Filipino subjection.

The 1898 Treaty of Paris would bring the Philippines under U.S. imperial control, consolidated by the Philippine-American war, as vast numbers of troops were deployed to quell the organized resistance against the occupation in what was one of the more bloody and brutal wars of colonial conquest. Famously referred to as "little brown brothers" in a ubiquitous formulation of imperialist paternalism attributed to William Howard Taft, Filipinos were also subject to a range of primitivist stereotypes (including the epithet "dogeater").[56] These derogations made their way into a diasporic context. Yen Le Espiritu's ethnography of Filipino migrants reveals the extent to which Filipino racialization as "brown" shaped their personal histories. For instance, Juanita Santos, who immigrated in 1952, refers to her "inferiority complex—being short, and very brown, and very Filipino."[57] In a little-known memoir entitled *I Have Lived with the American People* (1948), Manuel Buaken describes being turned away as a prospective tenant because "the place was not meant to be occupied by 'monkeys' like us"; "it was only because of our brown skins that we were not wanted."[58] Hysteria around the figure of the hypersexualized (yet paradoxically effete) Filipino male circulated in this context, combining primitivist fears with nativist anxieties about miscegenation and racial mixing.[59]

As a revenant from Villa's past, the brown dog might well represent the biography that dogs Villa, try as he might to elude it. Despite Villa's disavowal of "epidermal" reality, an emblematic figure of coloniality and race enters into his work. The fear of the narrator in this moment is perhaps the fear of his own racist caricature, suffused with trauma and constraint. It is not only the father but also the fatherland that denies the narrator the possibility of self-determination. The dog represents the familial trauma as well as the trauma of colonization that violently subjugates the Philippines to U.S. tyranny in the guise of benevolent paternalism. Its appearance in *Footnote to Youth* occasions the imagined reconciliation of father and son and opens up the possibility of transmuting an old world attachment (to his father) into a new world attachment (to Jack). By naming the brown dog after Jack, the narrator tries to remake the emblem of colonial subjection into that of metropolitan belonging. Jack, with his Swedish background and breezy masculinity, represents the allure of whiteness. If the narrator can only hold on to Wicki, he can hold on to Jack and through him to his dream of assimilation.

Villa admits to none of this in *Footnote to Youth*, nor would he have countenanced this sort of reading. What we get instead is a grotesque character who, like some of the other grotesques in the stories, is repulsive and comical by turns. In one scene, Wicki terrifies the narrator, and in another, he delights everyone around him, "gaily dressed" in paper garlands (*FTY*, 111). Wicki is also linked to various human characters—to the narrator whom he follows, to the narrator's father through the reminiscences of the narrator, to Jack by name, and to Johnny who also adopts him. This combinative figure becomes apparent in one scene in which the narrator and Jack play with Wicki in Jack's room, and Jack notices something about the dog: "Jack felt Wicki's skin and found it was loose and Jack said Wicki was half dog and half duck because the skin under Wicki's arms flapped like a web" (*FTY*, 112). It is not clear whether we are meant to be amused or disturbed by this grotesque tableau, for Wicki is made ridiculous by the very feature that points to his deprivation. What we see is not only the proximity of human and animal forms, but the animal as chimera, composed of many animals, part dog, part duck, part "panthery eyes."

Even though Villa refuses the burden of representation, *Footnote to Youth* exposes how this burden works. John Frow's notion of the paredros seems calibrated for Villa's brown dog: "uncanny double," "daemonic other," "the non-human but figured absence from which all narrative figuration emerges."[60] The paredros mobilizes the other of character, breaking down the illusion of a coherent self into a transindividual realm of history, element, and structure. The brown dog works similarly to interrupt the linkage of art to biography that would conjoin the outer appearance of character to inner personality. As Abdur-Rahman puts it, "collage is a technique of substitution, corruption, and denaturalization in art production."[61] We cannot track the straight path from literary persona to social representation that the indexical notion of ethnic character presents. Rather, the brown dog represents this contextual reality without directly doing so in the circuitous forms of the grotesque. *Footnote to Youth* draws us into a tableau of grotesque proportions, bringing us through emblems to more emblems. It shows us how the characterization of minorities works, on literal and allegorical levels, and at the level of the reading itself. In making sense of the symbolic geography of the grotesque, we become enmeshed within it. This is not a bad thing. The fundamental instability of the grotesque means that we do not simply behold its forms but are also solicited by them. As we become part of the scene of exposure, our hermeneutic desires are also exposed. "One name for this daemonic other is the reader," Frow writes, cryptically.[62] The reader, too, reaches the other of character by reading characters that challenge the received wisdom about how characterization works.

Character, Self

"Do not try to be an American," advised Anderson, when he responded to Villa. "I will not try to be an American," Villa wrote back, appearing to acquiesce.[63] Becoming American was not something Villa could choose to do, as a colonial subject of U.S. empire. Historically, Filipinos were part of "unincorporated" colonial territories and had limited constitutional rights, as the Insular Cases held. Classified as "U.S. nationals," they were neither citizens nor aliens, possessing freedom of movement within the United States but not the full rights of citizenship.[64] The Tydings-McDuffie Act paved the way for Philippine independence under terms grossly favorable to the United States, finding Filipino migrants to be aliens who would henceforth be subject to deportation and coerced repatriation and be denied reentry. It was not until independence was achieved in 1946 that Filipinos were able to naturalize.[65] Asked in a 1982 interview if he was considered an American poet by critics, Villa answered in the negative, citing the fact that he was denied the Bollingen Prize in 1949 (which went to Wallace Stevens instead) because he was not an American citizen: he said that he considered himself "a Filipino, but an American resident," acknowledging his asymptotic relationship to the privileges of being American.[66]

In another sense, however, Anderson's response hit at the heart of the matter. Villa's salability was a direct function of his otherness. As he struggled to get published in the narrowed Depression-era market, Villa's stories were accepted and featured for their exotic allure. When "Malakas" appeared in the *New Mexico Quarterly*, a new subtitle was appended, denoting its setting in no uncertain terms: "A Story of Old-Time Philippines."[67] Villa's correspondence with the editors of *Scribner's Magazine* and its publishing house reveals their paternalistic condescension, as they contrast the stories set in the United States unfavorably to those set in the Philippines and encourage Villa, now cut off from his allowance by his father and increasingly desperate for both support and approbation, to return to the Philippines for his own good.[68] Charles Scribner's Sons finally agreed to publish *Footnote to Youth*, but they did so at Villa's expense. The resulting book, subtitled "Tales of the Philippines and Others," and embellished with palm trees and arrowheads, emphasized the exotic provenance of the stories even as Edward O'Brien capitalized on Villa's otherness in his introduction, describing Villa as ineluctably foreign. Reviews of the collection pointedly identified its author as a native of the Philippines, found the best stories to be those set in the Philippines, and treated stories of his life in the United States with sarcastic condescension.[69] Villa's popularity in the exoticist modernist milieu continued to be linked to his primitivist and Orientalist appeal.[70] Despite her mixed feelings about his poems, Sitwell found it "so extraordinary to think of this presumably minute, dark green creature, the colour of New Zealand jade, spinning these sharp flame-like poems out of himself," as she wrote in a letter to her sister-in-law.[71]

Villa worked hard to negotiate the imperialist terms of his reception by creating new frameworks for his legibility. As Chua shows, Villa sought to frame his short stories by presenting himself as a rebel and a romantic, avoiding reference to his prior publication history in the Philippines, and excluding stories depicting urban, middle-class life in the Philippines.[72] Villa's relentless pursuit of formal and generic experimentation can be read as a protest against his primitivist and Orientalist reception, as he moved increasingly away from anything approaching realism toward more concise modes, ending with that sparsest of genres, the aphorism.[73] In brevity, he sought to make himself legible only in ways he saw fit. After the publication of "The Anchored Angel" in the *Times Literary Supplement* in 1954, "he stopped writing poetry" because, as Francia conjectures, he "had a great fear of repeating himself."[74] It was rumored that he was at work on a colossal volume of poetic philosophy that would remain unpublished during his lifetime.[75] Perhaps Villa feared becoming yet another iteration of imperialist caricature.

Literary criticism offered an expressive niche that Villa could fill on his own terms. How empowering it must have felt to be the self-appointed and increasingly well-regarded arbiter of fiction and poetry in the Philippines through his eagerly awaited collection of selected "bests." Villa embraced this project, which set a standard for interpreting Villa's work and provided a forum where he could take his critics to task for what he believed to be their myopic assessments. Through these eclectic and haughty rejoinders, he could try to guide readings of his work and regulate its reception. He could voice the American dream of the artist by claiming to sever art from biography, promoting an aesthetics of transcendence and sublimation, and deriding surfaces and appearances.

It is in his critical writings that Villa links his rarefied aesthetics to the figure of the artist through an expressive theory of art. "Personality," he argues in the annual selection for 1934, "is *personal force, flavor*: the emergence of the man in the work of art: *the reflection of the artist as man: the man behind the work of art.*"[76] "A true personality is the only valid style. Style is not the undergraduate conception of it as rhetorical flourish or external embellishments—but *Character, Self.* . . . the splendour of the Man behind the artist."[77] "Great art springs from great living," he goes on to clarify in the 1935 preamble, which eschews mathematics and science, the genetical and the physical, outward appearance, status and wealth, for "substance," "*deep awareness*," "the grand scale," "essence," "profundity of self" ("the higher reality being the reality of *idea*, of *essence*, the lower reality the reality of fact, of externality").[78] Literary character is an expression of authorial character, Villa suggests. But he does not advance an indexical model of ethnic character, adjudged by fidelity to the identity of the author or to the group to which he belongs. Next to "character" is indeed the artist's "self," but in the form of abstract and universal "Man," concerned not with facts or appearances but with ideas and essences.

The way character works in Villa's short stories contravenes his framing, as *Footnote to Youth* eviscerates personality rather than affirming its transcendental plenitude. As grotesques, Villa's characters are fitted and reduced to their emblematic function, enmeshed within the very reality that they purportedly transcend. They are denied "profundity of the self." Through the distorted forms of its characters, *Footnote to Youth* shows how minorities, and Filipinos in particular, are characterized in society. They are rendered grotesque, legible not through the inner attributes of character but through its outward mark.

The narrator—as the nearest "Character" to the artist's "Self"—is also grotesque. He is obsessed with his own emblematic function as a character. This obsession is revealed by the conceit of the narrator's fabricated journey to New York, which appears across several of the stories. One morning, at the breakfast table with his friends, he tells them that he plans to quit the school and leave for New York that afternoon. After a maudlin farewell, he goes back to his room and lies down on his bed and admits that he does not plan to leave. "I knew I was not truly leaving for New York yet I felt greatly hurt," he admits, confirming again that "I had said I was leaving for New York but it was not true" (*FTY*, 82, 83). Although the evidence suggests that the narrator never leaves his room in Albuquerque, the stories devote a considerable amount of space to this fabricated adventure, as the narrator recounts his exploits despite not having actually had them. Villa thus prioritizes inner action (the "adventure" of "personality") above outer action. "In the big city New York, where I had never been, I was hungry and without money," he writes, "I lived in a little dark room and it was dark and ugly for the rent was cheap. There was only one little window in the room and it was tight to open" (*FTY*, 83). Here, where the narrator has "never been," he longs for a new suit and to see a German film, gazes at store windows, watches rich men and women pouring out of a theater, and eventually returns to his dismal room. He then turns on the light and reads a book about a liar that reminds him of himself: "The story was about a liar. I thought of myself. I had lied to Joe and Wiley and to Aurora and Louise and to every one at the table. It had occurred to me to lie and I did and now I was living up to my lie" (*FTY*, 85). At the close of this imagined adventure, he reaffirms the original lie: "All these adventures in New York I have been telling you about happened in my room as I lay on the bed crying because I was a liar" (*FTY*, 85–86). At this point, he ostensibly stops pretending and goes to the bus station, where another elaborate farewell scene ensues. When he arrives at the train station, however, he does not board the train but watches it leave instead ("I watched it till I could not see it. I wondered if I was in it") (*FTY*, 88). "Had I bidden myself good-bye?" he asks, "Afterwards I walked through the town as if I had gone out of myself. I looked for myself vainly. I was nowhere. I was now only a shell, a house. The house of myself was empty" (*FTY*, 88). The next morning he meets his friends on campus, and they admit to being convinced that he had indeed left. Subsequent stories work to allay any doubts as to whether or not his trip has actually taken place: "In fancy I went to New York, where I had never been, and there I starved"; "All my adventures in New York happened in my room in Albuquerque as I lay quietly in bed" (*FTY*, 249, 250).

These twists and turns in the narrator's itinerary show a character transfixed by his own characterization. He repeatedly ponders the making of himself into an emblem, whether in the overarching frame of his fabricated adventure to New York or in many local moments within it—reading a book featuring a character who reminds him of himself, standing immobile on the train platform imagining another version of himself speed away, or searching through town for himself and finding only a shell, an empty house. Fashioning these imagined itineraries, the narrator is intensely aware of his role as a made-up character. After a fight with Georgia, he says, "I walked the streets muttering to myself. I did not know what I was saying. I called myself, 'You . . .' but the sentence did not get finished" (*FTY*, 79). In this metafictional moment, the narrator inhabits the recursive mirror of characterization. Riveted by the fiction of his character, he sees himself as a literary emblem, as an author or a reader might—the sum of finished and unfinished sentences.

Alongside *Footnote to Youth*, Villa's biography reads like the making of a grotesque. As the character function of Villa, the narrator is prescient, for Villa would be overtaken by his own cult of personality and reduced to an

Boy with Bird by José Garcia Villa (1935). Courtesy of Lance Villa and Filipinas Heritage Library.

"empty" "shell." The fantasy of a "white cool birth" never materialized for Villa, who was ever the marked artist. Sitwell's appraisal of Villa as a "creature" indicates the grotesque terms upon which Villa would be taken into the modernist fold. The life of the once famed writer would end in penurious, solipsistic isolation in New York, as Villa was barely able to support himself and unwilling to see even the few friends and disciples who sought him out in his decline for fear that they would see the reality of his circumstances. The reminiscences about Villa in his later life are telling: to Hagedorn, he seemed "a grotesque parody of his former elegant self"; on his deathbed, Francia finds him "wraith-like, comatose, and gaunt, almost a parody of his youthful slenderness."[79]

Like the narrator, Villa, too, was reduced to contemplating highly stylized emblems of character. In the 1930s, when Villa was living in a destitute state in New York, he was reputed to have made several paintings of a face that confirmed to his mind his unequalled prowess as a painter. He was apparently very secretive about these paintings and kept them with him at all

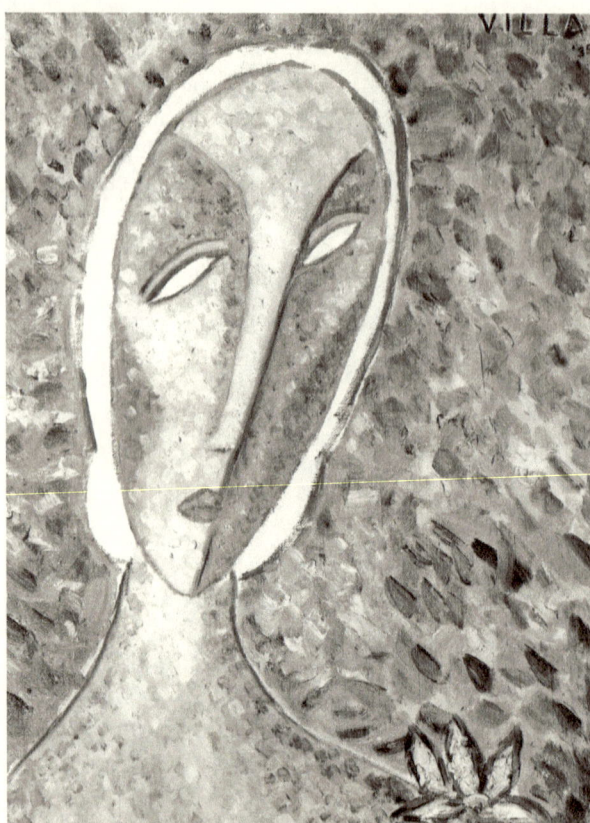

Woman's Face by José Garcia Villa (1935). Courtesy of Lance Villa and Filipinas Heritage Library.

times. "Those paintings had become a legend among his friends in New York," Joaquin writes, "Everyone had heard of them (he was always talking about them) but nobody had seen them (he wouldn't show them) and people wondered if they really existed or were like the emperor's new clothes."[80] Critic Federico Mangahas saw them and described them thus: "I notice that the face to which he had called my attention was really one and the same thing in every canvas whether of a woman or a child or a man—a highly simplified geometric-like gesture that struck me as a much stylised representation of the artist's face intensely idealised. It must be said to be the human face, perfected in the artist's own, liberated of all human handicaps."[81] San Juan Jr.'s gloss on this description is suggestive: Villa is "Narcissus," laid bare in the course of his migration from New Mexico to New York to the unanswerable demands of the literary marketplace, and now, on the verge of Europe's fascist outbreak, "withdrawn to the contemplative study of his persona, his mask," "seduced by the hermaphroditic body of the artist, now an emblem of reconciliation."[82]

These paintings are striking as an expression of the grotesque. Featuring human figures alongside plant and animal icons, they recall the symbolic geography of *Footnote to Youth*. Villa's narcissistic attachment to these paintings is also grotesque. The caution with which Anderson closes his preface comes to mind: the "subject would become so big in his mind that he himself would be in danger of becoming a grotesque." The paintings seem to have grown all out of proportion to the point that Villa bases upon them his exaggerated sense of his importance as an artist. The reluctance Villa had around showing these paintings suggests that they expose too much: not reconciliation, but its failure, not the "human face . . . liberated" in the form of universal man (or "Boy" or "Woman"), as Mangahas's equivocal description suggests, but the "artist's own" face, "simplified" and "stylised." To reveal these paintings would be to reveal that what we see is all there is—Villa, fixated by his own emblematic character.

Reading Villa through his characters shows that he is much like them. But race character critique also reframes his legacy within the literary historical record. Villa's book of grotesques reveals his consummate character to be a function of necessity rather than choice. Villa was not merely idiosyncratic or misguided in his attempt to sever art from biography. Rather, he sought ways to make himself legible as other than grotesque, delimited by Orientalist and primitivist caricature with which he, as a Filipino subject at the heart of the colonial metropole, continually had to contend. His rarefied aesthetics were an attempt to sublimate the reality that *Footnote to Youth* shows to be inescapable. Villa's characters expose, rather than efface, the strictures of biography. To the pull of "Upward Gravity" they counterpose another force: their grotesque revelation of how the characterization of minorities works, particularly that of Filipinos. Through these characters, we can read the paradoxes and excesses of Villa's career—whether his brief lionization or his unforgettable yet disappearing glare—as attempts to grapple with the burden of representation even as Villa refused to take up this burden. "You . . ." the narrator calls out to himself, but also to Villa, calling out the impossible dream of the unmarked artist.

CHAPTER THREE

Many Parts of Pocho
The Discontinuous Characters of José Antonio Villarreal

Pocho (1959) declares its own character. The cover of the original edition of the novel features the title emblazoned above the image of a man whose back is turned. He faces the low mountains of what looks to be a rural California landscape. The subtitle announces that this is "a novel about a young Mexican American coming of age in California." We surmise that the pocho named in the title and evoked by the image is the same as the "Mexican American" featured in the novel.

The protagonist and author both reference this definition of the term, as does the apparatus surrounding the text. When Richard, admits to being a pocho, he does so to account for his hybrid Spanish, "which was a CaliforniaMexicanAmerican Castilian": "I am a Pocho," he says to Pilar, a young woman recently arrived from Mexico, explaining that "we speak like this because here in California we make Castilian words out of English words. But I can read and write in the Spanish, and I taught myself from the time I had but eight years."[1] This admission does not faze Pilar. "It matters not . . . I understand you perfectly well," she responds, and they "enjoy their conversation" as though nothing intervenes between them. In a 1959 article about the publication of his novel, José Antonio Villarreal's definition of the term is also straightforward: "Pocho, which means a Mexican born in California."[2] The apparatus surrounding the text affirms this meaning, as the dust jacket of the 1959 edition proclaims this to be "the story of the 'Pocho'—the Mexican-Californian-American," and the back cover of the 1989 edition states that "Villarreal here illuminates the world of the 'pochos,' Americans whose parents came to the United States from Mexico."

But the meaning of the term is not as stable as it is made out to be, as the quotation marks around its usage suggest. Richard is "flushed" when he first perceives Pilar's amusement: "he knew she was laughing at his Spanish" (PO, 165). While he deflects this embarrassment by admitting to being a pocho, he cannot eclipse the initial awkwardness, which registers in the clumsy phrase that describes his hybrid Spanish. In a 2001 interview, Villarreal struggles to corral this term. Recalling his experience growing up,

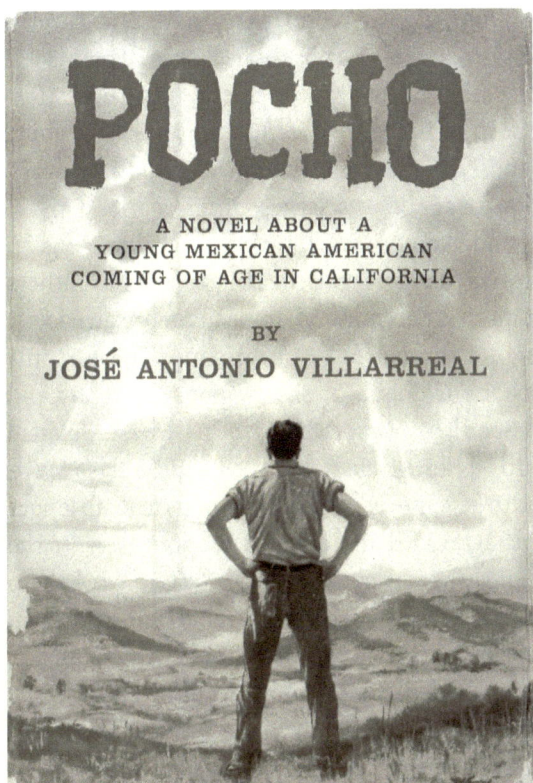

Front cover of the original edition of José Antonio Villarreal's *Pocho*, featuring art by Charles McCurry (1959).

like Richard, in the Santa Clara Valley of the 1930s and 1940s, he says that the term was a loving one ("pocho was really a term of endearment. Our parents called us 'pocho.' Or even 'pochita.' It was a love title") and its usage differed from that of the "Chicanos" who "came around and changed the definition of the term. They made it up. And they refuse to understand it in the way which I have used it. They use new definitions."[3] Villarreal attempts to ground his usage of the term in his autobiographical experience, which has shaped the novel, wanting to guide how his work is interpreted. But he recognizes, with some frustration, that the concept has meanings beyond his control.

"Pocho" is far from a neutral term, as Villarreal's interview suggests. Roberto Cantú captures its range of signification, including its dictionary meaning as "colorless" or "faded," its broader figurative sense as "sad, disillusioned," and its associations with "historical or cultural treachery... by Mexicans in reference to other Mexicans—native or U.S. born—who feign being other than what they are."[4] It is "a pejorative Mexican term for an

'Americanized' Chicano," Ramón Saldívar writes.⁵ Arturo Madrid-Barela's revealing excursus contradicts Villarreal's recollections at several points. He ventures beyond the "strictest sense of the word" ("pochos were those Mexicans who had either been born or had grown up in California") to which Villarreal tries to adhere, and elaborates the fraught meanings of pochismo. "It was not an affectionate apodo," he writes, describing how those who lived across the border and claimed authentic links to being Mexican "could never understand why we did not speak the language of our fathers and mothers, or of our abuelitos. Our accommodations to American society were traiciones in their eyes, era agringarse."⁶ The term mediates not only the national border, but divisions of language, class, region, geography, and immigrant succession ("To Spanish-speakers those of us whose Spanish was deficient were pochos. To working class mexicanos middle class Mexican Americans were pochos. To la gente del barrio those of us who no longer lived there were pochos. To rural raza urban dwellers were pochos. . . . To the newly arrived all those previously here were pochos").⁷

The pocho embraces a particular telos of the American dream. The term does not describe the Mexican American so much as the Americanized Mexican, signifying a process of deracination and acculturation that is highly contentious. By becoming American ("agringarse"), the pocho betrays racial identity as it intersects with class, nation, language, and geography. In order for Chicano consciousness to emerge, Madrid-Barela argues, this shameful past must be overcome. "Before we were Chicanos many of us were Pochos," he points out, "It is doubtful any of us readily volunteered we were Pochos. It was not a name we gave ourselves. It never became a term of pride. Nobody ever rallied to the cry of Pocho Power."⁸ While he takes a frank look at pochismo, he does so with the hope that, in grappling with their "Pocho past," Chicanos might "cure" their "traumas" and "be Pochos no more."⁹

There is a fascinating slippage in this essay between the figure of the pocho and Villarreal's life and work, which Madrid-Barela enlists in order to make sense of the term. He describes how pochos attempt to overcome the shame associated with speaking Spanish in the classroom by studying the dictionary and learning the idioms of an affected English, citing the example of the novel. "Richard Rubio had his own 50¢ word—sundries—and his older self, José Antonio Villarreal clearly had his too, as we see in his description of an old barn: 'Like all inutile inanimates it gives no hint that it too, has a past.'"¹⁰ This passage assumes that Villarreal is Richard's "older self," that fictive and authorial characters exist on a continuum with one another and share similar desires and failings.

This assumption is facilitated by the semiautobiographical nature of the novel, which takes the form of a künstlerroman partly modeled on James Joyce's *A Portrait of the Artist as a Young Man* (1916). The autobiographical continuities between the life of Richard and Villarreal are apparent.[11] Villarreal's parents were born and raised in peonage in Zacatecas, and his father fought for seven years in Pancho Villa's army. Born in Los Angeles in 1924, Villarreal moved throughout California with his family as they worked as seasonal farmworkers, living primarily in Mexican encampments until they settled in Santa Clara in 1930, where Villarreal spent the early decades of his life. In successive interviews, Villarreal has ascribed a testimonial function to the novel. "In *Pocho* it was very important to me to show things that I had seen," he claims, affirming that "everything I wrote was truth: it was fiction, but it was truth."[12] The Chicano movement has also salvaged the book as a product of its own specific history.

But there is something particular to the act of writing *Pocho* that structures the apparent continuity between Villarreal and his protagonist. Despite the fact that the Chicano movement was instrumental in rediscovering Villarreal, he had many detractors and little praise. "*Pocho* has always been somewhat of an embarrassment to Chicanos," Saldívar writes.[13] The novel has been denounced as "an American book with Mexican American characters and themes," featuring characters with "clichéd Mexican male values" who "assert an Americanized individuality" and uncritically accept "dominant ideologies," and its author has been described as "influential but accommodationist precursor."[14]

In a 2001 interview, Villarreal continues to be rankled by his early encounters with Chicano nationalism: "Chicanos thought that I was a traitor to the cause. They didn't say I was no better than the son of a bitch, they said I was a son of a bitch. I mean it was really terrible. It upset my wife more than it upset me."[15] He registers the slippage of fiction and biography in his refusal to "perform as they would have me in either my writing or my personal life," going on to say that he does not "perform things that I do not believe in. And I certainly do not believe that, just because we are Mexican-Americans, we deserve special rights."[16] The conflation of work and writer brings Villarreal into the orbit of condemnation and recrimination. He exhibits a version of machismo, attributing his "upset" to his wife and retreating from the prospect of a broader social collective into the heteronormative ideal of family

("I think that my family is the most important part of my life").[17] He also enacts a form of racial betrayal, championing colorblindness by elevating his own personal experience to the level of political doctrine and refusing to recognize the particular history of Mexican American subjection. He uses an awkward and somewhat endearing turn of phrase—"I can't be a turncoat if I don't have the coat"—that imagines racial identity as an article of clothing he happens never to have owned, rather than an indelible feature of his skin.[18] In taking the measure of critical responses to his fiction, Villarreal takes on the proportions of his fictional characters.

Villarreal's biography bears out a version of this betrayal, as does his subsequent work. Villarreal left the United States and settled in Mexico, eventually becoming a Mexican citizen. His subsequent novels can be said to build upon the stereotypes that *Pocho* features. *The Fifth Horseman* (1974) takes the reader back into the world of the Mexican Revolution that Richard's father leaves behind, based in part on Villarreal's travels to the hacienda where his parents were raised. *Clemente Chacón* (1984) features the Horatio Alger type that Richard prefigures, as he rises up from the streets of Juárez and moves to El Paso, eventually becoming a successful businessman while coming to terms with his upward mobility and his embrace of the American dream.

In effect, the character of "pocho" is overburdened. As the title of Villarreal's novel, it appears to emblematize its protagonist and to encapsulate the work as a whole, as the maelstrom of critical responses to the novel suggests. Villarreal, too, is drawn into the ambit of betrayal, for he does not answer to the burden of representation of the Chicano movement as it seeks to empower itself ("Nobody ever rallied to the cry of Pocho Power"). There is an interpretive excess at work here, as the characters in the title implicate the title character and the author's character in turn. Is the character of pocho coextensive with its fictive incarnation? In representing racial betrayal, is Villarreal betraying his own racial identity?

Race character critique offers a new view upon this overdetermined character by mapping it out across Villarreal's life and work. As a figure for racial betrayal, pocho has many parts. These are best encapsulated not through one or another person, as the mirroring of Richard and Villarreal would suggest, but rather through aggregates of character within the text. *Pocho* encompasses two fields of characterization. The first, El Macho, is arrayed around the figure of Richard's father, and generates a homophobic and misogynist caricature of machismo even as it is riven by feminized and queer desire. The second, El Malinche, is arrayed around Richard. It proliferates queer characters and queers heteronormative characters, refashioning the relationship they have to their masculinity. As heir to La Malinche, Richard disidentifies with minority masculinity. Even as he accedes to assimilation, he elicits critiques of racism and colonialism. The novel does not affirm the archetype of racial betrayal in the continuity of pocho, Richard, and Villarreal, but exposes the gaps and disjunctures between these figures. These discontinuous betrayals amount in the aggregate of characterization to a fuller view upon the social and culture spheres within which minority resistance takes shape.

Aggregates of Character

Pocho tells the story of the coming of age of Richard in Depression-era California between the Mexican Revolution and World War II. The novel begins with Richard's father, Juan Manuel Rubio, who served as a cavalry officer in Villa's army, as he grapples with the breakdown of the Mexican Revolution and eventually heads north of the border from El Paso to Los Angeles where he is joined by his wife, Consuelo, and his children. The family follows the harvest of California crops until Richard is born. Then they settle in Santa Clara, where Juan's dream of returning to Mexico recedes. Juan eventually buys a house, hastening the Rubio family's assimilation into the middle class, their estrangement from what Richard perceives to be traditional Mexican values, and their embrace of Americanism, whether in recitals of the pledge of allegiance at the table or the growing refusal of the women of the family to submit to patriarchy. The ensuing breach between Consuelo and Juan heads toward a divorce, as Juan moves in with Pilar, who, having recently arrived from Mexico, appears to represent the ideal of the traditional Mexican woman.

Meanwhile, the narrative tracks Richard's consciousness from the age of nine to his eventual enlistment in the war. Even as he rebels against institutional authority (his family, teachers, and the Catholic church), he develops a sense of the broader sociopolitical forces shaping his community as it grapples with destitution and unemployment through mass organizing, strikes, and marches. He comes to terms with the racial and sexual politics of friendship and romance among a motley crew of school friends who share the same rural, working-class background, including his best friend and rival, Ricky, who is Italian; Thomas, who is Japanese and often bears the brunt of bullying along with Richard; and Zelda, who commands the crew with the sheer force of her tomboyishness until Richard eventually asserts his sexual dominance over her. In an ongoing social experiment, he joins and then leaves behind other figures and groups on the fringes, including the Portuguese émigré and local pariah "Joe Pete"; the new Mexican American arrivals who bring with them pachuco fashion and ethos to Santa Clara; and a group of white liberals he meets through a creative writing class. The novel culminates with his decision to leave his family and join the war, rejecting the role of dutiful provider for an uncertain future.

The novel's initial appeal is due in part to the fact that it peddles one version of the American dream, as Richard embraces individualism and turns his back on his community. *Pocho* was one of the first Chicano novels to be accepted by a major publishing house. José Saldívar has a damning assessment of the novel's mainstream draw. He argues that Villarreal wrote "according to New York editors' standards about certain U.S. ethnic themes—social maladjustment, the individual and the environment, the pathological character of the Chicano family, illegals, violence, and criminal behavior—that dominant cultural practices define as worthy and 'universal.'"[19] In his brief assessment of *Pocho*, Saldívar touches on many of the problems with the text: the fact that "the author (unwittingly) projects a stereotypical view," that Juan is "an arrogant, callous *macho*," "a one-dimensional character" (by implication) who leaves Richard no recourse but to "assert an Americanized individuality, or succumb to the burden of machismo and cultural nationalism imposed on him by his father and his community."[20] Richard's tragic assimilation is leavened by enough local color and hyperbole to confirm the projections of *Pocho*'s readers. In the novel, they find the archetype of racial betrayal, whose shifting allegiances affirm the dominant American ideal.

Pocho also represents a problem for the Chicano movement. The novel was republished in 1970, with an introduction by Ramón Ruiz that sought to conjoin aesthetics to the politics of the Chicano struggle for empowerment and self-determination. While in sympathy with its characters (the novel's "character portrait" of Juan "demonstrates both knowledge and a profound insight" into the first generation and treats "with gusto and sureness of the *pochos*"), Ruiz justifies *Pocho*'s existence as a historical document and limits its vagaries to a function of its time: Villarreal wrote out of an "'assimilationist' phase," he claims, when "most Mexican-Americans had rebelled against traditional values in their urge to join the American mainstream"; the "book needs no apologies because it mirrors faithfully the sentiment of its age" and "stands for a piece of the past, a document written by a university-educated man of Mexican ancestry who interprets the struggle of his 'people' in the light of his day."[21] Ruiz struggles to hold on to a sense of *Pocho*'s historical relevance and continuity while relieving Chicanos of this burdensome inheritance. Those in his present audience, who are "awakened" and "call themselves chicanos," share "a common historical foundation" with the novel, but they are no longer "'lost' Richards" as they build "an identity to replace that sense of inferiority" that Richard represents.[22]

Critics have grappled with the vexed legacy of *Pocho* in different ways. Some read *Pocho*'s rugged, masculinist individualism as a view upon "man's hopes and frustrations in his incessant struggle to live life to its fullest extent" (Francisco Jiménez) or as featuring "a Mexican American Adam" who "fulfills the American Adamic destiny of alienation and solitude that echoes across generations of U.S. American literature" (Timothy Sedore).[23] For other critics, the novel is anticipatory. "As soldiers and men, Juan and Richard thus symmetrically oppose and reflect one another," Saldívar writes; they represent "a dialectic of developing protopolitical understanding," as Richard transforms "his father's idealist concept of history" into "the materialist concept of history."[24] Melissa Hidalgo argues that the novel has "queer potential"; Richard serves "as a prototype for queer and nonnormative masculine figures" even as "*Pocho* anticipates a queer Chicana/o literary bildungsroman heritage."[25] John Alba Cutler shifts the terms of "controversy" around the "putative assimilationism" of *Pocho*, arguing that the novel depicts "a society in flux," where "Richard does not simply cross a boundary separating his 'ethnic' community from the white mainstream" but inhabits "a world in which the boundaries are themselves unstable" and a multiracial, immigrant working class is selectively incorporated into whiteness.[26]

In this context, what might it mean to focus on the literary characterization of Juan and Richard, to ask how they serve not as "soldiers and men" but as literary figurations who inhabit *Pocho*'s narrative world? Doubtless, *Pocho* is a book in two minds—two masculine, discrete, anthropomorphic minds. Villarreal himself sets up this expectation in a 1976 interview, describing *Pocho* as the "specific story of Juan Rubio, which was the fall of man, and that of Richard Rubio, which was the hope of man."[27] As Villarreal would have it, Juan and Richard are not only exclusive of one another but also squarely within the general and gendered realm of "man." Assuming the equivalence of character and "man" reproduces this schematic plotting of the novel and its teleological imperative, as father gives way to son. Even if Richard is incorporated into a canonical American tradition, this tradition stands, along with the ideology of masculinist individualism into which *Pocho* is then subsumed.

Sociformal approaches to character have helped to disarticulate literary persona from individual personhood. As Elizabeth Fowler points out, literary representations encompass multiple "social persons," and "verbal portraiture" is but one among a myriad of ways that a literary text does the work of characterization.[28] Alex Woloch proposes that we read characters in a "distributional matrix" in which they occupy a "structured position within the literary totality."[29] He navigates this totality using two key concepts: "character-space" ("the dynamic interaction between a discretely implied individual and the overall narrative form"), and "character-system" ("a constellation of intersecting and simultaneously unfolding character-spaces").[30] These concepts illuminate "the peripheral 'character-spaces' of early Chicana/o texts," Jayson Gonzales Sae-Saue finds, showing how marginal Asian American characters shape the development of Chicano political consciousness in *Pocho* and related works.[31] These concepts also draw attention to sites where protagonist and author are conflated, where criticism of *Pocho* "expands the space of the protagonist beyond even the boundaries of the novel," as in Cutler's assessment (via Woloch) of Saldívar's reading.[32]

In the analysis that follows, I read *Pocho* through the notion of a "distributed field of characterization," following Woloch.[33] Juan and Richard are not coextensive with "soldier" or "man," nor is their range as characters solely anthropomorphic. Rather, they are aggregates of character—"character-spaces" within a "character-system"—that are overlapping and counterposed. El Macho is the field Juan inhabits within the novel. In some respects, he is a cliché as a type of virile, warmongering jinete (horseman) who shoots Spaniards and beds women with impunity. In this sense, he is flat, "constructed round a single idea or quality," per E. M. Forster.[34] Such characters are not absolute, however, but variable. Flat characters can "curve towards the round," Forster allows.[35] If we look beyond Juan to his field of characterization, we can see how his character is fleshed out and this emblem of machismo feminized and rendered queer.

Key to this variability is the proximity of El Macho to El Malinche, the second major field of characterization within the novel. A word on this construct is in order, for it has been linked to another paradigmatic figure of the "pocho," Richard Rodriguez. "Rodriguez is critiqued and rejected," Randy Rodríguez writes, "because he is a *joto or puto*, a passive homosexual—a non-man in Mexican/Chicano/a-defined cultural terms," and he "serves much of the Chicano/a intellectual and artistic community as El Malinche, a masculine, but emasculated, updated version of the original version of the historical and mythologized La Malinche."[36] Rodríguez takes us back to the primal scene of new world colonization, positing a parallel between

Rodriguez and La Malinche, the archetype of female treachery whose notoriety has obscured the singular history of Malintzin Tenépal. Characterized as passive, violated, and abject, La Malinche has been reinterpreted through the lens of Chicana feminism as a transgressive meditator who skillfully negotiates the complex of desire, betrayal, violation, and retribution that mantles colonial border zones.[37] As Rodríguez suggests, we must build on this reinterpretation to rethink the figure of betrayal writ large.

Rodriguez himself explores the link between betrayal and emasculation in *Hunger of Memory* (1982) in ways that bring Villarreal's characters more sharply into focus. In one set of passages, he describes how relatives and friends come to terms with his inability to speak Spanish fluently. "*Pocho* then they called me. Sometimes playfully, teasingly, using the tender diminutive—*mi pochito*. Sometimes not so playfully, mockingly, *Pocho*."[38] He recalls that his maternal uncle visited from Mexico and was repulsed by the "disgrace" of his nephew's stilted Spanish.[39] In a 2003 interview, Rodriguez reflects on his uncle once again: "I remember feeling this enormous effeminacy—I don't know how else to put it, but there was some masculine quality lost in the boy already in that this man had no place for me. I was not his nephew. I was less, a real withering disdain. I've always heard in that word *pocho* a loss of some virility. It's hard to explain."[40] The thread of his response falters here. But Rodriguez has a sense that the embarrassments of the pocho are linked to the embarrassments of emasculation, that his lack of fluency represents a threat to nationalist pride.

The connotations of the term suggest as much, especially when understood through queer critique. Hidalgo links the term "queer" to the term "pocho" through "notions of being spoiled and ruined," pointing out that "*pocho*," "*agavachado*," and "*joto*" were synonymous in the era of Chicano nationalism.[41] She draws upon José Esteban Muñoz's theory of "disidentification," which charts a course between "identification, assimilation" and "counteridentification, utopianism" and entails working with and through dominant ideology in an oblique relation.[42] Repurposing this concept to think through intraracial relations within hegemony—essentially, dominance within domination—reveals a complex negotiation on the part of the pocho as concessions to assimilation generate critiques of cultural nationalism.

As a field of characterization, El Malinche does similar work, for it both reproduces and exposes the heteropatriarchal violence that mantles the new world colonial order. Richard and Juan are neither fully congruent nor directly opposed. While often in conflict at the level of plot and dialogue, they are obliquely conjoined by the overlapping spaces they occupy as characters. The neat schematics of "fall of man" and "hope of man" are reconfigured where El Macho and El Malinche adjoin each other. Aggregated around the figure of Richard, El Malinche is at once patriarchal and queer, assimilationist and nonnormative. Richard accedes to assimilation but also voices a queer perspective on machismo, and ultimately shows how minority masculinity takes its bearings from the dominant patriarchal order, eliciting from Juan a clearheaded critique of racism and coloniality. We cannot apportion betrayal or resistance to one or the other character. Rather, the pocho comes into view through their aggregation—how they are collated and divided, the forms through which they enter and exit the narrative, and the thematic and generic configurations of their exchange.

Enter El Macho

The first part of *Pocho* introduces the bellicose figure of Juan, whose revolutionary bravura, homophobia, and misogynistic violence combine to form a stereotypical portrait of machismo. The action moves from one set piece to another. The setting is Juárez, and a train from Mexico City is carrying Juan. He has been here twice before, under the command of Villa to take and retake the city. Wearing "the traditional tight-fitting costume of the Mexican charro" he is "ruddy," and his mackinaw and sombrero make him appear larger than he is (*PO*, 1). He enters a cantina, claims a prostitute, and handily wins a gunfight with her pimp, a "city-bred gachupín" whose murder lands Juan in jail (*PO*, 3). Upon realizing that he has ordered the arrest of one of the "old dogs of the Revolution," General Fuentes comes to meet with Juan, and they reminisce about the war and their status as fallen heroes: Fuentes has grown "fat" and "soft," and Juan finds himself without any useful occupation, having left the National Army training academy (where he was sent after the revolution) after roping and dragging behind a horse a "snotty cadet sergeant with the walk of a maricón" who dared attempt to teach him how to be a soldier (*PO*, 6, 8, 15).

Juan and the general's homophobia is barely disguised, as the figure of the sergeant and the cultured Spaniard ("gachupín") represent all that is perverse about the new social order against which Juan manfully asserts himself, with a measure of rural and Indigenous pride: "our ancestors were princes in a civilization that was possibly more advanced than this one"; "the india is still the most beautiful woman in the world" (*PO*, 8).[43] Riled by the general's capitulation to the new social hierarchies, Juan launches upon an uncompromising defense of his machismo. "If a man has been a man, he will always be a man," he claims. "I will never forget that which I believe is right. There must be a sense of honor or a man will have no dignity, and without the dignity a man is incomplete. I will always be a man" (PO, 15).

Looking beyond Juan to the preamble that introduces him reveals how precarious his position is within the new military and social order. Villarreal deploys his stock characters strategically, as Saldívar points out, reading in this opening the "stereotype of the corrido hero" who will serve as the "negative counterpoint" for the rest of the novel.[44] But the contradiction extends to the preamble as well. The stereotype is itself unsustainable, as the idealized figure of machismo is undermined by the plot. Even before Richard's arrival on the scene, fissures appear in the set and pageantry. While Juan's win in the bar fight represents a small victory, there is a sense that he has lost the war, that there is no place for him in post-revolutionary Mexico. He must now flee to El Paso and join the ranks of migrants fleeing the Mexican Revolution. For a time, he stays near the border involved in a conspiracy to overturn the new presidency with precisely those schemers and propagandists who constitute the new social order that he so detests. This ambition is brought to a swift end when Juan gets news of Villa's assassination and resolutely turns his back on his old life, deciding to head west.

Of particular interest are the homoerotic pairings that accompany Juan's decidedly homophobic rhetoric and actions. Paramount among these is Juan's relationship with Villa. Reminiscing about being under his command in battle, Juan imagines that he would offer his "backside" and "submit to him," this "man with such balls!" (PO, 11). News of Villa's death occasions a remarkable outpouring of grief and tears ("He was on his knees, holding his head in his hands, and he cried unrestrainedly, as a child would cry") (PO, 25). Juan and the general have a similarly suggestive relationship, as they reminisce about the homosocial camaraderie of the revolution. The pairing of Juan and the cadet sergeant is considerably more fraught, but Juan gets no uncertain pleasure from recounting the story to the general of how he roped and dragged around the screaming man. Among the exiled politicians whose scheme he joins is another model of the revolutionary: a gay journalist, René Soto, whose relationship with another of the generals of the revolution, General Carrillo, is an open secret.[45] Although Juan is discomfited by René, and does not trouble to hide his homophobic rancor for this lesser model of the revolutionary, the two travel to California together when news of Villa's death reaches them and dissolves their fledgling plot. Consuelo, who has thus far been relegated to the background of this homosocial post-revolutionary space, finally joins Juan in Los Angeles, filling in the void left by René's presumed departure.

These figures represent prototypes of El Malinche who, while maligned by Juan, occupy the "character-space" of El Macho. The structuring of their characters draws Juan into the ambit of their ruin and treachery. They not only violate the new political order but are violated by it (in the sense that Juan and the general are violated by the end of the revolution, the cadet sergeant is violated by Juan, and René, once violated by Carrillo, now seeks to violate Juan, and so on). At the level both of content and of form, Juan partners with these traitors to his revolutionary principles who scheme in conspiracy rather than waging open battle. While he embraces some of these men and repudiates others, they nonetheless introduce a queer element into the "character-space" that he occupies. Their presence opens the way to the dramatic scene of Richard's birth, which takes place at the end of this section, signaling the reconfiguration of El Macho.

This scene represents a queer and feminized space, governed by new formal conventions. Once Consuelo rejoins Juan in Los Angeles, the narrative takes an unexpected turn away from the heroic romance of the border corrido, rendered through the figure of Juan, to describe the story of Richard's birth in a dilatory fashion. The landscape comes into view, no longer serving as a backdrop for Juan's adventures, as Villarreal takes pains to describe Brawley, Richard's birthplace, and the harsh and exploitative conditions facing the migrants in the fields who die in the hot sun and bury their own dead for lack of money and resources. The location of these graves is not known to many, Villarreal writes, mentioning offhandedly "that when a witch was murdered (for there were witches in those days, as there are today), she was committed to the earth, and the English-speaking population knew nothing of her death, if, indeed, they had known of her existence" (*PO*, 29). He introduces a tear into the realist fabric of the novel, gesturing toward another reality that *Pocho* has not yet allowed.

The gendered turn is perceptible as the narrative brings Consuelo into focus, tracing her movement from the house to the scene of the birth. The predominance of dialogue, with meager glimpses into the characters' inner lives, gives way here to a narrative effusion that surrounds the absentminded Consuelo: "Now she walked on the creekbed, first on gravel, and the sound her shoes made on the pebbles penetrated her senses, and in her mind she was back on the hacienda in Zacatecas, walking on a dry creekbed such as this, although she did not know she was on a creekbed, on her way to a manantial for water" (*PO*, 30). As she follows the dry creek in a trance, we are invited to follow her thoughts all the way to Zacatecas and into the Spanish word for spring ("manantial"). "The urge to urinate, which had left her, returned with an intensity she could not resist," Villarreal writes, "and she undid her cotton drawers and squatted, holding the folds of her dress under her armpits. And there on the soft sand she dropped her child" (*PO*, 30). Even as Consuelo births Richard, the novel prepares the reader for the shifts in narration that will follow in the transition from realist to modernist modes, as the dry creek overflows with the stream of Richard's consciousness.

Richard's arrival transforms Juan, as we see when the latter arrives on the scene. Until now, the birth is unsentimental. But when Juan carries mother and child back to the house, he (and the narrative) are overwhelmed by feeling. Juan has the sense of having entered a female space, as his daughters help him to care for their mother and the newborn until a neighbor arrives. "He was very nearly overcome by emotion," Villarreal writes, having "never been this close to the birth of a child"; when he hands Richard over, he begins to cry, "not because it was a manchild, or because its genitalia seemed enormous in proportion to the little body, but because he was relaxed and because for a moment he had caught a glimpse of the cycle of life, lucidly not penumbrally, and he knew love and he knew also that this was good" (*PO*, 30, 31). Even as this moment affirms the phallic lineage, it presents once again the figure of the inconsolable Juan, weeping not for the death of Villa this time but for the birth of his son and for the view he has received into the cyclical nature of life.[46]

El Macho is fundamentally changed by El Malinche's emergence, marked by *Pocho*'s modernist turn. It is not only Juan who confronts the "cycle of life" but his field of characterization as well, which couples Richard's birth with the death of a version of Juan's character. The corrido hero has already become "a part of the great exodus" stemming from the Mexican Revolution, joining a "bewildered people" who move "west to New Mexico and Arizona and California, and as they moved, they planted their new seed" (*PO*, 15, 16). His son's birth "dropped" in the "soft sand" represents this "new seed," fashioning a link to the new world that Juan symbolically strengthens by returning to the creek to "deeper bury the afterbirth" (*PO*, 31). In the paragraphs immediately following, the prospect of Juan's heroic repatriation is finally put to rest as the family settles in Santa Clara: "Now this man who had lived by the gun all his adult life would sit on his haunches under the prune trees, rubbing his sore knees, and think, *Next year we will have enough money and we will return to our country*. But deep within he knew he was one of the lost ones" (*PO*, 31). "And the chains were incrementally heavier on his heart," Villarreal writes, foreshadowing the chain of events that will end in a very different character for Juan (with "prematurely white" hair, and a body that has "lost its solidity" and grown "flabby") as he grows increasingly emasculated, much like the fallen revolutionary heroes he abhors (*PO*, 31, 134).

The scene of Richard's birth mirrors the scene of farewell between father and son toward the end of the novel, as both represent a queer rendering of El Macho. Having struck his daughter and wife, and then Richard, when he tried to intercede, Juan finally resolves to leave his family. Father and son find themselves surrounded by women who are testing out the limits of the patriarchal order. In his decision to leave this setting, it seems Juan has recovered a sense of masculine pride ("I feel I am a man again") (*PO*, 169). But the departure is deeply felt by father and son. It highlights their homosocial attachment as they come to terms with the queer figure of René, who is once again evoked by Juan. In their brief, uninterrupted exchange, Juan sits by Richard who is lying on the bed to recover from the fight. They both find themselves in tears. Juan recalls "this man" (likely René) who once told him that Mexicans "are a lachrymose race" (*PO*, 168). Sensing a distance between his father and René, Richard asks his father whether or not he liked him, to which Juan responds, "He was a strange one; in fact I thought at times that he was one of 'those others'" (*PO*, 168). Then Juan confesses his fears as to Richard's homosexuality, describing his deep love for his son as maternal ("I feel about you as strongly as your mother does") (*PO*, 168). It is here that Richard tells his father he wants to be a writer, like René, and it is a vocation his father accepts. As Juan turns to leave, at the very moment when he feels him to be "a man again," Richard calls out to Juan for an embrace and they "put their arms around each other in the Mexican way. Then Juan Rubio kissed his son on the mouth" (*PO*, 169). Even as El Macho affirms his masculinity, El Malinche interpellates him into a homosocial order. The kiss is carefully choreographed. It cements not only the collusion of father and son with patriarchy but also reveals their effeminacy and their tolerance for what is nonnormative and queer.

Richard's Queer Counterpose

The transition in *Pocho* from the story of Juan to that of Richard reveals how these aggregates of character work. El Malinche poses an oblique challenge to El Macho. In one sense, Richard's arrival disrupts the homosocial "character-space" of the revolution and its range of homoerotic bonds, for René must depart the narrative frame in order for Consuelo to appear within it. Juan's apprehension of his son's disproportionately large genitalia would indicate that his "manchild" confirms (rather than challenges) his own masculinity. But Richard's appearance also has the effect of rendering El Macho queer, as the narrative veers decidedly away from the border romance and toward the modernist bildungsroman, and Juan enters into a feminized, maternal role. Even as Juan apprehends the cycle of life, the reader is made aware of the life cycle of Juan's character: apparently unassailable and static, in the stereotypical form of the corrido hero, he begins to undergo a transformation. While undeniably masculine at the point of his arrival, Richard is also queer. He does not directly oppose El Macho but works within his "character-space," straining Juan's relationship to his masculinity.

This complex structure of characterization is at work in the broader arc of the novel, as Richard assumes his birthright in machismo while also assuming El Malinche's queer counterpose. Only Zelda is close enough to him to see this "part of his character"—that his "sensitivity" and "gentleness" are coupled with a "great cruelty," which is the "fault in his makeup" (*PO*, 143, 144). In many ways he is his father's son. Privileged to be the only boy in a family of daughters, he continues his schooling while his sisters work at home, contravenes his mother's attempts at self-assertion, defends the patriarchal status quo, and beats his sister, even as he develops an awareness of his family's confinement within particular social roles ("he saw the demands of tradition, of culture, of the social structure on an individual") (*PO*, 95). Among his friends, his conquest of Zelda is exactly that: "You're my girl now," he tells her, as their last fight as coequals signals the end of one regime of oppression (in which she is sexually free but also sexually exploited by the boys in their circle) and the beginning of another as she accepts "his newfound and now everpresent dominance" as part of their monogamous relationship and makes "token resistance" to his advances only to please him (*PO*, 141, 143).

But Richard is also perceptible within *Pocho* as nonnormative, partly because of an extensive network of queer familiars that he cultivates. "In short, he was a sissy, really," Villarreal and Richard allow in the shared space of free indirect discourse, as Richard reflects on his self-image on the occasion of his twelfth birthday (*PO*, 95). His closest attachments are to figures who inhabit a spectrum of nonnormative masculinity and who, because they are part of very different social milieus, often appear "queer" to one another by contrast. He befriends Joe Pete, who comes from the Azores looking for the

Portuguese settlement in Santa Clara and settles on the fringes of society; he has an aura of aristocracy about him and is mostly left alone to graze and tend his cows, although people refer to him as "that queer one," or "that maluco João" (PO, 80). In a different context, Richard's declaration of love for Ricky meets with the latter's fear and suspicion: "Hey, you're not going queer, are you?" Ricky asks, as Richard tries to explain and deflect his attachment (PO, 112). Ricky perceives Richard's associations with anyone beyond their immediate circle of school friends as queer. He accuses Richard of associating with "funny people—all those pachucos you got for buddies" and of hanging out in San Jose with his creative writing friends, "a couple of guys that looked queer as hell" (PO, 177).

In the context of these relationships, Richard's masculinity is often put to the test and seems to win out, but not without destabilizing the idea of machismo altogether. The first clue to this dynamic appears as the young Richard is able to shift the terms of his bullying by the older children, who are especially derisive because he is Mexican. When the Depression plunges many of these already poor families into crisis, it appears that Richard's family is better equipped to make do with little, and Richard discovers a newfound popularity among his hungry friends. "The hated, oft-repeated cries of his schoolmates—'Frijoley bomber!' 'Tortilla strangler!'—now disappeared, as did the accompanying laughter, and he sometimes shared his lunch with them. He did this with a sense of triumph, because he felt he had defeated them by enduring their contempt and derision openly" (PO, 47). Although Villarreal suggests that the reason for his acceptance is due more to his lunch than to him, the narrative offers the reader a clue into Richard's approach to the male-dominated struggle for dominance: to weather publicly the torrent of insult and ridicule as proof of his own manly character. Even his declaration of love for Ricky, which subjects him to the charge of "going queer," ends by Richard affirming his superiority over Ricky, for Richard is able to comprehend the finer points of homosocial attachment and attraction while Ricky cannot ("And the thought that he had passed beyond Ricky made him confident once more. Confident and strangely powerful") (PO, 112, 113).

When it becomes generally known that Joe Pete has sexually assaulted a young girl, Richard is caught up in the police investigation. Although he refuses to join in the general condemnation, he is careful to detach himself from the stigma of this association. Questioned by a police officer under the watchful eye of his father, Richard perceives the underlying concern with his friendship with Joe Pete: "You mean was he a homosexual? No, he wasn't," Richard tells the police officer (announcing precociously to the latter that the "big word" means *"queer"*) despite Joe Pete's confessions to distinctly queer desire and his intimation of gay sexual encounters (PO, 89). "I have the feeling for girls already," he reassures his father, emerging relatively unscathed and secure in his sense of masculinity (PO, 90).

Another scene features the tense arena of the boxing match between Richard and Thomas, into which Richard enters reluctantly and only because he feels pressured to save face. The only opening he finds as he is being pummeled by his friend is by "looking real sadlike right into his eyes, as if to say, *Go ahead, kill me*," a look that disarms Thomas and enables Richard to land one solid punch; in the next round, Richard performs his failure, exaggerating his reactions to Thomas's punches while "sneaking looks at the people" and dramatizing his overwhelming defeat: "he had made it look pretty good" (PO, 105, 106). Ironically, Richard, rather than Thomas, is approached and praised by the referee who asks if he would like to become a professional fighter. It is Richard's elaborate performance of loss, his deliberate surrender, that wins the day and undermines the bravado of the whole enterprise. Reflecting on the fight, Richard realizes that an "unwritten code of honor" has pressed him to join the arena, and resolves to "never succumb to foolish social pressures again" and to do only what pleases him, because "what people thought was honorable was not important, because he was the important guy" (PO, 108). By losing, he has not only emerged the winner but has also thrown into crisis the whole logic that structures this masculine display.

Richard is recruited to another fight when he starts associating with pachuco subculture, and his ignominious fate once again serves to confirm the futility of machismo. By "this year of Our Lord 1940," in which Richard finds himself, this subculture had reached from Texas to California (PO, 153). Pachucos represented a fierce, if hybrid, cultural nationalism with its own markers of language, dress, and comportment: they spoke Caló, a slang fusing English and Spanish, and wore zoot suits, with a specific repertoire of accessories and hairstyles. Only a few years later, events such as the 1942 Sleepy Lagoon murder and the 1943 Zoot Suit Riots would bring pachucos into the national spotlight—targets of nativism and mob hysteria fomented by sensational media coverage, racist law enforcement, and biased public reports.[47] Richard is fascinated by this new group, and recognizes the pachucos as being different from the Mexicans he has encountered until now, set in opposition to white Americans as well as Mexican immigrants. But he maintains a studied distance, even as he remains something of an outlier from the perspective of the group, regarded by the women, especially, as "a traitor to his 'race'" (*PO*, 151). The very name of the group leader, Rooster, is a conspicuous index of masculinity. As Richard gazes upon him, he wonders "what errant knight from Castile had traveled four thousand miles to mate with a daughter of Cuahtémoc to produce this strain" (*PO*, 156). Rooster represents a variant on machismo, whose pedigree is shaped by colonialism and mestizaje. But Richard ranks the pachucos alongside his father: "They, like his father, were defeated—only more so, because they really never started to live. They, too, were but making a show of resistance" (*PO*, 151).

Although Richard tries to remain uninvolved, he is recruited to fight in a local orchard with another group from Ontario. Sitting in the back of a car on his way to the fight, his posture is decidedly unheroic, as he is "afraid that they might discover the growing terror inside him," or that "his fear" has "turned to panic" (*PO*, 154). The fight is over quickly as Richard, in blind terror, flails about with a bicycle chain and finds himself face down in the mud. When Rooster takes him home and helps him to the door, Richard elicits a surprising admission of fear from him. "I'll tell you, Rooster," he says, "I've never been afraid as much as I was tonight," to which Rooster responds, "Hell, that's no news. We all were" (*PO*, 157). Their conversation contrasts the bravado of the fight, as the aura of fearlessness around Rooster dissolves.

It falls to El Malinche to accept but also refigure the legacy of El Macho. Richard reveals the exploitative social order against which this masculinist resistance is being waged, and which is the real arena of the subaltern struggle. As he starts to rebel against his father, he has a keen awareness of the latter as a fallen man: "Richard knew that although his father was not one of the vanquished, as he claimed, there was little resistance left" (*PO*, 131–32). A life of drudgery has brought Juan low, Villarreal suggests, as he creates a stark picture of the life of farmers who work from morning to night during harvest season, are worn down with toil, and subsist through winter on government relief. Richard rails against "this thing—this horrible, inexplicable, merciless intangible—that held humanity in its power," compelled to provide and procreate ("they were feeding their families and their children would grow and raise their families. This was happiness!") (*PO*, 132).

Richard knows that the heroic template of El Macho falls apart in this social dispensation, where Mexican immigrants struggle to wrest a measure of self-determination and upward mobility from the clutches of a deeply exploitative system. In fact, he rejects this version of assimilation as a capitulation to the meager gains that the American dream (which he recognizes as a parody of "happiness") has to offer. The bullying to which Richard submits, much like the boxing arena and the fight in the orchard, all displace and reenact the violence of the social order, which pits brown men against brown men. But Richard refuses to take part in this cycle of violence. He has a sense that this is the wrong fight. To displays of machismo he responds with masochism, displacing hegemonic violence upon himself. As El Malinche, or the one who is violated, Richard is poised to expose the violations of the racist order. This is not a contest of men, where the "fall" of one gives way to the "hope" of another, but a systemic struggle between dominance and subordination.

Horse of a Different Color

El Macho and El Malinche encounter one another in a telling scene that reveals the dynamics of their characterization. On the day of Richard's twelfth birthday, he plans to ask his parents for money to go to the movies and sits down with them instead:

> He went inside the house to eat, and thought maybe his father would give him a dime to go see Buck Jones. He sat at the table with his chin in his hands and said aloud, in English, "I am Buck Jones and Ken Maynard and Fred Thompson, all rolled into one—I'm not Tom Mix, too, because I don't like brown horses." And he settled down to think some more....
>
> Richard was still thinking of Silver King. "Do you think, Papá," he said, "that when we go to México I could have a horse?"
>
> "That is understood."
>
> "A white one, and very big?"
>
> "If you want," said Juan Rubio. "But why do you want a white one?"
>
> "Because I want the best."
>
> "Who told you that? White horses are usually little more than useless."
>
> "You are playing with me," said Richard. "Everybody knows that a white horse is the best horse there is."
>
> Juan Rubio laughed. "Hoo, that shows how much you know. That is only in the moving pictures, but if you knew anything about horses, you would know that a good horse is not chosen for his color." (PO, 96-97)

In response, Richard teases his father and asks his mother if she really knows about horses. Consuelo's answer has the effect of reactivating the corrido hero stereotype, as she praises her husband's great skill, and their exchange begins to rekindle the romance between husband and wife. "That is the one thing he does know, son—that and about women," she answers. "Your father was the greatest horseman in our whole section of the country" (*PO*, 97). These reminiscences about their early life in Mexico have the effect of bringing husband and wife together. Richard looks up at one point to find that his mother has left the stove and is being caressed by his father. As their flirtation develops, he slips away from the kitchen, feeling elated by the prospect of their reconciliation.

Richard is overawed and aroused by this performance of machismo and the glimpse he gets into the primal scene. Consuelo's praise leaves him "warm with pleasure," and his parents' display of affection "speechless with happiness" (*PO*, 97, 102). The names Richard lists are those of actors known for their starring roles in Westerns of the era, who themselves represent a popular version of machismo. But the silver screen is eclipsed by the action unfolding before Richard, as he watches the character of El Macho come into his own in the figure of his father—who has worked at one time as an extra within these very movies—and his mother, serving primarily as her husband's foil. Enthralled by the drama playing out right before him, Richard "forgot about the movies," Villarreal writes (*PO*, 102).

There is a lot more here that prompts Richard's admiration, as the conversation between Juan and Consuelo rounds out El Macho's ostensibly flat character. We get a glimpse of Juan as a revolutionary nationalist with a thoroughgoing critique of colonialism and a sense of solidarity with the downtrodden that extends from Mexico to the United States. Consuelo describes how Juan gave his belongings away to those poorer than he was and sometimes took what he needed by force from those richer than he was. As their conversation turns to ancestry, Consuelo traces Richard's roots to Indigenous, Spanish, and possibly French sources. But Juan is adamant that he and his family are Mexican. "She has a love for Spaniards I could never have," he says, for they embody racialized colonialism: the rich European in collusion with the church to oppress the darker masses, precisely the exploitative structure that Juan in his capacity as revolutionary fighter, as well as the Zapatista narrative of political emancipation thematized in the novel, have sought to upend (*PO*, 99). When Richard points out that he is friends with many Spanish immigrants in Santa Clara, Juan reveals his fraternity with the exploited classes, his class solidarity that, ultimately, transcends racial difference: "these people are different—they are also from the lower class. . . . people who were stepped on, much the same as we were in our country" (PO, 99). "Richard looked at his father with a new respect," Villarreal writes, as Richard realizes that Juan has joined the revolution not for a "lark" but to take a principled stand for social reform against the exploitative aftereffects of colonialism (PO, 101).

Richard's desire for a white horse confounds Juan, for whom whiteness holds no corresponding allure. Even after his father tells him, with all the weight of his experience as a jinete, that "a good horse is not chosen for his color," Richard continues to insist upon the superiority of white horses. He describes seeing the infantry horses in an encampment nearby: "They were very pretty horses, but they were all brown." "What is this obsession about the brown?" Juan retorts, saying "Enough! A horse is a horse!" (PO, 97). There is more at work in this scene than the stubbornness of a pubescent boy challenging his father. Horses, here as in José Garcia Villa's *Footnote to Youth* (1933), are richly emblematic of racialized masculine power. This banter between father and son comes at a pivotal moment in the bildungsroman—Richard's twelfth birthday—and veers into a discussion about Richard's mongrel, new world pedigree. The white horse functions as an emblem of Richard's assimilative desire, revealing that he has a very different relationship to racialized power than his father does. It is no coincidence that the cowboy heroes who appeal to Richard rode white horses, whereas Mix rode a brown horse; the color of this horse becomes racialized as the undesirable other of whiteness partly by its proximity to the idea of racial mixing coded in Mix's name. Richard uncritically and unknowingly disavows the lineage of mestizaje that Consuelo attributes to him. Captivated by his son's interest in horses and what it affirms about his lineage as a jinete, Juan does not register this disavowal, but he is confounded by it. Words that he speaks to his daughter elsewhere as she breaks out in a recitation of the pledge of allegiance are apposite to this scene: "Just because your name is Rubio does not mean you are really blond" (PO, 133).

This scene is informed by the tenuous relationship that Mexican immigrants had to whiteness, given the particular history of colonization and annexation in the American Southwest. The 1848 Treaty of Guadalupe Hidalgo, which ceded approximately one-third of Mexican territory to the United States, was a milestone in U.S. expansionism. Scholars have traced the subjection of Mexican Americans and Chicanos to this date, when the model of "imported colonialism" that characterizes Mexican migration was shaped.[48] While Mexicans within the annexed territories were accorded U.S. citizenship and therefore made legally "white," their relationship to whiteness was tenuous and unstable. Distinguished from "Anglos," Mexicans were "borderline Americans," disenfranchised on every level as they came to occupy "an inferior, caste-like status" within the social hierarchies of the border zones.[49] A landmark 1897 ruling, *In re Rodriguez*, revealed these contradictions even as it affirmed the right of Mexican immigrants to naturalize. The court had difficulty reading the figure of the petitioner, Ricardo Rodriguez. "As to color," in the words of the District Court Judge, "he may be classed with the copper-colored or red men. He has dark eyes, straight black hair, and high cheek bones" although he "knows nothing of the Aztecs or Toltecs" and is "not an Indian."[50] The petitioner abutted different racial categories (most perceptibly that of the "Indian"), but the court was nonetheless obliged by treaty to find him to be eligible to naturalize. This "pure-blooded Mexican" applicant was admitted to citizenship despite the fact that, according to the court, "he would probably not be classed as white" by the racial pseudo-science of the period.[51] In this context, Mexicans defined the terms of their own whiteness where possible. Some professed Latin American or Spanish American heritage, claiming to be descended from "the first white race" to conquer the new world, while others supplemented this "Caucasian strategy" by relying on cultural modes of whitening, even as a new concept of "*La Raza*" arose out of a combination of racism, nativism, and segregationist violence, producing a pan-Hispanic consciousness and presaging the subsequent development of Chicanismo.[52]

Whereas Juan is well aware of his colonial subjection in both Mexico and the United States, Richard cherishes a fantasy of belonging. He wants to have the horse and have it be white: to claim the masculinist lineage that his father represents as the heroic jinete while also epitomizing the white cowboy who rides across the movie screen. But it is difficult to parse these characters as consistent. Juan, the cliché of machismo, proffers anticolonial, antiracist critique. Richard's assimilative desire is unsurprising, but this desire is what prompts Juan's critique, which in turn elicits Richard's admiration. At one level, these are two characters speaking in the confines of the Rubio kitchen. At another level, they are also two fields of characterization through which the social coordinates of power are being mapped.

Part of Nothing

Prior to the conversation about horses, Richard has an extended appraisal of himself on the occasion of his twelfth birthday, in which he affirms his masculinity while entertaining the fantasy of intersex identity. "I am a man," he declares, as he swaggers and fights off invisible assailants in an imagined arena, making a display of his manliness ("New clothes he had that day, and he strutted up and down the walk in front of his house, all along, his cap set at a rakish angle, occasionally striking a boxer's pose") (*PO*, 95). However, he is clear that his performance is just that: "he could fool a lot of people," but "he was a sissy, really," "afraid of the dark and afraid of ghosts," and also "afraid to fight" (*PO*, 95, 96). He recalls seeing a "hermaphrodite in the carnival at the Portagee fiesta," and, allowing that he has a "hardon, and it was a real good one," stands "in front of the mirror watching to see on which side he would have the breast and mustache" (*PO*, 96). His masculinity is burgeoning yet precarious. Even as he plays the sensational part of the macho, he anticipates signs of intersexuality.

This moment prefigures another later in the novel, when Richard decides to restrain his developing intimacy with the pachucos. "I can be a part of everything," he thinks, "because I am the only one capable of controlling my destiny.... Never—no, never—will I allow myself to become a part of a group—to become classified, to lose my individuality.... I will not become a follower, nor will I allow myself to become a leader, because I must be myself and accept for myself only that which I value, and not what is being valued by everyone else these days (*PO*, 152–53). Richard's intersex fantasy resonates here, as the desire to have all the parts. Even though these scenes are comparatively understated, they evoke Khalid's feminized body as well as his vision of the "Superman of America." For here too are the makings of the protagonist of the American dream, who imagines he can play all parts. Assimilation is the unspoken word: not to this or that group (a prospect that Richard emphatically rejects), but to the ideals of self making and individualism, which are part of the national fantasy of the American dream.

Villarreal has a similar fantasy that the novel is meant to encapsulate. He describes *Pocho* as reconciling different aspects of his hyphenated upbringing: "to share my experiences of growing up in an old country traditional way, breaking away from that culture and going on to a new way of life, yet still holding on to the traditional ways that were good and adding to them the new things I liked in the Anglo-American society."[53] In another interview, he positions his "parents who came from Mexico" as "American pioneers," who are "just as important to the development of America as the pioneers who beat their way across the prairies, the Western European immigrants, the black slaves, and the first English who came here."[54] Like Richard, Villarreal sees himself as part of a broad lineage that encompasses coerced and voluntary migrations, the slave trade and European resettlement, hemispheric flows as well as westward expansion. As an artist, he affirms the "idea of universality."⁵⁵ To his detractors, he responds in another interview, "I believe in all races. I have never had any kind of attitude about people because of race. I was taught by my parents that we were all alike. We are human beings, and we live in the same situation."⁵⁶ Villarreal's universalism resounds with that of Ameen Rihani, who also sought to bridge great social divides through his writing. Villa's transcendental humanism has an echo here as well, as "the hermaphroditic body of the artist" (following E. San Juan Jr.) is incarnated in Richard's anticipation of male and female physiognomy.⁵⁷

This is not only a naive fantasy but also an unsustainable one, as *Pocho* shows. The real barrier to Richard's desire becomes clear toward the end of the novel, when Richard confronts the racist brutality of the police. While roaming San Jose with his childhood friends to steal some skirts for Ricky's new car, Richard and his school friends are apprehended (before they actually break the law), arrested, and beaten by the police. "Goddam pachucos!" the officer says, assuming Richard is part of a gang from Los Angeles; the detective calls him "scum" and accuses him of a recent attack against a white woman, purportedly raped by Mexicans (*PO*, 158, 159). Richard presses the detective as to the validity of his assumption ("did she see their birth certificates? Maybe they were Americans?"), but there is no room in the detective's answer for a Mexican to be American ("she saw them" and "said they were Mexican, that's how we know") (*PO*, 161).

Richard's desire to be "part of everything" is perverted, for it appears there is only one part open to him: that of the stereotypical Mexican. Overdetermined by the outward appearance of his character, his ontology has no room to emerge. He has little room to determine the scope of own identifications, for he is subject to all sorts of misreadings of his character due to its physical impress upon his features and his skin. The American dream vanishes from his grasp along with his assimilative ideal in the figure of the cowboy who rides a white horse, as Richard discovers that he is decidedly not "the only one" who determines his "destiny." This is a pivotal episode, for it disabuses Richard of his amalgamative and masculinist desire. Unlike the bulk of his other encounters with male violence, this encounter does not take place within subaltern society. Violated by racism, El Malinche proffers a new view of masculinity. "'Man,' that is truly the worst thing he could possibly call him at this moment," says Richard of the detective, unable to salvage the ideal of manhood (*PO*, 163).

It turns out there is another part open to Richard, which would represent an apotheosis of sorts for the pocho. After the detective finds out that

Richard is a local, bound for college, he invites Richard to join the police force. "There are a lot of your people around now, and someone like you would be good to have on the side of law and order" (*PO*, 162). This is a fitting end for the "pocho," invited to assume the mantle of his own character. The detective's inducement ("There's a lot you can do for your people that way") has the opposite effect, given Richard's disdain for group identification and the detective's patently hypocritical concern, not to mention the fact that Richard's implicit faith in law enforcement has been drastically, and violently, challenged (*PO*, 162). This solicitation parodies Richard's desire to be "part of everything," for he can only join the broader social order on its coercive terms, forced to partner with the forces of repression that subjugate him and others who look like him.

Pocho fundamentally reorients the character of racial betrayal in this moment. Instead of dwelling on whether Richard has betrayed his race, we are asked to consider how his racialized appearance has betrayed him. His friends are already wary of Richard, because they sense that his presence has alerted the police to them and triggered the violent reprisal of the officers ("they were thinking that if he had not been there, they would not have been accused by association, and therefore not beaten") (*PO*, 163). Richard spends so long with the detective that his friends suspect him of having "betrayed their trust" (*PO*, 163). In a way, he admits to a betrayal, for his refusal to cooperate is motivated by self-preservation rather than fraternal loyalty. But *Pocho* underscores the fact that it is Richard's racialized appearance that betrays him, not only to his friends but also within the dominant social order. As the target of racism, Richard is drawn into the ambit of treachery. His racially motivated arrest subjects him to a barrage of verbal and physical abuse. Even though he refuses the detective's solicitation, he is typed as a traitor.

This scene throws into relief the difficulty of being part of anything—let alone everything—that Richard struggles with, as does Villarreal. The only part Richard seems to play is one that gets him out of playing a part, as we see in his fight with Thomas. Even when Richard imagines himself to be "part of everything," he assumes an anthropological distance from the subjects he encounters. Fascinated by pachuco subculture, he makes "explorations" and "deductions as to their character and makeup," as though undertaking a character study (*PO*, 151). He serves the character function of the author, conjuring the creative work of writing and the figure of Villarreal, who likewise makes "explorations" and "deductions" of character within the fictional world of the novel. Like Richard, Villarreal, too, wants to be "part of everything" without becoming "part of a group." In the 1976 interview, he addresses his designation as a Chicano writer: "I don't react at all to being called a Chicano writer, although I don't think of myself as one. The last is not only because of semantics—the word Chicano does not mean to me what it means to the movement. In its current meaning, the word strongly connotes political implications, and I am not a political hack. Lest I be misunderstood, however, I do not reject inclusion in this group, because certainly I'm a part of the movement."[58] Villarreal is much like Richard in his ambivalent desire and his quibble with the politics of the term. He, too, wishes to play "a part" while staying apart. As it turns out, he plays the overdetermined part of pocho as well, as he is conflated with the character he so vividly represents.

Pocho reveals the many parts of pocho. As a character, pocho does not reside within this or that person. Race character critique brings racial betrayal into focus through the novel's overlapping fields of characterization. Juan, the stereotype of the corrido hero, is one locus of betrayal who becomes in the aggregate of El Macho feminized and queer, antiracist and anticolonial. Richard, the avowed pocho, in the aggregate of El Malinche accepts the lineage of machismo but renders it queer; he concedes to assimilation while exposing the violence of the hegemonic order within which minority masculinity takes form. Racial betrayal is not, finally, coextensive with either Juan's masculinist anticolonialism or Richard's queer assimilationism. Rather, it is better understood through aggregations of character that are discontinuous, contradictory, and generative. "Pocho power" (following Madrid-Barela) inheres in these aggregations, where the betrayal of one ideal opens up the critique of another, and assimilative desire creates a crisis of subaltern masculinity. Reading Villarreal through the novel shows him to diverge from his own proclamations as he occupies another aggregate of character—the space of the author as character within the biographical and historical record. This field of characterization presides over *Pocho* but is fundamentally shaped by it. Even as Villarreal professes betrayal, he provides tools for critique.

CHAPTER FOUR

Building American Character
Dalip Singh Saund's Model of Minority

Congressman from India (1960) repeatedly makes an example of Dalip Singh Saund. The cover declares this to be the "inspiring autobiography of a man whose life is a vivid example of Democracy in action." Variants on this refrain reoccur at multiple points in Saund's autobiography. "Look, here I am. I am a living example of American democracy in action," Saund promises to tell global audiences while campaigning for his election, reaffirming this promise at the start of his travels abroad ("I would go to India and the Far East and present myself as a living example of American democracy in practice").[1] His devotion to his own example is disarming, as when he describes a speaking engagement at the Women's Press Club at the start of his very first term in Congress: "I touched on some of my campaign experiences and expressed my pleasure at serving as a living example of American democracy in action" (*CFI*, 116).

Saund's status as an example is shaped by his remarkable biography, which would prove serviceable in the context of the Cold War. In the forty-odd years after this farmer from Punjab immigrated to the United States, at a peak of racism and nativism against South Asian immigrants, he became an American citizen, was elected as a county judge in Westmorland, California, and went on to serve as representative for the Twenty-Ninth Congressional District of California for multiple terms. At midcentury, even as the model minority myth was being formed, Saund's spectacular success served a valuable propaganda function. He could regale people around the world with news of his unlikely election at a moment when the civil rights struggle had gained momentum and events like the crisis of desegregation in Little Rock were under scrutiny abroad.

The appeal of Saund is apparent, for he serves as a template for minorities who have entered into politics. When Hawai'i achieved statehood in 1959, aspiring Asian American political candidates (such as Daniel Inouye and Hiram Fong) were seen to be following in Saund's footsteps. Anxieties about the "apparition" of "a person of Oriental ancestry" in the U.S. Senate, as one article quipped, were moderated by reference to Saund having "broken the

Front cover of Dalip Singh Saund's *Congressman from India* (1960).

ground in Congress for persons of Asian descent."[2] Saund's example was brought up in comparisons as far as East Africa, whose Indian population sought to maintain government positions in the newly independent republics ("The fact that a son of India is an American congressman should aid recognition that a grandson of India may appropriately be a civil servant in Tanganyika").[3] Through the latter part of the twentieth century, Saund was evoked in newspapers in the diaspora concerned about Indian American political participation and the broader problem of Asian American apathy.[4] Recently, he comes up in more self-congratulatory contexts, as commentators applaud the increased political clout of these communities.[5] Any number of election campaigns at state and national levels by South Asian candidates have been likened to that of Saund, including G. M. "Bill" Quraishi, Kumar Barve, Eappan Peter Mathews, Neil Dhillon, Ram Uppuluri, Bobby Jindal (touted as the "'wonder-boy' of Punjabi heritage"), and Hansen Clarke.[6] Such comparisons are remarkably empty of content, for they often traverse party lines and political platforms. As Samuel Freedman points out, Jindal and Nikki Haley (who has been discredited as a "female Uncle Tom") are notably unlike Saund in that they trade on their conversion to Christianity and the anglicization of their names.[7]

As an example, Saund is illustrative and imitable. A flexible and manipulable archetype of the American dream, he can be put to many uses. He is a model minority who, through a rigorous program of self making, is able not only to join the American family but also to symbolize it as a broadly acclaimed public official. He represents the selective incorporation of difference: the transformation of race into ethnicity that is the exception to American democracy rather than its rule. His example conceals this fact—that the American dream is held out to a select few whose visibly racialized success obscures racism and structural barriers, and who are deployed against other minorities unable to achieve the same exceptional success. Saund's appeal is apparent in his many resurrections, which are varied as well as contradictory, and are often uncritical, for the substance of his politics is frequently disregarded.

This chapter grapples with the character of Saund, who assumes the mantle of model minority. My reading brings into view the archetypal function that Saund serves, linking *Congressman from India* to the emergence of the model minority myth in the Cold War arena. The autobiography uses discourses of character building to shape the character of Saund, obscuring racial inequality and creating the illusion of a level playing field in which Saund's success is assured. That *Congressman from India* insists on presenting Saund as a "vivid example" suggests that his exemplary status is precarious, for the autobiography also refracts the archetype of model minority into all its richness as a character, using elisions and contortions to manage how Saund is read. Ultimately, *Congressman from India* does not succeed in transforming race into ethnicity, but pivots around them. It guides us to a critical perspective upon the American dream and upon the role Saund plays within the biographical and historical record.

The Making of a Model

Saund was part of a migration that predates the emergence of the model minority myth. From 1900 to 1960, approximately thirteen thousand East Indians entered the United States.[8] This group included migrant workers and farmers (mostly from the Punjab region in the northwest from which Saund hailed) who came primarily to the West Coast, and much smaller numbers of students and political exiles who settled in major cities on the

East and West Coasts, establishing centers of anticolonial organizing there.[9] Generally described as "Hindu," a majority of these immigrants were in fact Sikhs, with some Muslims and even fewer Hindus among them.[10]

Although their numbers were relatively small, a series of events brought these immigrants into the public eye. In 1907, riots in Bellingham and elsewhere in the Pacific Northwest exposed nativist tensions, as Indians working in lumber mills were beaten, robbed, and driven from their homes and employment. In 1914, the *Komagata Maru* (a Japanese vessel chartered by Indian immigrants) languished for months in the Vancouver harbor before being forced to return with its passengers, exposing the limited right of Indians to immigrate as British subjects. The rise of the anticolonial Ghadar movement and the outbreak of hostilities between Germany and Great Britain in 1914 led to the exodus of hundreds of immigrants who returned in hopes of joining the fight for Indian independence. Wartime hysteria was brought to bear upon a largely unsuccessful collaboration between Indian revolutionaries and German agents, as a series of spectacular "Hindu-German conspiracy" trials roiled California from 1917 to 1918. A deportation drive at the close of the war caught up Indians in the growing federal dragnet against radicalism. Following the Bellingham riots, the San Francisco Japanese and Korean Exclusion League changed its name to the Asiatic Exclusion League in order to target Indian immigrants.[11] According to a 1910 article, it was no longer "a question of the yellow and the white, but of the Oriental and the Occidental" since the "threatening inundation of Hindoos over the Pacific Coast."[12] Efforts at exclusion culminated in the passage of the Immigration Act of 1917, which prohibited entrants from India as part of the "Asiatic barred zone." A 1923 Supreme Court decision in *United States v. Bhagat Singh Thind* found that "Hindus" were not white and were therefore ineligible for naturalization. The *Thind* decision would make Indians susceptible to the alien land laws passed in California and many other states that restricted ownership of land to aliens eligible for citizenship. As U.S. and Indian interests became more closely aligned with the outbreak of World War II, and thousands of American troops were deployed to India in 1943 in order to prevent Axis advancement in Asia, Indian immigrants (Saund among them) were able to push for avenues for naturalization. The Luce-Celler Act of 1946 granted naturalization to Indian immigrants while preserving the stringent quota limitations on the group.

Saund's biography in this context is exemplary and the catalog of his successes impressively long. He entered into the turmoil of nativist violence and juridical exclusion, arriving in the United States just three years before the passage of *Thind*. In 1920, he reached San Francisco, having journeyed through Europe and New York to the West. After studying agriculture and mathematics at the University of California, Berkeley, he moved to the Imperial Valley in 1925 to make his living as a farmer in the path of Indian immigrants before him.[13] By chance, he reunited with an acquaintance from his transatlantic voyage and her daughter, Marian Kosa. The two were married in 1928 and eventually raised a family, dividing their time between Los Angeles and the Imperial Valley. Already active as president of the Hindustan Association of America during his student days, Saund became a public figure in his new community, becoming involved with various public speaking clubs in Westmorland and Brawley. After he became an American citizen in 1949, he went on to campaign successfully for the position of county judge in Westmorland, although his election was voided on the grounds that he had not been a citizen for one year when he was elected. In 1952, after a successful campaign, he won, serving as county judge until 1957 when he assumed his position in Congress. What was then the Twenty-Ninth Congressional District (comprising Imperial and Riverside counties) presented its own challenges, for it had an entrenched Republican incumbent, John Phillips. When the Democratic Party entered its own candidate for the first time in 1954, Saund, who was serving as chairman of the Imperial County Democratic Central Committee at the time, managed his Imperial County campaign. Although the Democratic candidate was easily defeated, this gave Saund the experience he needed to make a push in 1956. Phillips's decision not to run opened up the race, and, after a hotly contested primary, in which Saund's opponent launched an unsuccessful effort to have him disqualified on the grounds that he had not been a citizen for seven years, Saund won the primary election. The ensuing contest against the considerably more wealthy, well-connected, and renowned aviator and businesswoman Jacqueline Cochran was featured in local and national media. Saund eventually won a seat in Congress by a slim margin of 3,300 votes, a considerable upset in a district that had not previously elected a Democrat to Congress. His public career was grounded in an intimate knowledge of his constituency, shaped by his range of experience from foreman to sharecropper to farmer to small businessman. As judge, he tackled issues such as gambling, border trafficking, prostitution, food safety, police misconduct, personal debt, and domestic abuse. Shaped by his experience of the Great Depression and the local successes of various New Deal reforms, his congressional work was devoted to matters directly affecting his constituents (farm subsidies, flood control, irrigation and reclamation, postal service), while he also committed himself to broader social issues (border enforcement, civil rights reform, targeted foreign assistance, global self-determination, Native American sovereignty, veterans' rights) and created opportunities for transnational collaboration (Mexico–United States Interparliamentary Group) as well as intercultural understanding (East-West Cultural Center). Saund was reelected for two more terms before a debilitating stroke in 1962 ended his public career.

Published during Saund's second congressional term, *Congressman from India* tells much of this story, doubtless serving Saund's campaign for reelection. The first line of the book indicates its scope: "This book is the simple story of the struggles, sorrows and joys, defeats and recoveries, of a twenty-year-old native of India who came to the United States and, nearly twoscore years later, became a United States congressman" (*CFI*, v). Part autobiography and part political treatise, *Congressman from India* details Saund's birth and upbringing, his immigration and studies, his early work as a farmer and small businessman, as well as his rise as a public figure, culminating in an account of his 1957 tour (that took him to East Asia, South Asia, and Southeast Asia, among other places) as a one-man subcommittee of the Foreign Affairs Committee, news of which was broadcast far and wide at the behest of the United States Information Agency (USIA). Throughout the text, Saund interprets for his readers and constituents his work as congressional representative, closing with his future political program.

Saund's autobiography also transforms the meaning of Saund's biography. Already a successful congressional representative, Saund was nonetheless driven to figure himself as a literary character. Although he presents the autobiography as a "simple story," Saund's awareness of himself in the third person and his deployment of the iconic phrasing of the Gettysburg Address suggest that his self-presentation is anything but simplistic. The literary example of Saund supplements and refigures the historical figure, revealing representation to be not just a result of social election and legal investiture but a metaphorical act and site of creative negotiation. *Congressman from India* authors Saund's spectacular transformation from a racialized and disenfranchised minority—unable to vote, unable even to hold many forms of public office—into a model minority and a representative American.

Thus far, *Congressman from India* has received little attention as a literary document in its own right. The autobiography has been cited primarily as a history, with insights into midcentury politics and the struggle for immigrants' rights.[14] Readings by Sandhya Shukla and Rajini Srikanth do much to attend to the ideological nuances of the figure of Saund and the limitations of positioning him within an assimilative framework in transnational postwar Indian diasporic and South Asian American contexts, respectively.[15] *Congressman from India* exceeds the "linear trajectory from one (old) land, into another (new) nation" that guides much of immigrant and ethnic autobiography, as Shukla points out, proposing that it be read as a "diasporic autobiography" with a "sustained relationship to homeland," where "Indianness is a foil for and a path into America."[16] In the context of autobiography studies, Saund's absence from the critical record might also be due to the fact that *Congressman from India* is difficult to situate between the polarities of Eurocentric and oppositional critique. Saund's troubling Americanism and his precarious status as an Asian American are difficult to bring into focus through interpretations emphasizing either ethnic assimilation or racial inassimilability.[17] *Congressman from India* throws into crisis this polarity between ethnicity and race.

My readings explore the character of Saund within and without the autobiography. While Shukla reads *Congressman from India* in terms of a diasporic "politics of relation," I focus on the work that the figure of Saund does within a national context.[18] The discourse of character helps to refigure Saund as a model minority, building on a genealogy that critics have traced to the colonial and early national period. Warren Susman famously argues that, in going from the nineteenth to the twentieth century, we go "from a culture of character to a culture of personality."[19] James Salazar has shown that the crisis of character's decline paradoxically led to its efflorescence, as the concept was refigured and redeployed. He traces the "rhetoric of character" through the late nineteenth and early twentieth centuries as "a privileged mediator of national identity and public culture in the United States," revolving around twin poles of "character representation" and "character building"—a "theory or concept of the self" and "a way of performing and practicing the self."[20] Similarly, Jeffrey Louis Decker argues that the shift from "character" to "personality" and, ultimately, to "image" in the postwar period repurposes the myth of the self-made man, which is "no longer principally the site of a utilitarian calling, behavior modification, or even economic production, but, increasingly, of body image and consumer desire."[21]

The model minority is an important, though unacknowledged, figure in this genealogy. As Robert Lee has shown, the Cold War era saw the rise of the myth of model minority, shaped by postwar geopolitics, Pacific Rim economic policy, the dissolving regime of Asian exclusion, the imperative to manage the "race problem" both domestically and abroad, and the political silence of Asian Americans. One key feature of the myth is its transformation of race into ethnicity: the "representation of Asian Americans as a *racial* minority whose apparently successful *ethnic* assimilation was a result of stoic patience, political obedience, and self-improvement."[22] This spectacle of success not only obscures structural racism but also produces its obverse in non-model minorities, particularly African Americans who become targets of discourses of black pathology.[23] Anne Anlin Cheng's analysis of the affective structure of this intermediary position is suggestive, for she describes the model minority as "the figure who has not only assimilated but also euphorically sings the praises of the American way."[24] This "manic relation to the American Dream" has a twofold function according to Cheng, in that it "serves to contain the history of Asian abjection, as well as to discipline other racial groups in America."[25] This "paradigm of Americanness" is based on the assimilation of European immigrants and is held out to immigrant groups generally, as Susan Koshy has shown, for they must contend with a "mythology of the American Dream that allows for their ethnicization rather than their racialization."[26] The "morphing of race into ethnicity" has been a crucial feature of the "new multiculturalism," Koshy argues, whereby "'white' serves only as a modifier of ethnicity, and, simultaneously, nonwhite capital-compatible ethnicities are promised incorporation into the American Dream."[27] In this context, the "myth of the model minority ... singles out Asian Americans, interpellating them as whites-to-be."[28]

Linking the model minority to the genealogy of character foregrounds not only the role of character in the construction of the model minority myth but also the literary structure of this myth. Saund's "simple story" partakes in what we might think of as the model minority *mythos*: the narrative through which success gets told, the assemblage of characters, themes, tropes, and plotting through which the myth of model minority takes ideological form. This is a character-driven mythos, which features the archetype of the model minority in a starring role and enlists discourses of character, whether in overt or implied form.[29] Lee highlights "stoic patience, political obedience, and self-improvement" as features of the model minority myth and the keys to the transformation of race into ethnicity. Although Salazar's readings do not extend as far as the period in which Saund is writing, *Congressman from India* exemplifies many of the rhetorical features that Salazar identifies as part of the discursive building of character: a sense of coherent self-mastery, ongoing self-disciplining toward the chimerical ends of upward mobility and equality, masculinist will power with a paradoxical embrace of adversity, all hinging upon characterizations of male adolescence.

In the postbellum period of racial uplift, as Salazar shows, Frederick Douglass, W. E. B. Du Bois, Pauline Hopkins, Booker T. Washington, and others turned to character to confront racial determinism. "The acquisition of character was meant to challenge the very epistemological and semiotic foundations of race itself," writes Salazar: "Such a challenge was grounded in the ability of the rhetoric of character to unmoor the meaning of race from the physiological body and to rearticulate racial identity in terms of the class indicators that signaled the presence or absence of the talents and capabilities of character."[30] By recourse to character, black social possibility could be disarticulated from race. Salazar reframes the famous debate between Washington and Du Bois as a debate about character in which the two men conceived racial progress through the work of character building, while disagreeing as to what precisely that work entailed. Washington's *Up from Slavery* (1901) is an instructive template for *Congressman from India*. Both are accommodationist texts, governed by the imperative of self-mastery and written strategically with white readers in mind. In both, the life story is interwoven with a rigorous program of self-discipline, texts of speeches, testimonials by famous people, and catalogs of public works. As Decker points out, Washington was a "representative American," who promulgated a "color-blind, character-based motto of American self-making."[31] This is not an imitative project but an inventive one, Houston Baker Jr. emphasizes, underscoring Washington's "mastery of form"—"a culturally specific and canny rhetorical appropriation" of the minstrel mask that was the precondition of black oratory in this period.[32]

In Saund's autobiography, character is a key, if largely unspoken, word. While *Congressman from India* does not directly engage with the discourse of character, this discourse permeates the literary characterization of Saund at every level. Seemingly trivial anecdotes about Saund brawling with village boys or witnessing a schoolyard fight lay the interpretive groundwork for the making of Saund into a model minority. As exercises in building character, these anecdotes dislodge racial identity and obscure the racial body, opening up the possibility of sociocultural mobility. They minimize structural barriers and depict a level playing field, where grievance is not only impermissible but unsportsmanlike. Saund is able to refigure himself on the ethnic pattern, maintaining a sense of cultural distinction (the congressman, after all, is from India) while reaping the benefits of the American dream through a combination of individual effort and deserved benevolence. His example diverges from that of Washington, for he represents the ascendance of a distinct archetype of American character not burdened by blackface minstrelsy and solicited, as an immigrant, to mediate black and white relations by obscuring racial slavery and affirming white hegemony. As a visibly racialized minority, Saund represents not the effacement of difference but its incorporation, for his spectacular success occludes structural racism and sustains the fantasy of the American dream.

Character-Building Exercises

Two schoolboy scenes set the foundation for building character in *Congressman from India*. In the first scene, Saund has returned for the summer to Chhajjalwaddi, the village where he was born, from boarding school in nearby Amritsar. He decides to join the local village boys in a game. "Grudgingly," the boys let him play, "but they resented my attitude and my dress, for I wore clean white clothes, and, as a student, I appeared altogether different" (*CFI*, 20). Envying his privilege, the boys bully Saund until he is reduced to tears and runs home to his mother. Rather than comforting him, Saund's mother impresses upon him a set of related maxims about grievance, self-reliance, and fair play: "Son, you went out to play with boys of your own age and came home crying. Let that be the first and the last time. When you go out to play with other boys, you've got to take care of yourself—if you can't, just stay away" (*CFI*, 21). There is no room to complain, Saund learns. He must rely upon himself in the playing field or stay away altogether. Saund's mother emphasizes his choice to play with boys of his "own age," presenting age as a leveling principle in an arena of presumed equals.

Saund's mother's response effaces the structural inequality that is built into this interaction, and which operates on two levels, as the advantaged Saund is only momentarily at a disadvantage. Because he is from a well-off family, Saund has the luxury of joining the game and not being refused (his father is a government contractor who helps endow the village schoolhouse and pay for the teacher). He also has the luxury of quitting not only this particular playing field but his small village altogether, having moved from the local primary school to the secondary boarding school in Amritsar and become poised to inherit the advantages of a comparatively wealthy family. Nonetheless, Saund experiences the game as an injustice in which the village boys conspire against him and target him in an expression of protest against his privileged position, likely because they cannot freely deny him entry into their own space of play. These complex hierarchies are elided in the lesson that he learns and extrapolates to other situations in the autobiography, that in joining the arena he must acquiesce to its terms: assume the illusion of fair play, ignore structural disadvantage (particularly when it has the effect of effacing his broader advantage), and rely, uncomplainingly, not on others but himself.

A second scene involving a fight between two American boys establishes the link between these minor skirmishes and the making of Saund's character. As a student in Berkeley, he observes a fight in which "not one among the spectators tried to help or hinder either of the fighters" (CFI, 41). He is astonished that, in the end, "the two boys walked arm in arm to the soda fountain nearby" and "shared" a drink from "the same bottle": "It was my first experience with sportsmanship as practiced in America. I vowed to myself that if I was going to acquire any of the characteristics of the American people, one of the most important ones would be to learn to be a good sport" (CFI, 41). The import of such scenes becomes clear, being no less than a matter of building American character by acquiring the right "characteristics." Exactly what this entails is established by the accretion of these scenes. The substance of the conflict does not matter, as Saund does not explain what the fight is about, or why one of the boys "had enough." Was he much weaker than the other, or did he tire of his own strength? Saund is not interested in such details. What matters, as in the village scene, is the illusion that the boys meet on equal terms, in an arena free from outside intervention. The performance of camaraderie is what captivates Saund, as both boys share "arm in arm" in the leveling privilege of capitalist consumption.

These character-building exercises enable Saund's ascendance as a model minority, which entails a series of "fights" in which Saund participates, developing his capacity for sportsmanship in the face of his many failures. Initially, he must "fight it through" insolvency, refusing to declare bankruptcy (as many other farmers do) after a series of poor investments and low prices (CFI, 67). His "fight for citizenship" is detailed in a chapter of that title (CFI, 69). The political contests for judge and congressional representative are directly modeled on the schoolboy scenes. The reader does not have to work hard to see this link, for Saund immediately moves from the description of the Berkeley fight to that of the 1920 presidential race, as "another example" of sportsmanship "on the political level" (CFI, 41). When he loses his "first political battle," his successful election overruled due to his ineligibility for the office, he recalls the schoolyard scene: "I remembered the fight that I had seen between two boys at the Berkeley High School grounds in 1920 and decided that this was the time for me to practice a little good sportsmanship

I remember standing on the Berkeley High School campus. A group of youngsters stood in a circle around two boys fighting. Those watching the fight kept their hands off. They wanted to see a good, clean fight, and to see the "better man" win. After the fight was over, I saw the two battered and bruised boys walk off arm-in-arm to drink one bottle of coke with two straws. This was my first experience with American sportsmanship. I vowed I'd rather lose ten times, and be called a good loser, than win each time and be considered a poor sport.

Illustrated anecdote from Dalip Singh Saund's campaign biography, *What America Means to Me* (1956). Courtesy of the Collection of the U.S. House of Representatives, gift of Dr. Eric Saund.

of my own" (*CFI*, 79). It is this memory that leads him to conclude that the "board had made their decision under their legal authority and I should have no basis for complaint" (*CFI*, 79). The scene echoes the Indian village scene as well, as Saund's entry onto that playing field presages his later entry into the public eye. He must learn to ignore his disadvantage, weather racially motivated attacks, and accept with equanimity all outcomes—or quit the competitive arena altogether. Saund's mother's injunction echoes here, suggesting that his legitimate grievance against a racist and nativist polity would be but the petulance of a relatively privileged village boy who comes crying to his mother. That Saund takes her teachings to heart is clear in his approach to many hotly contested political fights. "I harbored no bitterness against my opponents," he claims, seeking to run "on my own merits," and resolving to "not say a word against my opponent" (*CFI*, 81, 101).

Because we are primed for this illusion, it appears that in coming to the United States Saund has entered an equitable arena where there can be no grievance, where there is no racism or structural disenfranchisement, and where justice and fairness prevail. When a fellow Californian launches a strident objection to Saund's campaign for naturalization, telling him "you ought to have your head examined" for pursuing this course, Saund counters by evoking the rhetorics of fair play: "I laughed, but told my friend that I had great faith in the American sense of justice and fair play and the righteousness of my cause" (*CFI*, 73). When a friend and neighbor questions Saund's suitability to serve in the office of local judge because of his relatively recent naturalization (he wants an "American to be the judge in Westmorland"), tracing his own ancestry to the *Mayflower* pilgrims, Saund counters by asking him how many ballots he had been given in the last election. "What a foolish question for an educated man to ask," he condescends, "They gave me one ballot," to which Saund responds: "Well, Mr. Boarts. . . . Isn't that a strange coincidence. I just got one ballot, too" (*CFI*, 80). Though they claim different ancestries, Saund counts as much as any American. Because their votes are equal, Saund suggests that they are on equal footing. In the face of sustained opposition to his congressional campaign on the grounds of his birthplace and race, Saund avows that the "American people believe in giving contestants an even chance in any contest": "If I do not succeed in my objective to be elected to Congress, I shall know that it will not be because of the place of my birth or the color of my skin, but because the voters of the 29th Congressional District decided to send someone better than myself to Washington" (*CFI*, 101, 109).

The glaring contradiction of racially restrictive naturalization is elided, as Saund frames the Indian campaign for citizenship as yet another schoolboy fight. Its impetus appears to be his relative discomfort in encountering this barrier to his assimilation: "I was making America my home. Thus it was only natural that I felt very uncomfortable not being able to become a citizen of the United States" (*CFI*, 72). His mother's injunction hovers over this moment, leaving no opening for the adjudication of just demands, as Saund resolves, rather than "crying or complaining about the situation," "to do something about it" (*CFI*, 72). Apparently, all Saund needs do is make the plight of Indian immigrants known: "I felt certain that if only we could present our story to the representatives of the American people in the Congress of the United States there could never be a 'no' answer to our simple plea for rights to apply for American citizenship" (*CFI*, 73). This is a superficial account. The historical record attests that Saund helped to organize (and was elected the first president of) the India Association of America, which supported the extensive campaign for Indian naturalization that stretched from East Coast to West Coast, and involved grassroots, governmental, and transnational mobilizations.[33] In the autobiography, however, the "Fight for Citizenship" is compressed into a chapter of that title, telescoping "four years of long waiting and hard effort" into a brief account that barely mentions the concerted, collective organizing in which Saund was involved (*CFI*, 75). When it seems to Saund's reader that the bill will not pass, an unexplained boost from President Harry Truman appears to secure a victory.[34] The formidable, collective work of challenging a racist bar to naturalization seems to be the matter of a "simple plea" that cements

Building American Character 131

the illusion of fairness, justice, and reciprocal benevolence in the political arena.

The scene of Saund's naturalization affirms not the hard-won privilege of belonging and enfranchisement in a regime of racial nativism, but Saund's successful efforts at becoming a model American. Saund realizes that citizenship is "not an easy matter even with the permission to apply," for each application is subject to careful scrutiny of the "past behavior and character of each individual applicant" (*CFI*, 75–76). Given his support of Indian nationalism, it turns out that the government has "quite a file" on Saund, and he must answer to its details in a lengthy interview with an immigration inspector in Los Angeles (*CFI*, 76). The repressive surveillance apparatus of the U.S. government, which worked in tandem with the British government to monitor and suppress anticolonial organizing in the diaspora, patently contradicting the values of equal opportunity and fair play espoused by Saund, is reframed as due diligence that identifies as prospective citizens only those immigrants who can pass this test of "character."[35] Instead of being an indictment of a regime of politically motivated and racialized surveillance, the scene of naturalization becomes the culmination of Saund's exercises in building character, confirming his fitness for American citizenship.

It is significant that the immigration inspector is Irish, for he represents the ethnic pattern that Saund seeks to copy as an American. Questioned about the anticolonial content of his speeches, Saund is able to share a laugh with the inspector, whose background makes him amenable to Saund's anti-British proselytizing. Shared in this moment is not just anti-British sentiment, but two histories of immigration: an earlier genealogy of Irish immigration that saw the promise of the American dream fulfilled through successful ethnicization as an upwardly mobile, "white" minority, and a newer genealogy of racialized immigration from India that seeks similar terms of entrance into the American polity. Recalling the camaraderie of the sporting American boys who, initially on opposite sides, eventually share a soda, this scene suggests that such a transformation of race into ethnicity is not only possible but achievable as Saund prevails in his "fight for citizenship."

The complex structure of autobiography helps to build Saund's character. William Howarth shows that autobiographies motivated by *"oratorical* aims" ("devotion to doctrine, whether in religion, history, or politics") present an "allegorical" story, "seeking to represent in a single life an idealized pattern of human behavior"; they manifest a "strong and principled character" from out of the contrast of the "narrator," who "teaches his prime lesson," and the "protagonist," who "relives and learns from his days of sin or error."[36] The schoolboy scenes, then, are not mere incidents in a life story but parables in the discursive building of character that reveal gaps and continuities between the multiple actors within the autobiography—protagonist, narrator, author—whose presumed identity constitutes what Philippe Lejeune defines as the "autobiographical pact."[37] It is the "character narration" that mediates these various positions within the narrative, as James Phelan argues, identifying a fundamental mechanism of indirectness and unreliability ("Narration in fiction or nonfiction by a participant in the story events") that ranges across fiction and autobiography.[38] Lack of character within the autobiography affirms Saund's character without. The eight-year-old protagonist, for instance, has obviously misinterpreted the events of the game, even though his sense of injustice is palpable. This shortsighted view is revealed in part by his mother's response, but also because the narrator frames the episode through the protagonist's shortcomings: "I was not altogether a model boy in my younger years. I had my share of quarrels and fights and disappointments in the life of the village" (*CFI*, 20). The young protagonist is a "model" in the making who will not be realized as such until he becomes the author, a telos that the narrator mediates. The narrator's vantage in the Berkeley scene proves important as well, as the character narration supplies the promise to build character that the author presumably goes on to fulfill. In both cases, the narrator, not entirely coincident with the protagonist or the author, disarticulates these characters in order to dramatize their transformation and remake Saund in the American mold.

Distinct American Archetype

These exercises in building character take shape within the broader arc of *Congressman from India*, which creates a distinct American archetype. Saund's naturalization is but one step in the making of this character, who goes on to fashion ties to a polity implicitly racialized as white. It is significant that Saund's marriage and family are the preamble to his desire for citizenship: "I had become a close part of American life. I had married an American girl, and was the father of three American children. I was making America my home. Thus it was only natural that I felt very uncomfortable not being able to become a citizen of the United States" (*CFI*, 72). Whiteness is the unspoken word here, as Saund's "American" wife and children are tacitly racialized. Saund implies that he has married into whiteness, a connection that the autobiography works to develop without inflaming racial anxieties surrounding miscegenation. The "Preface" sets the stage for Saund's intermarriage in the generalized geospatial terms of Orientalism: "Kipling said, 'East is East and West is West, and never the twain shall meet.' Clearly, he was wrong, for a Saund from the East met a Kosa from the West. God blessed them with three marvelous children" (*CFI*, v).[39] It turns out that this multiracial family proves instrumental to his campaign for election, as his children and their spouses help to campaign and register voters on his behalf and make a "highly favorable impression" in general (*CFI*, 106). They are featured on the back cover of the autobiography, whose centerpiece is a photograph of Saund with his wife, his children, his son-in-law, and his daughter-in-law. The black-and-white images smooth the contrast of their racialized bodies, rendering whiteness and brownness in a palette of grays.

In the course of his move to Imperial Valley, Saund broadens the scope of his affiliation from his nuclear family to that of his constituents. Figures like "Uncle Ben" abound, lending their wisdom, their farming equipment, or their good will to help him make his start. Agrarian whiteness plays a key if implicit role, as the California farmer is presented as an honest yet beleaguered man, beset by economic woes and subject to the whims of nature, ranging from floods to drought, grasshoppers to blackbirds. Saund's concern extends even to Dust Bowl migrants in a version of the American georgic that does not admit of racial divides even as it is implicitly rendered as white. Early in the autobiography, at an event at a Berkeley minister's home welcoming foreign students, Saund tells those assembled that he does not want to be treated as a guest to whom the "best place" is given, but as a "close relative or friend," to "be merely members of the family and not feel we are strangers or foreigners" (*CFI*, 40). It seems he has achieved his desire, as the dutiful "American" son-in-law, the appreciative nephew of Uncle Ben, whose sympathies are with the implicitly white figures of the farmer and small businessman.

Saund's attachments are shaped by the history of South Asian racialization, which reveals the uncanny proximity of South Asians to whiteness. There was no adequate lexicon for the particular mode of difference represented by early immigrants from the Indian subcontinent. Those who wore turbans were particular targets of West Coast nativism, denounced as "rag-heads"; some availed themselves of a limited sartorial flexibility, doffing their turbans and passing as Italian or Portuguese.[40] Greeted in 1907 by what one Vancouver newspaper called a "Bumper Anti-Brownie Parade," and characterized by one California senator as a "brown horde," they confounded dichotomies of black and white racialization.[41] As one landlord

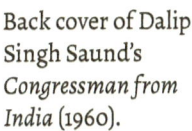

Back cover of Dalip Singh Saund's *Congressman from India* (1960).

Left. Judge Saund being welcomed back to his childhood home, Chhajalwadi. From the left, Mrs. Saund, the Judge's Indian sister, Ratan Kuar, his daughter Ellie. *Below.* The Saund family. Behind the Judge are his wife and daughters Ellie and Julie. In the rear row is Dalip Jr., his wife, Dorothy, and Julie's husband, Dr. Fred Fisher.

remarked in a 1924 interview, the "Hindu resembles us except that he is black—and we are shocked to see a black white man."[42] Over the course of the twentieth century, immigration from the Indian subcontinent would be classified variously as "Other," "Hindu," "White," "Asian Indian," and "Asian or Pacific Islander."[43] The courts took on the challenge of categorizing this immigration, finding Indians to be white for the purposes of naturalization in 1910, 1913, 1919, and 1920, but not in 1909, 1917, or 1923 and thereafter.[44] Thind's 1923 case involved a putative claim to Caucasian kinship and Aryan ancestry, which the courts worked assiduously to police.[45] It is possible that Saund subscribed to this view, for he gestures to the "exodus of the Aryans from central Asia to the plains of India" while explaining the caste system to

Building American Character 135

his reader (*CFI*, 16). A broader look at this history reveals both the proximity of South Asians to whiteness, for which their anomalous classification as "white" in the 1970 census represents something of a touchstone, as well as the extent to which claims to this privileged status were impracticable.[46]

The genealogy of American and Indian revolutionary nationalism provided Saund with yet another mode of filiation, as he fashions himself as heir to both the Founding Fathers and Mahatma Gandhi. Even as Saund schools the reader in the British colonization of India—telling the history of broken promises after World War I, violent suppression exemplified by the massacre at Jallianwala Bagh, and the rise of the Indian nationalist struggle under Gandhi—he describes his own schooling in U.S. history and the American revolution in particular. "I must confess that as late as 1917, when I was a junior in college," he writes, "my knowledge of the United States of America was next to nothing" (*CFI*, 29). There follows a voracious program of self-education, in the course of which Saund learns about the American Revolution, reads Woodrow Wilson's wartime speeches, pores over biographies of Abraham Lincoln and the text of the Gettysburg Address, and delights in stories of Theodore Roosevelt's exploits, culminating in his unshakeable resolve to go to the United States. Saund avoids mention of the Ghadar movement, which linked the exclusion and exploitation of Indian immigrants in the diaspora to their colonial status as British subjects and drew upon traditions of anticolonialism and radicalism in the United States, instead emphasizing bookish attachments to the distant ideal of an independent India.[47] At the end of the autobiography, Saund's filiation is nonthreatening and secure, for he observes the independence of India and Pakistan as though he is an outsider, identifying instead with "the fathers of our own great republic" who have inspired these revolutions (*CFI*, 185).

Congressman from India refigures Saund's character as explicitly American and implicitly white. The autobiography presents his affiliations carefully, downplaying race as a mode of ineradicable difference and fashioning class-based and cultural ties. As Shukla points out, "Saund's described sense of difference took the form of class position. As a farmer, Saund addressed a particular constituency" and was able to "engage his differences in ways that follow well in the traditions of U.S. politics, most notably like those of his hero Abraham Lincoln."[48] Shaping Saund's character along the lines of the beleaguered farmer or small businessman, or upon the heroic model of Lincoln and other historical luminaries, *Congressman of India* seeks to transcend racial divides. Racial barriers to naturalization notwithstanding, the autobiography proposes that one becomes American by being schooled in

American character. The figure of the young Saund poring over the archives of American revolutionary and nationalist history conjures up precisely this possibility: that to become a model minority one must cultivate the right cultural and ideological ties.

The congressional race testifies to the ascendance of this distinct American archetype, as the model minority wins out over the fairy-tale version of the American dream. Saund makes no secret of his admiration for Cochran in *Congressman from India*, claiming, if patronizingly, that he has "watched her meteoric career to fame within the last twenty years with pride" (*CFI*, 109). "My opponent was a colorful, world-famous aviatrix as well as a diligent, hardworking, capable, and imaginative campaigner," he tells his readers, not neglecting to point out that she "was the wife of one of the wealthiest men in the country" (*CFI*, 103). He frames their contrast thus: "Mrs. Odlum was a national figure, a colorful personality with a Cinderella-like success story, while I was a native of India, seeking a high office no one of my race had ever held" (*CFI*, 103). Although she, too, has a recognizable "success story" with its own "meteoric" rise and the hallmarks of self-reliance that he takes pains to ascribe to himself ("diligent," "hardworking"), hers is a fairy-tale romance in which rags are magically transformed to riches through the right marriage. Saund implies that he is, by contrast, a self-made man. Working his way from farmer to successful businessman, Saund suggests that he is more like his constituents than Cochran. As he emphasizes later on his world tour, he is "not a rich man; just a small businessman making a good living," who happens to win "against the wife of one of the richest men in America" (*CFI*, 158). Once again, Saund's description of the contrast between him and Cochran suggests that this is ultimately a race about race. His victory testifies to the power of this masculinist figure whose race is not only foregrounded ("native of India") but also under erasure, trailing the promise of social mobility and ethnicization.

Historically, coverage of the election bears out this contrast, while clarifying Saund's strategic self-presentation. The tenor of a 1956 *Los Angeles Times* article, "Hot Race Looms in 29th District," is echoed in many media outlets: "Seldom if ever has the American melting pot cooked up a spicier election dish than the contest now simmering in California's 29th Congressional District," the article proclaims. The "race pits a woman who dines with Presidents and royalty," "blond and bouncy" "Millionaire Flier Jacqueline Cochran," against "dark-hued Dalip S. Saund": a "Hindu justice of the peace," "rated a real spell-binder," who is not only the "first of his countrymen to hold public office in the United States," but who also "believes his color could be a big asset in combating Communist propaganda."[49] Routinely linked to her rich husband, lawyer and industrialist Floyd Odlum (under whose name she campaigned), Cochran is identified as a rich, white woman with powerful backers and considerable renown as an aviator. Saund, on the other hand, is invariably linked to his Indian origins and to the many firsts of his public career, while his race is foregrounded as is his religion (often erroneously), as well as his relatively wealthy family background and prosperous business as a farming supply wholesaler.

Two gaps emerge between this coverage and Saund's account of the congressional race in *Congressman from India*. We see that behind Saund's characterization of Cochran as a consummate "aviatrix" and "campaigner" is the fact that she is herself a successful businesswoman with perhaps an even more compelling claim to self making, which the marriage plot overshadows within the autobiography.[50] The media does not shy from this version of the rags-to-riches formula, depicting Cochran as a "blond Florida orphan" with not inconsiderable business acumen; as she declared in a 1956 interview, "I figure that if I can run a two-bit cosmetic business into a nationwide cosmetic concern, I can make a success of politics."[51] Saund, conversely, cannot claim this formula for success. "While Mr. Saund's major theme, in the recent campaign and before, has been that America is the land of opportunity, his story is not the standard one of rags-to-riches," the *New York Times* puts it, pointing out (as do many other accounts of the election) that he "came from a well-off agricultural family in Amritsar in Punjab" and highlighting that "he surmounted a greater obstacle than the economic one" in his fight for naturalization and subsequent election to public office "in a race-conscious section" of the country.[52]

The romance of race, rather than rags to riches, drives Saund's appeal. The media describes Saund's bid for election in racialized, exoticist, and Orientalist terms. Although Saund makes Cochran out to be the "colorful" one in *Congressman from India*, coverage of the election dwells on the "Colorful Contest" and on the figure of Saund in particular—whether his foreign nativity, his appearance ("brown-skinned," "dark-hued," "dark skinned," "walnut skin"), his carriage ("a real spell-binder," "jaunty judge"), or his speech ("clipped and high-pitched, common to the English of most East Indians," with an "urgent tone, with just a faint alien accent").[53] For those who "regret that the fashionable 'Jackie' Cochran will not grace the house chamber in Washington," one facetious contributor offers some consolation: "Rep. Saund could . . . be pretty decorative himself" if he would "revert to the costume and customs of his former country."[54] If he "lets his beard grow and oils it until it shines, and puts his hair up under a bright red turban," the piece ominously concludes, "he can expect to be a marked man in the house."[55] Fundamentally, however, Saund's racialization serves a propaganda function that coverage of the election does not fail to highlight. "He said that if elected he will visit India to promote better relations between that country and the United States, and will work to counteract communist propaganda by displaying himself as 'living example of American democracy,'" claimed the *Chicago Daily Tribune* when Saund won the Democratic Party nomination, using language that also appears in the autobiography.[56] His successful election, Saund proclaims, with some false modesty, "just demonstrates that America is real."[57]

As this coverage suggests, Saund's appeal can only be fully apprehended through the lens of Cold War geopolitics. He is well aware of his propaganda function in *Congressman from India*, and evokes it in the course of his campaign to diffuse the stigma of his racial and national difference:

> My opposition, as I have said, made an attempt to use my Indian origin against me. I decided to turn it to my own advantage and announced on a television broadcast that if elected I would immediately fly to India and the Far East. I would appear before the people there and tell them, "You have been listening to the insidious propaganda of the Communists that there is prejudice and discrimination in the United States against your people. Look, here I am. I am a living example of American democracy in action. I was elected by the free vote of the people in a very conservative district of the state of California to membership in the most powerful legislative body on earth. Where else in the world could that happen?" (*CFI*, 108)

Presenting his victory as a self-fulfilling prophecy that confirms the American dream, he augurs his own usefulness as anti-Communist propaganda. Saund's reticence around Ghadar makes strategic sense, as the specter of links between the Ghadar movement and communism was being raised and investigated in the years leading up to his election.[58] Conversely, Saund is forthright about his scripted function. If elected, he promises to go forth in defense of the United States, joining the ranks of government officials and bureaucrats who traveled throughout the third world seeking to win the ideological battle against the Soviet Union.

The relationship between the United States and India was of particular significance at this historical juncture, as many saw a common cause between Indians and U.S. racial minorities. Secretary of State John Foster

Dulles went to India in 1953 hoping to enjoin India to sign on to the Baghdad Pact of 1955. India's prime minister, Jawaharlal Nehru, would go on to help found the Non-Aligned Movement in 1961, uniting those countries unwilling to join either superpower under the stated aim of "peaceful co-existence," motivated partly by the Afro-Asian alliance forged at Bandung.[59] The common cause of people of color in the first and third world was not lost on either side. Nehru, Gandhi, and Swami Vivekananda before them had spoken out against the subjugation of African Americans; in 1946, Nehru noted that "negroes, though they may be 100 per cent American, are a race apart, deprived of many opportunities and privileges, which others have as a matter of course."[60] On his first visit to India in 1959, Martin Luther King Jr. commented that "the strongest bond of fraternity was the common cause of minority and colonial peoples in America, Africa and Asia struggling to throw off racialism and imperialism."[61] Historian Jay Saunders Redding, author of *An American in India* (1954), went on a speaking tour sponsored by the State Department and found that Indians "told me that I was 'one of them;' that (obviously, because of my color) I looked like a 'Madrassi,' or a 'Bengali.'"[62] At the same time, they asked him, "Why has no colored person ever held high office in America?"[63] Justice William Douglas, part of the Warren Court that decided *Brown v. Board of Education*, toured India and noted in his travel narrative, *Strange Lands and Friendly People* (1951), that the "attitude of the United States toward its colored minorities is a powerful factor in our relations with India."[64]

As the coverage of Saund's tour testifies, Saund's success would prove eminently marketable. The media reports establish that Saund's proposed international tour was an important feature of his congressional campaign. In the days after his election, there was already talk of broadcasting news of Saund's victory beyond the United States, as plans were underway for the congressman-elect to visit India with a "State department goodwill troupe which will show films of his victorious campaign to his former countrymen."[65] The U.S. State Department apparently foresaw Saund's propaganda value and recorded his campaign in hopes of airing it abroad.[66] "Rep. Saund to Tell His Story to India," "Not a Standard Story," the newspapers proclaimed, as Saund prepared "to don the mantle of unofficial ambassador to India."[67] After some controversy surrounding an initial cancellation, the USIA went ahead with plans to feature Saund on the Voice of America (VOA), reportedly aiming to "show that the United States gives equal opportunity to everyone and that a native-born Indian could be elected to the chief governing body of the Nation."[68] As his itinerary started to take shape for the fall of 1957, Saund clarified his role in the newspapers: "'I'm not going to talk about U.S. foreign policy or India's foreign policy, I'm just going around and show [sic] myself as a living contradiction of the Communist lie that racial prejudice against Asians is rampant in America... I'm not trying to change the world. I just want to be a good freshman Congressman"; elsewhere, he claimed that "he hoped to undo at least some of the Communist propaganda in Asia by his mere appearance on the scene."[69] Coverage of the tour describes how he made "Salesmanship His Theme" and called on the U.S. government to do the same in its propaganda campaign in the Cold War.[70] In recognition of his work, Saund was honored as a pioneer in "race relations" (for being a "living example of democracy at work and a symbol to the world of this country's belief that all democratic rights belong to all of our people") and as an "unofficial ambassador" for his "recent highly effective tour of India."[71]

A *Reader's Digest* article published in 1958 offers a revealing retrospective of this period in Saund's public career. It sets the scene by evoking a joint session of India's Houses of Parliament, convened on the occasion of Saund's visit. "With a few words he spiked volumes of Soviet propaganda: 'Here am I, a living example of American democracy,'" J. Campbell Bruce writes. "Discrimination against Asians in America? He said simply, 'I was chosen by the people in a free election.'"[72] It is the example of Saund that is meant to eviscerate Soviet propaganda and the entrenched history of violence and discrimination against the minority populations of the United States. Bruce arrives directly at this subject a few lines later. "What was his secret?" he asks, "A Republican offered a clue: 'I believed him, and I believed *he* believed what he said.' This was a subtlety of character that had to be felt."[73] Saund's effectiveness as an emblem inheres not in the character that he is but the character that he believes himself to be. He is well aware of the limitations of his role, as even the newspaper articles indicate, for he does not plan to "talk about... foreign policy" but simply on "going around" to "show myself as a living contradiction," on making a "mere appearance on the scene." The work of diplomacy is not focused on substantive negotiation, but it begins and ends with the visibly racialized figure of Saund. In feting Saund, it turns out the people of the world are not only feting a representative of the American people but the American ideal itself. A quotation from Saund affirms the metonymy that links individual character to that of the nation: "The invitation to address Parliament and the receptions everywhere were a tribute not to D. S. Saund but to the American people. The thrilling fact is that throughout Asia, and especially in India, the people hold America in such great esteem they are proud that one of them has been freely elected to the United States Congress."⁷⁴ Speaking of himself in the third person, Saund is well aware of the production of his persona and its starring role in the promulgation of the American dream.⁷⁵

Coming back to *Congressman from India*, we can see that the autobiography delivers on Saund's campaign promise thematically and structurally, assuring the making of a distinct American archetype. As the title declares, Saund is a Congressman *from India*. This is not a contradiction in terms but a central feature of his character as a model minority, for he is able to deploy his Indian origins in service of his assimilation while positioning India as a district within the geopolitical purview of the United States. The "East" meets "West" formula that Saund uses to describe his marriage in the preface sets the terms for the developing synthesis of these constructs and for the circular structure of American Orientalism that shapes the autobiography. As one newspaper report declared in the wake of his election, "East is West."⁷⁶ The images on the cover frankly symbolize this synthesis, as a photograph on the top left corner shows a garlanded Saund and his family being welcomed to his village in India. Paired with the focal image of Saund with his wife and children, these images are meant to confirm one another, as Saund's triumphant return assures the making of his American character. This logic of return is built into the structure of the autobiography, for the very first line of *Congressman from India* finds the Congressman returning to India: "It was ten-thirty on the evening of November 24, 1957, when the plane from Rangoon, Burma, landed on the airport of Calcutta, India. I had strange feelings of joy and anticipation for I was about to set foot on the soil of India, the land of my birth, after an absence of thirty-seven years" (*CFI*, 11). Saund can be forthright about his empirical nativity (the "land of my birth") in the course of this tour as an American member of Congress. Yet he is careful to modulate his nostalgia: his visit to Chhajjalwaddi is brief and lasts for less than a day, barely interrupting his official itinerary.

Speaking to audiences in India and other parts of the third world, Saund denounces communist tyranny; rehearses Orientalist stereotypes; reframes U.S. intervention in terms of democracy and freedom; elides the thorny questions of nuclear fallout by appeals to "military necessity"; misreads targeted opposition to his unreliable testimony as the "restless and revolutionary temper" of the times; deflects sharp comments about U.S. government officials by reference to their character ("in all my dealings with him I had found his interest in India's continued welfare to be firm and sincere"); and attributes deep communal divides shaped and exploited by colonialism and neocolonialism to "misunderstanding" (*CFI*, 158, 171, 180, 182). On tour in Saund's travels and his autobiography is his "vivid example," meant to signify the transformation of the racial exception into the ethnic rule. As a model minority, he affirms American exceptionalism, promising by his own spectacle to convince even the most skeptical audiences that the United States is the land of colorblind opportunity.[77] This ideological fiction of national character is buttressed by the exceptional character of Saund.

The Inevitable Question

Saund's whirlwind tour recalls the "Superman of America," who also sallies forth in defense of his adoptive country, appearing to bridge "East" and "West" with ease. Much like Ameen Rihani's *The Book of Khalid* (1911), *The Congressman from India* generates its own critique of this sanguine mission. Passages that describe Saund's return to Chhajjalwaddi, while scant, are conspicuous for their expression of grief. "Like many diasporic subjects, Saund relates to India nostalgically," Shukla points out, noting that "the public self of Saund is stripped away" in these moments of "confessional" intimacy.[78] The recitation of a poem upon the occasion of his homecoming makes Saund quite emotional ("I could not hold back the tears"), as does the sight of an inscription that he helped paint before his departure in 1917: "Three of my cousins and I had inscribed the verse during a summer vacation that year. My three cousins have all since died: two by natural causes and one a victim of the mass slaughter at the time of the partition in 1947. But those lines were still legible and the blue paint visible from a distance. That, too, brought tears to my eyes" (*CFI*, 179). In a text that is otherwise invested in what Cheng calls the "manic relation to the American dream," these lines stand out for their acknowledgment of internecine violence and the upheaval of deracination. Saund assures us that he can contain this outpouring of emotion. "I had fully regained my composure," he notes, by the time he is called upon to publicly respond, while the official tour charges on after a "hurried lunch in the old family home" (*CFI*, 179, 180).

This interlude nonetheless invites us to develop a critical perspective on the archetypal figure of Saund. His profusion of "tears" tear at the ideological fabric of the text, emblematizing what Saund loses in his embrace of the American dream. Saund, as protagonist, struggles to compose himself in this scene and appears to succeed. But the scene also points to the broader work of characterization within the autobiography and the fact that *Congressman from India* itself struggles to maintain its hold on Saund's character. This is the double movement that enlivens race character critique—that character is shadowed by impersonal, structural forces that are beyond its reckoning as a stable self. In this way, the autobiography does not just build Saund's character but also unbuilds it through a selective vision that culminates in an unanswerable challenge.

In the course of its effort to figure Saund as a model minority, *Congressman from India* must manage a series of elisions and contradictions. In the preamble to his decision to pursue the fight for naturalization, Saund writes, "I was dedicated to what is called the American way of life and yet when I looked in front of me I saw that the bars of citizenship were shut tight against me. I knew if these bars were lifted I would see much wider gates of opportunity open to me, opportunity as existed for everybody else in the United States of America" (*CFI*, 72). The clash of tropes in this moment exemplifies not only Saund's struggle but that of the autobiography as a whole. In his avowed dedication to the "American way of life," Saund must look past the apparent contradictions that are staring him down: in this case, the fact that the "bars of citizenship" are "shut tight" not only against him but against all who do not meet the racial prerequisite to naturalization. He must see these "bars" as "gates," look beyond them to claim the "opportunity" that is available to "everybody else." Even as Saund dramatizes this farsighted vision, which continues in one form or another to be shaped by his self-reliant and uncomplaining character, the autobiography shows us all that he does not see—manifesting the gap between this blind ideal of equal opportunity and the very real history of racial oppression that obscures (literally "bars") this vision.

Returning to the "Fight for Citizenship," it becomes clear that Saund presents a selective history, one that emphasizes individual effort over collective mobilization. Saund's brief treatment does not address the history of racially restrictive naturalization, for Saund would have been hard-pressed to reconcile the racist arguments of *Thind* with his belief in the fairness and justice of U.S. courts, as the infamous verdict allowed for the shared ancestry of "the blond Scandinavian and the brown Hindu" in "the dim reaches of antiquity" but took recourse to "the average man" in finding "that there are unmistakable and profound differences between them today."[79] Midcentury mobilizations around Indian naturalization aimed for congressional rather than juridical remedy in what was a more favorable geopolitical climate. Congresswoman Clare Boothe Luce described Indian naturalization as "a diplomatic and political measure against our present and future enemies," highlighting India's substantial contributions to the war.[80] Although

Congress debated the findings of *Thind* once more, discussions emphasized political rather than racial grounds for naturalization, which was amenable to Saund's discursive building of character.[81] The "Fight for Citizenship" emphasizes Saund's "simple plea," affirming the illusion of fair play and equal opportunity rather than exposing this strategic and limited opening to naturalization.

Notwithstanding several gestures to the racist and nativist laws targeting Asian Americans and the backlash provoked by his campaigns, *Congressman from India* elides the racial history of South Asian immigration. Saund acknowledges briefly the "keen discrimination" he experienced and "the considerable prejudice against the people of Asia in California" (*CFI*, 40–41, 45).[82] He mentions restrictions on land ownership, noting that he has to lease property in his wife's name, but the autobiography does not convey the impact of the alien land laws in the wake of *Thind* for farmers like him who—after having reclaimed for agriculture by their own skill and hard work much of the land in California's Imperial, San Joaquin, and Sacramento valleys—were defrauded of what had become some of the most valuable acreage in the state.[83] He hints at the slander he endured in the course of his public campaigns, noting opposition to his candidacy for judge "on racial grounds," the "violent" opposition and "virulent full-page ad" launched against him in the course of the Democratic primaries, and the fact that the "Republican campaign also hit hard at my being born in India" (*CFI*, 82, 101). But the autobiography foregrounds the uncomplaining self-reliance that Saund's mother inculcates, presenting the history of racial nativism and exploitation as anomalous rather than constitutive. There is no mention of the fact that the celebrated union of "Saund from the East" and "Kosa from the West" in a climate hostile to intermarriage likely stripped Marian of her citizenship.[84] Or that Marian and the children probably moved from their home in Westmorland to Los Angeles because of how her children (stigmatized as "*halfbreeds*") were treated in local schools.[85]

The Mexican immigrant, positioned outside the bounds of the national polity, provides an important point of contrast. Saund recourses to nativism and protectionism while in public office, taking a moralistic approach to sex trafficking as he targets a local "den of vice" involving trafficked women from Mexico during his tenure as judge and works together with immigration authorities to institute stringent deportation measures to rid the town of Mexican migrants construed as undesirables who "drink, gamble, and visit the prostitutes" (*CFI*, 83, 88). While he is concerned about the exploitation of Mexican immigrants under Public Law 78, an extension of the Bracero Program, his appeal to the House Agriculture Committee strategically involves "the farmers, small businessmen, Indians—all those directly and personally affected," a list that does not include Mexican workers (*CFI*, 129). Although he will not countenance internal borders, writing in reference to the Dust Bowl migration that "it was inconceivable to me that an American would not be permitted to go wherever he pleased within the continental limits of the country," the sanctity of national borders must be maintained (*CFI*, 56). Saund's function as a congressional representative hinges on a defense of his constituency against the encroachments of Mexican immigrants, who remain outside his constituency.

The existence of a sizable group of Punjabi Mexicans is altogether elided, an omission that is all the more conspicuous because the Imperial Valley was home to a large number of such families.[86] Restrictive immigration and antimiscegenation laws policing whiteness led to intermarriage between Indian men and Mexican women, who worked and migrated alongside one another in farmlands across Texas and California. Stigmatized for being "half-breeds" or "mestizos," these Punjabi Mexican families constantly negotiated the effects of racial exclusion, as the women were denounced as *"Hindera"* (or Hindu lover) by other Mexicans and the men were ostracized by later generations of South Asian immigrants for having married non-Punjabi women.[87] Such racially overdetermined sites, representing both interracial romance and stigma, cannot be reconciled with Saund's marriage to a "Kosa from the West" and the vision of the implicitly white "American" household that this union conjures. In fact, Saund avoids mention of South Asian immigrants, and figures such as the "rich Singh" stand out as being dubious and untrustworthy (*CFI*, 63).[88] It is the absent presence of such figures, impermissible as characters within the autobiography, that secures the ethnicization of Saund. *Congressman from India* works hard to contain their threatening proximity, whether the specter of racial nativism that their inclusion would evoke or the prospect of interracial solidarity that might have menaced Saund's constituents.

Even at the sentence level, the autobiography works to manage these elisions by relying on a nonrestrictive grammar to circumvent the barriers Saund encounters as he seeks to transform race into ethnicity. Reflecting on the moment of his entry to the United States, he proclaims: "for as long as I have been in the United States, particularly in the early years, while I was cruelly discriminated against many a time because of the place of my birth, not once has my right to say what I pleased been questioned by any man" (*CFI*, 36). There is a more complex negation at work here than outright denial, for Saund acknowledges that he has been "cruelly discriminated against" for being Indian by birth. This confession is set off by commas, however, and does not appear to delimit the meaning of Saund's newfound freedom: he can mention but also circumvent the discrimination he faces.

In another instance, Saund writes: "America exemplified for me the highest form of democracy. Its people had developed a system based upon the Declaration of Independence and the belief that all men are created equal. Human dignity was recognized and (with some notable exceptions) the principles of democracy were practiced" (*CFI*, 44–45). Amid this encomium comes a discrepant parenthetical claim that appears not to substantially alter the overall meaning. Exceptions to the "principles of democracy" are themselves excepted within the sentence's frame. Saund can simply step outside this bracketed purview even though his ability to do so is unusual rather than typical. The sentence seeks to elide this constraint and to reaffirm the promise of American exceptionalism—to normalize as a rule a spectacular exception within American democracy even as the rule of discrimination is made out to be the exception.

Saund's international tour, which is the moment of his greatest triumph as the "vivid example of democracy in action," also presents the greatest challenge, as audiences interrogate Saund's implicit disavowal of the history of racial violence in the United States. Speaking to crowded and demanding audiences, Saund faces a range of concerns about U.S. intervention, foreign occupation, and nuclear testing. One issue that comes up repeatedly is the Little Rock crisis, which his audience has trouble squaring with his blandishments about American democracy and freedom.[89] "Before I left I spoke before a large group of students and was asked the inevitable question about Little Rock," Saund writes, being pressed to confront enforced desegregation in the South and the history of racial enslavement and violence in the United States (*CFI*, 161).

Addressing students at the University of Sendai, Saund responds by marshaling the discourse of character building that the autobiography has developed thus far. "I began my answer by reminding them that in thirty-five out of the forty-eight states of the Union there was no discrimination against Negroes in schools or public places," he writes, confining the problem of discrimination to *de jure* sites rather than acknowledging its reach throughout the country (*CFI*, 156). When one professor is skeptical of this account, he assures his audience that "the vast majority of the

American people disapproved of Governor Faubus's action" (*CFI*, 157). Next, he excerpts his speech as follows:

> Then I said: "My friends, no matter where we may live, whether it be in Japan, in India, or the United States of America, there exists in one form or another injustice of man toward man. And the people of the United States full well recognize they are faced with a very difficult race problem in their midst. They are trying to do the best they can, and I shall urge to my friends in Japan, and to people wherever I go, to try to understand this difficult problem of the people of the United States, just as they would want other people to study and understand their problems. Instead of finding fault with each other, it should be the duty of civilized men everywhere to resolve these injustices of man toward man. There is no denying that the segregation of races in any part of the world is wrong and cannot be condoned, and the people of the United States do not condone it." I ended by again pointing out that segregation was limited to one part of the country where its roots were deep and will take some time to dig up. Nevertheless, we were working hard at the job and were determined to get it done. (*CFI*, 157)

Saund harks back to the schoolboy scenes early in the autobiography, foreclosing the possibility of critique and claiming that hard work will suffice to root out racial segregation and violence. A rhetorical sleight of hand takes place here to suggest that, barring a few exceptions, the playing field is generally fair. There is an oblique evocation of national unity, whose subtext is the image of the two sporting schoolboys who fight and then share a drink from the soda fountain, as though their camaraderie can bridge racial divides, which are exposed precisely at such segregated sites of social consumption. It matters not that Saund's audience seems largely unconvinced. Rather, Saund seeks to convince his American readers, for whose benefit the latter part of his speech is quoted and bears repeating. His goal is not ultimately to change public opinion worldwide but to confirm the good opinion his own constituents have of themselves, to present a vision of the American dream that they can continue to rely upon.

This rendering of Saund's travels is a tour de force of self making that rests, finally, on the appeal of his character. The inclusion of excerpts of his speeches recalls Washington's inclusion of his 1895 Atlanta Exposition address in *Up from Slavery*. Washington's exhortation, "Cast down your bucket where you are," resonates here, particularly as it solicits white and non-white audiences very differently.[90] Saund suggests to his auditors in Japan that, rather than "finding fault" or casting aspersions, they look to their own situation and work "everywhere to resolve these injustices of man toward man." For his white readership the implications are different: it is in Saund's speech itself that they can find all they need to affirm their own view of American democracy. No matter that his well-meaning, apparently unsophisticated diplomacy is peppered by reservations about proxy wars and puppet dictatorships, as well as brief appeals to the "American people" to "accept" as "their equals in every respect" the inhabitants and nations of the third world who are "one and all writing their constitutions on the American pattern" (*CFI*, 154, 185). Such exhortations work more to ensure than to threaten the complacency of his American readership, appealing to the sporting nature of Saund's readers and to their sporting acceptance of Saund. In such scenes, Saund does not mention his support for civil rights legislation and the 1957 Civil Rights Act in particular.[91] He is less concerned to vindicate his own character than to vindicate American character through his example.

The chapter that details Saund's travels, "My Trip Abroad," ends with a remarkable coda. "When I tried to evaluate the results of my trip, I asked myself this question," Saund writes, "Why should the people in Japan be interested in seeing newsreel pictures of a freshman congressman from the United States arriving in Tokyo?" (*CFI*, 182). By his own account, Saund is welcomed with "particular consideration" by government officials and greeted by "great throngs" of masses, to which the cover image of Saund and his family weighed down by innumerable garlands testifies (*CFI*, 183). "There could be only one answer," he proposes: "The people of India and the Asiatic world knew the story of my election to the United States Congress in 1956 and were proud of the fact that a man born in India had been elected to that high office" (*CFI*, 183). Saund seeks to contain the ideological contradictions that emerge in the course of his tour by way of his characterization. To "evaluate" his diplomatic efforts, he suggests, we must take the measure of his character. Supplementing his speeches, Saund returns us once again to the "story" of his election and to the archetype at the heart of the autobiography whose spectacular example obscures the "race problem," tempering the disagreeable facts of black subjugation. On view here is not only the "freshman congressman" arriving in Tokyo, but "newsreel pictures" of this event: a spectacle of the spectacle through which Saund seeks to contain the ideological contradictions that confront him during his travels.

Saund tries to avail himself of the metonymy that comes out of the particular genealogy of American character. His ambition evokes the fictive protagonists of Rihani and José Antonio Villarreal, as he hopes no less than "to be part of all American life" (*CFI*, 72). The autobiography must work to transform this poor, immigrant farmer into a synecdoche for the white majority despite the fact that he is, as a racialized and historically disavowed member of the body politic, one of the least likely candidates for this transformation. It must create a "vivid example" for a public eager for precisely such an example—whose "simple story" of success can make success seem simple. As my reading shows, *Congressman from India* constructs this model of minority, aiming to effect the metonymic slippage between exception and rule, between individual and national character. Character could "name the underlying substance or material of the nation itself," Salazar points out: "individual character and national character were conceived as not simply reflective or 'analogical' measures of one another but rather as inextricably bound together in their very formation."[92] Becoming a "part" of America entails making America a part of him, and Saund does this by fashioning a complex familial and political genealogy that is implicitly white and by eliding the racial history of South Asian immigration and racialization. Through a series of exercises in building character, he conjures a level playing field that admits of no grievance but requires dedication, self-reliance, and sportsmanship in order to realize the promise of individual success, conjoining individual character and American character in a seamless alchemy. Through the autobiography, characterization is revealed to be an important technology of the American dream, which relies upon and cathects around the archetype of model minority.

But the autobiography must work diligently to manage the interpretive excess of Saund's character. Ultimately, *Congressman from India* pivots between race and ethnicity, rather than effecting their transformation. The racialized characters that call out from the margins of history, the exceptions and contortions of Saund's local grammar, not to mention the skepticism of his international audiences, indicate that Saund's figurative self-portrait cannot bridge the gap between his representation of the American dream and the reality facing people of color and African Americans in particular. Saund seems to misunderstand the "race problem" as being not about him, although this is precisely the connection that the audience probes: the want of practical racial solidarity implied by his comments, the lack of self-reflexivity around the structural rather than local nature of the problem, and the mounting sense that the model minority does not transcend racial divides but casts them sharply into relief. Even as Saund deflects the "inevitable question" from his incredulous audience by recourse to his own character, he cannot fully answer this question. The impressive edifice of Saund's character cannot, ultimately, occlude the significance of race within the autobiography.

In one telling scene, *Congressman from India* guides us to a particular reading of Saund and opens up the agency of the autobiography as it transforms the historical record. When "a prominent citizen" opposed to Saund's bid for judge confronts him in a local restaurant ("Doc, tell us, if you're elected, will you furnish the turbans or will we have to buy them ourselves in order to come into your court?"), Saund responds thus: "My friend...you know me for a tolerant man. I don't care what a man has on top of his head. All I'm interested in is what he's got inside of it" (*CFI*, 82). Saund redirects attention from what is "on top" to what is "inside" his head. He asks that the "citizen"—and, by extension, the reader—read his character not from its outward determinants but from his inner disposition, to which the autobiography, as an "inside" account, provides one point of access. "All the customers had a good laugh at that and the story became the talk of the town during the next few days," Saund emphasizes, as if to demonstrate that he is able to circulate a new standard for his legibility (*CFI*, 83).

Even so, Saund's gloss cannot fully govern how his character is read. "I had given up wearing a turban shortly after I came to the United States," he mentions earlier (*CFI*, 49). But he is not able so easily to remove this emblem of race. Although he no longer wears the turban, it envelops him and overdetermines his character. Try as he might to direct his critics away from this volatile misreading, he is unable to manage the interpretive excess of his visible racial difference. By dramatizing this scene, Saund not only gives voice to racial nativism but also portrays himself as ineluctably foreign. In effect, *Congressman from India* exposes the archetype of Saund as a complex character. Race character critique reveals how Saund's literary deployments exceed and reshape his function as a biographical and historical figure. The autobiography shows us what an unlikely candidate Saund is, not only for Congress, but also for the model of minority that he builds.

CHAPTER FIVE

Paule Marshall's Brown Girls
Structures of Character

Among the many memorable characters in Paule Marshall's work, Silla Boyce is conspicuous for her embrace of upward mobility. Featured in *Brown Girl, Brownstones* (1959), a novel about a community of Barbadian immigrants in World War II–era Brooklyn, Silla represents an attachment to the American dream that is both troubling and impossible to ignore. She views the United States as a site of economic advancement. "I ain saying that we don catch H in this country what with the discrimination and thing and how hard we does have to scrub the Jew floor to make a penny, but my Christ, at least you can make a head-way," she says, contrasting opportunities for betterment in the United States to colonial Barbados, which keeps Barbadians in a state of near-enslavement.[1] She models herself on Jewish immigrants before her, from whom she seeks to wrest the American dream by claiming ownership of her brownstone home. "Every West Indian out here taking a lesson from the Jew landlord and converting these old houses into rooming houses—making the closets-self into rooms some them!—and pulling down plenty-plenty money by the week," she tells her husband at one point, setting her sights on "a swell house in dichty Crown Heights" (BGB, 173). She follows this pattern of social advancement, as she comes eventually to own the brownstone home that the Boyces initially rent and is poised by the end of the novel to move to Crown Heights. Her awareness of exploitation notwithstanding, Silla's figure occludes systemic racism by highlighting the upward mobility of Afro-Caribbean immigrants. She is part of a community of Barbadians who acknowledge that they "ain white yet" and work to distinguish themselves from the "poor colored man with his hand always long out to the rich white one," aiming to secure their economic future by exploiting African Americans and other immigrant groups (BGB, 221).

The archetypal power of this figure is apparent in the opening pages of the novel, which reveal the mother through the daughter's perception. Sitting at the top of the stairs inside the brownstone, ten-year-old Selina appreciates the "silence which came when the mother was at work," even as she walks through the house and finds traces of her mother everywhere (BGB,

5). She peeks into her parents' bedroom where she is allowed to sleep when she is sick; recalls her mother's rebukes as she pesters her sister, Ina; stares at a family photograph featuring her young mother; chafes at her mother's rules about going out with her friends; and conspires with her father in the sun parlor in her mother's absence. As "the mother," Silla has considerable symbolic power. Selina anticipates her arrival ("before she looked up and over to the park she knew that she would see the mother there striding home under the trees"), which brings "the theme of winter" as "the park, the women, the sun even gave way to her dark force; the flushed summer colors ran together and faded as she passed" (*BGB*, 16). Silla transforms the fictive landscape, reshaping even the structure of its narration. Whereas the novel until now is relayed through the voice of an omniscient narrator, focused through Selina's perspective, Silla assumes an omniscient stance. Her appearance is followed by epigraphs that frame our introduction to the remaining characters: Suggie, the sensuous Bajan tenant who has difficulty holding down a job (who *"don know shame"*); Miss Mary, the old white servant of the family who used to live in the brownstone and who now rents an upstairs apartment (*"nothing but a living dead"*); her husband, Deighton (*"don know his own mind . . . always looking for something big and praying hard not to find it"*); and Miss Thompson, the African American hairdresser (who *"does break down work to support somebody else's wild-dog puppies"*) (*BGB*, 17, 19, 21, 27). As Patricia Saunders points out, "Silla Boyce is represented as an omniscient force who controls everything in the universe."[2] "You's God; you must know," Deighton says to her at one point, acknowledging the power of her grim judgments (*BGB*, 24).

As the protagonist of *Brown Girl, Brownstones*, whose life story shapes the arc of the bildungsroman, Selina seems diametrically opposed to her mother. Denounced as "Hitler" by her daughter, Silla is figured as Selina's absolute antagonist (*BGB*, 183). At a meeting of the Association of Barbadian Homeowners and Businessmen, Selina overhears her mother's justification for her exploitative role within the capitalist system, and struggles to respond: "If only there was a way to prove to them and herself how totally she disavowed their way!" (*BGB*, 225). *Brown Girl, Brownstones* sets about articulating Selina's rebellion, as Selina rejects the role that her mother has scripted for her, refusing the cutthroat terms of socioeconomic advancement and choosing instead to set off for the Caribbean and craft her own future.

Despite its title, the novel features not one "brown girl" but two. As brown girls, Silla and Selina are linked in an obverse, mirroring structure—like that of a chiasmus. Silla has a trenchant awareness and critique of colonialism and racism, but is nonetheless driven to work within capitalist power structures, to supplant whiteness by acquiring property without challenging racialized oppression. Although opposed to her mother, Selina is like Silla. Selina is haunted by the ghostly imprint of whiteness built into the very walls of the brownstone in which her mother is so deeply invested, and by the imagined appeal of the white families that inhabit the brownstone before her, even as her desire grows increasingly unsustainable and she seeks to flee these racially mediated spaces. Although Silla and Selina are opposed to one another within *Brown Girl, Brownstones*, their opposition unites them so they reflect one another in a distorted way.

Race character critique enables a critical perspective upon the character of Silla. The chiasmus of mother and daughter draws them together in their shared experience of racism, which reveals the embrace of upward mobility to be impelled not by a character flaw, or an individual shortcoming, but by social constraints. The brownstone is key here. As a character in its own right, it emblematizes the vexed succession of immigrants that shapes both mother and daughter, encouraging us to read their characters through structural imperatives. By refracting these brown girls through the architectural figure of the brownstone, *Brown Girl, Brownstones* opens up a powerful critique. The novel proposes that we attend to characters who emblematize the American dream and denounce instead the oppressive social structures within which their desires take shape.

Black Success Story

Marshall's parents were Barbadian immigrants who shaped a particular story of immigrant advancement. They were part of the first wave of immigration from the Caribbean, which consisted of approximately eighty-five thousand West Indians who came to the United States between 1900 and 1930 and settled primarily in Harlem and Brooklyn.[3] Most hailed from Jamaica and Barbados and were spurred by economic and environmental crises and oppressive colonial regimes.[4] Census data indicates that the foreign-born black population increased from 20,336 to 98,620 between 1900 and 1930.[5] In the Harlem Renaissance, these immigrants were recruited to a particular genealogy of immigration. W. A. Domingo's essay in *The New Negro* (1925) casts them as "pioneers and shock troops to open a way for Negroes into new fields of employment"; much like "the Jew," he writes, extending the "analogy," "they are both ambitious, eager for education, willing to engage in business, argumentative, aggressive and possessed of great proselytizing zeal for any cause they espouse."[6] As Domingo's comparison indicates, Afro-Caribbean immigrants had a reputation as "black Jews."[7] Marshall was well aware of this reputation, which attached to Barbadian immigrants in particular. "Bajans," she writes in *Triangular Road*, her 2009 memoir, "had no objection to being called 'the Jews of the West Indies' by the other islanders—the term based on their perceived ability 'to squeeze a penny till it cried "Murder! Murder!"' and to 'turn a dime into a dollar overnight.'"[8]

The question of whether or not there is a "black success story," as the subtitle of a 2008 study asks, has resonated with historians and sociologists concerned with whether racism limits class mobility or whether the American dream is indeed colorblind.[9] The appeal of the "immigrant analogy" is apparent here, as Afro-Caribbean immigrants are likened to European immigrants.[10] Upward mobility in this context (as with the model minority myth that Dalip Singh Saund represents) turns on the possibility of what Susan Koshy calls "the morphing of race into ethnicity."[11] The composite figure of the "black Jew" represents precisely this possibility: in excess of black racialization and white ethnicization, this figure holds out the promise of the triumphal erasure of racism and the promise of an egalitarian American dream. There has been much debate about the reasons for the relative socioeconomic success of West Indian immigrants in comparison to African Americans, but scholars generally agree that the "black success story" has been exaggerated. While Afro-Caribbean immigrants have a labor market advantage over African Americans, this difference not only coexists with entrenched racial discrimination but is attributable to a more complex set of structural and cultural factors than was previously understood, ranging from selective migration to socialization that deemphasizes racial identity.[12]

Brown Girl, Brownstones attempts to make sense of this "black success story," as its imbrication with Marshall's biography reveals. Set in Brooklyn in the 1930s and 1940s, the novel centers on Selina's coming of age in a brownstone at the edge of Fulton Park. Aiming to buy their brownstone, Silla sells Deighton's inherited land in Barbados behind his back, destroying his hopes of return. Deighton, in turn, retrieves the money from the bank and spends the whole of the sum in one extravagant shopping spree. After he is injured in a factory job, he finds temporary solace in the congregation of Father Peace, a local divine. But he is then deported at the behest of his wife and jumps overboard to his death in sight of Barbados, unable to bear the ignominy of his return. Eventually, Silla comes to own her home and becomes a proud member of the Association. Selina emerges out of a long period of grieving for her father only to fasten her desires around the dream of running away to the Caribbean with her lover, Clive. Selina plans to defraud the Association of its scholarship money for young members in order to fund their getaway. Her plans change following her successful solo dance performance of a birth-to-death cycle, when she has a racist altercation with her friend Margaret's mother. Eventually, Selina refuses the scholarship and sets out for the Caribbean by herself.

Marshall has made no secret of the fact that *Brown Girl, Brownstones* is shaped by her family's and her own experience. Her 1983 essay, "From the Poets in the Kitchen," figures her mother's kitchen as a "wordshop" where the Bajan women of her acquaintance grappled with their "triple invisibility" as "black, female and foreigners" through the "spoken word," teaching Marshall her "first lessons in the narrative art."[13] *Triangular Road* reveals the extent of the overlap between the fictive plot of *Brown Girl, Brownstones* and Marshall's biography: her own father, like Deighton, was undocumented; the family leased an old brownstone much like the brownstone featured in the novel, with fruit trees in the yards, a coveted sun parlor on the second floor, and upstairs apartments that could be rented; the "Mother Poets" are evocative of Marshall's mother, Adriana, and her friends who gathered together in the kitchen at 501 Hancock Street; and her father, too, abandoned the family for Father Divine (upon whom Father Peace is based), leaving his "devastated eleven-year-old" daughter behind.[14]

As her comments about the novel indicate, Marshall is ambivalent about the American dream and skeptical of the racial divides that *Brown Girl, Brownstones* probes. In a 1991 interview, she points out that the breakdown of her nuclear family and their inability to purchase a home meant that they were unlike many of the families she grew up with. Figures such as Silla's friend, Beryl, who seems to have all the luxuries denied Silla, represent a way of negotiating this gap, for even as the "Beryls ... have realized the immigrant dream" that Marshall, too, "longed for," she also "questioned it," she says, "and in a sense even rejected it because it seemed so narrow to my mind. And so using her as a character was a way for me to deal with some of those feelings."[15] Marshall said in a 1982 interview, and again in 1991, that Silla is meant to represent a critique of the "black success story" rather than its vindication: "Silla is symbolic of the kind of thing that makes me so unhappy about American society: this kind of almost blind absorption in the material which makes for a kind of diminishing of life, of feeling"; "I see her as someone who has perhaps foolishly or unquestioningly bought the whole

American materialistic ethic."[16] She has little patience for the disunity between Afro-Caribbean immigrants and African Americans that the novel dramatizes, remarking in a 1988 interview that this divide is utter "nonsense" given the history of segregation and entrenched racism in the United States ("I mean whites see only a black face until perhaps you open your mouth").[17] As she reiterates in 1992, "I don't make any distinction between African-American and West Indian. All o' we is one as far as I'm concerned. And I, myself, am both."[18]

In this sense, Marshall is incongruous with the other writers I study, because she is not herself a troubling figure; she fits well within an oppositional framework of ethnic literature. Nor is she easily confused with the vexed characters she represents. *Brown Girl, Brownstones* is something of an anomaly in a body of work committed to crafting a vision of black solidarity and decolonial feminism. Marshall's novels are peopled by characters such as Merle Kinbona in *The Chosen Place, The Timeless People* (1969), and Avey Johnson in *Praisesong for the Widow* (1983), who transform social divides entrenched by plantation slavery and find alternatives to materialism in the spiritual traditions of the Caribbean.

A brief view into Marshall's autobiography reveals her sustained commitment to civil rights activism, shaped by diasporic movements for black self-determination. Her own Cold War–era tour sponsored by the U.S. Department of State is a case in point. In a memorable scene from *Triangular Road*, she describes a government briefing in advance of her travels through Europe along with Langston Hughes, who invited her to accompany him. Confronted by her "dossier," she recounts the extensive scope of her political involvement: participation in the American Youth for Democracy and the Association of Artists for Freedom, for instance, and in various rallies and demonstrations that she attended, and at which she often spoke, including the first joint civil rights and anti–Vietnam War march in Times Square.[19] Unlike Saund, Marshall subverts her propaganda function, refusing to serve as a mouthpiece for American exceptionalism. She resolves, in her words, to "speak my mind about said government when asked, even though my freedom to criticize might, ironically, redound to Washington's good. No matter. Speaking out would be a way of making use of being used."[20] With audiences as far afield as Paris, London, Copenhagen, and Berlin, she was forthright about violent crackdowns on peaceful protests throughout the South, the importance of the struggle for voting rights, and the extent to which racism was socially and structurally entrenched in the United States.

Despite Marshall's countervailing biography, the archetypal allure of Silla is such that her character has been used to justify arguments about black pathology. In their controversial study, *Beyond the Melting Pot* (1963), Nathan Glazer and Daniel Moynihan cite *Brown Girl, Brownstones* as they attribute black poverty to behavioral and cultural factors. "The ethos of the West Indians, in contrast to that of the Southern Negro, emphasized saving, hard work, investment, education. Paule Marshall has described this ethos in a remarkably revealing novel about Barbadians in Brooklyn. Here is a wife denouncing a husband who has not measured up to Barbadian ('Bajan') ideals," they write, quoting a long passage in which Silla unfavorably compares Deighton to other men in the community.[21] Appropriated by scholars attempting to justify racist pathologies, a figure like Silla has a fraught legacy, particularly in the absence of a literary hermeneutic that would frame the reading of her character in such contexts. While Glazer and Moynihan's arguments have since been discredited for the highly subjective data upon which they are based, *Brown Girl, Brownstones* nonetheless lends itself to an indexical reading.[22] In her sociology of West Indian immigration, Mary Waters, for instance, explains how she bought a copy of *Brown Girl, Brownstones* for a student in the hope that it would help her better understand her intergenerational conflict with her mother.[23]

That Marshall ascribes a testimonial function to the novel encourages such an approach, but she also underscores that her work refigures rather than reflects reality. "I thought that if I remembered the poetry and drama I heard in the voices in my neighborhood, if I really tried to understand what their whole need was, in coming to America and purchasing houses and so on—if I could understand the sociology of their lives, I would maybe be able to make it real for the reader," she claims in a 2009 interview.[24] Sociology informs her work, as does the expressive horizon of the "real." This might well explain the particular uses to which the novel is put in studies of Caribbean immigration as a form of historical testimony, not least by Marshall herself whose essay on black immigrant women (collected in one volume under the rubric of Afro-Caribbean "case studies") cites *Brown Girl, Brownstones* liberally.[25] But Marshall also emphasizes her creative license. In interviews in 1979, 1991, and 1996, she reveals that the novel is "autobiographical," but its people are "composites"; while "a good deal of their emotional history is drawn from what I have experienced either personally or what I have seen in the community that shaped me," Selina is "not Paule Marshall, but a compilation of any number of young women I knew at that time."[26] In the 2009 interview, Marshall emphasizes the act of translation: "*Brown Girl,*

Brownstones was an attempt to be daring enough to see if I could translate onto the page some of the impressions and experiences and relationships that made up my world growing up."[27] There are important differences between Marshall's fiction and her biography. For instance, unlike Silla, Marshall's mother used money from her mother's sale of her land to take the children back to Barbados to visit their grandmother instead of putting it toward a down payment on their brownstone home.[28] As these interviews suggest, figuration rather than equivalence mediates Marshall's life and work. Her experiences are not just documented but reconfigured into the amalgamated characters and imagined plots of a fictive world beyond her personal history.

How does the novel, as a powerful fiction in its own right, transform the reality that it mediates? As Elda María Román points out, *Brown Girl, Brownstones* is among a set of novels that "theorize Black social mobility in ways that would later be echoed by major sociological works."[29] This potential is embedded in the studies of Caribbean immigration that showcase Marshall's work. While the introduction to a 1981 collection describes her fiction as "background" or "baseline," that "corroborates and complements much of what follows in the social science contributions," Marshall's essay throws down a gauntlet. She foregrounds the "triple invisibility" of black immigrant women who have not "been dealt with in any direct and substantial way in the social science literature," inviting this field to rethink its habits and parameters by way of her literary work.[30] As a theory of society, rather than sociological data, *Brown Girl, Brownstones* gives us a critical perspective upon the characters that it generates. Even as Marshall creates the archetype of Silla, she shows how to grapple with her embrace of upward mobility and her troubling attachments to the American dream. The dynamics of characterization are key to this critique, as my reading shows, focusing on the way that the characters of mother and daughter relate. This relationship has been the focus of much of the criticism on the novel, which tends to position these two figures in opposition to one another. The novel is ordered by conflict, for World War II is both its setting and its template. The feud between Silla and Deighton is built into the organization of the novel: one of its sections, entitled "The War," ends with Deighton's death, Silla's hollow triumph, and with Selina having to choose between whether she is "Deighton's Selina" or whether she will take the "mother's way" (*BGB*, 239, 247). In this context, Silla is read by Mary Helen Washington, Trudier Harris, and Sabine Bröck under the sign of tragic necessity, as an emblem of American materialism who—given her manifold subjugation as black, immigrant, woman, and working class—is trapped by her own assimilation into racist and capitalistic structures of power.[31] Selina, conversely, is positioned both as an antithesis to Silla and as a sublimation of the divide represented by mother and daughter.[32]

I build upon these arguments, emphasizing the alignment of Silla and Selina even as it is structured in opposition. As Heather Hathaway points out, while mother and daughter appear to be "Manichean adversaries," their "apparently simple contrasts . . . emerge in extraordinary complexity" that "prevents us from grouping characters along simple lines of opposition."[33] To capture this complexity, it helps to map Silla and Selina's relationship onto the rhetorical figure of the chiasmus, a figure of speech in which two or more clauses are repeated in a reversal that harnesses them in an inverse relation.[34] As a mode of characterization, the chiasmus brings into focus scenarios in which characters are opposed but bound together in their opposition. Adapted to think through the relationship between mother and daughter, the chiasmus reveals their apparent contrast to be a function of difference and of likeness. It registers the overlap of these characters—the twisted way in which they mirror one another. This doubling is built into the concept of character itself, which, as J. Hillis Miller points out, "will not keep out its differential other."[35] Across the figure of mother and daughter, the chiasmus serves to bring the archetype of Silla into view and refracts this archetype into its component parts. Mother and daughter are revealed as distorted reflections. Although distinct, they come to occupy a similar niche as characters who unmistakably parallel one another. We learn to see that Silla and Selina, while opposed, are not all that different, and that their likeness is an expression of shared social constraints.

Chiasmus of Character

The scene of the Association meeting that opens this chapter also helps frame the relationship between mother and daughter. Introducing the work of the Association to its newest members, along the trajectory of white ethnicization ("We ain white yet. We's small-timers! . . . But we got our eye on the big time . . ."), Cecil Osborne distances the upwardly mobile Barbadian immigrant from the stereotype of the indigent African American. "This then is the *Barbadian* Association. Still in its infancy. Still a little fish in a big white sea. But a sign. A sign that a people are banded together in a spirit of self-help. A sign that we are destroying that picture of the poor colored man with his hand always long out to the rich white one, begging: 'Please, mister, can you spare a dime?' It's a sign that we has a *business* mind! I thank you!" (*BGB*, 221). Partly an extension of Garveyism (Beryl's "father says it's going to be the biggest thing since Marcus Garvey"), the Association extolls the virtues of colorblind self-reliance (*BGB*, 196).[36] So Claremont Sealy's speech, which follows that of Osborne, draws the ire of the audience, for Sealy proposes to open the association to all black people ("You need to strike out that word *Barbadian* and put *Negro*") (*BGB*, 222).

Speaking with her friends about Sealy's proposal, Silla has an important gloss on their reflexive disdain. "People got to make their own way," she says, "And nearly always to make your own way in this Christ world you got to be hard and sometimes misuse others, even your own. Oh, nobody wun admit it. We don talk about it, but we does live by it—each in his own way" (*BGB*, 224). "We would like to do different," she allows, "But the way things arrange we can't, if not we lose out. . . . It's true the roomers is our own color. But if they was white or yellow and cun do better we'd still be overcharging them. Take when we had to scrub the Jew floor. He wasn't misusing us so much because our skin was black but because we cun do better" (*BGB*, 224). For her, "power is a thing that don really have nothing do to with color," and "people got a right to claw their way to the top" (*BGB*, 224, 225). "Take this world," she says, "It wun always be white. No, mahn. It gon be somebody else turn soon—maybe even people looking near like us. But plenty gon have to suffer to bring it about. And when they get up top they might not be so nice either, 'cause power is a thing that don make you nice. But it's the way of this Christ world best-proof!" (*BGB*, 225).

In this moment, the figure of Selina represents quite a contrast to that of her mother. Faced with this adept and irrepressible sermon, she sits with "her underlip clenched childishly between her teeth" (*BGB*, 225). She tries to voice her "own small truth that dimly envisioned a different world and a different way; a small belief—illusory and undefined still—which was slowly forming out of all she had lived" (*BGB*, 225). "If only she could turn and give the lie to that argument and shout her truth to them all!" she protests, "If only there was a way to prove to them and herself how totally she disavowed their way! But how, when her own truth was so uncertain and untried? How, when she knew nothing of the world or its ways? This was the gall and humiliation" (*BGB*, 225). Selina's repudiation is absolute, but she is unable to respond to her mother's wrathful eloquence.

The readings that follow complicate Silla and Selina's apparent antagonism, delineating the chiasmus of character through which mother and daughter are linked. Silla's archetypal appeal is apparent as she disidentifies with blackness and charts the course of upward mobility, claiming white power and privilege without challenging racist structures of exploitation. Although Selina positions herself as her mother's antagonist, she is also cast in the image of her mother. She, too, has an unsustainable dream of whiteness, as she imagines herself as one of the white family who used to live in the brownstone. Drawn to the appeal of their grace and gentility, Selina is ashamed of her own blackness even as she develops a nascent sense of black solidarity and pride. Mother and daughter are conjoined in their opposition, as they negotiate the challenge of being positioned as racialized immigrants along the continuum of white ethnicization.

Silla's troubling position within capitalist power structures reveals itself in her comments at the Association meeting, as she exploits her black boarders and disavows racial solidarity across class divides. There is very little identification across the gap between the business-minded Bajan and the "poor colored man." They "cun do better," Silla avows, as though class stratification is fated. Although she and her friends have mixed feelings about living by such exploitative codes, the shared color of their skin does not draw landlord and tenant together across the socioeconomic gap that separates them. Silla acknowledges her exploitation of African Americans and her ambivalence about that exploitation. But, for Silla, power corrupts irrespective of race, and she evokes the examples of the slave trade and child labor to make her point that group solidarity founders with the promise of individual gain.

However, Silla does not seek to be white and is quick to criticize particular modes of identification with whiteness. Anything that smacks of white idolatry or affectation evokes her outrage. When Iris expresses a patriotic fondness for Britain during the war, Silla castigates her for her misdirected loyalty: "But Iris you's one ignorant black woman! . . . What the king know 'bout you—or care?" (BGB, 69–70). She describes Deighton's romanticized dream of return to Barbados and his grand plans to build a dream house on his inherited land ("gon build all this fancy house like white people") as part of a "show" and a compulsion to "play like he's white" (BGB, 114, 175, 82). She has no false allegiance to the crown, no lingering obeisance to the British colonial enterprise. In contrast to the nostalgic tales of sporting and play with which Deighton regales his children, Silla presents them with a stark picture of her childhood in the "Third Class": "a set of little children picking grass in a cane field from the time God sun rise in his heaven till it set" (BGB, 45). Of all the characters, she has the most penetrating critiques of racialized structures of colonial power, where "white people treating we like slaves still and we taking it. The rum shop and the church join together to keep we pacify and in ignorance. That's Barbados" (*BGB*, 70).

Instead, Silla identifies with white power and privilege and seeks to supplant whiteness through her own upward mobility. She believes that the world "wun always be white." As long she accepts "the way things arrange," she, too, will rise. Power will change hands, irrespective of race. In contrast to colonial Barbados and its entrenched exploitation of black peasantry and workers, the United States presents opportunities for advancement that Silla views as deracialized. Here is a place where she can "make a head-way," as the novel in some sense shows, tracking her employment as a domestic laborer, a factory worker, and foreseeably, as a nurse, as she begins a new program of education after the factory closes at the end of the war. Selina's glimpse into her mother working on the assembly line suggests that industrial capitalism has finally met its match in Silla: "Only the mother's own formidable force could match that of the machines; only the mother could remain indifferent to the brutal noise" (*BGB*, 100). Even though Deighton squanders the money from her duplicitous sale of his land, Silla eventually goes from leasing to owning the brownstone, evicts her longstanding tenants, and is able to follow the upwardly mobile itinerary of Association members to Crown Heights. The brownstone is the emblem of her success. Of everyone in her family, she alone seems at ease within its white walls. "His wife stood easily amid the whiteness, at the sink," as Deighton observes, "in the relaxed unself-conscious pose of someone alone" (*BGB*, 22).

Silla's complex relationship to whiteness is illustrated by her obsession with Miss Mary, from whom she must wrest the promise of the American dream. With her perpetual dirge about the white family that once employed her, their soothing routines, and her eager service, Miss Mary testifies to one version of the American dream in which the former inhabitants of the house presumably moved on to bigger and better things, achieving socioeconomic mobility. Her tenacious hold on life infuriates Silla, who is eager to supplant this old order by dividing the upstairs rooms and charging more rent. In one remarkable scene, Silla bursts in one afternoon as Selina is sitting with Miss Mary in her apartment piled high with relics from the past, and begins to upend and destroy the old boxes, paintings, and furniture covered with dusty sheets. Silla and Miss Mary are locked in a symbolic contest that seems very real: "For a time they struggled silently, Silla's curved fingers drawing the life from Miss Mary, while Miss Mary strained to hold it. The old head with the skull transparent under the wisps of hair quivered up, the wasted body writhed out of Silla's reach. But as Silla leaned forward, her fingers tightening and her face becoming more menacing, Miss Mary slowly dropped back, weakening, until finally she lay still" (*BGB*, 203). A few months later, Miss Mary dies and Silla's dream comes that much closer.

Miss Mary represents not only the success of the American dream, but its palpable failure, which might well account for the particular vehemence that Silla directs against this figure. Her testament to the old white order notwithstanding, Miss Mary is also its remnant in that she and her daughter Maritze—the poor white servant and her illegitimate child—are left to fend for themselves by the employers Miss Mary helplessly adores. Trapped in the distorted fantasy of benevolent gentility, Miss Mary is the detritus of capitalism. Although Maritze tries to make a push for their family's advancement, enjoining her mother to quit the brownstone for a "nice little house on Long Island" (as her mother contemptuously describes it), Miss Mary refuses to relinquish her link to this past (*BGB*, 36). Silla hates Miss Mary not because she is white but because she is not upwardly mobile, her failure a grim reminder of the insupportable failure of the American dream.

What is even more terrifying about Miss Mary is that she opens up the possibility that Silla's read of capitalism is perhaps flawed, that class privilege is not in fact colorblind but deeply mediated by race. Miss Mary's tenacious hold at the top of the household, in what is likely the old servant's quarter, also represents the hold of a stubborn racist order that ranks the white servant above the black immigrant and impedes the "black success story." Despite her relative disempowerment as the illegitimate daughter of a single, working-class mother, Maritze is secure in her sense of superiority over the Boyces, or "that black foreign scum downstairs" as she refers to them (*BGB*, 35). It is not that Silla is deluded about racism ("the discrimination and thing"), for she is well aware of Miss Mary and her daughter's racist presuppositions ("Yes, and your long-face daughter too that never once count me to speak because my skin black") (*BGB*, 203). Rather, she imagines that, under capitalism, race and class privilege can be disarticulated, and it is this hope that is tested by Miss Mary and Maritze's stubborn sense of superiority over the Boyces, despite—and because of—their relative lack of power and privilege as poor whites.

Selina, on the other hand, has a very different relationship to Miss Mary, for she finds solace in the latter's memories of the white family that used to live in the brownstone home. While Silla is in a rush to supplant this history, Selina is captivated and lulled by Miss Mary's lament as she sits by her side "in the dust-yellow room while she wheezed and gasped her dirge of memories" (*BGB*, 51). Her attraction for this "rank, half-dead old woman" is incomprehensible to Silla, and hardly justified by the novel, which does not trouble to construct illusions of interracial communion, as Selina's attempts to communicate with Miss Mary are swept away by the relentless stream of her hallucinations (*BGB*, 202). But the past that Miss Mary evokes has a powerful hold upon Selina that is not relinquished until Miss Mary dies, and she realizes she "resented the old woman for having lured her as a child into her tomb with her crooning memories" (*BGB*, 204).

The attraction these memories hold for Selina is revealed in the opening pages of *Brown Girl, Brownstones*, where Selina imagines herself as one with this white family. As she rises from her familiar haunt at the top floor landing and descends the stairs, "pale footfalls," "white hands," and "mild voices" surround her, "fusing with her": "she was no longer a dark girl alone and dreaming at the top of an old house, but one of them, invested with their beauty and gentility. She threw her head back until it trembled proudly on the stalk of her neck and, holding up her imaginary gown, she swept downstairs to the parlor floor" (*BGB*, 5). Selina is "invested with" the ideal of the white family that once occupied the brownstone. The imaginary gown, symbol of rank and privilege, is the symbolic investiture of whiteness. But as she moves forward and sees her reflection, the vision shatters: "the mirror flung her back at herself. The mood was broken. The gown dropped from her limp hands. The illusory figures fled and she was only herself again. A truculent face and eyes too large and old, a flat body perched on legs that were too long. A torn middy blouse, dirty shorts, and socks that always worked down into the heel of her sneakers. That was all she was. She did not belong here. She was something vulgar in a holy place" (*BGB*, 5–6). Selina's unsustainable vision bespeaks a psychic identification with whiteness. That her flight of fancy takes place upon a flight of stairs heightens its irony. Selina's failed performance prefigures that of Deighton, as both represent variations of the "play" on whiteness that Silla impugns. But Selina continues to be captivated by this imagined past, a bulwark against the disarray of her life, and dreams of "the family who had lived there before them," a time when "nights had been safe and quiet" and "the heavy door locked against the chaos outside" (*BGB*, 51).

What is fascinating about these opening passages is that they figure Selina as different from yet like her mother. In our first introduction to Selina, she is described with eyes that are "not the eyes of the child": "Something too old lurked in their centers. They were weighted, it seemed, with scenes of a long life. . . . She seemed to know the world down there in the dark hall and beyond for what it was" (*BGB*, 4). The outside world is her mother's domain. Yet she knows more of it than her age and experience would suggest. The description of Selina's relative inexperience at the Association meeting echoes this passage ("How, when she knew nothing of the world or its ways?"). While her relative lack of experience contrasts with her mother's worldly knowledge, Selina is also old before her time and appears to possess her mother's worldliness. Her movement through the text is also similar yet different. Contrary to Silla's upwardly mobile climb, Selina moves downstairs. But, for both women, the staircase is an emblem of their troubling relationship to whiteness. Where Silla seeks to supplant white power, Selina imagines herself as white. They are in mirrored opposition, resembling one another in those moments where they appear to be dissimilar.

Where mother and daughter differ is in their relationship to blackness, for Selina cultivates relationships with people who do not fit the Association's template. Suggie introduces Selina to a life of pleasure, and draws Selina out of mourning for her father and into an awareness of her sensuality. Miss Thompson (a composite of Marshall's grandmother, her hairdresser, and one of her mother's few African American friends) introduces her to the violence of racial enslavement and the Jim Crow regime symbolized by the festering sore upon her foot, the result of an assault by a white man.[37] Clive opens up space around the Association's margins for artistic and sexual exploration, through his constant fiddling at the piano, his desultory attempts to make a life by painting, and his dispassionate reminiscences of Bohemian New York life. Taken together, these figures represent the possibility of a relationship to blackness that differs from that of Selina's mother, that takes a long view of black diasporic history and sees the possibility of community based in all of its parts instead of only those devoted to economic advancement. As Román notes, the novel features a particular character type in "conflicted artists" who are "both sympathetic and antagonistic to the community's demand that members share the quest for home ownership and material success."[38]

Even so, Selina is unable to share this alternate vision of black solidarity at the Association meeting. When, at her mother's urging, she joins a group of her own age, she is pressed by Julian Hurley to offer her response. She bursts forth, goaded in part by her homophobic reaction to Julian, inveighing against the Association as "the result of living by the most shameful codes possible—dog eat dog, exploitation, the strong over the weak, the end justifies the means—the whole kit and caboodle," comprising "a band of small frightened people. Clannish. Narrow-minded. Selfish. . . . Prejudiced. Pitiful—because who out there in that white world you're so feverishly courting gives one damn whether you change the word *Barbadian* to *Negro*? Provincial! That's your Association" (*BGB*, 227). The debate over Sealy's proposal strikes Selina as deluded. She lashes out at her peers for their misplaced concern but also simultaneously at her own limited understanding. She wants desperately to find an alternative to these "shameful codes" but is not able to articulate this alternative. Despite this outburst, her "own truth" continues to elude her, as does the possibility of a different relationship to blackness. In this, Selina is not dissimilar to her mother. When she finally leaves for the Caribbean at the end of the novel, it is precisely at the moment that the Association has begun to allow African Americans to join their ranks. As Gavin Jones points out, "Selina's final alienation from her 'own people' arises, ironically, at the very moment that a hopefully pluralistic definition of black identity comes into being."[39]

Although mother and daughter seem opposed, their opposition is articulated in likeness. Marshall builds this chiasmus of character into the very language of Selina's rebellion. On the one hand, Silla gives us an account of "the way things arrange," that people must make their "own way" (a phrase she repeats twice more), or "claw their way" as they negotiate the "way things arrange" and the "way of this Christ world." The repetition of this unassuming word indexes not only the intractable structures of capitalist exploitation but also Silla's entrapment within them. Thus, her "own way" reflects the "way" of the world in which she finds herself. Selina, on the other hand, would like to envision "a different way," to find "a way" to reject "their way." Even as she opposes her mother, Selina mirrors her mother's language and tries unsuccessfully to refigure it. The complex crossing of their voices reveals their antagonism to be structured in similitude. The rest of the novel lays out the contours of this chiasmus of character, as each act of rebellion draws Selina closer to Silla.

Two Head-Bulls

The chiasmus that structures the relationship between Silla and Selina manifests in the plotting of their characters within *Brown Girl, Brownstones*. Although the novel is in part a bildungsroman, almost half of the book is devoted to the dramatic plot of the struggle between Silla and Deighton over Deighton's inherited land. World War II forms the background for this epic battle, as Silla's plan to defraud Deighton of his land is mapped onto the outbreak of hostilities and Deighton's eventual suicide coincides with the end of the war. The final section, "Selina," begins under the shadow of this conflict, as Selina emerges out of a period of deep mourning for her father in seemingly intractable opposition to what Silla has done. In rebellion against her mother, Selina is drawn to dancing, the very opposite of the "practical" vocation that her mother intends for her (*BGB*, 201). She takes Clive as her lover, despite having internalized her mother's puritan injunctions and Silla's particular objection to Clive, a "man that wun work," who is very low in Silla's regard (*BGB*, 259). As a künstlerroman, the novel explores the marginalized figure of the artist within this upwardly mobile community.

But this seeming opposition between the plotting of mother and daughter is actually structured in likeness, as Selina comes increasingly to mirror her mother. In a dramatic reversal, she ingratiates herself with the Association and works to win its scholarship fund, planning to use the money to fund her journey with Clive. Her scheme rivals that of her mother. While Selina's artistic rebellion is opposed to the conformist materialism that Silla represents (and is intended specifically to deceive Silla), both dramatic arcs take similar form. Defined by betrayal, treachery, and deceit, they feature eminently capable protagonists who match each other in their capacity to orchestrate such intricate deceptions.

Even as she tries to articulate her opposition to her mother, Selina becomes more like her mother. Clive is the first to notice this resemblance. Admiring her willfulness, in contrast to his own inertia, he unwittingly reveals to her how much she is like her mother at the very moment when her rebellion is calculated to repudiate Silla. Recalling their first time having sex, he says: "Take that first night when you seized me in all my innocence. . . . It wasn't even me you were seizing. You might have been grabbing life itself by the throat, throttling it, cursing it" (*BGB*, 247). Selina is appalled by the "picture he had drawn of her—as someone ruthlessly seizing a way and using, then thrusting aside, others. It recalled the mother's argument at the Association. This was the mother's way!—which had seemed so opposed to her own small yet undefined truth, which had so infuriated her" (*BGB*, 247). In her single-minded pursuit of her plan to defraud the Association, Selina is even more like Silla. Like her mother, she declares her fierce resolve: "It's almost too easy in a way. I want to do more. Can you understand that? I want more intrigue, more deception, more duplicity!" (*BGB*, 272). Like her mother, she executes her deception masterfully, eventually winning the scholarship as a result of her tireless efforts. Mother and daughter are bound in a chiasmus, as Selina's "way" turns out to look a lot like "the mother's way."

It is her artistic rebellion that ironically brings Selina into deep communion with Silla, as she comes face to face with the racism that impels her mother's ruthless pursuit of upward mobility. After her solo dance recital, she goes to the home of one of the dancers, Margaret Benton, to celebrate with the other women in the show. Margaret's mother requests to see "the star of the show," partly out of resentment that her own daughter has been relegated to the chorus line (*BGB*, 285). In the "inquisition" that follows, she primly but devastatingly exploits Selina's foreign origins (*BGB*, 287). Upon discovering in answer to her probing questions that Selina's parents are from the West Indies, Margaret's mother slowly humiliates Selina by way of a motivated comparison to a West Indian woman named Ettie, who cleaned the Benton house. Her experience of this racist condescension opens up for Selina a vision of black solidarity, as she sees all of the figures she has known united with her in their shared experience of racism and oppression. She has now glimpsed the conditions that Silla and many of her friends, domestic workers at one time or another, have endured. Fleeing this demeaning encounter, she comes full circle to the "darkened Association building" and feels for the first time that she is "one with them: the mother and the Bajan women, who had lived each day what she had come to know" (*BGB*, 292–93).

A close reading of this scene reveals the particular violence of racist characterization, as Margaret's mother collapses Selina and Ettie into versions of the same character. At first, Margaret's mother struggles to read Selina, eventually discovering that her parents are from the West Indies. "Ah, I thought so," she says, claiming that there is "something different . . . about Negroes from the West Indies in general" and that she can "always spot it" (*BGB*, 287). In the particular spirit of racist and classist condescension, she goes on to label Ettie as a "girl" (although "she wasn't a girl, of course. We just call them that"), praise her as "efficient" and "reliable," and applaud her honesty ("I could leave my purse—anything—lying around and never worry") while bemoaning her "lack of proper training and education" (*BGB*, 287–88). Selina is conflated with Ettie even as she is made out to be the exception: "You can't help your color," Margaret's mother says, "You . . . well, dear . . . you don't even act colored. I mean, you speak so well and have such poise. And it's just wonderful how you've taken your race's natural talent for dancing and music and developed it. Your race needs more smart young people like you. Ettie used to say the same thing. We used to have these long discussions on the race problem and she always agreed with me. It was so amusing to hear her say things in that delightful West Indian accent . . ." (*BGB*, 288–89). In the face of this onslaught, Selina makes a mute plea for her unique self to become visible to Margaret's mother: "Why couldn't the woman *see*, she wondered—even as she drowned—that she was simply a girl of twenty with a slender body and slight breasts and no power with words, who loved spring and then the sere leaves falling and dim, old houses, who had tried, foolishly perhaps, to reach beyond herself?" (*BGB*, 289). But Margaret's mother's "pale eyes" are a "well-lighted mirror" that reveals to Selina "the full meaning of her black skin" (*BGB*, 289). Eventually, Margaret's mother exhorts Selina to perform a caricatured version of herself, to compensate for the powerful performance that has obscured her own daughter and triggered her spiteful jealousy. "Oh, please say something in that delightful West Indian accent for us!" she says, as she stands over Selina and smilingly shakes her hand (*BGB*, 289). Selina finally throws her off, and she falls back into the lamp, which crashes down, casting the room into darkness.

This scene recalls the Fanonian moment of racist apprehension, as Selina's outward character elicits a cascade of associations that makes it impossible for her inward character to emerge. The burden of signification of character is in full evidence here, as is the burden of representation that Selina bears. Once Margaret's mother marks Selina as a black West Indian, she ranges both metonymically and metaphorically from this impress of character, voicing one primitivist stereotype after another. Even as Selina is singled out as exceptional, she stands in not only for Ettie but for the whole of the "race" by extension. This surfeit of figuration entraps Selina, who is "imprisoned in the wing chair under the glaring lamp," and renders her hyper-visible in the "well-lighted mirror" of Margaret's mother's eyes (*BGB*, 287). Much like the scene Frantz Fanon dramatizes, she, too, is a specimen, "*fixed*" and "dissected under white eyes."[40] In the closed circuit of the "pale" screen of Margaret's mother's perception, Selina's personality cannot emerge. The darkness into which the reciprocal violence of Selina's gesture casts the room confirms that, despite the profusion of artificial light, she has not really been seen by Margaret's mother.

The novel does not reveal Selina's authentic character but the complexity of racial characterization itself. Rushing from the room, Selina pushes her way through the circle of her friends and runs out of the apartment and into the street, eventually ending up collapsed in the entrance of an empty store. "With trembling fingers she found her handkerchief and, wetting it, wiped off the stage make-up and then rubbed the dirt from the window," Marshall writes (*BGB*, 290). Here, in the "meager glow of a distant street light," Selina confronts the image that Margaret's mother sees: "the night, symbol of their ancient fears, which seethed with sin and harbored violence, which spawned the beast in its fen; with the heart of darkness within them and all its horror and fascination" (*BGB*, 290, 291). In this primitivist vision, Selina is horrified to find an affirmation of her "own dark depth," her "furtive pleasures with Clive on the sofa, her planned betrayal of the Association, the mosaic of deceit and lies she had built to delude the mother" (*BGB*, 291). Margaret's mother's racist apprehension triggers Selina's shameful apprehension of herself, an assessment of her character—in the sense of her moral makeup—that she finds wanting. All her attempts to destroy this image fail ("her arm slashed out, her fist smashed that mouth, those eyes; her flat hand tried to blot it out. . . . and still it remained") (*BGB*, 291). "Exhausted, she fell against the glass," Marshall writes, "her feverish face striking the cold one there": "She cried because, like all her kinsmen, she must somehow prevent it from destroying her inside and find a way for her real face to emerge. Rubbing her face against the ravaged image in the glass, she cried in outrage: that along with the fierce struggle of her humanity she must also battle illusions!" (*BGB*, 291–92). As Selina peels away layer upon layer of her character, one mask is stripped only to reveal another. She removes her makeup and cleans the dirt from the window only to find Margaret's mother's vision confirmed in her own. She cannot hold herself apart from this vision, as every attempt to strike it down brings her closer to it, until her face literally rubs up against the reflection in the window. Her "real face" is but a gesture, as elusive at the end of the scene as it is at the beginning. Instead, Selina understands that she must "find a way for her real face to emerge." To return to Miller, the storefront window is like an "inseparable ghostly companion, like a double reflection in a double-paned window at night," which obscures any access to a "fixed personality."[41] This recursive mirror of character invites us not to unmask character but to read character more fully. Selina does not see through the layers of racist caricature to an authentic vision. Instead, *Brown Girl, Brownstones* shows how these many masks of character irreducibly mediate Selina's sense of herself.

As a fundamental turn within the novel, this moment recalls Richard Rubio's violent arrest and Khalid's unceremonious jailing. In all three instances, the philosophical twinning of character and fate is reshaped. The idea that "character is fate"—sometimes translated as "one's bearing shapes one's fate"—is often attributed to Heraclitus and accompanied by exhortations to develop good character that emphasize the power of individual will over destiny.[42] But this self-determined outcome is delimited by structural power. The translation of the Heraclitan proverb in terms of "bearing" captures this double valence, in that bearing refers to the manner in which one carries oneself and how this carriage is perceived by others. Under the white gaze, outward character as "mark" or "brand" constrains inward character or "personality."[43] In the language of Fanon, the "racial epidermal schema" overpowers all others; the colonial subject is the "slave" of "appearance," legible only through the manifestation of character, ensnared by colonialist and primitivist discourses of race.[44] Thus Fanon calls for a "sociodiagnostic" that will help "get rid of the worm-eaten roots of the structure."[45]

This is precisely what *Brown Girl, Brownstones* offers in this meticulously arranged scene, revealing Silla's character to be shaped not by individual will but by social constraints. In some ways, the encounter with Margaret's mother confirms what Selina has already known, that the promise of the American dream is an empty promise, as "vacant" as the storefront window where she eventually finds herself (*BGB*, 290). But the overdetermination of Selina's character by race, which Marshall so carefully choreographs, like an extension of the dance performance itself, exposes the violence of the social arrangement in which mother and daughter are ensnared. Conjoined to her mother, in the experience of racism, Selina is able to see her troubling embrace of upward mobility for the mode of survival that it is. That familiar word, repeated once again in the storefront scene, is clarifying: for "the way things arrange" circumscribes the "way" these two women take.

The final scene cements this likeness, revealing mother and daughter to be linked in a chiasmus of character. When called upon at a lavish ceremony to accept the Association scholarship, Selina publicly declines the award. In the coatroom, on her way out, she confesses to her mother the details of her scheme. At this moment, when she has utterly rejected all that her mother and the Association represent, and appears as far as possible to be "Deighton's Selina," there is a remarkable reversal. "Poor-great like the father before you," Silla calls her, but Selina disagrees: "I'm truly your child," she says, revealing how she has always been captivated by the story of Silla's immigration ("Remember how you used to talk about how you left home and came here alone as a girl of eighteen and was your own woman? I used to love hearing that. And that's what I want. I want it!"); Silla relents briefly toward her daughter, as though "she somehow glimpsed in Selina the girl she had once been. For that moment . . . she became the girl who had stood, alone and innocent, at the ship's rail, watching the city rise glittering with promise from the sea" (*BGB*, 304, 307). This is precisely the journey that Selina proposes to undertake now, but in reverse. Like her mother, she will be "going alone" (*BGB*, 306). At this complex crossing, mother and daughter do not simply oppose one another. Rather, they are coupled in an obverse relation. Selina's journey does not just parallel Deighton's return but mirrors Silla's journey in reverse. What binds mother and daughter in this moment of separation is their knowledge of the depth and violence of racism. Silla asks her daughter if she knows "what it tis out there? How those white people does do yuh?": "At her solemn nod, at the sad knowing in her eyes, Silla's head slowly bowed" (*BGB*, 306, 307). Silla's bow is a reflection of Selina's "nod," affirming their shared experience. "G'long," say Silla, "my own mother did say two head-bulls can't reign in a flock" (*BGB*, 307).

A Structural Critique

As the readings above suggest, space is fundamental to characterization within *Brown Girl, Brownstones*. The characters of Silla and Selina are deeply mediated by the architecture of the brownstones. The title of the novel announces this relation, placing anthropomorphic figure alongside architectural figuration. There is something of an enigma in this parataxis. Both "brown girl" and "brownstones" appear to have a central role within the narrative, but how they connect across the comma that separates them is unclear. While critics have analyzed this relationship in different ways, we have yet to consider how the brownstones shape the dynamics of characterization within the text.[46] Essentially, the brownstones function as emblems of structural constraint. Personified as characters, they shape the other characters and transform the way characterization works in the novel.

From the very beginning, the brownstones feature prominently in the arc of the bildungsroman. The novel begins with the famous image of the brownstones as "an army massed at attention," whose "backs reared dark against the sky," variously "indifferent," "squat," "formidable," and "grim" (*BGB*, 3). Washington writes, "like the brownstones they inhabit," the Barbadians, too, "are a formidable army—huge, somber, watchful, ancient and beautiful."[47] "Indeed the brownstones are the first characters we meet," Hathaway points out, arguing that the brownstones personify aspects of the Barbadian immigrant community.[48] "Her house was alive to Selina," Marshall declares, and pursues that conceit at various points throughout the novel: the room "like a dark, fragrant mother tried to soothe" Selina, the brownstones "reared like a fortress wall guarding the city," they "joined in their conspiracy" as Ina spills her father's secrets to Silla, "leaned against the soft sky" as Selina races down Chauncey Street, "seemed to pull the night quickly down around them, like old women drawing heavy veils over their ruined faces," and "lowered down in disapproval" as she retells the story of her mother's betrayal and father's death to Clive (*BGB*, 4, 7, 34, 43, 53, 246, 249). The fate of the brownstones follows the figurative arc of Selina's birth-to-death cycle, as the novel ends with an image of gutted brownstones, destroyed to make way for new housing projects.

The brownstones mold the characters as well, as these are plotted in architectural terms. There are many instances of characters described through buildings and spaces. For instance, Selina likens Beryl to a "small well-lighted room with the furniture neatly arranged around it"; Florrie says of Deighton, "His mouth look like a house"; and descriptions of Silla ("back was stiff again") and Selina ("small back as unassailable as her own") resonate with the opening descriptions of the houses (*BGB*, 15, 75, 42, 47).[49] Silla and the brownstones "take shape from each other," Vanessa Dickerson notes, "as Marshall characterizes each by the attributes found in the other."[50] Marshall also takes pains to plot the characters architecturally, situating them in the opening pages of the book at various points throughout the brownstone: Selina on the top floor landing, Miss Mary in her room upstairs, Deighton in the sun parlor, and Ina in the basement bedroom. Selina's movements through the house are carefully choreographed, as she sweeps down the staircase through the entrance hall and parlor, sees herself in the full-length mirror, peeks into the master bedroom (where we are introduced to her mother in her absence), rushes into the bedroom she and her sister share, backs out into the dining room, and then joins Deighton on the sun parlor. What Alex Woloch calls "character-space," describing the space that the narrative allots to characters, has a literal meaning here, as the characters are enfolded by and apportioned into the space of the brownstone.[51]

Returning to the opening scene reveals an extended and contradictory personification of the brownstones as both uniform and distinctive:

> In the somnolent July afternoon the unbroken line of brownstone houses down the long Brooklyn street resembled an army massed at attention. They were all one uniform red-brown stone. All with high massive stone stoops and black iron-grille fences staving off the sun. All draped in ivy as though mourning. Their somber façades, indifferent to the summer's heat and passion, faced a park while their backs reared dark against the sky. They were only three or four stories tall—squat—yet they gave the impression of formidable height.
>
> Glancing down the interminable Brooklyn street you thought of those joined brownstones as one house reflected through a train of

Block of Brooklyn brownstones photographed by Danny Lyon (1974). Courtesy of the U.S. National Archives and Records Administration (412-DA-13468).

mirrors, with no walls between the houses but only vast rooms yawning endlessly one into the other. Yet, looking close, you saw that under the thick ivy each house had something distinctively its own. Some touch that was Gothic, Romanesque, baroque or Greek triumphed amid the Victorian clutter. Here, Ionic columns framed the windows while next door gargoyles scowled up at the sun. There, the cornices were hung with carved foliage while Gorgon heads decorated others. Many houses had bay windows or Gothic stonework; a few boasted turrets raised high above the other roofs. Yet they all shared the same brown monotony. All seemed doomed by the confusion in their design. (*BGB*, 3)

The houses are personified as an army massed at attention. Their anthropomorphic features liken them to the Barbadian community, and their outward appearance bespeaks uniformity. As in the 1974 photograph of the brownstone block, the row of houses appears to be a single house "reflected through a train of mirrors," an endless repetition of sameness upon sameness. But a tension develops, for the brownstones are "squat" and "*yet*" they suggest "formidable height." "*Yet*, looking close" reveals in fact that "each house had something distinctively its own," some small, unique variation.

"*Yet*" again, the narration claims, "they all shared the same brown monotony. All seemed doomed by the confusion in their design." This confusion is built into the confused narration itself, into its twists and turns. The brownstones are uniform yet distinctive, mournful yet formidable, massive yet squat, conjoined yet discrete, featuring a rich panoply of singular architectural styles even as they appear unvarying without and within.

While critics interpret this confusion as a tension between individualism and community, I foreground its relation to the succession of immigrants that Marshall identifies.[52] "Behind those grim façades, in those high rooms, life soared and ebbed," she writes: "First, there had been the Dutch-English and Scotch-Irish who had built the houses. There had been tea in the afternoon then and skirts rustling across the parquet floors and mild voices. For a long time it had been only the whites, each generation unraveling in a quiet skein of years behind the green shades" (*BGB*, 3, 4). European and Afro-Caribbean immigrations converge at the site of the brownstones. But the new immigration is markedly different: "the West Indians slowly edged their way in. Like a dark sea nudging its way onto a white beach and staining the sand, they came," and "with their coming, there was no longer tea in the afternoon, and their odd speech clashed in the hushed rooms" (*BGB*, 4).

At issue here is the relevance of the model of European immigrant assimilation to non-European migrations, or the relationship between race and ethnicity. The "race relations cycle" popularized by the Chicago school of sociology held out the promise of assimilation for all immigrant groups, setting up the assumption that European and non-European immigrations were analogous to one another.[53] *Brown Girl, Brownstones* is suspicious of this immigrant analogy and foregrounds the gap between ethnicity and race. The word "skein" signifies both thread and tangle, suggesting that the thread of succession snags with the arrival of the West Indians, who are described as incongruous ("edged"), discordant ("clashed"), and ignoble ("staining").[54] Their immigration represents a strain on the assimilation cycle that would see racialized immigrants incorporated on the model of white ethnicity. In the littoral zone of the novel's own imagery, the "dark sea," unlike prior tides of immigration, does not dissolve into the "white beach."[55]

Even as the novel stresses the disjunction of these successive immigrations, it explores their concatenation in the figure of the "black Jew" upon which many of the characters are modeled. Throughout the novel, Jewish immigration functions as a touchstone for Barbadian assimilation and upward mobility, precisely because it represents the possibility of transforming race into ethnicity. When a fellow Barbadian stops Deighton on one of his jaunts down Fulton Street, their talk turns immediately to Jewish immigrants. "Who say I faulting the Jew?" says Siefert Yearwood, "I lift my hat to him. He know how to make a dollar. He own all New York" (*BGB*, 38). While Silla and her friends are forced to journey daily to more affluent neighborhoods to clean homes, to dress their children in "the old clothes which the Jews had given them," and to "scrub the Jew floor," they admire the Jewish model of advancement (*BGB*, 11, 224). "Every West Indian out here taking a lesson from the Jew landlord," Silla tells Deighton, modeling her exploitation of boarders below her on the rungs of the socioeconomic hierarchy—whether newer immigrants or African Americans—upon the Jewish example.

In this context, the brownstones represent the pivot of race and ethnicity, signifying not only the impossibility of their transformation but also its possibility. A palimpsest of their consecutive inhabitants, they evoke the Barbadian immigration with their "backs reared dark against the sky," their rooms "like a dark, fragrant mother," and their aspect like "old women drawing heavy veils over their ruined faces." But they are also gothic entombments, a "museum of all the lives that had ever lived here," whose "frieze of cherubs and angels on the ceiling" and "antiseptic white furniture and enameled white walls" represent the former white inhabitants whose "ghost shapes" never quit the house (*BGB*, 5, 6, 22). Not a figuration of one or another immigrant group, the brownstones symbolize their negotiation of race and ethnicity. The "confusion in their design" denotes this pivot. They are not only irreducibly different from one another (each with "something distinctively its own"), but they are also alike to one another (partaking of the "same brown monotony"). Inasmuch as the succession of white and black immigration is disrupted, it is also conjoined in their "unbroken line," in the "train of mirrors" and the "vast rooms yawning endlessly one into the other." These contradictions signify both the sameness of white ethnicization and the difference of black racialization that Silla and Selina must negotiate.

This confluence of race and ethnicity finds an extension throughout *Brown Girl, Brownstones* in cross-hatchings of darkness and light, as well as their amalgam in brownness. The intertidal zone where "dark sea" meets "white beach" represents not only the incongruence of European and West Indian immigration but also its overlap. Similar imagery animates key moments in the novel: the "golden streak" of Deighton's trumpet flashes in the "twilit room" as he shares with Selina his dream of riches; the "brown envelope from home" brings news of Silla's betrayal; Deighton is deported through "dark streaks in the eddying sunlight"; Suggie prances with Selina out the doorway of her apartment in a "wide bar of light" as the "rich colors of their laughter painted the darkness"; and "fretwork of light and shadow" animates the brownstones in Selina's final farewell (*BGB*, 85, 108, 181, 210, 310).

The scenes where Silla's and Selina's schemes crystallize are instructive. In one of the more memorable episodes in the novel, Silla's vow to defraud Deighton of his land is latticed in light and darkness:

> With that she raised her arms, her body reared, and as she stood there pledging her whole self while the others sat struck silent, the day changed. The early winter sunset stained the sky beyond the pear trees with harsh yet lovely threads of mauve, wine rose, brassy yellow, and the last light reached in long attenuated strips into the kitchen. Shadows were there also, spreading their dark tentacles as the sun thinned. Silla, the barred sunlight and shade on her face, was imprisoned within this contradiction of dark and light. Indeed, like all men, she embodied it. Yet somehow it was more marked in her. Perhaps because the struggle was nearer the surface and more intense. (*BGB*, 76)

Silla's pledge ushers in the change of day into night, as the "last light" of sun contends with "dark tentacles" of shadows. Compelled by Iris's litany of Bajans who are putting down payments toward their houses, Silla resolves to sell Deighton's land in order to join their ranks, her arms "raised" in a symbolic embrace of upward mobility. The "contradiction of dark and light" is the contradiction of Silla's double aims: love and loyalty to her husband against the desire for social mobility on the other. In another sense, it also represents the contradiction between race and ethnicity that the figure of the "black Jew" inhabits and must "struggle" with. In another scene, Selina grapples with her mother's plan and forms her own resolve to oppose it. She flings herself into a chair at Miss Thompson's beauty parlor and turns it around at "a furious spin. Each time she sped past the mirror her face was more blurred until it was only a brown streak. She was blurring into nothingness and she deserved it" (*BGB*, 94). Although she is not in her house, the brownstones—named for the sandstone material with which they were overlaid—lend their color to her.[56] While Selina faces dissolution into the "nothingness" of her double negation as neither black nor white, Silla on the other hand is riven by the "contradiction of dark and light." As studies in black, brown, and white spectrums and contrasts, such scenes exceed the polarity of black racialization and white ethnicization. The pivot of race and ethnicity (around which Selina, in one sense, literally turns) finds something of a pause, as *Brown Girl, Brownstones* opens up a space of ideological indeterminacy and muddled allegiance and asks us to inhabit that space. The novel refigures that guiding trope of U.S. race relations, the color line, as a littoral zone awash in ambiguity and ambivalence, and inflected by the gradations of race in the Caribbean.[57] One name for this space is brown. As a precursor to Richard Rodriguez's "Brown Uncle Tom," it is here that the "brown girl" must find the coordinates of her "way."[58]

In such moments, the brownstones emblematize the structural constraints that Silla and Selina face. This is nowhere clearer than when Silla declares her resolve to steal Deighton's land, and she is "barred" and "imprisoned" by the "sunlight and shade on her face" as the light of the setting sun filters through the house. Inasmuch as Silla appears to be acting of her own volition, and indeed to be applying all the force of her willpower to the work of self making, there are forces at work upon her (superimposed upon her face) that are beyond her ken. As John Frow points out, character is shadowed by a "zone" that undoes character: "a world of random patterning" that is "beyond human control," involving "natural forces" ("of fate, and of the omens") or "transpersonal forces" ("'horizontal' patternings of the age cohort, of gender, of social class, of race and ethnicity").[59] It is precisely this other of character that the brownstone denotes, and the "patterning" of light and dark fills, enabling the "sociodiagnostic" that Fanon seeks. The title of the novel registers this double movement, as it names both individual and structure, character and its undoing.

Threat of the Artist

As the Boyces sit down to breakfast in the dining room, a "shaft of sunlight from the kitchen" shines on their "brown-faded family photograph on the buffet" (*BGB*, 171). Torn apart by Silla's deceit and Deighton's religious conversion, the family is on the verge of disintegration. The breakfast ends with Deighton's definitive departure from the brownstone home. Here, Marshall shows us a double vision of the family seated at the kitchen table alongside a photograph, one among many artifacts in the "museum" of the brownstone, as if to suggest that one is incomplete without the other. Illuminated by light refracted by the brownstone, this "brown-faded family" cannot help but be shaded by this symbolic structure. *Brown Girl, Brownstones* asks that we trace the confused designs of Silla and Selina to the "confusion" in the "design" of the brownstones pivoting between race and ethnicity. Silla's fraudulent sale of Deighton's land and Selina's scheme to abscond with the Association money are opposed yet similar attempts to negotiate their troubling succession. This insistent architectural mediation opens up a powerful structural critique, reshaping the embrace of upward mobility as a function of social forces rather than individual will.

The end of *Brown Girl, Brownstones* extends this structural critique through a recurrent dream that besieges Selina for a week after she runs from Margaret's mother's house. In this dream, Selina first feels at home in a Victorian parlor, whose description resonates with that of her own house. Hearing footsteps outside, she suddenly realizes she is an intruder: "Frantically, she searched for a window, but found none; nor was there a second door or a closet. In desperation she plunged through the grand piano, tearing her way through the wires until she reached the street" (*BGB*, 298). Unspecified "others" follow her for a time until she is chased by a "beast," a "low-slung, dark-furred animal" to whom she perversely wants to "surrender"; she climbs an empty bus, but not before "the beast caught her leg, slashing a deep furrow in the calf" and the "bus door closed on his bloody paw, and sent him tumbling—howling and snapping—into the gutter (*BGB*, 298).

Selina's encounter with Margaret's mother motivates the dream. The footsteps seem to belong to someone with a claim to the house, the ghostly white immigrants who haunt the brownstone, perhaps, or even Margaret's mother who has no compunction about making Selina feel out of place. Selina's pursuit undermines her claim to the brownstone home and, by extension, Barbadian assimilation on the model of whiteness, as the dream of ethnicity pivots back into race. The beast that chases Selina is an extension of Margaret's mother's racist imagination that hounds Selina even as she flees the initial scene of their exchange, the wound in her leg recalling the cramp that overtakes her in that earlier scene ("She ran until a stitch pierced her side and her leg cramped. Clutching her leg she limped—like an animal broken by a long hunt") (*BGB*, 290). The characterization of the beast references the illusions that Selina battles in the storefront window, recognizing herself in "the night, symbol of their ancient fears . . . which spawned the beast in its fen." It represents the screen of racist apprehension that Selina flees, then as now struggling with the impulse to surrender as she finds upon that screen a confirmation of "her own dark depth."

That Selina tears "a way" through the brownstone in her dream opens an alternative to "the way things arrange." She subsequently refuses the Association scholarship and resolves to set out for the Caribbean, supporting herself by working as a dancer on a cruise ship. Her dream of escape from the brownstone suggests that she has relinquished its hold upon her, even as she chooses to venture out in a ship, in some ways the complete antithesis of the brownstone house. But there is no escape from racist overdetermination, as the wound on her leg continues to hobble her along with the irony that she will now join the circuits of touristic consumption of the Caribbean.

Here, Marshall enters into *Brown Girl, Brownstones* as yet another brown girl. Selina's destruction of the piano foreshadows her resolve to go alone, for the piano is in some ways an extension of Clive. But the centrality of the piano in this dream suggests that art is instrumental to her break, as is the figure of the immigrant artist. Clive's painting, Selina's dancing, as well as Deighton's and Suggie's embrace of aesthetic pleasure, emblematize the character function of Marshall within the text. As Marshall points out in a 2001 interview, referring to a scene at a Barbadian wedding at which the community dramatically spurns Deighton, "they are really rejecting Deighton, the artist. They can't afford the threat he represents to their notion of the American dream. He is the sacrificial lamb to that dream. That's really one of the major themes of that first novel and of most of my work."[60] As Deighton's daughter, and an avatar for Marshall, Selina is poised upon the very journey that Marshall undertakes in subsequent novels as she tallies the losses of the American dream and finds alternative forms of black diasporic consciousness. In the end, Marshall creates the space for this journey within the novel, as an alternative to the determinative constraints of the brownstones. In Román's words, "the value of the ethnic artist . . . emerges through the text itself, in its rich and complex images gradating the insecurity of social and communal status."[61] Here, it seems, Selina's "own small truth" might be found, where the horizon of her travels extends into Marshall's subsequent fiction.

It is crucial that Selina's departure develops in similitude as well as opposition. When Osborne presents her with the scholarship in front of a crowded audience at the Association awards ceremony, she climbs upon the stage and announces her rejection. The award "means something I don't want for myself," she says, refusing in no uncertain terms the succession of upward mobility that the Association represents (*BGB*, 303). But her rejection is imbued with "admiration" and "love," as she sees before her a mirror of herself: "variations of her own dark face" whose "purposefulness" she is aware "charged her strength and underpinned her purpose" (*BGB*, 302, 303). This passage cements her likeness to the Barbadian community at the very moment of her farewell. Selina's view of the audience recalls the images that open the novel, for "the smiling faces" evoke "a dark sea—alive under the sun with endless mutations of the one color" (*BGB*, 302–3). As Selina is about to embark on her own sea voyage, the language of the novel brings us back to the littoral zone where "dark sea" meets "white beach" as if to suggest that this is where Selina's departure finds its coordinates, in the shared subjection of the Barbadians to racism and their resilience in the face of structural constraints. Art represents a break after all, not from characters like Silla but from our perspective upon them.

Conclusion
The Old Constellation

Race Characters reveals an archetype of the American dream and also refracts this archetype into all its complexity. My chapters feature visibly racialized immigrants who have an attenuated relationship to minority identity and accept the inducements of the American dream, identifying with imperialism, individualism, assimilation, or self making. As spectacles of incorporable difference, they appear interchangeable. Their specific histories seem to matter little. They perpetuate a particular notion of character—that of the selfsame, singular, masterful "I" whose success appears to prove the rule of American democracy.

Read through the framework of race character critique, such figures are transformed. They are no longer inert and interchangeable but protean. Adapted to the study of ethnic literature, theories of characterization open up a space within and around these figures, across the fictive and autobiographical worlds that they inhabit and between their literary and biographical manifestations. In dialogue with one another and with the social dynamics of racialization and characterization, the many parts of their character enliven the study of character and ethnic literature both. This work brings us to the other of character, a troubled zone of impersonal forces that shadows the illusion of mastery and constrains the ethnic "I." Reading in this way breaks down the archetype of the American dream and contests its appropriation, creating fuller portraits of ethnic identity.

The closing scene of *Brown Girl, Brownstones* (1959) exemplifies this double movement, as Paule Marshall returns us to the brownstone. Leaving the Association meeting, Selina walks down streets where new migrants have arrived. She recalls the cloistered occupancy of white immigrants and the Bajans who modeled themselves on this generation, thinking back to a time when "those houses would have been drawn within the darkness of themselves"; now "the staccato beat of Spanish voices, the frenzied sensuous music" and "the warm canorous Negro sounds" infuse the air, as Puerto Rican and African American tenants reshape the neighborhood.[1] Walking on, Selina arrives at the wreckage of a block of brownstones that is being cleared for "the new city houses" that already dot the horizon, "the lighted windows spangling the sky like a new constellation."[2]

Although the destruction of the brownstones signals a different social order, Selina is not particularly sanguine about these new buildings. In their oblique evocation of the national anthem, these "lighted windows" might well augur a new American dream. To the extent that these houses represent affordable public housing, linked to a commitment to racial integration in the postwar years, they are an alternative to the embrace of upward mobility that Silla personifies. But Selina is taken aback by their construction, by their "monolithic shapes," "concrete halls," and "close rooms," and she imagines "life moving in an oppressive round within those uniformly painted walls."[3] Her aversion is prescient, for the very communities such developments were meant to serve would end up being sidelined.[4]

Selina dwells less on this "new constellation" than the old. She pushes past the drama of succession that the canorous voices portend to the gutted brownstones themselves. Her view on this scene inflects all the readings in this book, for Marshall's description attests both to the archetype of the American dream and to its palpable failure. Portions of the building remain standing: "A solitary wall stood perversely amid the rubble, a stoop still imposed its massive grandeur, a carved oak staircase led only to the night sky."[5] Silla is not here but is everywhere, conjured especially through the ornate staircase that emblematizes the climb of upward mobility. The staircase is a grim monument to her stubborn endurance and her grueling ascent, as she identifies with white power and reproduces the racist exclusions of capitalism. As the young Selina's frequent haunt, the staircase also represents the imagined appeal of the white immigrants that lingers in the brownstones and threatens to cripple Selina's relationship to herself.

Traces of the other characters I study in my book can be read into this scene. Khalid also dreams "perversely" of an Arab empire founded on the American model, a dream that is partly countenanced by Ameen Rihani. José Garcia Villa's demurrals and those of his unmarked characters, abiding fantasies of artistic assimilation, continue to be "imposed" upon the ethnic canon. So too the "solitary" pocho reverberates through literary history, in the guise of Richard Rubio and José Antonio Villarreal and their calculated betrayal of racial identity. And the "grandeur" of Dalip Singh Saund's success makes itself felt through his vivid self-appraisal as a model minority.

Racialized immigrants, these characters nonetheless repudiate minority identity. They share the imperative to be anything but minor, each in his own way seeking to be all things. Thus Richard stands in front of the mirror and imagines himself with male and female parts. He calls to mind Villa's ambiguous portraits, his recusal from racial and national specificity, and his eventual retreat into a fictitious country. Doveglion, the name that Villa gives to himself and to this country, is itself a composite: "I meant it for Dove, Eagle, and Lion," Villa writes in a 1947 letter, "the dove for gentleness, the eagle for wisdom, the lion for courage. I just made the term up."[6] Khalid, too, is given to fantasies ("chimeras") and is himself a fantastical creature, in that his figuration as the American "Superman" represents an impossible synthesis of "East" and "West."[7] Silla and Saund also share in these visions, for they remake themselves in the broader pattern not of race but of ethnicity. As encompassing models, and spectacles of assimilable difference, they subtend American exceptionalism and white hegemony.

I locate these characters in an old constellation of ethnic literature, in a period of nascent ethnic and racial formation from 1900 to 1960. During this period, the civil rights movement had not yet voiced the crisis of the American dream and the categories that now guide the study of ethnic literature had not yet been formed. This period is more familiar to us as one in which Southern and Eastern Europeans assimilated into a socially constructed whiteness based on their shared experience of immigration and upward mobility. Although non-European immigrants have not been assimilated in the same pattern, they have also claimed this experience as shared, as my readings show. These readings tell a different story of immigration and race through the archive of ethnic literature, as non-Europeans imagine their relationship to whiteness and other forms of dominant identity as part of a troubling but important genealogy of becoming American. At the pivot of race and ethnicity, they inhabit sites of ambivalence and undecidability.

From the vantage of oppositional critique, such figures seem to be retrograde. Like the planets whose apparent reverse the term describes, they appear to hold fast against the revolutionary tide. As new dispensations surge forward, they often remain, isolated features, hard to approach yet impossible to excuse, part of a recalcitrant history that is easier to circumvent than to engage. Epithets cluster around them. Backward. Misguided. Treacherous. Compromised. Whether they receive very little attention or achieve a degree of notoriety, they tend to drop out of the study of ethnic literature, because they reject the categories and imperatives through which we often seek to understand them.

But the archetypal significance of these figures extends into the present, as the recent deployments of Rihani and Saund indicate. Susan Koshy has already shown how race and ethnicity are realigning since the 1960s, as historically racialized groups liminal to the dichotomies of black and white racialization are selectively incorporated into the American dream.[8] Lauren Berlant describes the millennial optimism around the future of race as part of a "masked hegemony of whiteness" that elides black, immigrant, gendered, Indigenous, and queer histories of exploitation and their repercussions by embracing a utopian ideal of racial hybridity.[9] Cracks in this ideal have deepened irreversibly with the resurgence of white nationalism and neofascism in recent decades. Still, the public spectacle of racialized minorities continues to sustain vestiges of postracial ideology. Figures who represent racial undecidability or testify to the irrelevance of race are called upon precisely when the American dream is deeply in question. Such figures reframe exceptions to the racial order as its rule and blur the imperative of structural critique, even as the revolutionary groundswell of the post-Ferguson era demands that we reckon with racialized inequity and disenfranchisement. Arundhati Roy encapsulates this role, refiguring the turkey-pardoning tradition at Thanksgiving—itself a veiled commemoration of settler colonialism—as an allegory for the "New Racism," which exonerates a select few turkeys ("the local elites of various countries, a community of wealthy immigrants, investment bankers, the occasional Colin Powell or Condoleezza Rice, some singers, some writers") while sacrificing the remaining millions to the violence and penury of corporate globalization: "Basically they're for the pot."[10]

Literary critique helps us to understand the new face of domination, as Roy's parable shows. She illustrates the concept of "New Racism" by way of the literary form of allegory, which highlights the preposterous spectacle of the new racial order, foregrounds the role of its corporate backers, and exposes its genocidal consequences. The construction of character is a central feature of this allegory and the ideology of American exceptionalism that it subtends. In "a show of ceremonial magnanimity," Roy points out, "the president spares that particular bird (and eats another one)"; the "lucky birds" are trained to put on a show, "to be sociable, to interact with dignitaries, school children, and the press," according to the company that supplies them.[11] These select turkeys are given a name, a voice, and an identity—essentially, a character, whose display is a key feature of their ceremonial pardon. Named "Liberty" or "Freedom," some are undisguised symbols of the nation.[12] That many (despite their overblown pardons) die from obesity and other physical afflictions related to their being bred and raised for size, testifies to the devastating ironies of the new racial order.[13]

As this parable shows, character is not incidental to the figures I study. Nor is it a way of talking about them loosely as people. The emphasis on building and displaying the character of the pardoned turkeys signals the importance of character, as does the portentous choice of their names. Character irreducibly mediates individual and national identity in the United States. Its discursive history extends from Benjamin Franklin through Horatio Alger to Booker T. Washington, a history my work develops through the figure of the model minority. This lineage captivates Richard Rodriguez ("the brown Uncle Tom"), who figures himself as an avatar of "Poor Richard."[14] The visibly racialized immigrant, shaped by immigration and changing racial demographics, plays a starring role in the American dream. As my readings show, the production of character mantles the pivot of race and ethnicity: by building character, immigrants dislodge the stigma of race and allow for their social mobility.

As a method, character emerges out of the problem studied here. J. Hillis Miller intuits this connection when he uses an odd choice of simile in his exegesis of character. Discussing Friedrich Nietzsche's dismantling of the idea of selfhood, Miller writes that the "whole structure of elements sustains itself in a constantly moving airy confabulation of self-generating and self-sustaining fictions, like a man lifting himself by his own bootstraps."[15] This gesture to bootstrap ideology in an otherwise abstract philosophical discussion implies the congruence of the fiction of character and fiction of self-reliant upward mobility that is so central to the American dream. Hélène Cixous's multiple cautions against the concept of character—its circuits of identification with the reader, its fetishization of wholeness, its collaboration with the myths of mastery, its attachment to the ego—read as inducements to the marginalized ethnic figure, who is denied such privileges.[16] Aspects that Cixous reviles represent openings for thinking about the work of writers who negotiate their own social character through the fiction of character. Through the dynamics of characterization in their work, they sustain and subvert the ideal of the American dream.

Character does additional work as a method, for it grounds the constellation of figures I consider. Writers and works that are usually differentiated as Arab, black, Chicano, Filipino, or South Asian are brought into comparison through the framework of character. Reading in this way challenges received habits of study. Holding these identities in abeyance can be difficult, for group formations have historically governed projects in ethnic studies. But such formations have difficulty encompassing writers who have vexed relationships to their identity. Their writing does not fulfill the terms of its identification and calls for new frameworks for its legibility. This is not at all to say that the work of building ethnic archives along ethnoracial lines is not crucial and ongoing. But it is also important to create new orientations toward the archive. Constellating ethnic literature through character allows otherwise inscrutable figures to manifest, figures who exceed the categories of literary criticism and inhabit race in unexpected ways. This method enables ethnic identity to develop from out of reading practice. It also captures the demurrals, refusals, concessions, and aberrations that have been marginal to the constitution of ethnic studies as a field.

Out of this constellation emerges both ubiquity and unevenness. A constellation is in one sense a complex articulation—the drawing of figures into an interrelated pattern. It performs the work of comparison, bringing into view something as yet unseen. As Rey Chow argues, comparison does not only inhere in customary sites. It need not involve variations on the world literature model. Nor must comparison necessarily take place across two national literatures or languages. Chow points to work by scholars on the peripheries of Europe who appear to be working within a single national literary tradition but are in fact reckoning with the historical fragment of European domination that shapes this tradition:

> ... the literary, cultural, and identitarian formations of non-Western modernity are, according to these critics, thoroughly immersed in, indeed predicated on, comparison. But this is not the kind of comparison that can be tabulated rationally or cumulatively so that differences are simply chronologically more recent variations to be incorporated into a familiar grid of reference. Instead, comparison now resembles the archaeological tracking of historical remnants that Foucault identifies as the modern order of things. To do its job properly, this kind of comparative practice must be willing to abandon inclusionary taxonomizing habits and ready to interpret cultural narratives symptomatically, as fragments that bear clues—often indirect, perverse, and prejudiced—to a history of ideological coercions and exclusions.[17]

This analysis informs my work, which is comparative not because it analyzes the literatures of various U.S. ethnic groups but because of the archetype of American character that structures the comparison. Because this archetype blurs the categories through which we generally read ethnic literature, it is all the more difficult to perceive. A replicable prototype of ethnic identity, it works as a norming mechanism upon which minorities are expected to pattern themselves, recruiting them to the ideology of the American dream. Through this archetype, certain kinds of difference are rendered stable within the social field. Ethnic literature always has this fragment, a resonant and reverberant figure for minority identity whose ubiquity these readings expose across literary and social worlds. "If racialization is inherently comparative," as Shu-mei Shih points out, then comparative reading is not "arbitrary juxtaposition" but "the recognition and activation of relations that entail two or more terms," which "brings submerged or displaced relationalities into view."[18]

In the passage above, Chow describes two modes of comparison. Based in a distinction made by Michel Foucault, the first is "a grid of intelligibility in the midst of infinite material variations" that is itself inert and unchanging, even as it continues to attach and subordinate new examples to itself.[19] In this vein, "literature as understood in Europe" forms the grid and "historical variations are often conceived of in terms of other cultures' welcome entries into or becoming synthesized with the European tradition."[20] The second approach is archaeological rather than taxonomic. Here, the "once assumed clear continuities (and unities) among differentiated knowledge items are displaced onto fissures, mutations, and subterranean genealogies" that must be tracked in the form of "broken lines, shapes, and patterns that may have become occluded, gone underground, or taken flight."[21] Gone is the "presumption of similarity, equivalence, and likeness," as "different things" are adjudged provisionally, as negotiable, *in sheer approximation to one another.*"[22] The grid can thus be taken apart so Europe is no longer the ground of comparison but "the referent of supremacy," "a memory, a cluster of lingering ideological and emotional effects whose force takes the form of a lived historical violation, a violation that preconditions linguistic and cultural consciousness."[23]

Undertaken in this way, comparison also brings out unevenness. Where ethnic identity is subordinated to an interchangeable archetype, comparison can help by foregrounding disjuncture. The norm can be refracted into its multiple parts, not to expand the array of types but to create studies in character—multiple literary portraits, complex biographical histories, and varied histories of immigration and race that flesh out the archetype of the American dream and reveal its many enigmatic faces. Within the literature, we can see how various parts play against one another, how seemingly unassailable models fail to hold and entrenched oppositions crumble across overlapping fields of character. Authors who appear aligned with their fictive characters undercut them through their character function within the text, and those who seem entirely coextensive with their biographical characters exhibit remarkable variations in and across their work. As against the specific histories of given ethnic groups, this archetype becomes other to itself. From the incommensurability of literary, authorial, and social character, critiques of the American dream can emerge. One revelation of race character critique is this, that no matter the effort to recruit ethnic identity to a stable norm, literature exceeds such appropriations. Literature does not reproduce the archetype but presents us with characters that a careful reading can engage.

This book builds on an ongoing recalibration in ethnic studies of its methods and its archives. Appraisals of our analytical categories are not new. Koshy wrote "The Fiction of Asian American Literature" in 1996, in which she argued that "'Asian American' offers us a rubric we cannot not use."[24] This double negative has put pressure on Asian Americanists to redefine their object. It has cautioned against "failing endlessly to put into question" the "category 'Asian American,'" in Kandice Chuh's words, "rather than looking to complete" it.[25] The fields of Latinx and black literary studies have taken up a similar challenge. "What is it that labeling a work of literature *Latinx* allows us to know?" asks Ralph Rodriguez in *Latinx Literature Unbound* (2018), proposing a taxonomy based on literary genre instead.[26] In *What Was African American Literature?* (2011), Kenneth Warren offers another answer, dating the end of African American literature to the end of Jim Crow segregation.[27] Warren's controversial argument has provoked broad discussions of retrospective paradigms, considering what affective and political desires organize readings in the archives of ethnic literature.[28] Of late, Stephen Best asks that black studies relinquish the "recovery imperative" and the "melancholy historicism" that attends it and recourse to mourning instead, "the very kind of mourning... that affiliates with a waking or dawning rooted in repetitive divestment" and "throws into question the idea that the slave past provides a ready prism for understanding and apprehending the black political present."[29] This proposition takes its bearings from new models of reading (which Best has helped to develop), which question commonplaces of interpretation that consider "meaning to be hidden, repressed, deep, and in need of detection and disclosure by an interpreter" who is often positioned as "a hero who performs interpretive feats of demystification," as Best and Sharon Marcus put it.[30] There is a growing sense that habits of suspicion limit rather than enlarge the scope of critique, that critics would do well to adopt a "comportment that involves thinking *like* a work of art."[31]

In this context, character points to display rather than demystification. While Cixous's damning assessment appears to leave little to do but unmask character, there is much other work besides. Neither the appeal of particular characters nor the pervasiveness of the discourse of character can be explained by demystification. "What matters then, is not the demystification of race or character in return to the authenticity of the pre-cultural body, but rather an attention to how character can be the bearer of authenticity *because* its cultural work is recognized rather than disavowed," James Salazar argues.[32] Similarly, Deirdre Shauna Lynch notes that "the merely demystificatory critique of the psychologized character dismisses the plenitude it should explain" without accounting for the "excesses" of character over time.[33] As John Frow points out, the face (long thought to be "expressive of inner character") is actually "better understood as a semiotic instrument for the display of messages, and it is thus, in principle, akin to the mask, to which it is often opposed."[34] The mask of character presents as a display. Houston Baker Jr. theorizes the mask as "form" in the sense of "a symbolizing fluidity," a "designated space—presumably, that between traditionally formulated dichotomies such as self and other," to which I would add surface and depth.[35] While character prospects hidden interiors, it also draws to the surface. This solicitation is built into the concept itself, for character is known through its appearance. As Salazar writes, "an individual who was seen to 'have' character was thus one who reliably *was* just what he or she *appeared* to be."[36] So, we start rather than end with the "mask as mask" (to return to Cixous), a phrase that signifies not the death of character as a concept but its ongoing uses.[37]

Frantz Fanon's governing tropes in *Black Skin, White Masks* (1952) are instructive. He shows how racial subjects are particularly vulnerable to their own display. The visible appearance of "black skin" overdetermines the character of the colonial subject, as assumptions about personality are extrapolated from the outer impress of race. Thus, the colonial subject is "the eternal victim of an essence, of an *appearance* for which he is not responsible," attached to "the effigy of him," a "slave" to his "archetypes."[38] Upon this screen of blackness, Fanon superimposes the "white mask"—that paradox of colonialism that takes the form of violent, self-alienating desire. "The black man wants to be white."[39] What has been understood as a complex of individual dependency, Fanon traces to society—to French love songs and magazines, to the dictates of colonial schooling, and ultimately to the whole of the conscious and unconscious colonial enterprise. As a structural feature, the "white mask" cannot readily be removed. In *Black Skin, White Masks*, it appears everywhere and nowhere. It cannot be localized and objectified, and therefore stripped, because it is inseparable from colonialism itself. The "white mask" emblematizes psychosocial structures of alienation that cleave the colonial subject. It is the screen that mediates racial perception. Demystification is not enough, because the mask exists as a device that makes race happen in certain ways. We must develop new and inventive readings of its display, understand its overwhelming effect upon the colonial psyche, and consider what critiques might emerge out of such readings.

There is a role for art here, as for interpretation. "The *eye* is not merely a mirror, but a correcting mirror," Fanon writes, "I do not say the *eyes*, I say the *eye*, and there is no mystery about what the eye refers to; not to the crevice in the skull but to that very uniform light that wells out of the reds of Van Gogh, that glides through a concerto of Tschaikowsky, that fastens itself desperately to Schiller's *Ode to Joy*, that allows itself to be conveyed by the worm-ridden bawling of Césaire."[40] To this inventory of artistic revelation, we might add *Black Skin, White Masks* itself. "This book, it is hoped," Fanon writes, "will be a mirror with a progressive infrastructure, in which it will be possible to discern the Negro on the road to disalienation."[41] Thus music, painting, and writing are the "correcting mirror" of the colonial display. Literature features prominently throughout Fanon's work, for he turns to Aimé Césaire, David Diop, Chester Himes, Jacques Roumain, Léopold Senghor, and Richard Wright to formulate a rejoinder to colonial racism and existential critique. Two of his chapters are based in literary texts: "The Woman of Color and the White Man" and "The Man of Color and the White Woman," which read the autobiographical novels of Mayotte Capécia, *Je suis Martiniquaise* (1948), and René Maran, *Un Homme pareil aux autres* (1947), respectively. As the chapter titles suggest, Fanon approaches these two novels as case studies, tracing the psychopathologies of their protagonists to racism and colonial oppression.

Black Skin, White Masks does not, however, explore the literary specificity of these texts. Although Fanon shows some hesitation about formulating "a general law" of human behavior based on these novels, perceiving a "touch of fraud" in such a move, he does not hesitate to collapse Capécia and Maran with their fictive characterization, reading their writing as unmediated expressions of their lives.[42] Despite the fact that the novels are not always obliging (the "personality of the author does not emerge quite as easily as one might wish"), it is "clear to me," Fanon writes, "that Jean Veneuse, alias René Maran, is neither more nor less than a black abandonment-neurotic."[43] These chapters do not scrutinize the formal opacity of literature in relation to reality, or the distinctions between literary characters and the writers who imagine them. In the absence of this literary hermeneutic, literature merely confirms rather than enriches Fanon's "sociodiagnostic."[44]

Through race character critique, however, literature is vitalized. Recall the final scene from *Brown Girl, Brownstones*, where Marshall emblematizes the futility of Silla's embrace of upward mobility and the empty promise of the American dream ("a carved oak staircase led only to the night sky"). "The spring wind, moaning over the emptiness, shifted the dust and bore up the odor of crushed brick and plaster, the dank exhalations from the cellars," Marshall writes, "while the moonlight played over the heaped rubble in a fretwork of light and shadow, and glinted with cold iridescence on the splintered glass."[45] The contrast of "light" and "shadow" evokes the indeterminate brown space in which both mother and daughter are enmeshed as they negotiate the pivot of ethnicity and race. Strikingly, Marshall frames Silla's aspirations through the physical structure of the brownstone, which orients us away from denouncing individuals and toward social critique. The brownstones are anthropomorphized: they stand "perversely" and breathe "dank exhalations." Selina conflates the topped buildings with "the bodies of all the people she had ever known broken."[46] They are part of the wreckage: "all the familiar voices" and "the pieces" (of the people and the brownstones) "piled into this giant cairn of stone and silence."[47] In this remarkable moment, the "brick and plaster" of the brownstones becomes flesh and blood. These entwined figures emblematize Marshall's structural critique, as human forms—and their potentials—are shaped by and entombed within the architectural forms of the brownstones and the social forces that these forms represent.

Characterization is also contestation, as the readings in *Race Characters* show. The entombment of the characters within the brownstone buildings recalls the parade of grotesques in Villa's work, which interweaves human, animal, and natural forms, revealing the social tapestry of Filipino subjection. While Khalid dreams of empire, the hyperproduction of his character casts his ambition into profound question and exposes the madness of the American dream, unmaking even as it makes Khalid into the American "Superman." This "subtranscendental" movement is part of Saund's autobiography as well, for the representative American pivots between race and ethnicity even as he builds up his character as a bulwark against the precariousness of his assimilation, revealing the gaps and elisions in the American dream.[48] In Villarreal's writing as in Marshall's, the complex interplay of character fields and spaces tells a different story about racial betrayal and upward mobility: the characters who identify in these troubling ways are not so dissimilar from the characters to whom they are opposed, and these characters generate unexpected, though powerful, critiques of colonialism, racism, and patriarchy.

As a whole, these readings foreground social constraint and oppose discourses of individual or group pathology. Khalid's representation is exemplary, for his madness is not an individual indictment but a social indictment of the impossible identifications that the American dream demands of its ethnic subjects. Try as he might to cultivate his rarefied legibility, Villa, too, becomes grotesque in light of his work. In attempting to evade the particulars of identity, he grows ever more deeply entrapped by his own caricature. He is compelled to his negation of biography. What appears to be an eccentric choice, an abundance of character, a guarantee, even, of liberal democracy, is exposed as an inescapable feature of Filipino life at the heart of empire. Recall that Villarreal writes of Richard, "I can be a part of everything, he thought, because I am the only one capable of controlling my destiny."[49] The hinge between these two clauses is weak. Richard believes himself to be ubiquitous not because he can control his destiny but because he cannot. He wants to play all the parts because he has no part, or perhaps because he has just one overdetermined part. The archetype of the American dream is revealed in these readings to be a grotesque assemblage ordered by hegemony.

Character is key to this "sociodiagnostic," following Fanon. As the interplay of many parts, the dynamics of characterization give us the fullest window into them. By bridging formal characters with their sociohistorical contexts, we can see how power gets worked out imaginatively. The juridical history of immigration, the social history of nativism, the politics of the borderlands, the geopolitics of empire, and the racial history of the United States are not incidental but represent the imperative of necessity through which these characters are shaped. Character as person, as manifestation of a social problem and often as a ready scapegoat, is refigured as a formal set of social forces whose workings are often obscured by the character of character itself. Marshall's treatment of the brownstones illustrates this point, that the emplacement of persons (particularly personalities like Silla that appear invulnerable) within architectural sites shows how history acts upon them. So we find determinative social traces in figures who appear to be reactionary or misguided.

Race Characters underscores this agency of literature and of literary critique. Ethnic literature takes up the burden of ethnic character in that it constructs untenable postures, imagines attachments that are appealing but unsustainable, and voices impermissible desires. If character in its basic sense describes an engraving or a mark, the challenge for ethnic literature is to produce a new mark, to set a different type, to create an original impress of character upon the page. Even as this literature traffics in the archetype of the American dream, it intervenes in the appropriations of this archetype, transforming the ways in which ethnic subjects are marked out (as characters) by their difference. Close and situated readings reveal this intervention, not in the mode of a narrow formalism but by linking biography, history, and sociology to literature.

Reading in this way generates new perspectives upon ethnic writers who are themselves characters, with an excess of eccentric and nonconformist personality. Such writers are both easily appropriable and hard to assimilate. I am thinking in particular of Rihani and Saund, who are made to champion U.S. exceptionalism within public culture but who make for difficult reading in the mode of oppositional or resistance-based literary critique. Returning to the recursive mirror of character ("To read character is to read character is to read character is to read character," following Miller), the multiple and layered meanings of the concept help ground readings in the archive.[50] The burden of signification of character elucidates the burden of representation of ethnic literature, helping to map out the continuities and disjunctures between what might appear to be one and the same: namely, ethnic writers, the groups to which they belong, and the figures that people their work. Reading the character function of the author within literary texts, alongside the space that the author occupies as a character within the historical and biographical record, reshapes reality through ethnic literature, rather than merely indexing it. Ethnic writers move in and out of the orbit of the fictive characters they create. They are not coextensive, even with their own character. By tracking their movements, we can reevaluate their social currency, particularly as it sustains the American dream.

This work points to attentiveness, even and perhaps especially under the sign of loss. Once again, Selina's portrayal in the final scene of *Brown Girl, Brownstones* is illuminating. The brownstones, like Selina, have weathered their own birth-to-death cycle in the arc of the novel and are now a "giant cairn" where "all the people she had ever known" are entombed. Selina is gripped by the desire "to leave something" to commemorate their destruction, and she throws upon the wreckage one of the two bangles that she has worn from birth and that are linked to her Barbadian identity: "She pushed up her coat sleeve and stretched one until it passed over her wrist, and, without turning, hurled it high over her shoulder. The bangle rose behind her, a bit of silver against the moon, then curved swiftly downward and struck a stone."[51] Selina takes nothing, instead choosing to give something of herself. Decidedly, she does not look back as she flings the bangle in her wake.

As a parable for critique, this scene intrigues. Selina does not model demystification or recovery, for she neither condemns the houses nor tries to salvage them. Here is "self-divestiture" and "leave-taking," in the words of Best, art governed by the "logic of immurement" that replaces "holding with letting go."[52] Selina acknowledges the loss of the brownstones, as well as her own attachment to this loss, leaving behind the bangle that is a part of herself—a metonym for her character. She finds "freedom in attentiveness," following Best and Marcus, mourning the personal and communal sacrifices tied to the acquisition of the brownstones and the tenuous hold on upward mobility that the buildings represent.[53] Alongside Selina's perspective, Marshall's description lingers over the brownstones, over their "fretwork of light and shadow" and fretful attachment to the American dream. Having attended to this attachment, Selina and Marshall now turn elsewhere.

Notes

Introduction

1. Patterson, "Triumph and Tragedy of Dalip Saund," 10; Phil Tajitsu Nash, "Dalip Singh Saund; An Asian Indian American Pioneer," *Asianweek*, September 22, 1999, 11; Inder Singh, "A Century Later, Remembering Congressman Dalip S. Saund," *India-West*, September 24, 1999, A5; Connie Kang, "Indian Americans Will Honor a Hero," *Los Angeles Times*, January 12, 2002, B4; Andrew Chow, "Inspiration to 1.7 Million," *Asianweek*, January 23, 2002, 17; Cheng, *Dalip Singh Saund*.

2. Ela Dutt, "Nearly 50 Years After Saund, Bobby Jindal Makes History," *News India Times*, November 12, 2004, 6; Aziz Haniffa, "Congress Passes Resolution to Name Federal Building After Saund," *India Abroad*, February 11, 2005, A4; Aziz Haniffa, "Obama Calls First Indian-American Congressman a Trailblazer," *India Abroad*, May 18, 2012, A15. See also Ela Dutt, "Obama's Outreach," *News India Times*, May 18, 2012, 4.

3. In some cases, writings by these politicians are plainly billed in terms of the American dream. See, for instance, Rubio, *An American Son*, which proves "that the American Dream is still alive for those who pursue it," according to the dust jacket; Obama, *The Audacity of Hope*, subtitled *Thoughts on Reclaiming the American Dream*; and Powell, *My American Journey*, which describes Powell as "the embodiment of the American dream" on the back cover of the paperback edition.

4. "Dalip Singh Saund," History, Art & Archives, http://history.house.gov/Collection/Detail/29982.

5. Joe Wilson, a congressman from South Carolina, pushed to feature Saund's portrait on Capitol Hill after he received a copy of *Congressman from India* (Aziz Haniffa, "Dalip Singh Saund's Portrait to Be Unveiled in Congress," *India Abroad*, November 9, 2007, A1, A16).

6. See generally Rihbany, *America Save the Near East*. For more on Rihbany's experience at the Paris Peace Conference, see Rihbany, *Wise Men from the East and from the West*, 201–25.

7. Rihbany, *A Far Journey*, 285.

8. See, for instance, Rizk, *Syrian Yankee*.

9. Buaken, *I Have Lived with the American People*, 293.

10. Villa, *Footnote to Youth*, 303.

11. Kang, *East Goes West*, 87.

12. Mukerji, *Caste and Outcast*, 223.

13. Mukerji, *Caste and Outcast*, 45.

14. See Chu, *Assimilating Asians*, which reads *Jasmine* as "Mukherjee's attempt to imagine a female immigrant version of the American Horatio Alger myth" (130).

15. Mukherjee, *Jasmine*, 240, 241.

16. Mukherjee, "American Dreamer," https://www.motherjones.com/politics/1997/01/american-dreamer/. For a sense of Mukherjee's controversial figure, see Grewal, *Transnational America*, 65–74.

17. Clack, "Introduction," https://usa.usembassy.de/etexts/writers/homepage.htm.

18. Rodriguez, *Brown*, 26, 35.

19. For a sense of Rodriguez's controversial figure, see Alarcón, "Tropology of Hunger."

20. Lee, *Native Speaker*, 328.

21. Sánchez, "Whiteness Invisible," 78; see also Aranda, "Contradictory Impulses," 553–56. On the appeal of resistance-based analysis and its pitfalls in a comparative ethnic studies context, see Parikh, *An Ethics of Betrayal*, 25, 79–80.

22. Nguyen, *Race and Resistance*, 7, 11, 29, 4. On the tendency to romanticize Asian America as a counterhegemonic formation, see also Lye, "Introduction," 5–6. Jinqi Ling has shown how the poststructuralist bent of Asian American literary criticism has dichotomized "traditional" writings of the pre-1980 archive, deemed oppressive and totalizing, and "contemporary" post-1980 writings deemed antiessentialist and oppositional (Ling, *Narrating Nationalisms*, 5).

23. Batiste, *Darkening Mirrors*, 8. See also Blake, *Black Love, Black Hate*, 20–21; Quashie, *The Sovereignty of Quiet*, 3–9; and Tate, *Psychoanalysis and Black Novels*, 3–4.

24. See generally Fanon, *Black Skin, White Masks*; Anzaldúa, *Borderlands/La Frontera*; Baker Jr., *Modernism and the Harlem Renaissance*; and chapter 4 of Bhabha, *The Location of Culture*, 121–31.

25. See, for instance, Wu, *Sticky Rice*, which excavates an intraracial queer Asian American archive; Batiste, *Darkening Mirrors*, which investigates Depression-era black performance and its enactments of imperialist identification; Parikh, *An Ethics of Betrayal*, which reads acts of Asian American, Chicano, and Latino betrayal with a view to develop an ethics of otherness; Love, *Feeling Backward*, which rereads queer novels and their "politics of refusal"; Chen, *Double Agency*, which studies Asian American literature and performance culture and the transformative possibilities of impersonation; Ngai, *Ugly Feelings*, which reads canonically minor texts cataloging ugly feelings; Cheng, *The Melancholy of Race*, which reads African American and Asian American literature as the basis for a theory of racial melancholia; Muñoz, *Disidentifications*, which explores through queer of color performance the survival strategies of minority subjects in deidealizing public spheres; and Tate, *Psychoanalysis and Black Novels*, which offers a psychoanalytic reading of novels that do not fit a protest-based tradition of African American literature.

26. See, for instance, Lim, *Bilingual Brokers*, which explores "bilingual brokering" in Asian American and Latino literature; Chu, *Assimilating Asians*, which reads Asian American bildungsroman as both employing and destabilizing the Americanization story; and Ling, *Narrating Nationalisms*, which explores the many "negotiations" of Asian American literature between literary and social worlds. Lee, *The Semblance of Identity*, and Chiang, *The Cultural Capital of Asian American Studies*, displace the dyad of resistance and accommodation by reconfiguring Asian American studies as a field through the work of Georg Lukács and Pierre Bourdieu, respectively.

27. See, for instance, Ty, *Asianfail*, which counterposes Asian North American failure narratives to the model minority myth; Cutler, *Ends of Assimilation*, which explores the afterimage of assimilation in Chicano literature; Mani, *Aspiring to Home*, which reads South Asian middle-class literary and cultural production through the diasporic analytic of locality; Ninh, *Ingratitude*, which situates the model minority at the locus of the immigrant family through narratives of intergenerational conflict; Schlund-Vials, *Modeling Citizenship*, which reconfigures Jewish and Asian American literature by way of the naturalization trope; Bascara, *Model-Minority Imperialism*, which links critiques of the model minority myth to critiques of U.S. imperialism; and Hattori, "Model Minority Discourse," which unearths a strain of "model minority discourse" in Asian American cultural criticism.

28. Love, *Feeling Backward*, 58.

29. See generally Lye, "Racial Form." Scholarship that participates in this turn includes Tsou, *Unquiet Tropes*; Lee, *Modern Minority*; Jeon, *Racial Things, Racial Forms*; and Yao, *Foreign Accents*.

30. Chuh, *Imagine Otherwise*, 27.

31. Chuh, *Imagine Otherwise*, 9, 10.

32. Sohn, *Racial Asymmetries*, 4, 5.

33. Lee, *The Semblance of Identity*, 3–4, 11.

34. Jarrett, *Deans and Truants*, 14.

35. Rodriguez, *Latinx Literature Unbound*, 20, 3.

36. Chuh, *Imagine Otherwise*, 10, 9.

37. Rodriguez, *Hunger of Memory*, 3.

38. Rodriguez, *Hunger of Memory*, 51.

39. "Tio Taco," Urban Dictionary, https://www.urbandictionary.com/define.php?term=Tio%20Taco.

40. Rodriguez, *Hunger of Memory*, 174.

41. Morrison, *Playing in the Dark*, 39.

42. Morrison, *Playing in the Dark*, 46–47, 48.

43. Woloch, *The One vs. the Many*, 345n18.

44. Woloch, *The One vs. the Many*, 372n2.

45. Anjaria, *Realism in the Twentieth-Century Novel*, 24. See also Sohn, "Minor Character, Minority Orientalisms," which reads "minor character" as an opening onto "minority Orientalism," attending to cross-racial representation by way of the peripheral figure of the Asian American in Chicano literature.

46. *Oxford English Dictionary (OED) Online*, s.v. "character, n.," Oxford University Press, March 2020.

47. Miller, *Ariadne's Thread*, 55, 58.

48. Miller, *Ariadne's Thread*, 58.

49. Frow, *Character and Person*, 8.

50. Morrison, *Playing in the Dark*, 68.

51. Cixous, "The Character of 'Character,'" 384, 387. See also Knights, *How Many Children Had Lady Macbeth?* and Fuchs, *The Death of Character*.

52. Felski, "Introduction," ix, v.

53. Several periods in literary studies have been reinvigorated through the lens of character in the past two decades: postwar cultural studies (Román, *Race and Upward Mobility*); postwar American fiction (Konstantinou, *Cool Characters*); transatlantic romanticism (Manning, *Poetics of Character*); modernism (Moses, *Out of Character*); Indian realism (Anjaria, *Realism in the Twentieth-Century Novel*); Gilded Age (Salazar, *Bodies of Reform*); medieval and early modern (Fowler, *Literary Character*); nineteenth-century novel (Woloch, *The One vs. the Many*); and sentimental fiction and American realism (Boeckmann, *A Question of Character*). For accounts of the appeal and function of fictional minds shaped by cognitive poetics, see Vermeule, *Why Do We Care about Literary Characters?* On ethical and moral aspects of character narration, see Phelan, *Living to Tell about It*. On the elaboration of genre through minor character literature, see Rosen, *Minor Characters Have Their Day*. On the reinvention of literary criticism and theory as a discourse of character, see Harpham, *The Character of Criticism*, and Anderson, *The Way We Argue Now*.

54. Woloch, *The One vs. the Many*, 17.

55. Woloch, *The One vs. the Many*, 17, 18.

56. For their proposed resolution to these theoretical contradictions, see Woloch, *The One vs. the Many*, 14–17; and Lynch, *The Economy of Character*, 14–18. Similarly, Elizabeth Fowler attends to "larger conditions of characterization" in order to address the relation between textual figures and their extratextual effects (Fowler, *Literary Character*, 4).

57. Jarrett, *Deans and Truants*, 16.

58. Brody, *Punctuation*, 70, 64.

59. Miller, *Ariadne's Thread*, 32.

60. Marlowe, *Tamburlaine the Great*, 56.

61. *OED Online*, s.v. "character, n.," Oxford University Press, March 2020.

62. I rely upon the 1967 translation by Charles Lam Markmann throughout. The 2008 version by Richard Philcox translates the chapter title as "The Lived Experience of the Black Man" (Fanon, *Black Skin, White Masks*, trans. Philcox). The original title is "L'expérience vécue du Noir" (Fanon, *Peau noire masques blancs*).

63. Fanon, *Black Skin, White Masks*, trans. Markmann, 116.

64. Fanon, *Black Skin, White Masks*, trans. Markmann, 111, 112.

65. Fanon, *Black Skin, White Masks*, trans. Markmann, 116.

66. Fanon, *Black Skin, White Masks*, trans. Markmann, 116. See also Gordon, *What Fanon Said*, 49–50.

67. I have in mind here E. M. Forster's distinction between "round" and "flat" characters, the latter being "types" or "caricatures" who are "constructed around a single idea or quality" (Forster, *Aspects of the Novel*, 67).

68. *OED Online*, s.v. "character, n.," Oxford University Press, March 2020.

69. Ahmed, "Willful Parts," 232.

70. Ahmed, "Willful Parts," 232.

71. Omi and Winant, *Racial Formation in the United States*, 3rd ed., 110, 112.

72. Mercer, *Welcome to the Jungle*, 214.

73. Shohat and Stam, *Unthinking Eurocentrism*, 183.

74. Ahmad, *In Theory*, 98.

75. Chow, *The Protestant Ethnic*, 189, 187, 189.

76. Locke, "Spiritual Truancy," 81.

77. Tate, *Psychoanalysis and Black Novels*, 4. For more on Alain Locke's evolution during this period, and the evolution of Locke and Claude McKay's relationship, see chapter 38 of Stewart, *The New Negro*, 740–54.

78. Wong, "Autobiography as Guided Chinatown Tour?" 38, 42.

79. Wong, "Autobiography as Guided Chinatown Tour?" 37–38. See also Cheung, *Articulate Silences*, which addresses the "peculiar burden" of cultural authenticity (12–13).

80. See, respectively, Chiang, *The Cultural Capital of Asian American Studies*, 140; Wu, *Sticky Rice*, 17; Rodriguez, *Latinx Literature Unbound*, 15.

81. For a comprehensive overview of this history focused on the Gilded Age, see Salazar, *Bodies of Reform*, 9–17. See also Decker, *Made in America*, which picks up in some ways where Salazar leaves off and traces the links between character and the myth of self-made success (xiii–xxix).

82. Schlund-Vials, *Modeling Citizenship*, 6.

83. See, respectively, Gross, *What Blood Won't Tell*; Boeckmann, *A Question of Character*; Salazar, *Bodies of Reform*; and Decker, *Made in America*.

84. Salazar, *Bodies of Reform*, 161. On the performance of character as a key determinant of racial identity, see chapter 2 of Gross, *What Blood Won't Tell*, 48–72; for more on how the "pseudo-sciences of character" reshaped scientific racism, see chapter 1 of Boeckmann, *A Question of Character*, 11–62.

85. Rihbany, *A Far Journey*, 248.

86. Rihbany, *A Far Journey*, 248.

87. Miller, *Ariadne's Thread*, 94, 66, 75.

88. See generally, Román, *Race and Upward Mobility*; Frow, *Character and Person*; Salazar, *Bodies of Reform*; Woloch, *The One vs. the Many*; Fowler, *Literary Character*; and Lynch, *The Economy of Character*.

89. Forster, *Aspects of the Novel*, 44.

90. Williams, *Marxism and Literature*, 196. See Beardsley and Wimsatt, "The Intentional Fallacy"; Barthes, *Image, Music, Text*, 142–48; Foucault, *Aesthetics, Method, and Epistemology*, 205–22.

91. On the assumed identity of author, narrator, and protagonist ("autobiographical pact") as a contractual function of autobiography, see chapter 1 of Lejeune, *On Autobiography*, 3–30. See also Smith and Watson, *Reading Autobiography*, which provides a useful mapping of the multiple subject positions autobiography implicates (71–78).

92. Wong, "Autobiography as Guided Chinatown Tour?" 42–43.

93. Foucault, *Aesthetics, Method, and Epistemology*, 216.

94. Foucault, *Aesthetics, Method, and Epistemology*, 215.

95. Woloch, *The One vs. the Many*, 14.

96. Woloch, *The One vs. the Many*, 13.

97. Fowler, *Literary Character*, 91.

98. Aranda, "Contradictory Impulses," 555; Tate, *Psychoanalysis and Black Novels*, 5; Jarrett, *Deans and Truants*, 21; Sohn, *Racial Asymmetries*, 16. See also Lee, *The Semblance of Identity*, which relies on a similar understanding of character (although his

focus is not on character per se but the role of aesthetics broadly) when he tracks the "semblance character" of the "idealized critical subject" as divided against itself (141).

99. See, for instance, Lu, *Pamela*; Vuong, *On Earth We're Briefly Gorgeous*; Anzaldúa, *Borderlands / La Frontera*; Du Bois, *The Souls of Black Folk*; and Lorde, *Zami*.

100. For a useful overview of archetypal criticism, see Abrams and Harpham, *A Glossary of Literary Terms*, 13–15.

101. *OED Online*, s.v. "archetype, n.," Oxford University Press, March 2020.

102. For an overview of this history, see Gutierrez, "Ethnic Studies."

103. Koshy, "Morphing Race into Ethnicity," 188.

104. Jacobson, *Whiteness of a Different Color*, 12.

105. See chapter 4 of Boelhower, *Autobiographical Transactions in Modernist America*, 95–114.

106. See, respectively, Sollors, *Beyond Ethnicity*, and Ferraro, *Ethnic Passages*.

107. See generally Adams, *The Epic of America*. See also Adams, "'Rugged Individualism' Analyzed," *New York Times*, March 18, 1934, SM1, which offers his own excursus on the concept, tracing the legacy of American individualism and its hypocritical but indisputable significance for the New Deal moment.

108. For more on these permutations, see generally Churchwell, *Behold, America*; Cullen, *The American Dream*; and Decker, *Made in America*, particularly as it relates to discourse of character. On the development of American exceptionalism and its links to the American dream, see Pease, *The New American Exceptionalism*, 7–14, 209–11.

109. Berlant, *The Queen of America Goes to Washington City*, 14, 162.

110. See the introduction of Pease, *The New American Exceptionalism*, 1–39.

111. Churchwell, *Behold, America*, 171.

112. Adams, "'Rugged Individualism' Analyzed," *New York Times*, March 18, 1934, SM1, SM2.

113. Cullen, *The American Dream*, 188; Decker, *Made in America*, 53.

114. Adams, *The Epic of America*, 416.

115. For a summary of this critique, see chapter 1 of Omi and Winant, *Racial Formation in the United States*, 3rd ed., 21–51. On the importance of race for European immigration history, in disagreement with Michael Omi and Howard Winant's fundamental demarcation, see Jacobson, *Whiteness of a Different Color*, 7–9. See also Treitler, *The Ethnic Project*, which argues that "[a]ll ethnic groups are initially racialized" (10).

116. Ngai, *Impossible Subjects*, 8.

117. Omi and Winant, *Racial Formation in the United States*, 2nd ed., 48.

118. Treitler, *The Ethnic Project*, 5–7; see also chapters 4, 5, and 6, which explore "successful," "struggling," and "failed" ethnic projects, respectively (67–101, 103–36, 139–69).

119. San Juan Jr., "In Search of Filipino Writing," 229; Wong, "Immigrant Autobiography," 159; Nguyen, *Race and Resistance*, 21.

120. Lye, "Introduction," 2.

121. Koshy, "Morphing Race into Ethnicity," 181, 156, 189. See also Hsu, "'Will the Model Minority Please Identify Itself?'", which tracks how Asian Americans are interpellated as American ethnics in a transnational capitalist order shaped by the Asia-Pacific frontier.

122. Treitler, *The Ethnic Project*, 7, 8.

123. López, *White by Law*, 3, 36; Act to Establish an Uniform Rule of Naturalization, ch. 3, § 1, 1 Stat. 103, 103 (1790); Act to Amend the Naturalization Laws and to Punish Crimes Against the Same, and for Other Purposes, ch. 254, § 7, 16 Stat. 254, 256 (1870).

124. Brown, *The Literature of Immigration and Racial Formation*, xv.

125. Clark, *The Asian American Avant-Garde*, 15–16, 19.

126. Tolentino, *America's Experts*, xiii.

127. Cullen, *The American Dream*, 10.

128. Ahmed, "Willful Parts," 231.

129. Miller, *Ariadne's Thread*, 79.

130. Frow, *Character and Person*, x.

131. Frow, *Character and Person*, 6–7.

Chapter One

1. Allam, "Bush Mideast Speech Draws Cool Response," https://www.mcclatchydc.com/news/politics-government/white-house/article24474625.html.

2. "President Bush Discusses Importance of Freedom in the Middle East," White House Archives, http://georgewbush-whitehouse.archives.gov/news/releases/2008/01/20080113-1.html.

3. Rihani, *The Book of Khalid*, 95. Further references to this work are cited parenthetically in the text.

4. For more on these early critiques, see Hajjar, *The Politics and Poetics of Ameen Rihani*, 101–8.

5. Rihani, *Excerpts from Ar-Rihaniyat*, 11.

6. Rihani, *The Path of Vision*, 90.

7. Born into a Maronite family, Ameen Rihani was also excommunicated, and identified with a self-described mix of "Animistic, Adonistic, Monotheistic, Christian, Islamic, and Sufi" beliefs (Rihani, *Excerpts from Ar-Rihaniyat*, 5). For a detailed intellectual biography of Rihani, see chapter 1 of Hajjar, *The Politics and Poetics of Ameen Rihani*, 21–42.

8. Karpat, "The Ottoman Emigration to America," 185.

9. Naff, *Becoming American*, 34–36.

10. For more on Rihani's work on behalf of what he saw as the joint cause of war and Syrian independence, see Hajjar, *The Politics and Poetics of Ameen Rihani*, 60–62, 138–42. On Rihani's subsequent travels in the Arabian peninsula from 1922 to 1923, which he framed as a diplomatic mission between American and Arabia, see Shahid, "Amīn al-Rīhānī and King 'Abdul-'Azīz Ibn Sa'ūd."

11. Rihani, *Letters to Uncle Sam*, 12, 13. Further references to this work are cited parenthetically in the text.

12. See, generally, Funk and Sitka, *Ameen Rihani*.

13. Marshall and Keyes, "Forward [sic]," d. See also Hajjar, "Ameen Rihani's Humanist Vision of Arab Nationalism," which views *The Book of Khalid* as the "culmination" of Rihani's "concern with bridging East and West" and the "best expression of his aspirations to universal citizenship" (136); and Oueijan, "The Formation of a

Universal Self," which reads Khalid alongside Childe Harold, both driven by "laborious quests for universal identities" that "are, then, quests for universal love" (87).

14. "The 100th Anniversary of the First Arab-American Novel," Project Khalid, http://projectkhalid.org/.

15. "Tributes to Rihani," The Ameen Rihani Organization, http://www.ameenrihani.org/index.php?page=tributes; H. Res. 608, 112th Cong. (March 29, 2012).

16. Barakat, "Ameen Rihani," 102.

17. See for instance, Gana, "Introduction," which argues that the "task of Muslim and Arab American writing is nowadays to wager more programmatically on formal adventurousness in order to wrest the universal humanity of Muslim and Arab suffering from the grinding machinery of the war on terror" (1580).

18. For more on Orientalism's new modes, see Behdad and Williams, "Neo-Orientalism."

19. See, for instance, Todd Fine's suggestion that Khalid is a "dialectical synthesis" of emergent historical contradictions (Fine, "Introduction," 5). On the links between Rihani's intellectual training and his combinative agenda, see Schumann, "Ameen Rihani's *The Book of Khalid* in its Historical and Political Context," 278. For notes on Rihani's emergent "hybrid Arab Americanism," see Bawardi, "Reading *The Book of Khalid*," 306.

20. Jahshan, *100 Years of Selected Writings*, 2.

21. Hassan, "The Rise of Arab-American Literature," 273–74n19, 252.

22. Hassan, "The Rise of Arab-American Literature," 271.

23. For more on the intertextual range of *The Book of Khalid*, see Al Maleh, "The Literary Parentage of *The Book of Khalid*"; and Hassan, *Immigrant Narratives*, 49–53. Studies that pursue specific influences and connections include Choueiri, "The Romantic Discourse of Ameen Rihani and Percy Shelley"; Fine, "*The Book of Khalid* and *The Rise of David Levinsky*"; Dunnavent III, "Rihani, Emerson, and Thoreau"; Rodionov, "Leo Tolstoy and Ameen Rihani"; Oueijan, "The Formation of a Universal Self"; and Rihani, "Cross-Cultural Approaches to Reconciliation."

24. "A Syrian Poet in New York," *Sun*, July 11, 1911, 8.

25. For more on pack peddling, see Naff, *Becoming American*, 128–60.

26. For more on the Holy Land and the "Orient" as a repository of American desire, see, respectively, Obenzinger, *American Palestine*, xi–xiii; and McAlister, *Epic Encounters*, 20–29.

27. For a precursor to this figure in transcendentalist thought, see chapter 4 of Morse, *American Romanticism*, 119–68.

28. Bourne, "Trans-National America," 96, 93, 95.

29. Gualtieri, *Between Arab and White*, 23.

30. See generally Hanioğlu, "Turkism and the Young Turks." For more on Rihani's ambivalent relationship to the Young Turk Rebellion, see Hajjar, *The Politics and Poetics of Ameen Rihani*, 122–24.

31. Freud, *General Psychological Theory*, 175, 176.

32. Freud, *General Psychological Theory*, 165.

33. Freud, *Group Psychology and the Analysis of the Ego*, 41, 42.

34. Freud, *General Psychological Theory*, 175.

35. Freud, *General Psychological Theory*, 175–76.

36. Freud, *Group Psychology and the Analysis of the Ego*, 64.

37. Fanon, *Black Skin, White Masks*, trans. Markmann, 11. See also Cheng, *The Melancholy of Race*, which shows that the relationship of racialized subjects to the American dream is a melancholic relation.

38. Frow, *Character and Person*, 4.

39. "Asl al-hunud wal-'arab fi amirka," *al-Hilal* 9, no. 19 (1901): 536–41, quoted in Gualtieri, *Between Arab and White*, 23.

40. Dolores Courtemanche, "Worcester's Lebanese-Syrian Community: An Ethnic Success Story," *Sunday Telegram*, September 14, 1980, 8, quoted in Naff, *Becoming American*, 252; "Minister for Syrians," *New York Times*, September 15, 1895, 16.

41. Naff, *Becoming American*, 249–51, 108–9, 252–53, 117. Naff cites the 1929 census in what appears to be an error; see Majaj, "Arab-Americans and the Meanings of Race," which also provides a useful overview of the "liminality" of Arab American racialization (333n8).

42. Gualtieri, *Between Arab and White*, 77.

43. *In re Najour*, 174 F. 735, 735 (N.D. Ga. 1909).

44. *Dow v. United States*, 226 F. 145, 148 (4th Cir. 1915). For more on the Syrian campaign for naturalization, see Gualtieri, *Between Arab and White*, 52–77. See also Naff, *Becoming American*, 247–59, and Gross, *What Blood Won't Tell*, 231–36.

45. Gualtieri, *Between Arab and White*, 156. For more on the tenuous relationship of Syrians to whiteness, see Gualtieri, *Between Arab and White*, 110–12, 113–34.

46. For more on the balance of "scientific evidence" versus "common knowledge" in the racial prerequisite cases, see López, *White by Law*, 65–72.

47. Phelan, *Living to Tell about It*, 68, 69.

48. Compare this to the manuscript version of *Letters to Uncle Sam*, which reads in the past tense: "remained on deck" (Ameen Rihani, Ameen Fares Rihani Papers, Library of Congress, box 4).

49. Miller, *Ariadne's Thread*, 79.

50. For an illuminating treatment of Rihani's political evolution, see generally Hajjar, *The Politics and Poetics of Ameen Rihani*.

51. Rihani, *The White Way and the Desert*, 31.

52. Nash, "Rihani and Carlyle on Revolution and Modernity," 51. For more on these shifts in Rihani's perspective over the course of his career, see generally Nash, *The Arab Writer in English*.

Chapter Two

1. Villa, *Footnote to Youth*, 300, 301. Further references to this work are cited parenthetically in the text.

2. Rihani, *The Book of Khalid*, 95.

3. Villa, ,,A Composition,, *Literary Apprentice* (1953): 59–61, repr. Tabios, *The Anchored Angel*, 136. Subsequent citations to this work refer to the latter.

4. Tabios, *The Anchored Angel*, 134.

5. Tabios, *The Anchored Angel*, 135.

6. Francia, "Villanelles," 171; Villa, *Doveglion*, xxxv.

7. Lee, *The Semblance of Identity*, 149.

8. Chua, *Critical Villa*, 59.

9. Chua, *Critical Villa*, 108, 109.

10. Chua, *Critical Villa*, 110.

11. Yu, "'The Hand of a Chinese Master,'" 43–46.

12. For more on José Garcia Villa's influence in the postwar era, see Chua, *Critical Villa*, 17–22.

13. For more on the significance of Villa's career in the Philippines, see Chua, *Critical Villa*, 27–28; on the coverage of *Footnote to Youth* in particular, see Chua, "The Making of José Garcia Villa's *Footnote to Youth*," 20–21.

14. San Juan Jr., *Toward Filipino Self-Determination*, 86. See also San Juan Jr., *From Exile to Diaspora*, 187–89.

15. Chua, *Critical Villa*, 23. For an overview of Villa's critical reception in the Philippines, see Chua, *Critical Villa*, 7–25.

16. Chua, "The Making of José Garcia Villa's *Footnote to Youth*," 21; San Juan Jr., "José Garcia Villa," 8.

17. For an explanation of this technique, see "A Note on the Commas" at the beginning of Villa, *Volume Two*.

18. Yu, "'The Hand of a Chinese Master,'" 54.

19. For a brief overview of Villa's initial popularity and subsequent obscurity in the United States, see San Juan Jr., "In Search of Filipino Writing," 228–31. On Villa's absence from the archives of Asian American literature and literary criticism prior to the 1990s, see Yu, "'The Hand of a Chinese Master,'" 57n5. For a useful gloss on this absence, see Cruz, "José Garcia Villa's Collection of 'Others,'" 18.

20. Ponce, "José Garcia Villa's Modernism," 577; Ponce, *Beyond the Nation*, 60.

21. San Juan Jr., *The Philippine Temptation*, 171.

22. San Juan Jr., "José Garcia Villa," 13, 14.

23. San Juan Jr., *From Exile to Diaspora*, 86, 87.

24. On Villa's challenge to colonial binaries, see Chua, *Critical Villa*, 26–28. On Villa's capitulation to and resistance against Orientalism, see Yu, "'The Hand of a Chinese Master,'" and Chua, "The Making of José Garcia Villa's *Footnote to Youth*." On Villa's queer modernism, see Cruz, "José Garcia Villa's Collection of 'Others'"; Ponce, "José Garcia Villa's Modernism"; and Ponce, *Beyond the Nation*, 58–88. On the challenge Villa poses for Asian American studies, see Lee, *The Semblance of Identity*, 145–52.

25. Hagedorn, "The Time of Mirrors," xv.

26. Yuson, "Villaesque," 226.

27. Cruz, "José Garcia Villa's Collection of 'Others,'" 17.

28. San Juan Jr., *The Philippine Temptation*, 171; San Juan Jr., *From Exile to Diaspora*, 72; San Juan Jr., "José Garcia Villa," 3.

29. Tabios, "Editor's Afterword," 150; Yu, "'The Hand of a Chinese Master,'" 41; Cruz, "José Garcia Villa's Collection of 'Others,'" 35; Ponce, "José Garcia Villa's Modernism," 592.

30. For a clarifying analysis of the "forgotten" Filipino, see Isaac, *American Tropics*, 5–8; see also Campomanes, "The New Empire's Forgetful and Forgotten Citizens," 147.

31. See also San Juan Jr., "José Garcia Villa," which reads this photograph as a "palimpsest or tell-tale rebus in itself" (7).

32. Chua, *Critical Villa*, 51, 79.

33. Chua, *Critical Villa*, 78, 139.

34. Letter to Sherwood Anderson, February 7, 1930, Sherwood Anderson Papers, Newberry Library, quoted in Chua, "The Making of José Garcia Villa's *Footnote to Youth*," 6.

35. Chua, *Critical Villa*, 301.

36. Chua, *Critical Villa*, 71–72.

37. Ruskin, *Modern Painters Volume the Third*, 131–32; see also chapter 3 of Ruskin, *The Stones of Venice Volume the Third*, which develops this distinction (112–65).

38. Anderson, *Winesburg, Ohio*, 23.

39. Anderson, *Winesburg, Ohio*, 23, 24.

40. Anderson, *Winesburg, Ohio*, 24, 21.

41. Anderson, *Winesburg, Ohio*, 34, 36, 103.

42. Anderson, *Winesburg, Ohio*, 28.

43. Ruskin, *The Stones of Venice Volume the Third*, 136.

44. Villa, *Volume Two*, 5; Villa, *Doveglion*, 227; see, for instance, Villa, *Have Come, Am Here*, which addresses Pablo Picasso and Marc Chagall in poem 40 (58); and Villa, *Selected Poems and New*, which addresses Piet Mondrian and Ben Nicholson in poems 202 and 204 (198, 200–201).

45. Ruskin, *Modern Painters Volume the Third*, 132.

46. *Oxford English Dictionary (OED) Online*, s.v. "grotesque, n. and adj.," Oxford University Press, March 2020; Dictionary.com, s.v. "grotesque," 2012, https://www.dictionary.com/browse/grotesque?s=t.

47. Ponce, "José Garcia Villa's Modernism," 595; Cruz, "José Garcia Villa's Collection of 'Others,'" 14. Similarly, for Dunne, *The New Book of the Grotesques*, Sherwood Anderson's grotesques index not individual deviance but modern subjection and alienation.

48. Cassuto, *The Inhuman Race*, 6.

49. Edwards and Graulund, *Grotesque*, 1–15.

50. *OED Online*, s.v. "character, n.," Oxford University Press, March 2020.

51. Forster, *Aspects of the Novel*, 67, 73.

52. Cassuto, *The Inhuman Race*, xiii.

53. Abdur-Rahman, "Black Grotesquerie," 683, 684.

54. Fanon, *Black Skin, White Masks*, trans. Markmann, 116.

55. Joaquin, "Excerpt from Viva Villa," 160.

56. Miller, *Benevolent Assimilation*, 134. On primitivist and Orientalist contours of Filipino subjection, see generally Brody, *Visualizing American Empire*; Okihiro, "Colonial Vision, Racial Visibility"; and chapters 1, 2, and 3 of Rafael, *White Love and Other Events in Filipino History*, 19–102.

57. Espiritu, *Filipino American Lives*, 46.

58. Buaken, *I Have Lived with the American People*, 71.

59. Ngai, *Impossible Subjects*, 109–16.

60. Frow, *Character and Person*, 4, 290, x.

61. Abdur-Rahman, "Black Grotesquerie," 690.

62. Frow, *Character and Person*, x.

63. Chua, "The Making of José Garcia Villa's *Footnote to Youth*," 8, 25n12.

64. For more on their liminal status as "*noncitizen nonaliens*," see Isaac, *American Tropics*, 7.

65. For an overview of the Filipino struggle for citizenship, see Melendy, *Asians in America*, 46–57. On the broader transformation of Filipinos "from colonial subjects to undesirable aliens," see chapter 3 of Ngai, *Impossible Subjects*, 96–126.

66. Alegre and Fernandez, *Writers & Their Milieu*, 308.

67. Chua, "The Making of José Garcia Villa's *Footnote to Youth*," 10.

68. Chua, "The Making of José Garcia Villa's *Footnote to Youth*," 7–12.

69. For more on the framing and reception of *Footnote to Youth*, see Chua, "The Making of José Garcia Villa's *Footnote to Youth*," 13–14, 16–17.

70. See generally Yu, "'The Hand of a Chinese Master,'" which charts the rise and fall of Villa's status as a modernist poet through the Orientalist framework of American modernism.

71. Glendinning, *Edith Sitwell*, 246.

72. Chua, "The Making of José Garcia Villa's *Footnote to Youth*," 14–16.

73. See, for instance, Villa's notes mapping out "The Evolution of Good Writing" from "expansiveness" through "economy" to "essence" (Villa, *Doveglion*, 242).

74. Francia, "Villanelles," 174.

75. For more on the unpublished work, see Villa, *Doveglion*, 240–41.

76. Chua, *Critical Villa*, 103.

77. Chua, *Critical Villa*, 105.

78. Chua, *Critical Villa*, 134, 130, 132, 133, 136.

79. Francia, "Villanelles," 175.

80. Joaquin, "Excerpt from Viva Villa," 156.

81. Mangahas, "Doveglion in New York," iii.

82. San Juan Jr., *The Philippine Temptation*, 197–98.

Chapter Three

1. Villarreal, *Pocho*, 165. Further references to this work are cited parenthetically in the text.

2. "Cannery Worker Writes Novel About Mexican-Americans' Life," *San Jose Evening News*, October 28, 1959, 12, quoted in Jiménez and Villarreal, "An Interview," 66.

3. Sedore, "'Everything I Wrote Was Truth,'" 79–80.

4. Cantú, "Villarreal, José Antonio," 421.

5. Saldívar, *Chicano Narrative*, 61.

6. Madrid-Barela, "Pochos," 52.

7. Madrid-Barela, "Pochos," 52.

8. Madrid-Barela, "Pochos," 51.
9. Madrid-Barela, "Pochos," 61.
10. Madrid-Barela, "Pochos," 57.
11. For a brief biography of José Antonio Villarreal, see Vallejos, "José Antonio Villarreal."
12. Sedore, "'Everything I Wrote Was Truth,'" 82, 78.
13. Saldívar, *Chicano Narrative*, 65.
14. See, respectively, Paredes, "Mexican American Literature," 806; Saldívar, *The Dialectics of Our America*, 110; Sánchez, "Ideological Discourses," 115; and Hernández-G., "Villarreal's *Clemente Chacon*," 35. For a useful recapitulation of the critical controversy around *Pocho*, see Sedore, "Solace in Solitude," 240–41.
15. Sedore, "Everything I Wrote Was Truth," 81.
16. Sedore, "Everything I Wrote Was Truth," 79.
17. Sedore, "Everything I Wrote Was Truth," 83.
18. Sedore, "Everything I Wrote Was Truth," 80.
19. Saldívar, *The Dialectics of Our America*, 111–12.
20. Saldívar, *The Dialectics of Our America*, 110, 111.
21. Ruiz, "On the Meaning of Pocho," ix, viii.
22. Ruiz, "On the Meaning of Pocho," viii, xii.
23. Jiménez and Villarreal, "An Interview," 67; Sedore, "Solace in Solitude," 245.
24. Saldívar, *Chicano Narrative*, 65, 67.
25. Hidalgo, "'He Was a Sissy, Really,'" 9, 31, 31–32.
26. Cutler, *Ends of Assimilation*, 55, 34.
27. Jiménez and Villarreal, "An Interview," 70.
28. Fowler, *Literary Character*, 2, 16.
29. Woloch, *The One vs. the Many*, 13, 12.
30. Woloch, *The One vs. the Many*, 18, 36.
31. Sae-Saue, "Aztlán's Asians," 566. See also Sae-Saue, *Southwest Asia*, which develops this argument.
32. Cutler, *Ends of Assimilation*, 227n23.
33. Woloch, *The One vs. the Many*, 6.
34. Forster, *Aspects of the Novel*, 67.
35. Forster, *Aspects of the Novel*, 67, 76.
36. Rodríguez, "Richard Rodriguez Reconsidered," 403. See also Parikh, *An Ethics of Betrayal*, which positions Richard Rodriguez among "failed men in the diaspora" who represent "a feminizing identification that hastens their entrance into America"; Villarreal's *Pocho* features briefly in this analysis as a precursor to contemporary cultural politics (81, 65).
37. See, for instance, Paz, *The Labyrinth of Solitude*, which infamously characterizes La Malinche as "the *Chingada*" ("passive," "abject," "an inert heap of bones, blood and dust," "Nothingness") (85, 86). For critiques of Octavio Paz and reconceptualizations of this figure from Chicana feminist perspectives, see generally Del Castillo, "Malintzin Tenépal"; Moraga, *Loving in the War Years*; Alarcón, "Traddutora, Traditora"; and Cutler, "Malinche's Legacy."
38. Rodriguez, *Hunger of Memory*, 29.

39. Rodriguez, *Hunger of Memory*, 29.

40. Torres and Rodriguez, "'I Don't Think I Exist,'" 173.

41. Hidalgo, "'He Was a Sissy, Really,'" 14, 15.

42. Hidalgo, "'He Was a Sissy, Really,'" 29; Muñoz, *Disidentifications*, 11.

43. See also Hidalgo, "'He Was a Sissy, Really,'" 17–18.

44. Saldívar, *Chicano Narrative*, 61, 71.

45. For more on René's challenge to El Macho and his function as Richard's "textual progenitor," see Hidalgo, "'He Was a Sissy, Really,'" 19, 16.

46. For more on the ambivalence of this scene, see Hidalgo, "'He Was a Sissy, Really,'" 20.

47. For more on this history, see Gutiérrez, *Walls and Mirrors*, 121–26.

48. Ngai, *Impossible Subjects*, 129. For a useful overview of traditional Chicano historiography that locates 1848 as a point of origination, and also reframes this perspective in terms of the subsequent capitalist reorganization of the U.S. Southwest, see generally González and Fernandez, *A Century of Chicano History*.

49. Benton-Cohen, *Borderline Americans*, 7; Gutiérrez, *Walls and Mirrors*, 13.

50. *In re Rodriguez*, 81 F. 337, 337–38 (W.D. Tex. 1897).

51. *In re Rodriguez*, 81 F. 337, 349 (W.D. Tex. 1897).

52. *LULAC News* 1, no. 9 (April 1932): 7, quoted in Ngai, *Impossible Subjects*, 74; Weise, "Mexican Nationalisms, Southern Racisms," 752–53; Gutiérrez, *Walls and Mirrors*, 35.

53. "Cannery Worker Writes Novel About Mexican-Americans' Life," *San Jose Evening News*, October 28, 1959, 12, quoted in Jiménez and Villarreal, "An Interview," 67.

54. Jiménez and Villarreal, "An Interview," 69–70.

55. Jiménez and Villarreal, "An Interview," 71.

56. Sedore, "Everything I Wrote Was Truth," 80.

57. San Juan Jr., *The Philippine Temptation*, 198.

58. Jiménez and Villarreal, "An Interview," 68–69.

Chapter Four

1. Saund, *Congressman from India*, 108, 152. Further references to this work are cited parenthetically in the text.

2. Lawrence E. Davies, "A Nisei of Hawaii Aims for Senate," *New York Times*, March 17, 1959, 20. See also Robert Trumbull, "Senator Fong Shows Asia the Twain Meet," *New York Times*, October 11, 1959, 20, which notes that Senator Hiram Fong, about to embark on his own international tour, is "following in the path of another member of Congress with an Asian heritage, Representative Dalip Singh Saund."

3. "Tanganyikans," *Chicago Daily Tribune*, October 12, 1961, 16.

4. See "Political Participation," *India-West*, November 3, 1978, 4; Bina Murarka, "Political Activism in Yuba City," *India-West*, February 6, 1981, 8; Bina Murarka, "Need for a Strong Asian Indian Lobby Stressed at AIA Banquet," *India-West*, July 16, 1982, 1; Jeff Burbank, "3rd Asian Indian Convention Meets to Plan, Promote Political Involvement," *India-West*, June 1, 1984, 21; Kanak Dutta, "Participation the Key to Politics," *India-West*, July 20, 1984, 4; Vora Batuk, "NFIA Convention A Fruitful Meeting on Key Issues," *India Abroad*, September 7, 1990, 22; Angela Anand, "Migration of Asian

Indians to the United States," *Asianweek*, June 18, 1993, 1. On the broader Asian American context, see Stanley Karnow, "Apathetic Asian Americans?" *Washington Post*, November 29, 1992, C1; Connie Kang, "Asian Americans Slow to Flex Their Political Muscle," *Los Angeles Times*, October 31, 1996, 1.

5. See, for instance, Connie Kang, "Indo-Americans Begin to Flex Political Muscle," *Los Angeles Times*, October 30, 2000, A3; "One of Our Own," *News India Times*, May 11, 2001, 51; Jyotirmoy Datta, "'Congressman from India,' Saund's Life, Told in His Own Words," *News India Times*, January 9, 2004, 27.

6. Ela Dutt, "Nearly 50 Years after Saund, Bobby Jindal Makes History," *News India Times*, November 12, 2004, 6. For coverage of these various campaigns, see Vincent Digirolamo, "Immigrant Chases American Dream in Run for Congress," *India-West*, November 15, 1985, 14; Ela Dutt, "Indians Seek Legislative Posts," *India Abroad*, January 5, 1990, 29; Richard Springer, "Barve Elected to Md. House of Delegates," *India-West*, November 16, 1990, 1; Richard Springer, "California Candidates," *India-West*, June 12, 1992, 1; Sonali Vepa, "New Growth, New Challenges," *India Currents Magazine*, October 31, 1992, M19; "Dhillon, Matthews Confident of Winning Campaigns," *India-West*, August 20, 1993, 64; Richard Springer, "Congressional Candidate Campaigns in Bay Area," *India-West*, February 25, 1994, 35; Michel Potts, "Mathews, Horn Debate Taxes, Jobs—and India," *India-West*, September 2, 1994, A1; Edmund Newton, "Advanced Lesson in Poly Sci," *Los Angeles Times*, October 20, 1994, 8; Ela Dutt, "1st Asian in Congress, Saund Provided Strength to Indian-Americans in Politics," *News India Times*, November 12, 2004, 8; George Joseph, "Hansen Clarke is the First Bangladeshi American Elected to Congress," *India Abroad*, November 12, 2010, A19.

7. Samuel G. Freedman, "Pride and Concern Follow Success of Indian-Americans," *New York Times*, July 10, 2010, A17.

8. Helweg and Helweg, *An Immigrant Success Story*, 53; for an overview of census figures during this period, see Melendy, *Asians in America*, 202–6, 225–26.

9. For more on this early South Asian immigration, see generally Shankar and Balgopal, "South Asian Immigrants before 1950"; Jensen, *Passage from India*; and Hess, "The Asian Indian Immigrants in the United States."

10. Leonard, *Making Ethnic Choices*, 30.

11. Jensen, *Passage from India*, 101.

12. Scheffauer, "The Tide of Turbans," 616.

13. For more on Indian farmers in the Imperial Valley and California, see Leonard, *The South Asian Americans*, 43–45; Jensen, *Passage from India*, 36–39.

14. Jensen, *Passage from India*, 280; Helweg and Helweg, *An Immigrant Success Story*, 56; Leonard, *Making Ethnic Choices*, 165–66; Varma, *Indian Immigrants in USA*, 148, 189, 295, 296.

15. Shukla, *India Abroad*, 141–49; Srikanth, *The World Next Door*, 238–42.

16. Shukla, "Indian Diasporic Autobiography," 107, 108.

17. See Boelhower, "The Brave New World of Immigrant Autobiography"; and Wong, "Immigrant Autobiography," which critiques this Eurocentric modeling of immigrant autobiography in terms of progressive Americanization by reading Chinese American autobiographies that deviate from this teleology.

18. Shukla, "Indian Diasporic Autobiography," 117.

19. Susman, *Culture as History*, 275.

20. Salazar, *Bodies of Reform*, 2, 11.

21. Decker, *Made in America*, xxix.

22. Lee, *Orientals*, 145.

23. On the model minority myth and its links to the racial policy debates of the 1960s, see Lee, *Orientals*, 150–51.

24. Cheng, *The Melancholy of Race*, 23.

25. Cheng, *The Melancholy of Race*, 23.

26. Koshy, "Morphing Race into Ethnicity," 189.

27. Koshy, "Morphing Race into Ethnicity," 156, 194.

28. Koshy, "Morphing Race into Ethnicity," 187.

29. For more on character as a residual formation, following Raymond Williams, see Decker, *Made in America*, xxv; Salazar, *Bodies of Reform*, 12.

30. Salazar, *Bodies of Reform*, 161.

31. Decker, *Made in America*, xv, 54.

32. Baker Jr., *Modernism and the Harlem Renaissance*, 31.

33. For more on the naturalization movement, see Jensen, *Passage from India*, 276–79; and chapter 19 of Melendy, *Asians in America*, 216–25. For a contextualization of this campaign in terms of a broader "India Lobby" in the United States, see Gould, *Sikhs, Swamis, Students, and Spies*. On Dalip Singh Saund's role in the campaign, see Gould, *Sikhs, Swamis, Students, and Spies*, 315; Varma, *Indian Immigrants in USA*, 220n50, 292, 295, 302, 304; and Puri, *Ghadar Movement*, 271. Note that there is a discrepancy about the exact name of Saund's organization, which Saund gives in his autobiography as the "India Association of America," Gould refers to as the "Indian National Congress Association," and Puri refers to as the "India Congress Association" (CFI, 73).

34. For more on this "deus ex machina intervention," see Srikanth, *The World Next Door*, 239.

35. For more on this history of political surveillance, see Jensen, *Passage from India*, 163–93, 243–44, 273–75.

36. Howarth, "Some Principles of Autobiography," 368.

37. See chapter 1 of Lejeune, *On Autobiography*, 3–30.

38. Phelan, *Living to Tell about It*, 214.

39. For more on this Asian man–white woman dyad, which has "typically emplotted the cultural impossibility and sexual danger of incorporating Asians into the nation," see Koshy, *Sexual Naturalization*, 22.

40. Jensen, *Passage from India*, 44–45.

41. "Will Be Bumper Anti-Brownie Parade," *Vancouver Daily Province*, September 7, 1907, 1; *Bellingham Herald*, September 30, 1907, 1, quoted in Jensen, *Passage from India*, 141.

42. William Smith, "Interview with Dr. E. E. Chandler," August 23, 1924, Survey of Race Relations Records, Hoover Institution Archives, box 25, image 513, https://purl.stanford.edu/wd698xd8121.

43. Koshy, "Category Crisis," 294.

44. López, *White by Law*, 48.

45. For more on this Aryan race theory, see Koshy, "Category Crisis," 295–98.

46. For more on the relationship of South Asians to whiteness, see generally Koshy, "South Asians and the Complex Interstices of Whiteness."

47. For more on the links between diasporic and colonial subjection, and the convergence of the Ghadar movement with anticolonialism and radicalism in the United States, see Jensen, *Passage from India*, 172, 19–20, 176.

48. Shukla, *India Abroad*, 146.

49. "Hot Race Looms in 29th District," *Los Angeles Times*, May 6, 1956, 45. See also "Mrs. Odlum, Saund Wage Hot Race," *Washington Post and Times Herald*, October 14, 1956, A12.

50. For more on how women entrepreneurs transformed traditional narratives of self making, see chapters 2 and 6 of Decker, *Made in America*, 15–30, 102–26.

51. "Mrs. Odlum, Saund Wage Hot Race," *Washington Post and Times Herald*, October 14, 1956, A12; "Congress Only Goal of Jacqueline Cochran," *Los Angeles Times*, October 25, 1956, A14. Jacqueline Cochran was not in fact orphaned, although she often claimed to be, and this erroneous biographical detail was popularized during the election; see Rich, *Jackie Cochran*, 3.

52. "A Sikh in Congress," *New York Times*, November 10, 1956, 13. See also Gladwin Hill, "Colorful Contest Shaping on Coast," *New York Times*, December 27, 1955, 17, which claims that "Judge Saund had it easier" than Cochran.

53. Gladwin Hill, "Colorful Contest Shaping on Coast," *New York Times*, December 27, 1955, 17; "Hot Race Looms in 29th District," *Los Angeles Times*, May 6, 1956, 45; "Mrs. Odlum, Saund Wage Hot Race," *Washington Post and Times Herald*, October 14, 1956, A12; Gladwin Hill, "California Leans Strongly to G.O.P.," *New York Times*, October 21, 1956, 68; "1st Native of India Wins House Seat," *Daily Defender*, November 8, 1956, 4; "Upset Victor," *Chicago Daily Tribune*, November 8, 1956, 11; "A Sikh in Congress," *New York Times*, November 10, 1956, 13.

54. "Advice to the Sikh Congressman," *Chicago Daily Tribune*, November 14, 1956, 16.

55. "Advice to the Sikh Congressman," *Chicago Daily Tribune*, November 14, 1956, 16.

56. Seymour Korman, "Adlai Top Man after Victory in California," *Chicago Daily Tribune*, June 7, 1956, 16.

57. "Upset Victor," *Chicago Daily Tribune*, November 8, 1956, 11.

58. On Saund's alleged ties to Ghadar being "a serious campaign issue, since Gadar had become linked with international communism," see Juergensmeyer, "The Gadar Syndrome," 54. See also Sood, "Expatriate Nationalism and Ethnic Radicalism," which points out that the California legislature investigated the Ghadar Party in 1953 (284).

59. Prashad, *The Darker Nations*, 95.

60. Nehru, *The Discovery of India*, 251.

61. King Jr., "My Trip to the Land of Gandhi," 24.

62. Dudziak, *Cold War Civil Rights*, 58.

63. Dudziak, *Cold War Civil Rights*, 58.

64. Douglas, *Strange Lands and Friendly People*, 296.

65. "Success Story," *Los Angeles Times*, November 9, 1956, 22.

66. "Winner on Coast Plans India Trip," *New York Times*, November 10, 1956, 13. See also Warren Unna, "'Not Mad,' Saund Says of Broadcast," *Washington Post and Times Herald*, November 28, 1956, B7, in which Saund reports that the United States

Information Agency (USIA) filmed Saund before and after the election and was already showing the footage in India.

67. "Rep. Saund to Tell His Story to India," *Washington Post and Times Herald*, November 9, 1956, C4; "A Sikh in Congress," *New York Times*, November 10, 1956, 13; "Winner on Coast Plans India Trip," *New York Times*, November 10, 1956, 13.

68. Drew Pearson, "Saund in Trouble Over Vote Funds," *Washington Post and Times Herald*, November 22, 1956, A3. For more on the controversy, see also Warren Unna, "'Not Mad,' Saund Says of Broadcast," *Washington Post and Times Herald*, November 28, 1956, B7.

69. "Congressman Born in India to Visit There," *Los Angeles Times*, May 3, 1957, 7; "Saund Visits Japan," *New York Times*, October 31, 1957, 8.

70. "Rep. Saund Sells U.S. On His Tour," *New York Times*, December 18, 1957, 19; "U.S. Should Sell Itself to Asians, Says Saund," *Los Angeles Times*, December 23, 1957, 6.

71. See "Race Relations Leaders Given Urban Awards," *Los Angeles Times*, February 8, 1958, B8; "Store Honors 'Unofficial Ambassadors'; 6 Individuals and 4 Companies Named," *New York Times*, May 8, 1958, 22.

72. J. Campbell Bruce, "Our Congressman from India," *Reader's Digest*, September 1, 1959, 175.

73. J. Campbell Bruce, "Our Congressman from India," *Reader's Digest*, September 1, 1959, 176. See also Peggy Streit and Pierre Streit, "The Man Who Came to Zindpur," *Christian Herald*, December 1959, repr. *Reader's Digest*, in which Saund solicits the stereotypical figure of the indolent Indian villager to learn from the example of his own character.

74. J. Campbell Bruce, "Our Congressman from India," *Reader's Digest*, September 1, 1959, 180.

75. See also Saund's 1960 campaign handbill, which catalogs the national and international media coverage of his "life story" ("He Works—He Cares," 1960, Collection of the U.S. House of Representatives).

76. "East is West," *Washington Post and Times Herald*, November 10, 1956, A8.

77. For more on how the geopolitics of the Cold War consolidated American exceptionalism, see Pease, *The New American Exceptionalism*, 7–13.

78. Shukla, "Indian Diasporic Autobiography," 118.

79. *United States v. Bhagat Singh Thind*, 261 U.S. 204, 209 (1923).

80. Gould, *Sikhs, Swamis, Students, and Spies*, 401, 415.

81. Gould, *Sikhs, Swamis, Students, and Spies*, 399–415.

82. For more on Saund's pan-Asian identifications, see Shukla, *India Abroad*, 144.

83. For more on the impact of these laws on Indian immigrants in California, see Leonard, *Making Ethnic Choices*, 55–57; Jensen, *Passage from India*, 265–67.

84. For more on antimiscegenation and immigration laws in this period, see Koshy, *Sexual Naturalization*, 3–12.

85. Patterson, "Triumph and Tragedy of Dalip Saund," 11; this oral history supplements the autobiography and reveals the extent of the prejudice the family faced in Imperial Valley.

86. For an overview of the distribution of these families, see Leonard, *Making Ethnic Choices*, 66–73.

87. Shankar and Balgopal, "South Asian Immigrants before 1950," 75–76; Leonard, *Making Ethnic Choices*, 209.

88. Karen Isaksen Leonard suggests that Saund "seemed only loosely connected to the Sikh networks" because he was of the Ramgarhia or artisan caste (Leonard, *Making Ethnic Choices*, 276–77n10). Ramgarhias were a minority among the "Jat-dominated migration to the Pacific Rim" (Dusenbery, "Introduction," 6).

89. For more on how the Little Rock crisis shaped global perceptions of the United States during this period, see chapter 4 of Dudziak, *Cold War Civil Rights*, 115–51.

90. Washington, *Up from Slavery*, 128.

91. See the transcript of Saund's impassioned address to the House of Representatives, which employs a similar rhetoric of sportsmanship ("Speech Delivered on Floor of the House of Representatives," June 14, 1957, Collection of the U.S. House of Representatives).

92. Salazar, *Bodies of Reform*, 13, 14.

Chapter Five

1. Marshall, *Brown Girl, Brownstones*, 70. Further references to this work are cited parenthetically in the text.

2. Saunders, "Woman Overboard," 210.

3. Waters, *Black Identities*, 34–35.

4. For a detailed analysis of economic, environmental, and political push factors contributing to emigration from this region, see chapter 1 of James, *Holding Aloft the Banner of Ethiopia*, 9–49.

5. Kasinitz, *Caribbean New York*, 25.

6. Locke, *The New Negro*, 345.

7. Waters, *Black Identities*, 98.

8. Marshall, *Triangular Road*, 86–87.

9. See generally Model, *West Indian Immigrants*.

10. For more on the European immigrant analogy and its extension in the post–World War II period to African Americans and other non-European groups, see Omi and Winant, *Racial Formation in the United States*, 3rd ed., 7, 29–37.

11. Koshy, "Morphing Race into Ethnicity," 156. See also Treitler, *The Ethnic Project*, which situates Afro-Caribbean immigrants as part of an "ongoing and struggling" ethnic project (135).

12. For a useful recapitulation of these debates, see Shaw-Taylor, "The Intersection of Assimilation," 3–6; and Waters, *Black Identities*, 95–103. For more on the selectivity thesis, see generally Model, *West Indian Immigrants*; and James, "Explaining Afro-Caribbean Social Mobility in the United States." For more on "conservative socialization" of immigrants, see Vickerman, *Crosscurrents*, 5.

13. Marshall, *Reena and Other Stories*, 12, 7, 12.

14. Marshall, *Triangular Road*, 89, 93.

15. Pettis and Marshall, "A *MELUS* Interview," 121.

16. Bröck, "Talk as a Form of Action," 199; Baer and Marshall, "Holding onto the Vision," 25.

17. Russell, "Interview," 15.

18. Dance, "An Interview," 7.

19. Marshall, *Triangular Road*, 6. See also Hall and Hathaway, "The Art and Politics of Paule Marshall," in which Marshall traces her politicization to her mother and her friends and their commitment to Garveyism (182).

20. Marshall, *Triangular Road*, 11.

21. Glazer and Moynihan, *Beyond the Melting Pot*, 35.

22. For a critique of their work, see Waters, *Black Identities*, 96–97.

23. Waters, *Black Identities*, 370.

24. Raffel, "Paule Marshall on Race and Memory," 191.

25. Sutton and Chaney, *Caribbean Life in New York City*, 85; see also Mortimer and Bryce-Laporte, *Female Immigrants to the United States*, for both collections include Marshall's essay and are peppered by references to *Brown Girl, Brownstones* and other fiction by Marshall.

26. De Veaux, "In Celebration of Our Triumph," 44; Baer and Marshall, "Holding onto the Vision," 25; Elam, "To Be in the World," 101.

27. Raffel, "Paule Marshall on Race and Memory," 191.

28. Marshall, *Triangular Road*, 69, 90.

29. Román, *Race and Upward Mobility*, 63.

30. Bryce-Laporte, "The New Immigration," xxvi; Marshall, "Black Immigrant Women," 3.

31. Washington, "Afterword," 313; Harris, "No Outlet for the Blues," 57; and Bröck, "Transcending the 'Loophole of Retreat,'" 86.

32. See, for instance, Brown, "The Rhythms of Power," 162; Byerman, "Gender, Culture, and Identity," 146; Japtok, "Paule Marshall's *Brown Girl, Brownstones*," 314; Meehan, "Caribbean versus United States Racial Categories," 269.

33. Hathaway, *Caribbean Waves*, 90.

34. For more on the "natural internal dynamic that draws the parts closer together" in a chiasmus, see Lanham, *A Handlist of Rhetorical Terms*, 33.

35. Miller, *Ariadne's Thread*, 79. See also Frow, *Character and Person*, which points out that character is "shadowed by a daemonic other" (x).

36. For more on Marcus Garvey's version of self making, and its links to Booker T. Washington, see Decker, *Made in America*, 53–62.

37. On the various historical figures that inspire Miss Thompson, see Marshall, *Reena and Other Stories*, 95; Graulich, Sisco, and Marshall, "Meditations on Language and the Self," 286–87; and Russell, "Interview," 15.

38. Román, *Race and Upward Mobility*, 31, 50.

39. Jones, "'The Sea Ain' Got No Back Door,'" 599.

40. Fanon, *Black Skin, White Masks*, trans. Markmann, 116.

41. Miller, *Ariadne's Thread*, 79.

42. On the fragment and its translations, see *Fragments*, trans. Haxton, 83, 97.

43. *Oxford English Dictionary (OED) Online*, s.v. "character, n.," Oxford University Press, March 2020.

44. Fanon, *Black Skin, White Masks*, trans. Markmann, 112, 116.

45. Fanon, *Black Skin, White Masks*, trans. Markmann, 11.

46. On architectural imagery as a unifying principle for the novel, see Benston, "Architectural Imagery and Unity." See also Bröck, "Transcending the 'Loophole of Retreat,'" which explores Marshall's careful placement of female characters as a way to create space for them; Dickerson, "The Property of Being," which reads the brownstones as a "property of being" that enables the Barbadian immigrants to secure their own progress and that of the community; and chapter 1 of Román, *Race and Upward Mobility*, which understands the house as a metaphor for "mortgaged status" that shapes middle-class minority subjectivity from one generation to the next (29–65).

47. Washington, "Afterword," 312.

48. Hathaway, *Caribbean Waves*, 90.

49. For a more detailed account of how characters are described in architectural terms, and how Marshall's language is generally architectural, see Benston, "Architectural Imagery and Unity," 68–69.

50. Dickerson, "The Property of Being," 3.

51. Woloch, *The One vs. the Many*, 13; see also Woloch's discussion of how the boardinghouse in Honoré de Balzac's *Le Père Goriot* (1835) reconfigures its characters (247).

52. See, for instance, Hathaway, *Caribbean Waves*, 91, 97; Dickerson, "The Property of Being," 3.

53. For more on this Chicago school thesis, see Omi and Winant, *Racial Formation in the United States*, 3rd ed., 26–29.

54. For more on the incongruence of this black immigration with the flow of white succession, see Román, *Race and Upward Mobility*, 43–44; Saunders, "Woman Overboard," 211; Hathaway, *Caribbean Waves*, 91–92; Jones, "'The Sea Ain' Got No Back Door,'" 598–99.

55. For a clarifying mapping of this succession of inhabitants, and shifts in the spatialization of brownstone Brooklyn from terms of ethnicity to those of race, see Osman, *The Invention of Brownstone Brooklyn*, 40–44.

56. For more on the "brownstone fronts," see Osman, *The Invention of Brownstone Brooklyn*, 27.

57. See also Jones, "'The Sea Ain' Got No Back Door,'" which frames *Brown Girl, Brownstones* as a departure from the major figures and tropes of black theorization in the United States (from the Du Boisian veil to Ellisonian invisibility), concerning "not so much the American idea of 'blackness' as a wider notion of 'brownness' which is diasporic in scope" (597).

58. Rodriguez, *Hunger of Memory*, 3.

59. Frow, *Character and Person*, 4, 6, 7.

60. Hall and Hathaway, "The Art and Politics of Paule Marshall," 188.

61. Román, *Race and Upward Mobility*, 51.

Conclusion

1. Marshall, *Brown Girl, Brownstones*, 309.
2. Marshall, *Brown Girl, Brownstones*, 310.
3. Marshall, *Brown Girl, Brownstones*, 310.

4. For more on the Manhattanization of Brooklyn and its eventual failure as a cultural project, see Osman, *The Invention of Brownstone Brooklyn*, 76–78.

5. Marshall, *Brown Girl, Brownstones*, 309.

6. Chua, *Critical Villa*, 183.

7. Rihani, *The Book of Khalid*, 248.

8. See generally Koshy, "Morphing Race into Ethnicity."

9. Berlant, *The Queen of America Goes to Washington City*, 207.

10. Roy, *An Ordinary Person's Guide to Empire*, 88.

11. Roy, *An Ordinary Person's Guide to Empire*, 87–88.

12. Trivedi, "Where Do Turkeys Go After Being Pardoned by the President?," http://news.nationalgeographic.com/news/2001/11/1120_TVprezturkeys.html.

13. Merica, "Where Pardoned Turkeys Go to Die," CNN, November 27, 2013, http://www.cnn.com/2013/11/27/politics/pardoned-turkeys/.

14. Rodriguez, *Hunger of Memory*, 3; see chapter 4 of Rodriguez, Brown, 81–101.

15. Miller, *Ariadne's Thread*, 46.

16. See generally Cixous, "The Character of 'Character.'"

17. Chow, *The Age of the World Target*, 84–85.

18. Shih, "Comparative Racialization," 1350.

19. Chow, *The Age of the World Target*, 76.

20. Chow, *The Age of the World Target*, 76.

21. Chow, *The Age of the World Target*, 81.

22. Chow, *The Age of the World Target*, 81.

23. Chow, *The Age of the World Target*, 89.

24. Koshy, "The Fiction of Asian American Literature," 342. See also Lye, "Introduction," which continues to ask why Asian American identity is necessary on strategic grounds, cautioning "against an ever-greater dependency on biological notions of identity to help us order our epistemological projects" (4).

25. Chuh, *Imagine Otherwise*, 10.

26. Rodriguez, *Latinx Literature Unbound*, 2.

27. See generally Warren, *What Was African American Literature?*

28. See, for instance, Carpio et al., "What Was African American Literature?"; Gruesz, "What Was Latino Literature?"; Michaels, Edwards, and Nielsen, "What Was African American Literature?," https://lareviewofbooks.org/article/what-was-african-american-literature-a-symposium/.

29. Best, *None Like Us*, 13, 15, 78, 79.

30. Best and Marcus, "Surface Reading," 1, 13. See also Love, "Close but not Deep," which proposes to read "close but not deep" by adapting methods from social sciences that emphasize observation (375).

31. Best, *None Like Us*, 62. On the "hermeneutics of suspicion," see generally Felski, *The Limits of Critique*.

32. Salazar, "A Good Judge of Character?" 331.

33. Lynch, *The Economy of Character*, 16. See also Culler, *Structuralist Poetics*, which points to a tendency in structuralism to treat the concept of character, and its particular appeal to readers, "as an ideological prejudice rather than to study it as a fact of reading" (230).

34. Frow, *Character and Person*, x.
35. Baker Jr., *Modernism and the Harlem Renaissance*, 17.
36. Salazar, *Bodies of Reform*, 19.
37. Cixous, "The Character of 'Character,'" 387.
38. Fanon, *Black Skin, White Masks*, trans. Markmann, 35.
39. Fanon, *Black Skin, White Masks*, trans. Markmann, 9.
40. Fanon, *Black Skin, White Masks*, trans. Markmann, 202.
41. Fanon, *Black Skin, White Masks*, trans. Markmann, 184.
42. Fanon, *Black Skin, White Masks*, trans. Markmann, 81.
43. Fanon, *Black Skin, White Masks*, trans. Markmann, 64, 79.
44. Fanon, *Black Skin, White Masks*, trans. Markmann, 11.
45. Marshall, *Brown Girl, Brownstones*, 309–10.
46. Marshall, *Brown Girl, Brownstones*, 310.
47. Marshall, *Brown Girl, Brownstones*, 310.
48. Rihani, *The Book of Khalid*, 96.
49. Villarreal, *Pocho*, 152.
50. Miller, *Ariadne's Thread*, 58.
51. Marshall, *Brown Girl, Brownstones*, 310.
52. Best, *None Like Us*, 23, 54, 65.
53. Best and Marcus, "Surface Reading," 13.

Bibliography

Archival Collections

Stanford, CA
    Survey of Race Relations Records, Hoover Institution Archives
Washington, DC
    Ameen Fares Rihani Papers, Library of Congress
    Dalip Singh Saund, Collection of the U.S. House of Representatives

Government Documents and Reports

Act to Establish an Uniform Rule of Naturalization, ch. 3, 1 Stat. 103 (1790)
Act to Amend the Naturalization Laws and to Punish Crimes Against the Same, and for Other Purposes, ch. 254, 16 Stat. 254 (1870)
H. Res. 608, 112th Cong. (March 29, 2012)

Legal Cases

Dow v. United States, 226 F. 145 (4th Cir. 1915)
In re Najour, 174 F. 735 (N.D. Ga. 1909)
In re Rodriguez, 81 F. 337 (W.D. Tex. 1897)
United States v. Bhagat Singh Thind, 261 U.S. 204 (1923)

Newspapers

Asianweek
Chicago Daily Tribune
Daily Defender (Chicago, IL)
India Abroad
India Currents Magazine
India-West
Los Angeles Times
New York Times
News India Times
Reader's Digest
Sun (New York, NY)
Vancouver Daily Province
Washington Post
Washington Post and Times Herald

Books, Articles, Dissertations, and Theses

Abdur-Rahman, Aliyyah I. "Black Grotesquerie." *American Literary History* 29, no. 4 (2017): 682–703.
Abrams, M. H., and Geoffrey Galt Harpham. *A Glossary of Literary Terms*. Boston: Thomson Wadsworth, 2005.
Adams, James Truslow. *The Epic of America*. Boston: Little, Brown, and Company, 1931.

Ahmad, Aijaz. *In Theory: Classes, Nations, Literatures*. London: Verso, 1992.

Ahmed, Sara. "Willful Parts: Problem Characters or the Problem of Character." *New Literary History* 42, no. 2 (2011): 231–53.

Alarcón, Norma. "Traddutora, Traditora: A Paradigmatic Figure of Chicana Feminism." *Cultural Critique* 13 (1989): 57–87.

———. "Tropology of Hunger: The 'Miseducation' of Richard Rodríguez." In *The Ethnic Canon: Histories, Institutions, and Interventions*, edited by David Palumbo-Liu, 140–52. Minneapolis: University of Minnesota Press, 1995.

Alegre, Edilberto N., and Doreen G. Fernandez. *Writers & Their Milieu: An Oral History of First Generation Writers in English*. Manila, Philippines: De La Salle University Press, 1984.

Al Maleh, Layla. "The Literary Parentage of *The Book of Khalid*: A Genealogical Study." In *The Book of Khalid: A Critical Edition*, edited by Todd Fine, 311–37. Syracuse, NY: Syracuse University Press, 2016.

Anderson, Amanda. *The Way We Argue Now: A Study in the Cultures of Theory*. Princeton, NJ: Princeton University Press, 2006.

Anderson, Sherwood. *Winesburg, Ohio*. New York: Penguin Books, 1960.

Anjaria, Ulka. *Realism in the Twentieth-Century Novel: Colonial Difference and Literary Form*. Cambridge: Cambridge University Press, 2012.

Anzaldúa, Gloria. *Borderlands / La Frontera*. San Francisco: Aunt Lute Books, 2007.

Aranda, José F., Jr. "Contradictory Impulses: María Amparo Ruiz de Burton, Resistance Theory, and the Politics of Chicano/a Studies." *American Literature* 70, no. 3 (1998): 551–79.

Baer, Sylvia, and Paule Marshall. "Holding onto the Vision: Sylvia Baer Interviews Paule Marshall." *The Women's Review of Books* 8, no. 10/11 (1991): 24–25.

Baker, Houston A., Jr. *Modernism and the Harlem Renaissance*. Chicago: University of Chicago Press, 1987.

Barakat, Halim. "Ameen Rihani: Daring to Dream." In *Ameen Rihani: Bridging East and West*, edited by Nathan C. Funk and Betty J. Sitka, 102–9. Lanham, MD: University Press of America, 2004.

Barthes, Roland. *Image, Music, Text*. New York: Hill and Wang, 1977.

Bascara, Victor. *Model-Minority Imperialism*. Minneapolis: University of Minnesota Press, 2006.

Batiste, Stephanie Leigh. *Darkening Mirrors: Imperial Representation in Depression-Era African American Performance*. Durham, NC: Duke University Press, 2011.

Bawardi, Hani J. "Reading *The Book of Khalid*, Writing Arab American History." In *The Book of Khalid: A Critical Edition*, edited by Todd Fine, 287–307. Syracuse, NY: Syracuse University Press, 2016.

Beardsley, Monroe C., and W. K. Wimsatt. "The Intentional Fallacy." In *The Verbal Icon: Studies in the Meaning of Poetry*, 3–18. Lexington, KY: University of Kentucky Press, 1954.

Behdad, Ali, and Juliet Williams. "Neo-Orientalism." In *Globalizing American Studies*, edited by Brian T. Edwards and Dilip Parameshwar Gaonkar, 283–99. Chicago: University of Chicago Press, 2010.

Benston, Kimberly W. "Architectural Imagery and Unity in Paule Marshall's *Brown Girl, Brownstones*." *Negro American Literature Forum* 9, no. 3 (1975): 67–70.

Benton-Cohen, Katherine. *Borderline Americans: Racial Division and Labor War in the Arizona Borderlands*. Cambridge, MA: Harvard University Press, 2009.

Berlant, Lauren. *The Queen of America Goes to Washington City: Essays on Sex and Citizenship*. Durham, NC: Duke University Press, 1997.

Best, Stephen, and Sharon Marcus. "Surface Reading: An Introduction." *Representations* 108, no. 1 (2009): 1–21.

Best, Stephen. *None Like Us: Blackness, Belonging, Aesthetic Life*. Durham, NC: Duke University Press, 2018.

Bhabha, Homi. *The Location of Culture*. London: Routledge, 1994.

Blake, Felice D. *Black Love, Black Hate: Intimate Antagonisms in African American Literature*. Columbus: Ohio State University Press, 2018.

Boeckmann, Catherine Ann. *A Question of Character: Scientific Racism and the Genres of American Fiction, 1892–1912*. Tuscaloosa: University of Alabama Press, 2000.

Boelhower, William. "The Brave New World of Immigrant Autobiography." *MELUS* 9, no. 2 (1982): 5–23.

———. *Autobiographical Transactions in Modernist America: The Immigrant, The Architect, The Artist, The Citizen*. Udine, Italy: Del Bianco Editore, 1992.

Bourne, Randolph S. "Trans-National America." *Atlantic Monthly* 118, no. 1 (1916): 86–97.

Bröck, Sabine. "Talk as a Form of Action: An Interview with Paule Marshall, September 1982." In *History and Tradition in Afro-American Culture*, edited by Günter H. Lenz, 194–206. Frankfurt: Campus Verlag, 1982.

———. "Transcending the 'Loophole of Retreat': Paule Marshall's Placing of Female Generations." *Callaloo*, no. 30 (1987): 79–90.

Brody, David. *Visualizing American Empire: Orientalism and Imperialism in the Philippines*. Chicago: University of Chicago Press, 2010.

Brody, Jennifer DeVere. *Punctuation: Art, Politics, and Play*. Durham, NC: Duke University Press, 2008.

Brown, Linda Joyce. *The Literature of Immigration and Racial Formation: Becoming White, Becoming Other, Becoming American in the Late Progressive Era*. New York: Routledge, 2004.

Brown, Lloyd W. "The Rhythms of Power in Paule Marshall's Fiction." *NOVEL* 7, no. 2 (1974): 159–67.

Bryce-Laporte, Roy S. "The New Immigration: The Female Majority." In *Female Immigrants to the United States: Caribbean, Latin American, and African Experiences*, edited by Dolores M. Mortimer and Roy S. Bryce-Laporte, vii–xxxix. Washington, DC: Smithsonian Institution, 1981.

Buaken, Manuel. *I Have Lived with the American People*. Caldwell, ID: Caxton Printers, 1948.

Byerman, Keith E. "Gender, Culture, and Identity in Paule Marshall's *Brown Girl, Brownstones*." In *Redefining Autobiography in Twentieth-Century Women's*

Fiction, edited by Janice Morgan and Colette T. Hall, 135–47. New York: Garland Publishing, 1991.

Campomanes, Oscar V. "The New Empire's Forgetful and Forgotten Citizens: Unrepresentability and Unassimilability in Filipino-American Postcolonialities." *Critical Mass* 2, no. 2 (1995): 145–200.

Cantú, Roberto. "Villarreal, José Antonio." In *Chicano Literature: A Reference Guide*, edited by Julio A. Martínez and Francisco A. Lomelí, 420–32. Westport, CT: Greenwood, 1985.

Carpio, Glenda R., Gene Andrew Jarrett, R. Baxter Miller, Sonnet Retman, Marlon B. Ross, Xiomara Santamarina, Rafia Zafar, and Kenneth W. Warren. "What Was African American Literature?" *PMLA* 128, no. 2 (2013): 386–408.

Cassuto, Leonard. *The Inhuman Race: The Racial Grotesque in American Literature and Culture*. New York: Columbia University Press, 1997.

Chen, Tina. *Double Agency: Acts of Impersonation in Asian American Literature and Culture*. Stanford, CA: Stanford University Press, 2005.

Cheng, Anne Anlin. *The Melancholy of Race: Psychoanalysis, Assimilation, and Hidden Grief*. Oxford: Oxford University Press, 2001.

Cheung, King-Kok. *Articulate Silences: Hisaye Yamamoto, Maxine Hong Kingston, Joy Kogawa*. Ithaca, NY: Cornell University Press, 1993.

Chiang, Mark. *The Cultural Capital of Asian American Studies: Autonomy and Representation in the University*. New York: New York University Press, 2009.

Choueiri, Youssef M. "The Romantic Discourse of Ameen Rihani and Percy Shelley." In *The Book of Khalid: A Critical Edition*, edited by Todd Fine, 338–66. Syracuse, NY: Syracuse University Press, 2016.

Chow, Rey. *The Protestant Ethnic and the Spirit of Capitalism*. New York: Columbia University Press, 2002.

———. *The Age of the World Target: Self-Referentiality in War, Theory, and Comparative Work*. Durham, NC: Duke University Press, 2006.

Chu, Patricia P. *Assimilating Asians: Gendered Strategies of Authorship in Asian America*. Durham, NC: Duke University Press, 2000.

Chua, Jonathan. *Critical Villa: Essays in Literary Criticism by José Garcia Villa*. Quezon City: Ateneo de Manila University Press, 2002.

———. "The Making of José Garcia Villa's Footnote to Youth." *Kritika Kultura* 21/11 (2013): 1–31.

Chuh, Kandice. *Imagine Otherwise: On Asian Americanist Critique*. Durham, NC: Duke University, 2003.

Churchwell, Sarah. *Behold, America: A History of America First and the American Dream*. London: Bloomsbury Publishing, 2018.

Cixous, Hélène. "The Character of 'Character.'" Translated by Keith Cohen. *New Literary History* 5, no. 2 (1974): 383–402.

Clark, Audrey Wu. *The Asian American Avant-Garde: Universalist Aspirations in Modernist Literature and Art*. Philadelphia: Temple University Press, 2015.

Cruz, Denise. "José Garcia Villa's Collection of 'Others': Irreconcilabilities of a Queer Transpacific Modernism." *Modern Fiction Studies* 55, no. 1 (2009): 11–41.

Cullen, Jim. *The American Dream: A Short History of an Idea that Shaped a Nation.* Oxford: Oxford University Press, 2003.

Culler, Jonathan. *Structuralist Poetics: Structuralism, Linguistics and the Study of Literature.* Ithaca, NY: Cornell University Press, 1975.

Cutler, John Alba. *Ends of Assimilation: The Formation of Chicano Literature.* Oxford: Oxford University Press, 2015.

Cutter, Martha J. "Malinche's Legacy: Translation, Betrayal, and Interlingualism in Chicano/a Literature." *Arizona Quarterly* 66, no. 1 (2010): 1–33.

Dance, Daryl Cumber. "An Interview with Paule Marshall." *The Southern Review* 28, no. 1 (1992): 1–20.

Decker, Jeffrey Louis. *Made in America: Self-Styled Success from Horatio Alger to Oprah Winfrey.* Minneapolis: University of Minnesota Press, 1997.

Del Castillo, Adelaida R. "Malintzin Tenépal: A Preliminary Look into a New Perspective." In *Essays on La Mujer*, edited by Rosaura Sánchez, 124–49. Los Angeles: University of California, Los Angeles, 1977.

De Veaux, Alexis. "In Celebration of Our Triumph." *Essence* 10, no. 1 (1979). Reprinted in *Conversations with Paule Marshall*, edited by James C. Hall and Heather Hathaway, 40–53. Jackson: University Press of Mississippi, 2010.

Dickerson, Vanessa D. "The Property of Being in Paule Marshall's *Brown Girl, Brownstones.*" *Obsidian II: Black Literature in Review* 6, no. 3 (1991): 1–13.

Douglas, William O. *Strange Lands and Friendly People.* New York: Harper & Brothers, 1951.

Du Bois, W. E. B. *The Souls of Black Folk.* Oxford: Oxford University Press, 2007.

Dudziak, Mary L. *Cold War Civil Rights: Race and the Image of American Democracy.* Princeton, NJ: Princeton University Press, 2000.

Dunnavent, Walter Edward, III. "Rihani, Emerson, and Thoreau." In *Ameen Rihani: Bridging East and West*, edited by Nathan C. Funk and Betty J. Sitka, 55–71. Lanham, MD: University Press of America, 2004.

Dunne, Robert. *The New Book of the Grotesques: Contemporary Approaches to Sherwood Anderson's Early Fiction.* Kent, OH: Kent State University Press, 2005.

Dusenbery, Verne A. "Introduction: A Century of Sikhs beyond Punjab." In *The Sikh Diaspora: Migration and the Experience beyond Punjab*, edited by Gerald N. Barrier and Verne A. Dusenbery, 1–28. Delhi: Chanakya, 1989.

Edwards, Justin D., and Rune Graulund. *Grotesque.* London: Routledge, 2013.

Elam, Anjela. "To Be in the World: An Interview with Paule Marshall." *New Letters* 62, no. 4 (1996): 96–105.

Espiritu, Yen Le. *Filipino American Lives.* Philadelphia: Temple University Press, 1995.

Fanon, Frantz. *Black Skin, White Masks.* Translated by Charles Lam Markmann. New York: Grove Press, 1967.

———. *Peau noire masques blancs.* Paris: Éditions du Seuil, 1971.

———. *Black Skin, White Masks.* Translated by Richard Philcox. New York: Grove Press, 2008.

Felski, Rita. "Introduction." *New Literary History* 42 (2011): v–ix.

———. *The Limits of Critique.* Chicago: University of Chicago Press, 2015.

Ferraro, Thomas J. *Ethnic Passages: Literary Immigrants in Twentieth-Century America*. Chicago: University of Chicago Press, 1993.

Fine, Todd. "Introduction." In *The Book of Khalid: A Critical Edition*, edited by Todd Fine, 1–14. Syracuse, NY: Syracuse University Press, 2016.

———. "*The Book of Khalid* and *The Rise of David Levinsky*: Comparison as Ethnic Bildungsroman." In *The Book of Khalid: A Critical Edition*, edited by Todd Fine, 433–48. Syracuse, NY: Syracuse University Press, 2016.

Forster, E. M. *Aspects of the Novel*. San Diego: Harvest Book, 1927.

Foucault, Michel. *Aesthetics, Method, and Epistemology*. New York: The New Press, 1994.

Fowler, Elizabeth. *Literary Character: The Human Figure in Early English Writing*. Ithaca, NY: Cornell University Press, 2003.

Francia, Luis. "Villanelles." In *The Anchored Angel: Selected Writings by José Garcia Villa*, edited by Eileen Tabios, 166–75. New York: Kaya, 1999.

Freud, Sigmund. *Group Psychology and the Analysis of the Ego*. Translated by James Strachey. New York: W. W. Norton, 1959.

———. *General Psychological Theory: Papers on Metapsychology*. New York: Touchstone, 1997.

Frow, John. *Character and Person*. Oxford: Oxford University Press, 2014.

Fuchs, Elinor. *The Death of Character: Perspectives on Theater after Modernism*. Bloomington: Indiana University Press, 1996.

Funk, Nathan C., and Betty J. Sitka, eds. *Ameen Rihani: Bridging East and West*. Lanham, MD: University Press of America, 2004.

Gana, Nouri. "Introduction: Race, Islam, and the Task of Muslim and Arab American Writing." *PMLA* 123, no. 5 (2008): 1573–80.

Glazer, Nathan, and Daniel Patrick Moynihan. *Beyond the Melting Pot: The Negroes, Puerto Ricans, Jews, Italians, and Irish of New York City*. Cambridge, MA: M.I.T. Press & Harvard University Press, 1963.

Glendinning, Victoria. *Edith Sitwell: A Unicorn Among Lions*. New York: Alfred A. Knopf, 1981.

González, Gilbert G., and Raul A. Fernandez. *A Century of Chicano History: Empire, Nations, and Migration*. New York: Routledge, 2003.

Gordon, Lewis R. *What Fanon Said: A Philosophical Introduction to His Life and Thought*. New York: Fordham University Press, 2015.

Gould, Harold A. *Sikhs, Swamis, Students, and Spies: The India Lobby in the United States, 1900–1946*. New Delhi: Sage, 2006.

Graulich, Melody, Lisa Sisco, and Paule Marshall. "Meditations on Language and the Self: A Conversation with Paule Marshall." *NWSA Journal* 4, no. 3 (1992): 282–302.

Grewal, Inderpal. *Transnational America: Feminisms, Diasporas, Neoliberalisms*. Durham, NC: Duke University Press, 2005.

Gross, Ariela J. *What Blood Won't Tell: A History of Race on Trial in America*. Cambridge, MA: Harvard University Press, 2008.

Gruesz, Kirsten Silva. "What Was Latino Literature?" *PMLA* 127, no. 2 (2012): 335–41.

Gualtieri, Sarah M. A. *Between Arab and White: Race and Ethnicity in the Early Syrian American Diaspora*. Berkeley: University of California Press, 2009.

Gutiérrez, David G. *Walls and Mirrors: Mexican Americans, Mexican Immigrants, and the Politics of Ethnicity.* Berkeley: University of California Press, 1995.

Gutierrez, Ramon A. "Ethnic Studies: Its Evolution in American Colleges and Universities." In *Multiculturalism: A Critical Reader,* edited by David Theo Goldberg, 157–67. Cambridge, MA: Blackwell, 1994.

Hagedorn, Jessica. "The Time of Mirrors." In *The Anchored Angel: Selected Writings by José Garcia Villa,* edited by Eileen Tabios, xi–xv. New York: Kaya, 1999.

Hajjar, Nijmeh. "Ameen Rihani's Humanist Vision of Arab Nationalism." In *Ameen Rihani: Bridging East and West,* edited by Nathan C. Funk and Betty J. Sitka, 134–47. Lanham, MD: University Press of America, 2004.

———. *The Politics and Poetics of Ameen Rihani: The Humanist Ideology of an Arab-American Intellectual and Activist.* London: Tauris Academic Studies, 2010.

Hall, James C., and Heather Hathaway. "The Art and Politics of Paule Marshall: An Interview." In *Conversations with Paule Marshall,* edited by James C. Hall and Heather Hathaway, 157–88. Jackson: University Press of Mississippi, 2010.

Hanioğlu, M. Şükrü. "Turkism and the Young Turks, 1889–1908." In *Turkey Beyond Nationalism: Towards Post-Nationalist Identities,* edited by Hans-Lukas Kieser, 3–19. London: I. B. Tauris, 2006.

Harpham, Geoffrey Galt. *The Character of Criticism.* New York: Routledge, 2006.

Harris, Trudier. "No Outlet for the Blues: Silla Boyce's Plight in *Brown Girl, Brownstones.*" *Callaloo,* no. 18 (1983): 57–67.

Hassan, Waïl S. "The Rise of Arab-American Literature: Orientalism and Cultural Translation in the Work of Ameen Rihani." *American Literary History* 20, no. 1–2 (2008): 245–75.

———. *Immigrant Narratives: Orientalism and Cultural Translation in Arab American and Arab British Literature.* Oxford: Oxford University Press, 2011.

Hathaway, Heather. *Caribbean Waves: Relocating Claude McKay and Paule Marshall.* Bloomington: Indiana University Press, 1999.

Hattori, Tomo. "Model Minority Discourse and Asian American Jouis-Sense." *differences: A Journal of Feminist Cultural Studies* 11, no. 2 (1999): 228–47.

Helweg, Arthur W., and Usha M. Helweg. *An Immigrant Success Story: East Indians in America.* Philadelphia: University of Pennsylvania Press, 1990.

Heraclitus. *Fragments: The Collected Wisdom of Heraclitus.* Translated by Brooks Haxton. New York: Viking Penguin, 2001.

Hernández-G., Manuel de Jesús. "Villarreal's *Clemente Chacon* (1984): A Precursor's Accommodationist Dialogue." *Bilingual Review/La Revista Bilingüe* 16, no. 1 (1991): 35–43.

Hess, Gary R. "The Asian Indian Immigrants in the United States: The Early Phase, 1900–65." In *From India to America: A Brief History of Immigration; Problems of Discrimination; Admission and Assimilation,* edited by S. Chandrasekhar, 29–34. La Jolla, CA: Population Review, 1982.

Hidalgo, Melissa M. "'He Was a Sissy, Really': Queering *Pocho* by the Books." *Aztlán: A Journal of Chicano Studies* 40, no. 1 (2015): 7–36.

Howarth, William L. "Some Principles of Autobiography." *New Literary History* 5, no. 2 (1974): 363–81.

Hsu, Ruth Y. "'Will the Model Minority Please Identify Itself?': American Ethnic Identity and its Discontents." *Diaspora: A Journal of Transnational Studies* 5, no. 1 (1996): 37–63.

Isaac, Allan Punzalan. *American Tropics: Articulating Filipino America*. Minneapolis: University of Minnesota Press, 2006.

Jacobson, Matthew Frye. *Whiteness of a Different Color: European Immigrants and the Alchemy of Race*. Cambridge, MA: Harvard University Press, 1998.

Jahshan, Paul, ed. *100 Years of Selected Writings on Ameen Rihani's* The Book of Khalid. Washington, DC: Platform International, 2011.

James, Winston. *Holding Aloft the Banner of Ethiopia: Caribbean Radicalism in Early Twentieth-Century America*. London: Verso, 1998.

———. "Explaining Afro-Caribbean Social Mobility in the United States: Beyond the Sowell Thesis." *Comparative Studies in Society and History* 44, no. 2 (2002): 218–62.

Japtok, Martin. "Paule Marshall's *Brown Girl, Brownstones*: Reconciling Ethnicity and Individualism." *African American Review* 32, no. 2 (1998): 305–15.

Jarrett, Gene Andrew. *Deans and Truants: Race and Realism in African American Literature*. Philadelphia: University of Pennsylvania Press, 2007.

Jensen, Joan M. *Passage from India: Asian Indian Immigrants in North America*. New Haven, CT: Yale University Press, 1988.

Jeon, Joseph Jonghyun. *Racial Things, Racial Forms: Objecthood in Avant-Garde Asian American Poetry*. Iowa City: University of Iowa Press, 2012.

Jiménez, Francisco, and José Antonio Villarreal. "An Interview with José Antonio Villarreal." *Bilingual Review/La Revista Bilingüe* 3, no. 1 (1976): 66–72.

Joaquin, Nick. "Excerpt from Viva Villa." In *The Anchored Angel: Selected Writings by José Garcia Villa*, edited by Eileen Tabios, 154–65. New York: Kaya, 1999.

Jones, Gavin. "'The Sea Ain' Got No Back Door': The Problems of Black Consciousness in Paule Marshall's *Brown Girl, Brownstones*." *African American Review* 32, no. 4 (1998): 597–606.

Juergensmeyer, Mark. "The Gadar Syndrome: Ethnic Anger and Nationalist Pride." In *From India to America: A Brief History of Immigration; Problems of Discrimination; Admission and Assimilation*, edited by S. Chandrasekhar, 48–58. La Jolla, CA: Population Review, 1982.

Kang, Younghill. *East Goes West*. New York: Kaya Press, 1997.

Karpat, Kemal H. "The Ottoman Emigration to America, 1860–1914." *International Journal of Middle East Studies* 17, no. 2 (1985): 175–209.

Kasinitz, Philip. *Caribbean New York: Black Immigrants and the Politics of Race*. Ithaca, NY: Cornell University Press, 1992.

King, Martin Luther, Jr. "My Trip to the Land of Gandhi." In *A Testament of Hope: The Essential Writings of Martin Luther King, Jr.*, edited by James Melvin Washington, 23–30. San Francisco: Harper & Row, 1986.

Knights, L. C. *How Many Children Had Lady Macbeth? An Essay in the Theory and Practice of Shakespeare Criticism*. Cambridge, UK: The Minority Press, 1933.

Konstantinou, Lee. *Cool Characters: Irony and American Fiction*. Cambridge, MA: Harvard University Press, 2016.

Koshy, Susan. "The Fiction of Asian American Literature." *The Yale Journal of Criticism* 9 (1996): 315–46.

———. "Category Crisis: South Asian Americans and Questions of Race and Ethnicity." *Diaspora* 7, no. 3 (1998): 285–320.

———. "Morphing Race into Ethnicity: Asian Americans and Critical Transformations of Whiteness." *boundary 2* 28, no. 1 (2001): 153–94.

———. "South Asians and the Complex Interstices of Whiteness: Negotiating Public Sentiment in the United States and Britain." In *White Women in Racialized Spaces: Imaginative Transformation and Ethical Action in Literature*, edited by Samina Najmi and Rajini Srikanth, 29–50. Albany: State University of New York Press, 2002.

———. *Sexual Naturalization: Asian Americans and Miscegenation*. Stanford, CA: Stanford University Press, 2004.

Lanham, Richard A. *A Handlist of Rhetorical Terms*. Berkeley: University of California Press, 1991.

Lee, Chang-rae. *Native Speaker*. New York: Riverhead Books, 1995.

Lee, Christopher. *The Semblance of Identity: Aesthetic Mediation in Asian American Literature*. Stanford, CA: Stanford University Press, 2012.

Lee, Robert G. *Orientals: Asian Americans in Popular Culture*. Philadelphia: Temple University Press, 1999.

Lee, Yoon Sun. *Modern Minority: Asian American Literature and Everyday Life*. Oxford: Oxford University Press, 2013.

Lejeune, Philippe. *On Autobiography*. Minneapolis: University of Minnesota Press, 1989.

Leonard, Karen Isaksen. *Making Ethnic Choices: California's Punjabi Mexican Americans*. Philadelphia: Temple University Press, 1992.

———. *The South Asian Americans*. Westport, CT: Greenwood, 1997.

Lim, Jeehyun. *Bilingual Brokers: Race, Literature, and Language as Human Capital*. New York: Fordham University Press, 2017.

Ling, Jinqi. *Narrating Nationalisms: Ideology and Form in Asian American Literature*. New York: Oxford University Press, 1998.

Locke, Alain. "Spiritual Truancy." *New Challenge* 2, no. 2 (Fall 1937): 81–85.

———, ed. *The New Negro*. New York: Touchstone, 1992.

López, Ian Haney. *White by Law: The Legal Construction of Race*. New York: New York University Press, 2006.

Lorde, Audre. *Zami: A New Spelling of My Name*. New York: Quality Paperback Book Club, 1993.

Love, Heather. *Feeling Backward: Loss and the Politics of Queer History*. Cambridge, MA: Harvard University Press, 2007.

———. "Close but not Deep: Literary Ethics and the Descriptive Turn." *New Literary History* 41 (2010): 371–91.

Lu, Pamela. *Pamela: A Novel*. Berkeley, CA: Atelos, 1998.

Lye, Colleen. "Introduction: In Dialogue with Asian American Studies." *Representations* 99 (2007): 1–12.

———. "Racial Form." *Representations* 104, no. 1 (2008): 92–101.

Lynch, Deidre Shauna. *The Economy of Character: Novels, Market Culture, and the Business of Inner Meaning*. Chicago: University of Chicago Press, 1998.

Madrid-Barela, Arturo. "Pochos: The Different Mexicans, An Interpretive Essay, Part I." *Aztlán: A Journal of Chicano Studies* 7, no. 1 (1977): 51–64.
Majaj, Lisa Suhair. "Arab-Americans and the Meanings of Race." In *Postcolonial Theory and the United States: Race, Ethnicity, and Literature*, edited by Amritjit Singh and Peter Schmidt, 320–37. Jackson: University Press of Mississippi, 2000.
Mangahas, Federico. "Doveglion in New York." In *Poems by Doveglion*, ii–vi. Manila, Philippines: The Philippine Writers' League, 1941.
Mani, Bakirathi. *Aspiring to Home: South Asians in America*. Stanford: Stanford University Press, 2012.
Manning, Susan. *Poetics of Character: Transatlantic Encounters 1700–1900*. Cambridge: Cambridge University Press, 2014.
Marlowe, Christopher. *Tamburlaine the Great*. Edited by J. S. Cunningham and Eithne Henson. Manchester: Manchester University Press, 1998.
Marshall, Marguerite Mooers, and Helen Johnson Keyes. "Forward [sic]." In *The Book of Khalid*, by Ameen Rihani, a–d. Beirut, Lebanon: Librairie du Liban, 2000.
Marshall, Paule. "Black Immigrant Women in *Brown Girl, Brownstones*." In *Female Immigrants to the United States: Caribbean, Latin American, and African Experiences*, edited by Dolores M. Mortimer and Roy S. Bryce-Laporte, 3–13. Washington, DC: Smithsonian Institution, 1981.
———. *Brown Girl, Brownstones*. New York: Feminist Press, 1981.
———. *Reena and Other Stories*. New York: The Feminist Press, 1983.
———. *Triangular Road: A Memoir*. New York: Basic Books, 2009.
McAlister, Melani. *Epic Encounters: Culture, Media, & U.S. Interests in the Middle East since 1945*. Berkeley: University of California Press, 2005.
Meehan, Kevin. "Caribbean versus United States Racial Categories in Three Caribbean American Coming of Age Stories." *Narrative* 7, no. 3 (1999): 259–71.
Melendy, H. Brett. *Asians in America: Filipinos, Koreans, and East Indians*. Boston: Twayne, 1977.
Mercer, Kobena. *Welcome to the Jungle*. New York: Routledge, 1994.
Miller, J. Hillis. *Ariadne's Thread: Story Lines*. New Haven, CT: Yale University Press, 1992.
Miller, Stuart Creighton. *"Benevolent Assimilation": The American Conquest of the Philippines, 1899–1903*. New Haven, CT: Yale University Press, 1982.
Model, Suzanne. *West Indian Immigrants: A Black Success Story?* New York: Russell Sage Foundation, 2008.
Moraga, Cherríe L. *Loving in the War Years*. Boston: South End Press, 1983.
Morrison, Toni. *Playing in the Dark: Whiteness and the Literary Imagination*. New York: Vintage Books, 1993.
Morse, David. *American Romanticism*. Totowa, NJ: Barnes & Noble Books, 1987.
Mortimer, Dolores M., and Roy S. Bryce-Laporte, eds. *Female Immigrants to the United States: Caribbean, Latin American, and African Experiences*. Washington, DC: Smithsonian Institution, 1981.
Moses, Omri. *Out of Character: Modernism, Vitalism, Psychic Life*. Stanford, CA: Stanford University Press, 2014.

Mukerji, Dhan Gopal. *Caste and Outcast*. Stanford, CA: Stanford University Press, 2002.
Mukherjee, Bharati. *Jasmine*. New York: Grove Press, 1989.
Muñoz, José Esteban. *Disidentifications: Queers of Color and the Performance of Politics*. Minneapolis: University of Minnesota Press, 1999.
Naff, Alixa. *Becoming American: The Early Arab Immigrant Experience*. Carbondale: Southern Illinois University Press, 1985.
Nash, Geoffrey P. "Rihani and Carlyle on Revolution and Modernity." In *Ameen Rihani: Bridging East and West*, edited by Nathan C. Funk and Betty J. Sitka, 47–54. Lanham, MD: University Press of America, 2004.
———. *The Arab Writer in English: Arab Themes in a Metropolitan Language, 1908–1958*. Brighton: Sussex Academic Press, 1998.
Nehru, Jawaharlal. *The Discovery of India*. Delhi: Oxford University Press, 1989.
Ngai, Mae M. *Impossible Subjects: Illegal Aliens and the Making of Modern America*. Princeton, NJ: Princeton University Press, 2004.
Ngai, Sianne. *Ugly Feelings*. Cambridge, MA: Harvard University Press, 2005.
Nguyen, Viet Thanh. *Race and Resistance: Literature and Politics in Asian America*. Oxford: Oxford University Press, 2002.
Ninh, erin Khuê. *Ingratitude: The Debt-Bound Daughter in Asian American Literature*. New York: New York University Press, 2011.
Obama, Barack. *The Audacity of Hope: Thoughts on Reclaiming the American Dream*. New York: Crown Publishers, 2006.
Obenzinger, Hilton. *American Palestine: Melville, Twain, and the Holy Land Mania*. Princeton, NJ: Princeton University Press, 1999.
Okihiro, Gary Y. "Colonial Vision, Racial Visibility: Racializations in Puerto Rico and the Philippines during the Initial Period of U.S. Colonization." In *Racial Transformations: Latinos and Asians Remaking the United States*, edited by Nicholas De Genova, 23–39. Durham, NC: Duke University Press, 2006.
Omi, Michael, and Howard Winant. *Racial Formation in the United States: From the 1960s to the 1990s*. 2nd ed. New York: Routledge, 1994.
———. *Racial Formation in the United States*. 3rd ed. New York: Routledge, 2015.
Osman, Suleiman. *The Invention of Brownstone Brooklyn: Gentrification and the Search for Authenticity in Postwar New York*. Oxford: Oxford University Press, 2011.
Oueijan, Naji. "The Formation of a Universal Self: Rihani and Byron." In *Ameen Rihani: Bridging East and West*, edited by Nathan C. Funk and Betty J. Sitka, 83–92. Lanham, MD: University Press of America, 2004.
Paredes, Raymund A. "Mexican American Literature." In *Columbia Literary History of the United States*, edited by Emory Elliott, 800–810. New York: Columbia University Press, 1988.
Parikh, Crystal. *An Ethics of Betrayal: The Politics of Otherness in Emergent U.S. Literatures and Culture*. New York: Fordham University Press, 2009.
Patterson, Tom. "Triumph and Tragedy of Dalip Saund." *California Historian* 38, no. 4 (1992): 9–13.
Paz, Octavio. *The Labyrinth of Solitude and Other Writings*. New York: Grove Press, 1985.

Pease, Donald E. *The New American Exceptionalism*. Minneapolis: University of Minnesota Press, 2009.

Pettis, Joyce, and Paule Marshall. "A *MELUS* Interview: Paule Marshall." *MELUS* 17, no. 4 (1991): 117–29.

Phelan, James. *Living to Tell about It: A Rhetoric and Ethics of Character Narration*. Ithaca, NY: Cornell University Press, 2005.

Ponce, Martin Joseph. "José Garcia Villa's Modernism and the Politics of Queer Diasporic Reading." *GLQ* 17, no. 4 (2011): 575–602.

———. *Beyond the Nation: Diasporic Filipino Literature and Queer Reading*. New York: New York University Press, 2012.

Powell, Colin. *My American Journey*. New York: Ballantine Books, 1995.

Prashad, Vijay. *The Darker Nations: A People's History of the Third World*. New York: The New Press, 2007.

Puri, Harish K. *Ghadar Movement: Ideology Organisation and Strategy*. Amritsar: Guru Nanak Dev University, 1993.

Quashie, Kevin. *The Sovereignty of Quiet: Beyond Resistance in Black Culture*. New Brunswick, NJ: Rutgers University Press, 2012.

Rafael, Vicente L. *White Love and Other Events in Filipino History*. Durham, NC: Duke University Press, 2000.

Raffel, Dawn. "Paule Marshall on Race and Memory." More (more.com), April 23, 2009. Reprinted in *Conversations with Paule Marshall*, edited by James C. Hall and Heather Hathaway, 189–91. Jackson: University Press of Mississippi, 2010.

Rich, Doris L. *Jackie Cochran: Pilot in the Fastest Lane*. Gainesville: University Press of Florida, 2007.

Rihani, Ameen Albert. "Cross-Cultural Approaches to Reconciliation: Ameen Rihani and H. G. Wells." In *Ameen Rihani: Bridging East and West*, edited by Nathan C. Funk and Betty J. Sitka, 16–24. Lanham, MD: University Press of America, 2004.

Rihani, Ameen. *Excerpts from Ar-Rihaniyat*. Louaize, Lebanon: Notre Dame University Press, 1998.

———. *The Book of Khalid: A Critical Edition*. Edited by Todd Fine. Syracuse, NY: Syracuse University Press, 2016.

———. *Letters to Uncle Sam*. Washington, DC: Platform International, 2001.

———. *The White Way and the Desert*. Washington, DC: Platform International, 2002.

———. *The Path of Vision*. Washington, DC: Platform International, 2008.

Rihbany, Abraham Mitrie. *A Far Journey: An Autobiography*. Boston: Houghton Mifflin, 1914.

———. *America Save the Near East*. Boston: Beacon, 1918.

———. *Wise Men from the East and from the West*. Boston: Houghton Mifflin, 1922.

Rizk, Salom. *Syrian Yankee*. Garden City, NY: Doubleday & Company, 1943.

Rodionov, Mikhail. "Leo Tolstoy and Ameen Rihani: The Interaction between Two Creative Worlds." In *Ameen Rihani: Bridging East and West*, edited by Nathan C. Funk and Betty J. Sitka, 72–80. Lanham, MD: University Press of America, 2004.

Rodriguez, Ralph E. *Latinx Literature Unbound: Undoing Ethnic Expectation.* New York: Fordham University Press, 2018.

Rodríguez, Randy A. "Richard Rodriguez Reconsidered: Queering the Sissy (Ethnic) Subject." *Texas Studies in Literature and Language* 40, no. 4 (1998): 396–423.

Rodriguez, Richard. *Brown: The Last Discovery of America.* New York: Viking, 2002.

———. *Hunger of Memory: The Education of Richard Rodriguez.* New York: The Dial Press, 2005.

Román, Elda María. *Race and Upward Mobility: Seeking, Gatekeeping, and other Class Strategies in Postwar America.* Stanford, CA: Stanford University Press, 2018.

Rosen, Jeremy. *Minor Characters Have Their Day: Genre and the Contemporary Literary Marketplace.* New York: Columbia University Press, 2016.

Roy, Arundhati. *An Ordinary Person's Guide to Empire.* Cambridge, MA: South End Press, 2004.

Rubio, Marco. *An American Son: A Memoir.* New York: Sentinel, 2012.

Ruiz, Ramón E. "On the Meaning of Pocho." In *Pocho*, vii–xii. Garden City, NY: Anchor Books, 1970.

Ruskin, John. *The Stones of Venice Volume the Third: The Fall.* London: Smith, Elder, and Company, 1853.

———. *Modern Painters Volume the Third: Of Many Things.* New York: Brian, Taylor & Company, 1894.

Russell, Sandi. "Interview with Paule Marshall." *Wasafiri* 4, no. 8 (1988): 14–16.

Sae-Saue, Jayson Gonzales. "Aztlán's Asians: Forging and Forgetting Cross-Racial Relations in the Chicana/o Literary Imagination." *American Literature* 85, no. 3 (2013): 563–89.

———. *Southwest Asia: The Transpacific Geographies of Chicana/o Literature.* New Brunswick, NJ: Rutgers University Press, 2016.

Salazar, James B. "A Good Judge of Character?" *American Quarterly* 54, no. 2 (2002): 325–31.

———. *Bodies of Reform: The Rhetoric of Character in Gilded Age America.* New York: New York University Press, 2010.

Saldívar, José David. *The Dialectics of Our America: Genealogy, Cultural Critique, and Literary History.* Durham, NC: Duke University Press, 1991.

Saldívar, Ramón. *Chicano Narrative: The Dialectics of Difference.* Madison: University of Wisconsin Press, 1990.

San Juan, E., Jr. "In Search of Filipino Writing: Reclaiming Whose 'America'?" In *The Ethnic Canon: Histories, Institutions, and Interventions*, edited by David Palumbo-Liu, 213–40. Minneapolis: University of Minnesota Press, 1995.

———. *The Philippine Temptation: Dialectics of Philippines-U.S. Literary Relations.* Philadelphia: Temple University Press, 1996.

———. *From Exile to Diaspora: Versions of the Filipino Experience in the United States.* Boulder, CO: Westview Press, 1998.

———. *Toward Filipino Self-Determination: Beyond Transnational Globalization.* New York: State University of New York Press, 2009.

———. "Jose Garcia Villa—Critique of a Subaltern Poetics." *EurAmerica* 40, no. 1 (2010): 1–29.

Sánchez, María Carla. "Whiteness Invisible: Early Mexican American Writing and the Color of Literary History." In *Passing: Identity and Interpretation in Sexuality, Race, and Religion*, edited by María Carla Sánchez and Linda Schlossberg, 64–91. New York: New York University Press, 2001.

Sánchez, Rosaura. "Ideological Discourses in Arturo Islas's *The Rain God*." In *Criticism in the Borderlands: Studies in Chicano Literature, Culture, and Ideology*, edited by Héctor Calderón and José David Saldívar, 114–26. Durham, NC: Duke University Press, 1991.

Saund, D. S. *Congressman from India*. New York: E. P. Dutton, 1960.

Saunders, Patricia J. "Woman Overboard: The Perils of Sailing the Black Atlantic, Deportation with Prejudice." *Small Axe* 13, no. 1 (2009): 203–16.

Scheffauer, Herman. "The Tide of Turbans." *Forum* 43 (1910): 616–18.

Schlund-Vials, Cathy J. *Modeling Citizenship: Jewish and Asian American Writing*. Philadelphia: Temple University Press, 2011.

Schumann, Christoph. "Ameen Rihani's *The Book of Khalid* in its Historical and Political Context." In *The Book of Khalid: A Critical Edition*, edited by Todd Fine, 272–86. Syracuse, NY: Syracuse University Press, 2016.

Sedore, Timothy S. "Solace in Solitude: An American Adamic Alienation and José Antonio Villarreal's *Pocho*." *Lit: Literature Interpretation Theory* 11, no. 2 (2000): 239–59.

———. "'Everything I Wrote Was Truth': An Interview with José Antonio Villarreal." *Northwest Review* 39, no. 1 (2001): 77–89.

Shahid, Irfan. "Amīn al-Rīhānī and King 'Abdul-'Azīz Ibn Sa'ūd." In *Arab Civilization: Challenges and Responses*, edited by George N. Atiyeh and Ibrahim M. Oweiss, 231–40. Albany, NY: State University of New York Press, 1988.

Shankar, Lavina Dhingra, and Pallassana R. Balgopal. "South Asian Immigrants before 1950: The Formation of Ethnic, Symbolic, and Group Identity." *Amerasia Journal* 27, no. 1 (2001): 55–84.

Shaw-Taylor, Yoku. "The Intersection of Assimilation, Race, Presentation of Self, and Transnationalism in America." In *The Other African Americans: Contemporary African and Caribbean Immigrants in the United States*, edited by Yoku Shaw-Taylor and Steven A. Tuch, 1–47. Lanham, MD: Rowman & Littlefield, 2007.

Shih, Shu-mei. "Comparative Racialization: An Introduction." *PMLA* 123, no. 5 (2008): 1347–62.

Shohat, Ella, and Robert Stam. *Unthinking Eurocentrism: Multiculturalism and the Media*. London: Routledge, 2014.

Shukla, Sandhya. *India Abroad: Diasporic Cultures of Postwar America and England*. Princeton, NJ: Princeton University Press, 2003.

———. "Indian Diasporic Autobiography: New Nations and New Selves." In *The Cambridge History of Asian American Literature*, edited by Rajini Srikanth and Min Hyoung Song, 107–22. New York: Cambridge University Press, 2016.

Smith, Sidonie, and Julia Watson. *Reading Autobiography: A Guide for Interpreting Life Narratives*. Minneapolis: University of Minnesota Press, 2010.

Sohn, Stephen Hong. "Minor Character, Minority Orientalisms, and the Borderlands of Asian America." *Cultural Critique* 82 (2012): 151–85.

———. *Racial Asymmetries: Asian American Fictional Worlds*. New York: New York University Press, 2014.

Sollors, Werner. *Beyond Ethnicity: Consent and Descent in American Culture*. New York: Oxford University Press, 1986.

Sood, Malini. "Expatriate Nationalism and Ethnic Radicalism: The Ghadar Party in North America, 1910–1920." Ph.D. diss., State University of New York at Stony Brook, 1995.

Srikanth, Rajini. *The World Next Door: South Asian American Literature and the Idea of America*. Philadelphia: Temple University Press, 2004.

Stewart, Jeffrey C. *The New Negro: The Life of Alain Locke*. Oxford: Oxford University Press, 2018.

Susman, Warren I. *Culture as History: The Transformation of American Society in the Twentieth Century*. New York: Pantheon, 1984.

Sutton, Constance R., and Elsa M. Chaney, eds. *Caribbean Life in New York City: Sociocultural Dimensions*. New York: Center for Migration Studies of New York, 1987.

Tabios, Eileen. "Editor's Afterword: An Angel's Invitation to a House of Song." In *The Anchored Angel: Selected Writings by José Garcia Villa*, edited by Eileen Tabios, 141–53. New York: Kaya, 1999.

———, ed. *The Anchored Angel: Selected Writings by José Garcia Villa*. New York: Kaya, 1999.

Tate, Claudia. *Psychoanalysis and Black Novels: Desire and the Protocols of Race*. New York: Oxford University Press, 1998.

Tolentino, Cynthia H. *America's Experts: Race and the Fictions of Sociology*. Minneapolis: University of Minnesota Press, 2009.

Torres, Hector A., and Richard Rodriguez. "'I Don't Think I Exist': Interview with Richard Rodriguez." *MELUS* 28, no. 2 (2003): 164–202.

Treitler, Vilna Bashi. *The Ethnic Project: Transforming Racial Fiction into Ethnic Factions*. Stanford, CA: Stanford University Press, 2013.

Tsou, Elda E. *Unquiet Tropes: Form, Race, and Asian American Literature*. Philadelphia: Temple University Press, 2015.

Ty, Eleanor. *Asianfail: Narratives of Disenchantment and the Model Minority*. Urbana: University of Illinois Press, 2017.

Vallejos, Tomás. "José Antonio Villarreal." In *Dictionary of Literary Biography: Chicano Writers*, edited by Francisco A. Lomelí and Carl R. Shirley, 282–88. Detroit, MI: Gale Research, 1989.

Varma, Premdatta. *Indian Immigrants in USA: Struggle for Equality*. New Delhi: Heritage, 1995.

Vermeule, Blakey. *Why Do We Care about Literary Characters?* Baltimore: Johns Hopkins University Press, 2010.

Vickerman, Milton. *Crosscurrents: West Indian Immigrants and Race*. New York: Oxford University Press, 1999.

Villa, José Garcia. *Footnote to Youth: Tales of the Philippines and Others*. New York: Charles Scribner's Sons, 1933.

———. *Have Come, Am Here: Poems by José Garcia Villa*. New York: Viking Press, 1942.

———. *Volume Two*. New York: A New Directions Book, 1949.

———. *Selected Poems and New*. New York: McDowell, Obolensky, 1958.

———. *Doveglion: Collected Poems*. New York: Penguin Books, 2008.

Villarreal, José Antonio. *Pocho*. New York: Anchor Books, 1989.

Vuong, Ocean. *On Earth We're Briefly Gorgeous: A Novel*. New York: Penguin Press, 2019.

Warren, Kenneth W. *What Was African American Literature?* Cambridge, MA: Harvard University Press, 2011.

Washington, Booker T. *Up from Slavery*. Oxford: Oxford University Press, 1995.

Washington, Mary Helen. "Afterword." In *Brown Girl, Brownstones*, 311–24. New York: Feminist Press, 1981.

Waters, Mary C. *Black Identities: West Indian Immigrant Dreams and American Realities*. Cambridge, MA: Harvard University Press, 2004.

Weise, Julie M. "Mexican Nationalisms, Southern Racisms: Mexicans and Mexican Americans in the U.S. South, 1908–1939." *American Quarterly* 60, no. 3 (2008): 749–77.

Williams, Raymond. *Marxism and Literature*. Oxford: Oxford University Press, 1977.

Woloch, Alex. *The One vs. the Many: Minor Characters and the Space of the Protagonist in the Novel*. Princeton, NJ: Princeton University Press, 2003.

Wong, Sau-ling Cynthia. "Immigrant Autobiography: Some Questions of Definition and Approach." In *American Autobiography: Retrospect and Prospect*, 142–70. Madison: University of Wisconsin Press, 1991.

———. "Autobiography as Guided Chinatown Tour? Maxine Hong Kingston's *The Woman Warrior* and the Chinese American Autobiographical Controversy." In *Maxine Hong Kingston's The Woman Warrior: A Casebook*, edited by Sau-ling Cynthia Wong, 29–56. New York: Oxford University Press, 1999.

Wu, Cynthia. *Sticky Rice: A Politics of Intraracial Desire*. Philadelphia: Temple University Press, 2018.

Yao, Steve. *Foreign Accents: Chinese American Verse from Exclusion to Postethnicity*. Oxford: Oxford University Press, 2010.

Yu, Timothy. "'The Hand of a Chinese Master': José Garcia Villa and Modernist Orientalism." *MELUS* 29, no. 1 (2004): 41–59.

Yuson, Alfred A. "Villaesque: The Father As Villain." In *The Anchored Angel: Selected Writings by José Garcia Villa*, edited by Eileen Tabios, 226–32. New York: Kaya, 1999.

Online Sources

Allam, Hannah. "Bush Mideast Speech Draws Cool Response." McClatchy Newspapers, January 13, 2008, https://www.mcclatchydc.com/news/politics-government/white-house/article24474625.html.

Clack, George. "Introduction." *Writers on America*, U.S. Department of State, December 2002, https://usa.usembassy.de/etexts/writers/homepage.htm.

"Dalip Singh Saund." History, Art & Archives, United States House of Representatives, http://history.house.gov/Collection/Detail/29982.

Merica, Dan. "Where Pardoned Turkeys Go to Die," *CNN*, November 27, 2013, http://www.cnn.com/2013/11/27/politics/pardoned-turkeys/.

Michaels, Walter Benn, Erica Edwards, and Aldon Lynn Nielsen. "What Was African American Literature? A Symposium." *Los Angeles Review of Books*, June 13, 2011, https://lareviewofbooks.org/article/what-was-african-american-literature-a-symposium/.

Mukherjee, Bharati. "American Dreamer." *Mother Jones*, January/February 1997, https://www.motherjones.com/politics/1997/01/american-dreamer/.

"President Bush Discusses Importance of Freedom in the Middle East." White House Archives, January 13, 2008, http://georgewbush-whitehouse.archives.gov/news/releases/2008/01/20080113-1.html.

"The 100th Anniversary of the First Arab-American Novel," Project Khalid, 2010, accessed September 12, 2016, http://projectkhalid.org/ (site discontinued).

"Tributes to Rihani," The Ameen Rihani Organization, 2016, http://www.ameenrihani.org/index.php?page=tributes.

Trivedi, Bijal P. "Where Do Turkeys Go After Being Pardoned by the President?" *National Geographic Today*, November 20, 2001, accessed June 21, 2017, http://news.nationalgeographic.com/news/2001/11/1120_TVprezturkeys.html (site discontinued).

Films

Cheng, E. Samantha. *Dalip Singh Saund: His Life, His Legacy*. Silver Spring, MD: Heritage Series, 2014, DVD.

Index

Page numbers in italics refer to illustrations.

Abdülhamid II, 54
Abdur-Rahman, Aliyyah, 80–81, 84
absence, space of, 38, 84
Adams, James Truslow, 29–30
aesthetics, 10, 14, 181, 201–2n98; politics and, 98–99; rarefied, 70–71, 74, 78–79, 86–87, 90–91, 194; sublimation and, 90–91; of transcendence, 78, 86; Villa's, 70–71
African American literature, 11, 190
African Americans, 32–33; in *Brown Girl, Brownstones*, 152, 153, 155, 157, 160–62, 166, 167, 183; complicated configurations of power and, 9; in connection to India, 140; Saund's failure to address racism, 150–51; as targets of black pathology discourses, 37, 126. *See also* Afro-Caribbean immigrants; *Brown Girl, Brownstones* (Marshall); Marshall, Paule
African diasporic cultural production, 80–81
Africanist persona, 13, 15
Afro-Asian alliance (Bandung), 140
Afro-Caribbean immigrants, 152, 154–55; as "black Jews," 155, 176–78; divide with African Americans, 157; literature as form of testimony, 158. *See also* African Americans; *Brown Girl, Brownstones* (Marshall); Marshall, Paule
Aguinaldo, Emilio, 70
Ahmad, Aijaz, 20
Ahmed, Sara, 19, 38
Alger, Horatio, 2, 7, 21, 29, 96, 187

allegory, 20, 22, 24, 75, 84, 132–33; constitutional allegoresis, 28–29; New Racism and turkey pardoning, 186–87
Althusserian ideology, 29
Ameen Rihani Organization, 46
American Center Library (New Delhi), 2
American character, 21, 34–39, 42, 61–64, 188–89; archetypes of, 4–5, 12–13, 21, 27; character building, 125–33, 137, 142, 148–50; national, ideological fiction of, 43, 61, 143, 150; Saund as distinct archetype of, 133–43
American dream: alternative forms of black diasporic consciousness and, 181; Americanized Mexican and, 94; antecedents, 29; of being unmarked, 35, 67; character and, 21, 29–30; as "diminishing of life," 156–57; impossibility and unsustainability of, 5, 35, 43, 58, 65, 172, 193–95; "manic relation to," 126, 143; as norming mechanism, 38, 188–89; as psychosocial condition, 58; Saund as archetype of, 2, 121, 126–29; stalled protagonists of, 59–65; as state fantasy, 29; "white ethnicity" model, 28
American exceptionalism, 29, 32, 185–86; Marshall's refusal to support, 157; in Rihani's work, 34, 44, 52; in Saund's autobiography, 143, 147, 195
American in India, An (Redding), 140
American Youth for Democracy, 157
Americanization, 3, 22; "agringarse," 94; relation to whiteness as central to, 28–32; teleology of, 29, 43, 46, 49,

Index 239

59, 65, 99; white ethnicization, 3, 28, 31–32, 155, 160, 162, 176–79

Anchored Angel, The (Villa), 71, 86

Anderson, Sherwood, 35, 67, 74–75, 85. Works: "The Book of the Grotesque," 75–76, 82; "Hands," 75; *Winesburg, Ohio*, 35, 67, 75

Anjaria, Ulka, 14

anthropomorphism, 76–78, 100, 117, 173, 175, 193

Antin, Mary, 28, 30

Anzaldúa, Gloria, 9

appropriation, 4, 28; of Rihani by Bush, 34, 42–44, 47, 65; shared burden of, 39–40

Arab Americans. See *The Book of Khalid* (Rihani); *Letters to Uncle Sam* (Rihani); Rihani, Ameen; Syrian diaspora; Syrian immigrants

Arab American studies, 32, 34, 47

Arab diasporic literature, 43

Arab self-determination, 43–45, 65

Aranda, José, Jr., 26

archaeological approaches, 188–89

archetypes: American, in *Congressman from India*, 133–43; of American character, 4–5, 12, 27; of American dream, racialized, 5, 27, 183; appropriation of, 28, 34; family in relation to, 133–35, *135*; immigrant who champions imperialism, 34, 42–43; refracted into heterogeneous parts, 5, 26–27, 37, 39–40, 56, 64–65, 121, 154, 160, 179, 183, 189; ubiquity and unevenness of, 37, 188–89

architecture: characters refracted through, 154, 173–76, 180, 193, 194–95; grotesque and, 75, 77–78; Saund placed within neoclassical, 2, 3

archive of ethnic literature, 4, 9–11, 190; ambivalent, 9–10, 188; Asian American literature, 32; as basis for oppositional politics and pedagogies, 39; black literature, 21, 32; deconstructive readings of, 32; recalibration of, 190. *See also* ethnic literature

artist, as threat, 180–82

Asian American, as term, 10, 32, 67, 190

Asian American literature, 9–11

Asian Americans: political candidates, 119–20; political silence of, 125–26. See also *Congressman from India* (Saund); Filipinos; *Footnote to Youth* (Villa); Indian Americans; Saund, Dalip Singh; South Asian Americans; Villa, José Garcia

Asian American studies, 9–10, 32, 71

"Asiatic barred zone" (Immigration Act of 1917), 62–63, 122

assimilation, 183–84, 194; in *Brown Girl, Brownstones*, 160, 176–77, 180; disidentification and, 97, 101; by early twentieth-century writers, 32; ethnicity vs. race, 30–31; European immigration and, 28–29, 176, 185; exploitative social order and, 110–11, 177; to ideals, 115; of minorities into capitalism, 153–54, 160, 162–64, 167; in *Pocho*, 36, 97–99, 101–2, 110–11, 115, 118; racial, 3, 6–9; as racial betrayal, 98; Rihani and, 63; Saund and, 70, 125–26, 131, 142; Villa and, 70, 83

Association of Artists for Freedom, 157

author function, 24–25

authors: "alter ego," narrator as, 25; as characters, 4–5, 12–14, 19–20, 24, 26–27, 33–36, 192–93; characters as authorial and textual, 10–11, 40; "death of," 24; excess of personality attributed to, 24, 26, 195; as historical persons and literary personas, 12–13; identity not coextensive with fictional characters, 10, 48, 59–60, 94–95, 189–90, 195; "implied authorial I," 64; overlap with literary characters, 10, 14, 87, 192–93; self-representation assumed, 8, 19–20. *See also individual authors*

240   Index

autobiography, 5–6, 23, 25, 28–29, 125; allegory in, 132–33; in Villa's "Young Writer in a New Country," 73–74
autofiction, 26

backwardness, as alternative form of politics, 10
Baker, Houston, Jr., 9, 127, 191
Barakat, Halim, 47
Barbadian immigrants, 37, 152, 154–55. See also *Brown Girl, Brownstones* (Marshall)
Barbados, 152, 154
Barthes, Roland, 24
Batiste, Stephanie Leigh, 9
"bearing," 171–72
Bellingham riots (1907), 122
Berlant, Lauren, 29, 186
Bertha Mason (character, *Jane Eyre*), 13–14
Best, Stephen, 190, 196
betrayal of racial identity, 4, 33, 35–36, 94–97, 101–2, 117, 121
Beyond the Melting Pot (Glazer and Moynihan), 157
Bhabha, Homi, 9
bildungsroman: *The Book of Khalid* as, 49–53; *Brown Girl, Brownstones* as, 37, 153, 167, 173; *Pocho* as, 99, 107, 113
binaries: aestheticism/proletarianism, 70; colonialism/nationalism, 7; domination/resistance, 9; El Macho/El Malinche opposition, 111–14; "fall of man"/"hope of man," 99, 101–2, 110–11
biography, negation of, 35
black British culture, 20
"black Jew," figure of, 155, 176–78
Black Skin, White Masks (Fanon), 9, 17, 82, 191–93
black solidarity, 157, 162, 166, 169, 181–82
black studies, 11, 190–92
blackness: in *Black Skin, White Masks*, 17–19, 191; in *Brown Girl, Brownstones*, 161–62; 166–67; typography as, 17

Boelhower, William, 28–29
Bollingen Prize, 85
Book of Khalid, The (Rihani), 34–35, 36, 43–65, 143, 184; "Al-Fatihah" prelude, 49; American dream critiqued in, 43–44, 48, 58, 115, 193, 194; American materialism critiqued in, 51, 55; as bildungsroman, 49–53; "Dream of Cyclamens," 50; editions, 46–47, 64; Gibran's illustrations for, 51, 52; "hand of Fate" motive in, 60, 63; *Histoire Intime*, 48, 51; "Khalidism," 50, 54, 59; making and unmaking in, 48–59; multiple literary traditions in, 48–49; natal tropes in, 43, 50, 59; origins in, 50–51, 61–62; palingenesis theme in, 50–51, 53; picaresque in, 49, 54; stalled protagonists in, 59–65; "subtranscendental" movement in, 56, 59, 193; "Superman of America" figure, 43, 44–45, 51, 54, 59–60, 66, 115, 143, 193; weaving, conceit of, 54–55. See also Khalid (character, *The Book of Khalid*); Rihani, Ameen
"Book of the Grotesque, The" (Anderson), 75–76
bootstrap ideology, 2, 3, 29, 31, 187
Bourne, Randolph, 51, 52
Bracero Program, 146
British Empire, 122, 132, 136
Bröck, Sabine, 159–60
Brody, Jennifer DeVere, 17
Brontë, Charlotte, 13
Brown (Rodriguez), 7–8
Brown Girl, Brownstones (Marshall), 34, 36–38, 152–82; artists in, 166, 168, 179–82; as bildungsroman, 37, 153, 167, 173; birth-to-death cycle in, 156, 174, 195; blackness, relationship of characters to, 161–62, 166–67; black pathology arguments drawn from, 37, 158; black solidarity in, 162, 166, 169, 181–82; brownstones as characters in, 154, 173–79, 175;

chiasmus of character in, 37, 153–54, 160–68, 172–73; closing scene, 183–84, 193, 196; colonial power in 162–63; confusion as theme in, 175–77, 179–80; exploitation of African Americans and immigrants in, 152, 153, 161, 177; Margaret's mother scene, 169–71, 180; mirroring structure in, 153–54, 160, 166–68; social constraint in, 37–38, 154, 160, 172–73, 181–82; staircase as emblem in, 152, 165–66, 174, 184, 193; structural critique in, 173–79; title, parataxis of, 173; white ethnicization in, 155, 162; whiteness, relationship of characters to, 161–66; whiteness as ghostly imprint in, 154, 164–65, 177; World War II as setting and template for, 159, 167–68. *See also* Marshall, Paule

Brown, Linda Joyce, 32

"brown Uncle Tom" characters, 6–12, 179, 187

Brown v. Board of Education, 140

brownness, 134, 177, 217n57; in *Brown*, 8; in *Brown Girl, Brownstones*, 177–80, 193; "brown" racial epithet, 62, 83, 134; in *Footnote to Youth*, 82–84; ideological indeterminacy and, 37, 179, 193; in *Pocho*, 111–13; racialization in terms of, 1, 12, 138, 144; transforming binaries, 12, 178–79, 193; Uncle Tom figure and, 11

Bruce, J. Campbell, 141

Buaken, Manuel, 6, 83

burden: of representation, 13, 24–25, 19–27, 84, 91, 96, 170, 195; of signification, 13–19, 22–23, 170, 195

Bush, George W., 34, 42–43, 44, 47, 48, 65

California: "Hindu-German conspiracy" trials, 122; Twenty-Ninth Congressional District, 1–2, 119, 123–24; Westmorland, 123

Cantú, Roberto, 93

Capécia, Mayotte, 192–93

capitalism: assimilation of minorities into, 153–54, 160, 162–64, 167; exploitative structures of, 153–54, 167, 177, 184; leveling privilege of, 129; resistance to, 9

Capitol, U.S. Cannon Rotunda, 1, 2

Cassuto, Leonard, 79–80

Caste and Outcast (Mukerji), 7

Cecil Osborne (character, *Brown Girl, Brownstones*), 160–61, 181

Cervantes, Miguel de, 49

character: aggregates of, 97–102; American, archetypes of, 4–5, 12–13, 21, 27; appearance and, 5, 17–18, 191; authorial and literary, overlap between, 10, 14, 87, 192–93; as authorial and textual, 10–11, 40; chiasmus of, 37, 153–54, 160–68, 172–73; constellation of ethnic literature through, 185, 187–88; cultural work of, 3, 191; as device, 12, 16, 19; distribution of, 13, 100; eccentric, 4, 13, 15, 33, 35, 68, 71, 194–95; embodiment of, 21–22, 36; as engraving/mark/stamp, 4, 14–19, 39, 195; as enigmatic, 8, 16; excess of, 70–71, 150–51; as fate, 63, 171–72, 179; flat, 13, 18, 19, 40, 80, 100, 112, 200n67; hyperproduction of, 35, 43, 58–59, 64–65, 76, 193; indexical function of, 23, 81, 84, 87, 158; individual identity mediated by, 125, 187; literal and figurative meanings of, 14–15, 19; literary as expression of authorial, 87; literary fictions of, 24, 38; mask of, 191–93; as method, 4, 12, 16, 24–27, 187–88; minor and minority linked, 13–14; multiplicity of, 26, 34, 39, 171; national identity mediated by, 125, 187; other of, 38–41, 59, 84, 183; overlapping fields of, 100–102, 114, 118, 189–90; personality, move to, 125; phenomenology of race and, 17–18; race linked to, 13–19; rebirthing of, 50–52, 54, 59; recursive mirror of interpretation, 15, 18, 22, 27, 60, 88, 171, 195; rhetoric of, 24, 125, 127; social characterization, 26, 31, 35, 67, 79–80; socioformal approaches to, 16, 24, 40–41, 99–100; types, 12–13, 15, 18, 80, 189, 200n67. *See also* characters, literary; persona, literary; race character critique

character building, 125–33, 142; sportsmanship and fair play, American rhetoric of, 129–32, 148–50; stigma of race dislodged by, 187. *See also* Saund, Dalip Singh

character function, authorial, 25, 151, 181, 189–90, 195; Marshall and, 155–56, 181; Rihani and, 43, 45, 60, 64–67; Saund and, 121, 128–37, 142–43, 150; Villa and, 74, 87–91; Villarreal and, 95–97, 115–16, 117–18

characterization: as contestation, 5, 193; literary structures of, 6; racialization disclosed by, 22; racist, 169–70; social, of minorities, 26, 31, 35, 67, 79–84, 87, 90–91; as technology of the American dream, 150

"character narration," 133

characterology, 17–18

"character representation," 125

characters, literary: absent presence of, 146; anthropomorphic, 76–78, 100; authors as, 4–5, 12–14, 20, 24, 26, 33–34, 36, 192–93; authors not coextensive with, 10, 48, 59–60, 94–95, 189–90, 195; distributional matrix of, 13, 24, 100; grotesque, 35, 67, 73–79; recentering marginalized subjects as, 10; as signs, 38; stock, 11, 14; as "word-masses," 24. *See also* character

"character-space," 25–26, 174, 194; in *Pocho*, 100, 104, 106–7

"character-system," 100

character theory, 12–14, 23, 38–41, 74–75

Cheng, Anne Anlin, 126, 143

Chiang, Mark, 21

Chicago Daily Tribune, 139

Chicago school of sociology, 30, 176

Chicano movement, 36, 93–94, 98, 101

Chow, Rey, 20, 188, 189

Chua, Jonathan, 70, 71, 86

Chuh, Kandice, 10, 11, 190

Churchwell, Sarah, 29–30

citizenship: in *Congressman from India*, 129, 131–33, 144–45; constitutional allegoresis, 28–29; denied to Indians, 122–23, 131–33, 144; Filipinos and, 85; Mexicans and, 31, 113–14; racist matrix of, 21; Saund becomes American citizen, 123; second-class, 2, 5, 39; stripped due to intermarriage, 145

Civil Rights Act (1957), 149

civil rights movement, 29, 119, 185

Cixous, Hélène, 16, 187, 191

Claremont Sealy (character, *Brown Girl, Brownstones*), 161, 167

Clark, Audrey Wu, 32

Clive (character, *Brown Girl, Brownstones*), 155, 156, 168, 181

close and situated analysis, 40, 195

Cochran, Jacqueline, 123, 137–38

Cold War, 36, 119; model minority myth, emergence of, 121, 125–26

colonial mimicry, 9

colonialism: anticolonial organizing, Indian, 122, 132, 136; Filipino colonial subjection, 35; heteropatriarchal violence of, 101–2; "imported," 113–14; racialization of appearance, 17–18, 191; subverted by Villa, 71, 102, 111–14; turkey-pardoning tradition as allegory of, 186–87; United States called on to intervene in, 6; West Indies, 154; "white mask" of, 191–92. *See also* decolonial critique

Columbus, 50

communism, fears of, 138–39, 141–42

comparative analysis, 4, 37, 38–39, 187–89

Congressman from India (Saund), 4, 36, 119–51; as accommodationist text, 127; American archetype in, 133–43;

Index 243

broader work of characterization within, 143–44; character-building discourse in, 36, 125–33, 150–51; confessional intimacy in, 143; destabilization of minority model in, 36; as "diasporic autobiography," 125; "East" meets "West" formula, 134, 142, 143; family in, 133–35, *135*; "fights" in, 128–29, 144; front cover, *120*; Gettysburg Address phrasing used in, 124; metonymy in, 150–51; nonrestrictive grammar at sentence level, 146–47; presidential race of 1920 in, 129; racial divides in, 147–48, 150–51; sportsmanship and fair play, rhetoric of, 129–32, 148–50. *See also* Saund, Dalip Singh

constellation, 37, 185, 187–88

constitutional allegoresis, 28–29

Consuelo (character, *Pocho*), 97, 103–5, 107, 110–11

contestation, 5, 193

Cruz, Denise, 71, 72, 79

Cullen, Jim, 30, 38

cultural materialism, 10, 24

Cutler, John Alba, 99, 100

"death of the author," 24

Decker, Jeffrey Louis, 30, 125

Declaration of Independence, 147

decolonial critique, 71, 157

Deighton Boyce (character, *Brown Girl, Brownstones*), 152, 155–56, 158–59, 162–63, 176–78

democracy: in *Congressman from India*, 119, 121, 139, 141–42, 147; as corrupted, in *The Book of Khalid*, 51

Democratic Party, 123, 139

demystification, 190–92, 196

Depression era, 73, 81, 85, 97, 108

Dickerson, Vanessa, 174

difference, 13; character in, 26; racial, 3; selective incorporation of, 3, 121, 126, 128; visible, 11, 19–20. *See also* visibly racialized subjects

"differential other," 38, 64, 160

disidentification, 97, 101, 161–62

displacement, 15, 20, 66, 79, 82, 111, 189

display, vs. demystification, 190–92

Domingo, W. A., 154–55

Don Quixote (Cervantes), 49

double consciousness, 25

Douglas, William, 140

Du Bois, W. E. B., 25, 127

Dulles, John Foster, 140

Dust Bowl migration, 146

East Goes West (Kang), 6

eccentric character, 4, 13, 15, 33, 195; Villa and, 35, 68, 71, 194

Editor (character, *The Book of Khalid*), 43, 48, 49, 54–55, 59–60, 64

Edwards, Justin, 80

ego, 39, 56–59, 187

ego ideal, 57–59

Ellis Island medical inspection, 58

Ellison, Ralph, 17

El Macho figure, 36, 96, 100, 102–7; queering of, 107, 111–14

El Malinche figure, 36, 96–97, 100–101, 104–7, 110–11, 116, 118

emblematization: in *Brown Girl, Brownstones*, 152, 165–66, 174, 184, 193; in Villarreal's work, 96; in Villa's work, 67, 73, 76–77, 80–84, 87–91

engraving/mark/stamp, character as, 4, 14–19, 39, 195

Epic of America, The (Adams), 29–30

essentialism, 10–11, 17, 32

ethnic literature: American dream and character confronted in, 4–5, 40, 51, 54–55, 64, 84, 127, 144, 147, 183, 193–95; art severed from biography, 35, 67, 86; autobiography, 5; "brown Uncle Tom" characters, 6–12, 179, 187; constellation of, through character, 37, 185, 187–88; minor and minority characters in, 14; oppositional framework of, 4, 7–12, 27–28, 33, 39, 125, 157, 185, 195; other of character in,

244 Index

38–41, 59, 84; propaganda function, 7–8, 36, 119, 138–41, 157; resistance-based model of, 4, 6, 8–10, 32, 39, 195; social minorness and, 11, 14, 21. *See also* archive of ethnic literature; literary criticism; *individual authors*
ethnic studies, 8–12, 20, 30, 33, 48, 187–88, 190; prehistory of, 28
ethnic writers. *See* authors
ethnicity: "ethnic projects," 30; race transformed into, 31, 36, 121, 126, 132, 143, 155, 160; racialization of non-European immigrants and, 30–33, 39; white ethnicization, 3, 28, 30–32, 126, 155, 160, 162, 176–79
Europe, as referent of supremacy, 189
European immigration, 28–30, 185
exceptionalism. *See* American exceptionalism
excess, 155; of character, 70–71, 150–51; interpretive, 15, 18–19, 22–24, 96, 150–51; of origins, 54; of personality, 24, 26, 195
exposure, 35, 72–73, 81, 84
exteriorization, 55–56, 60

face, as semiotic instrument, 191
"Fact of Blackness, The" (Fanon), 17–18
familiar: paredros ("daemonic other"), 38, 84, 216n35; queer, 107
family, American archetype and, 133–35, *135*
Fanon, Frantz, 9, 17–18, 22, 35, 58, 82, 170, 191–93; "racial epidermal schema," 18, 172; sociodiagnostic, 58, 172, 179, 193–94
Far Journey, A (Rihbany), 6, 22–23
Felski, Rita, 16
feminist critique, 14, 36; Chicana, 101, 209n37
Ferguson, Missouri, 186
"Fiction of Asian American Literature, The" (Koshy), 190
figuration, 14–15, 38–39, 84, 99, 159, 173, 177, 185; "figure for figure,"

15; hypervisibility, 18; surfeit of, 15, 18, 170
Filipinos: as colonial subjects, 35, 83, 85, 194; social characterization of, 79, 87, 91, 193; subjection of, 67, 73, 82–83, 193; as type of ideal American, 6; as U.S. nationals, 31, 85. *See also* Asian Americans; *Footnote to Youth* (Villa); Villa, José Garcia
flat character, 13, 18, 19, 40, 80, 100, 112, 200n67
Fong, Hiram, 119
Footnote to Youth (Villa), 35, 66–91, 112; anthropomorphism in, 76–78; character and self in, 85–91; characterizing the grotesque in, 73–79; collage technique in, 84; emblematic in, 67, 73, 76–77, 80–84, 87–91; exposure of social characterization of minorities, 79–84; immanent symbology in, 80; reviews of, 85–86; "Tales of the Philippines and Others" as subtitle, 85. *See also* Villa, José Garcia
Foreign Affairs Committee, 124
formalism, 10–11, 70, 195; social analysis transformed by, 11, 40–41
Forster, E. M., 24, 80, 100
Foucault, Michel, 24, 25, 188, 189
Fowler, Elizabeth, 24, 26, 99–100
Francia, Luis, 67, 86, 90
Franklin, Benjamin, 21, 29, 187
Freedman, Samuel, 120–21
Freike (Lebanon), 43
French mandate, 44, 45
Freud, Sigmund, 56–57
Frow, John, 15, 24, 191; paredros, concept of, 38, 84; "zone" of characterization, 59, 179

Gandhi, Mahatma, 136, 140
Garveyism, 161
gaze: colonial, 17–18, 35; microscopic, 18, 35
General Carrillo (character, *Pocho*), 103, 104

Index 245

General Fuentes (character, *Pocho*), 102–3
Ghadar movement, 122, 136, 139
Gibran, Kahlil, 49, 51, 52
Glazer, Nathan, 157
Grace Poole (character, *Jane Eyre*), 13
Graulund, Rune, 80
grid of intelligibility, 189
grotesque, the, 35, 73–79, 194; in African diasporic cultural production, 80–81; anthropomorphic characters, 76–78; emblematic in, 67, 73, 76–77, 80–84, 87–91; fixation as feature of, 75–76, 79; incongruousness of, 67–68; "noble" form of, 75; painterly sense of, 76; as site of racial objectification, 80–81; social characterization of Filipinos and minorities, 67, 79–84; as violation of basic categories, 80–81
group formations, 187–88
Group Psychology and the Analysis of the Ego (Freud), 57
Gualtieri, Sarah, 53, 63

Hagedorn, Jessica, 71, 72, 90
Haley, Nikki, 121
"Hands" (Anderson), 75
Harlem Renaissance, 154
Harris, Trudier, 159–60
Hassan, Waïl, 47–48
Hathaway, Heather, 160
Hawai'i, 119
Heraclitan maxim, 63
Heraclitus, 171
hermeneutic, literary, 11–12, 84, 158, 193
Hidalgo, Melissa, 99
hierarchy: racial, 30; social, 81, 102–103, 114, 128–29, 177
"Hindu-German conspiracy" trials, 122
Hindustan Association of America, 123
homophobia, 96, 102, 103, 166
homosociality, 103–4, 106–8
Hopkins, Pauline, 127
Howarth, William, 132
Hughes, Langston, 157
Hughes, Thomas, 11–12
Hunger of Memory (Rodriguez), 11, 101
hyperproduction of character, 35, 43, 58–59, 64–65, 76, 193

identity: authorial not coextensive with fictional characters, 10, 48, 59–60, 94–95, 189–90, 195; disidentification, 97, 101, 161–62; hyphenated, 7–8, 10, 12, 115; intersection of race, class, nation, language, and geography, 94; racial, betrayal of, 4, 33, 35–36, 94–97, 101–2, 117; subaltern, 9; Villa's disavowal of, 71. *See also* minority identity
I Have Lived with the American People (Buaken), 6, 83
"image," 125
immigrant analogy, 155, 176
immigration: Afro-Caribbean, 154–55, 176; as broad lineage, 115–16; European, 3, 28–30, 185; first-and second-generation, 33; Filipino, 83; as form of testimony, 158; genealogy of, 154, 177; hegemonic ideals reinforced by, 4; imperialism linked to, 34, 42–44, 51; "imported colonialism," 113–14; Irish, 132; noble discourse of, 53; non-European, 28, 30–33, 37–39, 177; post-Mexican Revolution, 103, 105; "race relations cycle," 30, 176; racialized, 3–4; South Asian, 145, 150, 121–22; succession of, 37, 94, 154, 176–77, 181, 184; symbology of, 42; Syrian, 45; white European model of, 3, 28, 176, 180; whiteness, categorization of, 135–36
Immigration Act of 1917, 62–63, 122
immurement, logic of, 196
Imperial County Democratic Central Committee, 123
imperialism: immigration linked to, 34, 42–44, 51; whiteness as requisite for, 61–63
"implied authorial I," 64
In re Rodriguez, 114

Ina Boyce (character, *Brown Girl, Brownstones*), 152, 173, 174
India: Ghadar movement, 122, 136, 139; relationship with United States, 139–42; revolutionary nationalism, 136
India Association of America, 131
Indian Americans, 120; alien land laws and, 145; claims to Caucasian kinship and Aryan ancestry, 135–36. *See also* Asian Americans; *Congressman from India* (Saund); Saund, Dalip Singh; South Asian Americans
Indian diaspora, 120, 143; anticolonial organizing, 122, 132, 136; East Indian migration to United States, 121–22
Indian realism, 14
individuality, 5–6, 25, 34, 95, 98, 114–18
industrialization, 13
Inouye, Daniel, 119
intentional fallacy, 24
interpretation: categories of, 12–13; of character through race, 37; eye as correcting mirror, 192; recursive mirror of, 15, 18, 22, 27, 60, 88, 171, 195
interpretive excess, 15, 18–19, 22–24, 96, 150–51
intersexuality, 114–16
Invisible Man (Ellison), 17
Irish immigration, 132

Jacobson, Matthew Frye, 28
Jahshan, Paul, 47
Jane Eyre (Brontë), 13–14
Jarrett, Gene Andrew, 10–11, 17, 26
Jasmine (Mukherjee), 7
Jean Veneuse (character, *Un Homme pareil aux autres*), 193
Je suis Martiniquaise (Capécia), 192–93
Jewish immigrants, 37, 152, 177
Jewish stereotypes, 155, 176–77
Jim Crow segregation, 28, 166, 190
Jiménez, Francisco, 99
Jindal, Bobby, 2, 120–21
Joaquin, Nick, 82, 90
Joe Pete (character, *Pocho*), 98, 107–9
Jones, Gavin, 167
Joyce, James, 95
Juan Manuel Rubio (character, *Pocho*), 97–118; birth scene, 104–6; colonialism, critique of, 102, 112–13; as fallen man, 105–6, 110–11
Julian Hurley (character, *Brown Girl, Brownstones*), 166–67

Kang, Younghill, 6
Khalid (character, *The Book of Khalid*), 44–45; as feminized, 50–51, 115; imperial mission of, 52–53; inward character of, 55–56; madness of, 56–58; origins of, 50–51, 61–62; as picaro, 49; rebirthing of, 50–52, 54, 59; as stalled protagonist, 59–65; "Superman of America" vision of, 43, 44–45, 51, 54, 59–60, 115, 143, 193; tripartite structure of characterization, 54–55. *See also The Book of Khalid* (Rihani)
King, Martin Luther, Jr., 140
Kingston, Maxine Hong, 21, 25
Komagata Maru (Japanese vessel), 122
Koshy, Susan, 31, 126, 155, 185–86, 190

La Malinche figure, 9, 97, 100–101, 209n37
"La Raza," 114
Latinx Literature Unbound (Rodriguez), 190
Latinx studies, 11, 190
Lee, Chang-rae, 8
Lee, Christopher, 10, 67, 71
Lee, Robert, 125, 126
Lejeune, Philippe, 133
Letters to Uncle Sam (Rihani), 34, 43, 45–46, 60–65, 66; white officer, encounter with, 60–64, 66. *See also* Rihani, Ameen
Lincoln, Abraham, 136
literary criticism, 9, 13, 186–87, 195; Eurocentric readings of immigrant literature, 28–29, 30; resistance-based, 4, 6, 8–10, 32, 39, 195.

See also ethnic literature; race character critique
literary text, as autonomous, 24, 27
literary worlds, social worlds and, 13, 16, 20–21, 26, 38, 189, 198n26
Little Rock crisis, 147–48
Locke, Alain, 20–21
López, Ian Haney, 31
Los Angeles Times, 137
Love, Heather, 10
Luce, Clare Boothe, 144–45
Luce-Celler Act of 1946, 122
Lye, Colleen, 10, 31
Lynch, Deirdre Shauna, 24, 191

machismo, 36, 95–96, 98; corrido hero, 103–5, 111–12; honor, code of, 103, 109; masochism as counter to, 111; stereotypical, 102–3. *See also* masculinity
Madrid-Barela, Arturo, 94
Mangahas, Federico, 90
mania and melancholia, 56–58
maqāma, genre of, 49
Maran, René, 192–93
Marcos, Ferdinand, 69
Marcus, Sharon, 190, 196
Margaret (character, *Brown Girl, Brownstones*), 169
Margaret's mother (character, *Brown Girl, Brownstones*), 156, 169–72, 180
Maritze (character, *Brown Girl, Brownstones*), 164
Marshall, Paule, 4, 152–82; background of, 154–56; black solidarity and, 157; on black women's triple invisibility, 156, 159; character function of, 181; civil rights activism of, 157; international tour, 36–37; interviews with, 156, 157, 158–59, 181; propaganda function subverted by, 157; reconfiguring of biography in novel, 158–59; on testimonial function of novel, 158. Works: "From the Poets in the Kitchen," 155; *Triangular Road*, 155,

157. *See also Brown Girl, Brownstones* (Marshall)
masculinity: El Macho and El Malinche conjoined, 101–2; horses as symbolic of, 113; minority based on dominant patriarchal order, 102; nonnormative, 71; queering of, 96–97, 99, 101–4. *See also* machismo
mask of character, 191–93
materialistic ethic, 156–57, 159–60
Mayflowerism, 53, 131
McKay, Claude, 20–21
melting pot trope, 44
Mercer, Kobena, 20
mestizaje, 110, 113
method: authorial character and, 25–26; character as, 12, 187–88; of race character critique, 4, 26–27; recalibration in ethnic studies of, 190; "socioformal," 16, 24
metonymy, 15, 19, 22, 61, 141, 149–50, 170, 196; expansionist, 44, 47, 51
Mexican Americans, 8–9; as "American pioneers," 115; "'assimilationist' phase" and, 98; divisions of language, class, region, geography, and immigrant succession, 93–4; exploitation of, 145–46; pachuco subculture, 109–10; racism against, 116, 145–46; whiteness, relationship to, 112–14. *See also* Chicano movement; *Pocho* (Villarreal); Villarreal, José Antonio
Mexican Revolution, 96, 97, 103, 105
Mexicans: citizenship and, 31, 113–14; Punjabi, 146
Miller, J. Hillis, 15, 17, 18, 23; differential other, concept of, 38, 64, 160; on reading character, 195
minorities: assimilation of into capitalism, 153–54, 160, 162–64, 167; minor and minority linked, 13–14; social characterization of, 26, 31, 35, 67, 79–84, 87, 90–91
minority identity, 3–9, 28, 183, 189; as anachronism for early

twentieth-century writers, 32–33; appropriation, shared burden of, 39–40; erasure of, 12–13, 40–41; rejection of, 6–8, 12–13, 32, 39–40, 184–85; under the sign of its own erasure, 12, 137. *See also* identity

minorness, 14, 21

mirror of interpretation, recursive, 15, 18, 22, 27, 60, 88, 171, 195

Miss Mary (character, *Brown Girl, Brownstones*), 153, 163–64

Miss Thompson (character, *Brown Girl, Brownstones*), 153, 166, 178

Mix, Tom (movie actor), 111, 113

model minority, 2–4, 9, 31, 187; destabilization of, 36; emergence of myth in Cold War era, 121, 125–26; non-model minority produced by, 126; Saund as example of, 119–29, 137, 142–44, 150, 155, 184

modernism, 35; in *Pocho*, 105, 107; Villa and, 68–70, 72, 86, 89

modernist minstrelsy, 9

Morrison, Toni, 13, 15

mourning, 190

"Mourning and Melancholia" (Freud), 57

Moynihan, Daniel, 157

Mukerji, Dhan Gopal, 6–7

Mukherjee, Bharati, 7

multiculturalism, 3, 126, 186

Muñoz, José Esteban, 101

mythos, character-driven, 126

Naff, Alixa, 62

Najour, Costa (*In re Najour* petitioner), 63

narrative form, 16, 26, 79, 100

narrator: as alter ego, 25; character narration, 133; "implied authorial I" and, 64

Nash, Geoffrey, 65

natal tropes, 43, 50, 59

nation: individual, slippage with, 5

national origins quota system (1924 to 1965), 30

nationalism, 136

Native Speaker (Lee), 8

nativism, 1, 39, 63, 109; South Asian immigrants and, 122–23, 130, 132, 134–35

naturalization: in *Congressman from India*, 144–45; as effortless, 6; of Filipinos, 85; of Mexican Americans, 114; *In re Rodriguez*, 114; right to, 31; Supreme Court cases, 122–23, 135, 144; Syrian immigrants and, 62–63

Naturalization Act of 1790, 21

Near or Middle East, as new construction, 62

Nehru, Jawaharlal, 140

New Criticism, 24

New Mexico Quarterly, 85

New Negro, The (Locke, ed.), 154–55

New Negro, The (Stewart), 201n77

New Racism, 186

New York Times, 138

Ngai, Mae, 30

Nguyen, Viet Thanh, 9

Nietzsche, Friedrich, 187

nineteenth-century literature, 13, 23, 200n53

Non-Aligned Movement, 140

non-European immigrants, 28, 37–39, 176–77, 185; liminal position of, 31, 185; racialization of, 30–33, 128

non-model minorities, 126

Obama, Barack, 2, 3

object-cathexis, 57

O'Brien, Edward, 85

Odlum, Floyd, 138

Odlum, Jacqueline, 137–38

Omi, Michael, 19, 30–31

ontology, 16, 18–19, 116

oppositional frameworks, 4, 7–12, 27–28, 33, 39, 125, 157, 185, 195

Orientalism, 7; circular structure of, 142; in Rihani's work, 35, 44, 47–49, 51, 58; Saidian paradigm of, 47; Saund and, 134, 137–39, 142; Villa's subversion of, 71, 82–83, 86, 90–91

Index 249

other: of character, 38–41, 59, 84, 183; differential, 38, 64, 160; paredros/daemonic, 38, 84, 216n35; Villa as, 67, 85–86
Ottoman Empire, 44, 45, 52–53
Oxford English Dictionary (OED) taxonomy of character, 14–15, 17

pachuco subculture, 98, 108, 109–10, 115–17
paredros (daemonic other), 38, 84, 216n35
Paris Peace Conference (1919), 6
paternalism, 85–86
Pease, Donald, 29
persona, literary, 3, 12–13, 24, 33, 59, 142; plural and heterogeneous, 26; socioformal approaches to, 99–100; in Villa's work, 72, 84, 90–91. *See also* character
personality, 125, 171–72; excess of, 24, 26, 195
Phelan, James, 64, 133
Philippine-American war, 83
Philippines: Anglophone literature in, 68; anticolonial struggle, 70; Treaty of Paris (1898), 83; Tydings-McDuffie Act of 1934, 68, 85
Phillips, John, 123
Phoenicianism, 53, 62
picaresque, 49, 54
Pilar (character, *Pocho*), 92
Playing in the Dark (Morrison), 13
pocho, 12, 35–36, 117, 184; contested meaning of, 92–94; queer critique and, 101; two fields of characterization, 96–97, 102, 114, 118. See also *Pocho* (Villarreal)
Pocho (Villarreal), 34–36, 92–118; American dream in, 94, 96, 98, 110–11, 115–16; as bildungsroman, 99, 107, 113; birth scene, 104–6; Chicano movement and, 98–99; colonialism subverted in, 102, 111–14; corrido hero stereotype, 103–5, 111–12; critical responses to, 95–96, 98–99; editions, 92, 93, 98–99; "fall of man"/"hope of man" binary in, 99, 101–2, 110–11; free indirect discourse in, 107; homophobia in, 102–3; homosociality in, 103–4, 106–8; horse figure in, 111–14; individuality in, 114–18; intersex fantasy in, 114–16; new social order in, 102–6; pachuco subculture in, 98, 108, 109–10, 115–17; plot, 97–98; queering of masculinity in, 103–4, 106–11; transition from realist to modernist modes in, 104–5, 107. *See also* Villarreal, José Antonio
Ponce, Martin Joseph, 27, 70, 71, 79
"Poor Richard," 187
Portrait of the Artist as a Young Man, A (Joyce), 95
postracial ideology, 186
power, 13; archetype and, 27, 30; capitalism and, 161–64; of character, 30, 37; racialized, 9, 113; structural, 162, 171–72, 180, 184
primitivism, 83, 170–71, 172
Project Khalid, 46
Promised Land, The (Antin), 28
propaganda function of race and ethnicity, 7–8, 36, 119, 138–41, 157
Prophet, The (Gibran), 49
psychological constructs in ethnic literature: alter ego, 25; cathexes, 35, 56–58, 65; ego, 39, 56–59, 71, 187; ego ideal, 56–59; narcissism, 57, 90–91; repetition compulsion, 58, 72
public figures, 3, 123–24
Public Law 78 (Mexican immigrants exploited under), 146
punctuation, blackness and, 17
Punjabi Mexicans, 146

queer critiques, 9, 36, 71, 79, 96–97, 99–102

race: character linked to, 17–19; connection between India and United

States, 139–40; as overdetermined, 5, 15, 17–19, 22, 26–27, 96, 116, 118, 146, 151, 172, 181, 191, 194; phenomenology of, 17–18; pivot with ethnicity, 32, 36, 121, 150, 177–80, 185, 187, 193; social reading of, 18–19; transformed into ethnicity, 31, 36, 121, 126, 132, 143, 155; fantasy of whiteness and, 62–64, 66, 89, 113–14, 133–34, 162–65

race character critique, 4, 6, 25–27, 40, 183, 190, 193; burden of signification and, 13, 91; conceptual links, 17; double move of, 12, 13, 37–39, 53, 59, 144, 179, 183; literary representations linked to contexts and histories, 4, 91; Marshall and, 154; plural and heterogeneous literary personas, 26; *Pocho*'s two fields of characterization, 96–97, 114, 118; protean figures of, 183; Rihani and, 63–68; Saund and, 144, 151; Villarreal and, 96, 118; Villa and, 67, 90–91. *See also* literary criticism

"race relations cycle," 30, 176

racial determinism, 127

racial epidermal schema, 18, 172

racial form, 10

racialization: black, 155, 177–79, 183; characterization and, 5, 18–19, 22–23, 60–62, 81–84, 111–14, 116–17, 133–37, 145–51; 161–67, 169–73, 176–80, 191–93; as comparative, 189; Filipino, 82–83; interpretive excess and, 18–19, 150–51; Mexican, 113–24; of non-European immigrants, 30–33, 128; South Asian, 134–36, 150; of success, 36, 119, 121, 126, 150, 155–57, 164; Syrian, 62–63. *See also* visibly racialized subjects

racial profiling, 19

racial realism, 11

racial uplift, 21, 127

racism: characterization and, 116–17, 169–70; essentialization based on "mark" or type, 17–18; hierarchies of, 164, 202n121; against Indian immigrants, 122; Jim Crow segregation, 28, 166, 190; Little Rock crisis, 119, 147–48; against Mexican Americans, 116, 145–46; New Racism, 186; pathologization of black people, 37, 126, 158; primitivistic discourses, 82–83, 170–72; structural, not challenged by authors, 3, 126, 128, 152, 162. *See also* visibly racialized subjects

racist apprehension, 170–71, 180

rags-to-riches romance, 29, 36, 137, 138

Reader's Digest, 141–42

realism: Indian, 14; racial, 11

Redding, Jay Saunders, 140

relation, politics of, 125

René Soto (character, *Pocho*), 103–4, 106–7

representation: assumption of, 20–21; burden of, 13, 24–25, 19–27, 84, 91, 96, 170, 195; burden of, and Villa, 67–68, 84, 91; burden of, and Villarreal, 96, 98–99; burden of signification and, 13, 19–20, 22–23, 170, 195; character and, 125; contestation and, 5, 79, 81; demand for, 20–21; logics of, 81; Saund and, 124

representative character, 20

"resistance theory," 9

ressentiment, ethnic, 20

rhetoric of character, 24, 125, 127

Rhys, Jean, 14

Richard Rubio (character, *Pocho*), 35–36, 92–118, 184, 194; queer counterpose of, 106–11

Ricky (character, *Pocho*), 97, 108, 116

Rihani, Ameen, 4, 6, 34–35, 203n7; American dream embraced by, 43–48; Arab self-determination, commitment to, 42, 65; archetypal function of, 34, 47; Bush appropriates in Abu Dhabi speech, 34, 42–43, 44, 47, 48, 65; character function of, 43, 45, 60, 64–67, 150; commemorative critique of, 46–47; complexity of, 43–44; edited collection, 2011, 47; international advocacy work of, 65;

Index 251

on nature of *The Book of Khalid*, 49;
Orientalism of, 44, 47–48; promotion
of Allied cause among Syrians
in Mexico, 45, 46, 62; as stalled
protagonist of American dream,
64–65; universalism attributed to,
46–47, 65, 116. Works: "From Brooklyn
Bridge," 44; *Letters to Uncle Sam*, 34,
43, 45–46, 60–61, 64; *Ar-Rihaniyat*, 44.
See also *The Book of Khalid* (Rihani);
Letters to Uncle Sam (Rihani)
Rihbany, Abraham Mitrie, 6, 7, 22–23
Rizk, Salom, 6
Rodriguez, Ralph, 11, 21, 190
Rodriguez, Randy, 100–101
Rodriguez, Ricardo (*In re Rodriguez* petitioner), 114
Rodriguez, Richard, 3, 7–8, 11–12, 100–101, 179, 187
Román, Elda María, 24, 159, 166, 181
Roosevelt, Theodore, 45
Rooster (character, *Pocho*), 110
Rose, Jacqueline, 29
Roy, Arundhati, 186
Ruiz, Ramón, 98–99
Ruskin, John, 75, 76

Sae-Saue, Jayson Gonzales, 100
Said, Edward, 47
Salazar, James, 21–22, 24, 125, 126–27, 191
Saldívar, José, 95, 98, 99, 100, 103
Saldívar, Ramón, 93–94
San Francisco Japanese and Korean Exclusion League, 122
San Juan, E., Jr., 70–71, 72, 90, 116
Sánchez, María Carla, 8–9
Santos, Juanita, 83
Saund, Dalip Singh, 27, 119–51;
1949 election and, 123, 129–31; as archetype of American dream, 2, 121, 126–29; autobiography transforms biography, 124; becomes American citizen, 123; campaign of 1956, 123, 137–38; as character, 4–5, 8, 39, 124; congressional work of, 123–24; disavowal of racial violence in United States, 147–51; as distinct American archetype, 133–43; ethnicization of, 133–36, 146; as example of model minority, 119–29, 137, 142–44, 150, 155, 184; first term in Congress, 119; Indian naturalization efforts and, 131–32; international tour, 1957, 119, 124, 140–43, 147–49; Little Rock crisis challenged by international audience, 147–48; as "living example of American democracy in action," 119, 139, 141; media coverage of, 137–38; making of, as model minority, 121–28; "manic relation to" American dream, 126, 143; portrait of, 1–5, *2*, 39, 70; propaganda function of, 119, 138–41; *Reader's Digest* article on, 141–42; schoolboy trope in autobiography of, 128–33, *130*, 148; subtranscendental movement in, 193–94; *What America Means to Me* campaign biography, 129–30, *130*. See also character building; *Congressman from India* (Saund)
Saunders, Patricia, 152
Schlund-Vials, Cathy, 21
"scholarship boy," 12
schoolboy trope, 11–12, 128–33, *130*, 148
scientific racism, 18, 21, 201n84
Scribner's Magazine, 85
second-class citizenship, 2, 5, 39
Sedore, Timothy, 99
self: as abstraction, 87; character as stand-in for, 23; in *Footnote to Youth*, 85–91
self making, 5, 29–30, 183; in *Brown Girl, Brownstones*, 179; constrained by social forces, 37; postwar myth of, 125; Rihani and, 47; Saund and, 121, 137–38, 148; Villarreal and, 115
Selina Boyce (character, *Brown Girl, Brownstones*), 37, 152–82; closing scene of *Brown Girl, Brownstones* and, 183–84, 193, 195–96; dream of escape from brownstone, 180–81

252   *Index*

Seurat, Georges, 76
Shakespeare, William, 56
Shakib (character, *The Book of Khalid*), 48–50, 51, 55–56
Shih, Shu-mei, 189
Shohat, Ella, 20, 23
Shukla, Sandhya, 124–25, 136, 143
Siefert Yearwood (character, *Brown Girl, Brownstones*), 177
signification, 29, 38; burden of, 13–19, 22–23, 170; burden of representation and, 13, 19–20, 22–23, 170, 195; trap of for ethnic writers, 19–20
Silla Boyce (character, *Brown Girl, Brownstones*), 37, 152–82; whiteness, relationship with, 161–63, 184, 185, 193, 194
Sitwell, Edith, 69, 69, 86, 89
Sitwell, Osbert, 69, 69
social analysis, formalist analysis transformed by, 11, 40–41
social characterization of minorities, 26, 31, 35, 67, 79–84, 90–91
social constraints, 6, 9, 29–30, 40, 83, 194; in *Brown Girl, Brownstones*, 37–38, 154, 160, 172–73, 181–82; in *Congressman from India*, 147
social field, 9, 20, 33, 38, 189–90; "character-space" and, 25–26
social minorness, 11, 14, 21
social mobility, 4, 21–22, 31; "black success story," 155; in *Brown Girl, Brownstones*, 152–53, 155, 159; disidentification with blackness, 161–62; staircase emblem of, 165–66, 184
social movements, 28
social persons, 21, 24, 26, 33, 99–100
social reading, 18–19
social stratification, 13, 24
social worlds, literary worlds and, 13, 16, 20–21, 26, 38, 189, 198n26
"sociodiagnostic," 58, 172, 179, 193–94
socioformal approaches to character, 16, 24, 40–41, 99–100

sociology, 158–59
Sohn, Stephen Hong, 10, 11, 14, 26
solidarity: black, 157, 162, 166, 169; with colonized classes, 112–13; as critical imperative, 8; interracial, as threatening to whites, 146; rejection of, 39, 150
South Asian Americans: citizenship and, 2; in *Congressman from India*, 146; political candidates, 120–21; racialization of, 134–36. *See also* Asian Americans; *Congressman from India* (Saund); Indian Americans; Saund, Dalip Singh
South Asian American studies, 32
space, characterization of, 173–79
spectrum from fiction to autobiography, 20, 25–26
sportsmanship and fair play, American rhetoric of, 129–32, 148–50
Srikanth, Rajini, 124–25
Stam, Robert, 20, 23
Statue of Liberty, 42, 44, 46, 55
Stevens, Wallace, 85
stock characters, 11–12, 14, 103
Stowe, Harriet Beecher, 12
Strange Lands and Friendly People (Douglas), 140
subaltern identity, 9, 73
subject: entomological forms for, 17, 82; idealized, 10. *See also* character; visibly racialized subjects
subjectlessness, 10–11
sublimation of minority status, 35, 47, 67, 68, 71, 73, 75, 80–81, 86, 90–91
"subtranscendental" movement, 56, 59, 193–94
success, racialized, 36, 119, 121, 126, 150, 183; "black success story," 155–57, 164
Suggie (character, *Brown Girl, Brownstones*), 153, 166, 178
Supreme Court, 31, 140; *United States v. Bhagat Singh Thind*, 122–23, 135, 144
Susman, Warren, 125
Syria, 44–45, 54

Syrian diaspora, 6, 42; Phoenician past, discourse of, 53. *See also* Arab Americans; *The Book of Khalid* (Rihani); *Letters to Uncle Sam* (Rihani); Rihani, Ameen; Syrian immigrants

Syrian immigrants, 34–35; naturalization laws and, 31; racialization and naturalization of, 62–63; "'yellow race' crisis," 63. *See also* Arab Americans; *The Book of Khalid* (Rihani); *Letters to Uncle Sam* (Rihani); Rihani, Ameen; Syrian diaspora

Tabios, Eileen, 72
Taft, William Howard, 83
Tamburlaine (character, *Tamburlaine the Great*), 17
Tanganyika, 120
Tate, Claudia, 21, 26
taxonomies, 11, 15, 188–90
Theridamas (character, *Tamburlaine the Great*), 17
Thind, Bhagat Singh, 31
Thomas (character, *Pocho*), 97, 109
Tolentino, Cynthia, 32–33
Tom Brown (character, *Tom Brown's School Days*), 11–12
Tom Brown's School Days (Hughes), 11–12
totality, literary, 100
tragic necessity, 159–60
transcendence: in Rihani's work, 35, 47, 56–59; in Villa's work, 67–68, 74–75, 78–80, 86–87, 116; in Villarreal's work, 112–13, 116; in Saund's work, 136–37, 150–51, 193–94
Treaty of Guadalupe Hidalgo (1848), 113–14
Treaty of Paris (1898), 83
Treitler, Vilna Bashi, 30, 31
Triangular Road (Marshall), 155, 157
Truman, Harry, 131
truth, grotesque and, 75–76
turkey-pardoning tradition, 186–87
Turner, Frederick Jackson, 51

twentieth-century fiction, 14
Tydings-McDuffie Act of 1934, 68, 85
types, 12–13, 15, 18, 80, 189, 200n67
typography, 17, 66

Uncle Tom (character, *Uncle Tom's Cabin*), 12
Uncle Tom figure, 11–12, 121, 179, 187; pocho and, 12; "Tio Taco" and, 12
Uncle Tom's Cabin (Stowe), 12
Un Homme pareil aux autres (Maran), 192–93
United States: American revolution, 136; character of, 5; empire, 34–35, 85; end of the American century, 8; expansionism, 113; global domination by, 8; hypocrisies of imperialism, 34, 42; India, relationship with, 139–42; materialistic ethic, 156–57, 159–60; melting pot trope, 44; Philippine-American war, 83; racism as foundational to, 31; second-class citizenship in, 2, 5, 39; as site of economic advancement, 152; sportsmanship and fair play, rhetoric of, 129–32, 148–50; surveillance apparatus, 132; transnationalism of, 51
United States Information Agency (USIA), 124, 140–41
United States v. Bhagat Singh Thind, 122–23, 135, 144
universalism, 115–16; attributed to Rihani, 46–47, 65, 116
Up from Slavery (Washington), 127–28, 148–49
U.S. State Department, 7, 140, 157

Villa, José Garcia, 4, 6, 66–91, 184; accolades, 69; aesthetics of, rarified, 35, 66, 70–71, 73–74, 78–79, 86–87, 90–91, 194; American dream of, 67, 86; Anderson, letter to, 74–75, 85; aphorisms, 86; art severed from biography in, 35, 67, 86; avant-gardism of, 68–69; brown dog emblem in, 82–84; burden of representation refused by, 84, 90–91; "comma poems," 70, 76; compulsion in criticism of, 72; critical writings of, 74, 86–87; cult of personality of, 88–89; as cultural attaché to United Nations, 69; as "disappearing," 69, 71–72, 88; "Doveglion" as fictitious retreat for, 185; duo-technique, 76; exposure, work of, 35, 72–73, 81, 84; Filipino identity disavowed by, 35, 68, 70; final years, 90; genres used by, 86; Gotham Book Mart photograph, 35, 69, 69–70; as grotesque, 194; grotesque characters of, 35, 67, 73–79; historical-materialist context, 71; humanism, literary, 68, 116; incongruousness of position, 67–68; neologisms, use of, 66, 67; otherness of as salable, 85–86; paintings by, 89, 89–92, 90; on personality, 86–87; persona of, 71–72; poetic philosophy volume, 86; primitivist and Orientalist reception of, 85–86; reception based on political milieu, 70–71; social compulsion of, 68. Works: *The Anchored Angel*, 71, 86; *Boy with Bird* (painting), 89; ,,A Composition,, 67; "Malakas," 85; Philippine short stories and poems, 68; short story compilations, 74; "Song I Did Not Hear," 73; "A Story of Old-Time Philippines," 85; "Wings and Blue Flame: A Trilogy," 66, 73, 75, 76; *Woman's Face* (painting), 90; "Young Writer in a New Country," 6, 66, 73–75, 78. See also *Footnote to Youth* (Villa)

Villa, Pancho, 95, 97, 102, 103

Villa, Simeon, 70

Villarreal, José Antonio, 4, 35, 92–118, 184; burden of representation refused by, 96; Chicano movement and, 95–96, 98; machismo, version of, 95–96; as Mexican citizen, 96; "part of everything," 36, 115–18, 150, 194; on *Pocho*'s plot, 99; queer characters and queering by, 96–97; racial identity, rejection of, 95–96; universalism of, 115–16. Works: *Clemente Chacón*, 96; *The Fifth Horseman*, 96. See also *Pocho* (Villarreal)

visibly racialized subjects, 3, 11–12, 17–19, 22, 121, 128, 141; American dream mediated by, 5, 36, 187; appearance overdetermines character, 5, 15, 17–19, 22, 26–27, 96, 116, 118, 146, 151, 172, 181, 191, 194. See also racialization

Vivekananda, Swami, 140

Voice of America (VOA), 140–41

war on terror, 44

Warren, Kenneth, 190

Washington, Booker T., 127–28, 148–49, 187

Washington, Mary Helen, 159–60, 173

Waters, Mary, 158

West Indians, 154

What Was African American Literature? (Warren), 190

white ethnicization, 3, 28, 31–32, 155, 160, 162, 176–79

"white mask," 191–92

whiteness: critique of, 162; as erasure of race, 66, 89; identification with, 8–9, 61–62, 83, 113–14, 133–34, 163–64; Mexican American relationship to, 112–14; negotiation with, 8, 12, 28, 32, 64, 185; of the page, 66; psychic identification with, 165–66; racial and cultural capital, 61; South Asian relationship to, 134–36; Syrian relationship to, 62–63; unspoken, 133–34

"Whiteness Invisible: Early Mexican American Writing and the Color of Literary History" (Sánchez), 8–9

whites, racist apprehension of, 170–71, 180

white supremacy, 186

Wide Sargasso Sea (Rhys), 14
Williams, Raymond, 24
Wilson, Woodrow, 45, 136
Winant, Howard, 19, 30–31
Winesburg, Ohio (Anderson), 35, 67, 75–76
Woloch, Alex, 13–14, 16, 24; "character-space," concept of, 25–26, 100, 174
Woman Warrior, The (Kingston), 21, 25
Wong, Sau-ling Cynthia, 21, 25
worker, as character, 13
world literature model, 188
World War I, 34, 43, 45, 122
World's Columbian Exposition (Chicago, 1893), 51

Wright, Richard, 26
Writers on America (U.S. State Department), 7
Wu, Cynthia, 21

Young Turk Revolution of 1908, 54
"Young Writer in a New Country" (Villa), 6, 66, 73–75, 78
Yu, Timothy, 70, 71, 72
Yuson, Alfred, 71

Zapatista narrative, 112
Zelda (character, *Pocho*), 97, 107

www.ingramcontent.com/pod-product-compliance
Lightning Source LLC
Chambersburg PA
CBHW030533230426
43665CB00010B/875